Thinking of Amitābha Buddha

Selected Mahāyāna Sūtras
Translated by Rulu

authorHOUSE®

AuthorHouse™
1663 Liberty Drive
Bloomington, IN 47403
www.authorhouse.com
Phone: 1-800-839-8640

Published by AuthorHouse 1/17/2012

ISBN: 978-1-4685-4089-5 (sc)
ISBN: 978-1-4685-4088-8 (e)

Library of Congress Control Number: 2012900527

To those who read and recite sūtras
pronounced by the Buddha

Contents

Preface xi

Translator's Introduction 1

PART I Five Sūtras and One Treatise 33

Five Sūtras and One Treatise 35

1 Buddha Pronounces the Sūtra of Amitāyus Buddha (in 2 fascicles) 佛說無量壽經 (T12n0360) 41

2 Buddha Pronounces the Sūtra of Amitābha Buddha 佛說阿彌陀經 (T12n0366) 84

3 Buddha Pronounces the Sūtra of Visualization of Amitāyus Buddha 佛說觀無量壽佛經 (T12n0365) 89

4 Great Might Arrived Bodhisattva's Thinking-of-Buddhas as the Perfect Passage (a subsection in the Śūraṅgama Sūtra) 大勢至菩薩念佛圓通章 (T19n0945) 106

5 Mahāvaipulya Sūtra of Buddha Adornment, fascicle 40 大方廣佛華嚴經: 入不思議解脫境界普賢行願品卷四十 (T10n0293) 107

6 Upadeśa on the Sūtra of Amitāyus Buddha 無量壽經優波提舍 (T26n1524) 121

PART II Four Other Sūtras 131

Four Other Sūtras 133

7 Buddha Pronounces the Sūtra of the Pratyutpanna Buddha Sammukhāvasthita Samādhi 佛說般舟三昧經 (T13n0417) 137

8 Sūtra of Mahā-Prajñā-Pāramitā Pronounced by Mañjuśrī Bodhisattva (in 2 fascicles) 文殊師利所說摩訶般若波羅蜜經 (T08n0232) 153

9 Mahāvaipulya Sūtra of the Inconceivable State of Tathāgatas 大方廣如來不思議境界經 (T10n0301) 171

10 Sūtra of the Prophecy Bestowed upon Avalokiteśvara Bodhisattva 觀世音菩薩授記經 (T12n0371) 181

PART III The Patriarchs, Ancient Translators, Prayers, Mantras 195

The Patriarchs of the Pure Land School 197

Nāgārjuna (circa 150–250). Vasubandhu (circa 320–80). Huiyuan (334–416). Shandao (613–81). Chengyuan (712–802). Fazhao (circa 747–821?). Shaokang (?–805). Yanshou (904–75). Xingchang (959–1020). Zhuhong (1535–1615). Zhixu (1599–1655). Xingce (1626–82). Shixian (1686–1734). Chewu (1740–1810). Yinguang (1861–1940). 197

Ancient Translators 227

Lokakṣema (147–?). Saṅghavarman (3rd century). Kumārajīva (344–413). Kālayaśas (383–442). Dharmodgata (4th–5th centuries). Mandra (5th–6th centuries). Bodhiruci (5th–6th centuries). Śikṣānanda (652–710). Pramiti (7th–8th centuries). Prajñā (734–?). 227

Prayers 233

Opening the Sūtra. Transferring Merit. Four Vast Vows. Universally Worthy Vow of the Ten Great Actions. Always Walking the Bodhisattva Way. Repenting of All Sins. Wishing to Be Reborn in the Pure Land. Supplicating to Be Reborn in the Pure Land. Ascending the Golden Steps. Praising Amitābha Buddha. 233

Mantras 237

How to Recite a Mantra 237

Introduction to the Eleven Mantras 238

The Eleven Mantras 240

1 Buddha-Crown Superb Victory Dhāraṇī 佛頂尊勝陀羅尼 240

2 Great Cundī Dhāraṇī 准提神咒 240

3 Whole-Body Relic Treasure Chest Seal Dhāraṇī 全身舍利寶篋印陀羅尼 240

4 Dhāraṇī of Infinite-Life Resolute Radiance King Tathāgata 聖無量壽決定光明王如來陀羅尼 241

5 Dhāraṇī for Rebirth in the Pure Land 往生咒 241

6 Root Dhāraṇī of Infinite Life Tathāgata 無量壽如來根本陀羅尼 241
7 Mantra of Medicine Master Tathāgata 藥師灌頂真言 241
8 Heart Mantra of the White Umbrella Dhāraṇī 楞嚴咒心 242
9 Samantabhadra Bodhisattva's Mantra 普賢菩薩所說咒 242
10 Great Compassion-Mind Dhāraṇī 大悲咒 242
11 Prajñā-Pāramitā Mantra 般若波羅蜜多咒 242

Appendix 243
Table A. The Sanskrit Alphabet 243
Table B. Pronunciation of the 13 Vowels 244
Table C. Pronunciation of the 33 Consonants 245
Glossary 247
Reference 277

Preface

The Mahāyāna Buddhist doctrine teaches that all sentient beings have Buddha nature and will eventually attain Buddhahood. For the spiritual training of those who are resolved to become Buddhas to benefit themselves and others, Śākyamuni Buddha recommends a Pure Land—Amitābha Buddha's Land of Ultimate Bliss. One can arrive there only by being reborn there. However, one may choose to return to our impure world any time for delivering sentient beings if one feels compelled and able to do so. In that splendid environment and in the excellent company of advanced Bodhisattvas, one will attain Buddhahood with Amitābha Buddha's training and support, bypassing the long and difficult path to Buddhahood through one's cycle of birth and death in the Three Realms of Existence.

Buddhists generally recognize that we are well into the Dharma-ending age, as reflected in the agonizing events in the world, such as epidemics, terrorism, war, and financial crises, as well as ravages of earth, water, fire, and wind. In the *Sūtra of the Total Annihilation of the Dharma*, the Buddha predicts that the *Śūraṅgama Sūtra* and the *Pratyutpanna Buddha Sammukhāvasthita Samādhi Sūtra* will be destroyed, to be followed by all other sūtras (Rulu 2012a, 73). However, one may find some comfort in His words in the *Amitāyus Sūtra* (Sūtra 1 in this book). The Buddha says, "In times to come, the Dharma will be annihilated. Out of lovingkindness and compassion, I will specially save this sūtra and make it stay for a hundred years more. Sentient beings that encounter this sūtra will all be delivered as they wish."

Therefore, the devotees of the Pure Land School, one of the Mahāyāna Schools originated in China, as their immediate goal, strive to be reborn in Sukhāvatī, the Land of Ultimate Bliss. To them, rebirth in the Pure Land is not only the Easy Path to Buddhahood, but the emergency flight out of this impure world.

The translator's introduction to this book presents Pure Land teachings in an organized manner, based on both the words of the Buddha and the works of exalted Chinese masters. I rely on canonical citations (translated or paraphrased by me) for authentication, and refrain from discussing Pure Land teachings in comparison with non-Buddhist doctrines. For the reader's interest and inspiration, the biographies of the patriarchs of the Pure Land School are presented in another chapter.

The Pure Land School is founded on five sūtras and one treatise. This book presents these six texts and four other sūtras in English, all of which are posted on my website at http://www.sutrasmantras.info. These ten English translations are based on texts in the digital Chinese Canon on a DVD-ROM (2009 version) produced by the Chinese Buddhist Electronic Text Association (CBETA) in Taiwan. Each text is identified by its volume and text numbers according to the CBETA system. For example, the epigraph in the translator's introduction is excerpted and translated from T09n0262, which corresponds to the Taishō edition of the Chinese Canon, volume 9, text 262. Any passage in a text can also be found by its page, column, and line numbers in the Taishō. For example, 0007a22–28 means page 7, column a, lines 22 to 28.

Five of these ten translations have never before been published in book form. Following the rules of translation stated in "Translator's Note" in my first book, *Teachings of the Buddha,* I have done my best to render the English translation as faithful to the Chinese text, yet as clear, as possible. As the Buddha teaches with one tone, all sentient beings receive benefits according to their needs and preferences. This book will benefit readers at all levels and serve as a basis for scholarly research. For those who aspire to be reborn in the Pure Land, it is the only English guidebook available.

For the generous help I have received, I thank the following beneficent learned friends: Shi Yinhai (釋印海), who discussed with me the Chinese texts of Sūtras 7–10; Mark Nguyen, who volunteered to proof Sūtra 1 against the Chinese text and made valuable suggestions; Anne Moses, who edited Sūtras 4, 8–10; Stephen Colley, who edited the other six sūtras and the entire manuscript of this book; Kottegoda S. Warnasuriya, who helped correct errors in the texts of the mantras; Avinash Sathaye, who with infinite patience further edited the mantras; the Amida Society, Temple City, CA, which provided for the cover of this book a picture of its statue of Amitābha Buddha; visitors to my website, who appreciate the teachings of the Buddha; and earlier translators, who have benefited readers and inspired later translators.

Any flaws in my translations are my sole responsibility. May the merit of all contributors be transferred to all sentient beings for their rebirth in the Western Pure Land of Ultimate Bliss and for their ultimate enlightenment!

Rulu (如露)
January 21, 2011

Translator's Introduction

Śāriputra, what is meant by the one grave matter as the only reason Buddha-Bhagavāns appear in worlds? Buddha-Bhagavāns appear in worlds because they wish to expose sentient beings to Buddhas' knowledge and views, and to have them acquire purity; because they wish to indicate to sentient beings Buddhas' knowledge and views; and because they wish sentient beings to enter the path to Buddhas' knowledge and views.

—*The Lotus Sūtra,* fascicle 1, chapter 2
Translated from the Chinese Canon (T09n0262, 0007a22–28)

It is well said that while the *Śūraṅgama Sūtra* is for one to realize one's true mind, the *Lotus Sūtra* is for all to attain Buddhahood. After speaking the above words, the Buddha declares the One Buddha Vehicle for all. One can ride this vehicle to Buddhahood through any of the 84,000 Dharma Doors taught by the Buddha, especially the supreme Dharma Door of thinking of Buddhas.

In the days of Śākyamuni Buddha (circa 563–483 BCE), it is Him that a disciple should think of and hold in memory. In the Ekottarika Āgama (discourses ordered by the number of dharmas in each discourse), fascicle 2, the Buddha tells the bhikṣus, "You should train in the one dharma and disseminate the one dharma. Once you have trained in this one dharma, you will have renown, achieve great fruits . . . , and attain nirvāṇa. What is this one dharma? It is thinking of the Buddha" (T02n0125, 0554a8–12). Thinking of the Buddha as one's spiritual training is implicit in the Three Refuges. As one finds comfort and guidance by taking refuge in the Buddha, the Dharma, and the Saṅgha, one thinks of the Buddha, the Dharma, and the Saṅgha, as a form of meditation.

How does one think of the Buddha? In the same fascicle, the Buddha says that one should tirelessly observe the Tathāgata's unsurpassed physical features and think of His virtues (ibid., 0554a20–25). Moreover, in a separate translation of the Saṁyukta Āgama (connected discourses), fascicle 9, the Buddha teaches that those who train in the six remembrances should also remember a Buddha's ten epithets (T02n0100, 0441b13–14).

In the Mahāyāna doctrine, the Buddha teaches us to think of all Buddhas of the past, present, and future, in worlds in the ten directions. In particular, He teaches us to think of Amitābha Buddha and the splendors of His Pure Land, recommending all to seek rebirth in that land and to attain Buddhahood there. However, these teachings are unknown to riders of the Two Vehicles, who refuse to hear them.

Types of Buddha Lands

The Tiantai School of China classifies innumerable Buddha Lands into four types: (1) lands inhabited by both ordinary and holy beings, (2) lands for those with remaining ignorance, (3) true reward lands, and (4) the land of eternal silent radiance.

(1) Lands inhabited by both ordinary and holy beings can be impure or pure, based on ordinary beings' life forms. For example, sentient beings in an impure land, such as this Sahā World, transmigrate in the Three Realms of Existence in five life forms: god, human, animal, hungry ghost, and hell-dweller, the last three being the impure (unfortunate) forms. Asuras are not included here as a sixth life form, because they may assume any of the first four life forms and live among sentient beings in these forms. Holy beings in an impure land, such as Buddhas, holy Bodhisattvas on the First Ground or above, Pratyekabuddhas, and voice-hearers who have achieved any of the four holy fruits, stay with ordinary beings only temporarily; their numbers are few, and most ordinary beings do not have the good fortune to see them. By contrast, a pure Buddha Land is a place where its inhabitants never assume any of the three impure life forms. Ordinary beings there live with innumerable holy beings and magically manifested holy beings all the time.

(2) Lands for those with remaining ignorance are for holy voice-hearers and Pratyekabuddhas, who have taken the Holy Path to end their afflictions, are mentioned in the *Lotus Sūtra*. In fascicle 3, chapter 7, the Buddha says that voice-hearers in this land who do not know the Bodhisattva Way will choose to enter nirvāṇa according to their understanding of the Small Vehicle. Then they will seek their Buddha wisdom in another land where the Buddha will appear under a different name (T09n0262, 0025c14–20). Although they have ended their karmic birth and death, because of remaining ignorance, they have not ended their changeable birth and death (see "two types of birth and death" in the glossary).

(3) True reward lands are Pure Lands of Buddhas, and Bodhisattvas who have partly realized the dharma body (dharmakāya). As the true reward for their spiritual training when they were on the Cause Ground, they assume their reward bodies (saṁbhogakāya) and live in a true reward land (visualizations 9–11 in Sūtra 3). Unrestrained by space and time, they see that all lands are hindrance free, like jewels in the god-king Indra's net.

(4) The land of eternal silent radiance is the state of a Buddha's dharma body. The world of Buddhas is true suchness with these three virtues: eternity, silence, and radiance. This is the secret land of Buddhas, the substance of which is the dharma body, liberation, and prajñā (wisdom), beyond the concept of purity or impurity. Just as the dharma body is not physical, this land is not material. A Bodhisattva who has partly realized the dharma body also partly experiences this land. Just as all inhabitants of the first three types of lands have the dharma body, whether or not they have realized it, their lands in true reality are the land of eternal silent radiance.

In an impure Buddha Land, each sentient being is repeatedly reborn in the three realms of a small world according to its karmas, and causes and conditions. The specific life form of a karmic rebirth is the main requital of a sentient being, and the environment its life relies on is the reliance requital, which comes with the main requital as a package, like a birdcage keeping a bird or a fishbowl holding a fish (Rulu 2012a, 5). In a pure Buddha Land, one is reborn in a magnificent body as one's main requital and lives in a splendid environment as one's reliance requital. In the *Vimalakīrti-nirdeśa Sūtra*, the Buddha explains: "If a Bodhisattva wishes to reach a Pure Land, he should purify his mind. In accord with the purity of his mind, his Buddha Land is pure" (T14n0475, 0538c4–5). This is the doctrine that a Pure Land is only one's pure mind. According to one's mind, pure or impure, one lives in a Buddha Land of a certain type.

Pure Lands Introduced by the Buddha

In Sūtra 1, the *Amitāyus Sūtra*, World Sovereign King Buddha displays to the bhikṣu Dharmākara 210 koṭi wonderful Buddha Lands. However, few Pure Lands are known to us. For example, as stated in the *Vimalakīrti-nirdeśa Sūtra* (T14n0475, 0555b5–7), in the distant east is Akṣobhya Buddha, who resides in His land called Abhirati (embracing joy). Although Vimalakīrti is a holy Bodhisattva from that Pure Land, it is not known how anyone here can be reborn there. In addition, according to the *Sūtra of the Original Vows of Seven Medicine Buddhas* (T14n0451), east of here, beyond countless Buddha Lands, seven Medicine Buddhas reside in their respective lands, each farther from here than the one before. The seventh Medicine Buddha is called Medicine Master Vaiḍurya Light King, and His land is called Pure Vaiḍurya (aquamarine). This Buddha originally made twelve vows before he attained Buddhahood, but none of them says anything about welcoming people to be reborn in His land. In China, this Buddha is always revered along with Śākyamuni Buddha and Amitābha Buddha, and people look to Him as physician and patron for their health and prosperity in their present worldly life.

Moreover, Maitreya Bodhisattva, the next Buddha to come, resides in his Pure Land, which is the inner court of Tuṣita Heaven, the fourth heaven in the desire realm of the Three Realms of Existence. He is teaching the gods there. In the *Sūtra of Maitreya Bodhisattva's Ascension to Tuṣita Heaven* (T14n0452), the Buddha says that those who wish to be reborn in Maitreya's Pure Land should think of Maitreya and his Pure Land, observe their precepts with purity, and transfer their merits with a wish to be reborn in the presence of Maitreya Bodhisattva. Then they will be reborn there and achieve the spiritual level of avinivartanīya (no regress). However, Maitreya Bodhisattva has not invited anyone here to be reborn there. It would be entirely dependent on one's wish and effort to be reborn as a god, specifically in the inner court of Tuṣita Heaven.

By contrast, Śākyamuni Buddha has given extensive teachings on Amitābha Buddha and His Pure Land, west of this world. Declaring His forty-eight great vows, Amitābha Buddha has extended an invitation to all sentient beings with all kinds of karma to be reborn in His land.

The Origin of the Pure Land School

Dharma Master Dao-an (道安, 312–85), who lived during the Eastern Jin Dynasty (317–420), was the first to promote Maitreya Bodhisattva's Pure Land. He and his disciples vowed to be reborn there. This school, called the Maitreya School (慈宗), thrived during the Southern and Northern Dynasties (420–589).

It is interesting that, Dharma Master Huiyuan (慧遠, 334–416), a disciple of Dao-an, chose instead to promote Amitābha Buddha's land. In 402, together with 123 Dharma friends training for rebirth in this Pure Land, Huiyuan founded a White Lotus Society on Lushan (廬山), the Lu Mountain, in Jiangxi Province. For this reason, the Pure Land School was initially called the Lotus School (蓮宗). One should distinguish it from the Japanese Lotus Sect (日蓮宗), or Nichiren Buddhism, which branched out of the Tiantai School in the 13th century, with its focus on the name of the *Lotus Sūtra*.

As the Pure Land School grew into a major Mahāyāna School in China, the Maitreya School went into decline after the Sui Dynasty (581–618). Nowadays, when the Pure Land is spoken of, it is understood to be Amitābha Buddha's land. The Pure Land School is founded on Śākyamuni Buddha's teachings on Amitābha Buddha and His land, and it continues to flourish with the support of its teachers and students, through their training, writing, and promoting.

Texts of the Pure Land School

Transmittal of the Buddha Dharma from India to China began in the first century CE, in the Eastern Han Dynasty (25–220). The two Indian monks Dharmāraṇya (竺法蘭) and Kāśyapamātaṅga (竺攝摩騰) arrived in Luoyang (洛陽), China's capital, in 67, the tenth year of the Yongping (永平) years of Emperor Ming (漢明帝). Staying at the White Horse Temple, they translated the *Sūtra in Forty-two Sections* (T17n0784). An Shigao (安世高), a prince of the kingdom of Anxi, the Arsacid Empire, in present-day northeastern Iran, arrived in Luoyang in 148, the second year of the Janho (建和) years of Emperor Huan (漢桓帝). Between 148 and 170, he translated many Sanskrit texts into Chinese, mostly Hīnayāna (Small Vehicle) sūtras. Fifty-five texts in the Chinese Canon are attributed to him.

It is generally accepted that Mahāyāna texts began to emerge in India after the first century BCE. In the second century CE, carrying the first batch of Mahāyāna texts, Lokakṣema (支婁迦讖 or 支讖, 147–?) arrived in Luoyang in 167, the last year of Emperor Huan. He was the first Indian master who went to China to disseminate Mahāyāna teachings. Included in his Chinese translations are Pure Land sūtras: text 361 (T12n0361) is one of the five versions of the *Amitāyus Sūtra* (Sūtra 1 in this book is translated from text 360), and texts 417–18 (T13n0417–18) are two of the four versions of the *Pratyutpanna Samādhi Sūtra* (Sūtra 7 in this book is translated from text 417). Therefore, Pure Land sūtras were among the earliest Mahāyāna texts that arrived in China.

The Five Sūtras and the One Treatise

The Pure Land School is founded on five sūtras and one treatise, but it was initially founded on only three sūtras and one treatise. These four Chinese texts were translated from Sanskrit over a period of about three hundred years. First, in the Cao Wei Kingdom (220–65), Saṅghavarman (康僧鎧, 3rd century) translated text 360, the *Amitāyus Sūtra*. Second, in the Later Qin Dynasty (384–417), Kumārajīva (鳩摩羅什, 344–413) translated text 366, the *Amitābha Sūtra*.

Third, in the Liu Song Dynasty (420–79), Kālayaśas (畺良耶舍, 383–442) translated text 365, the *Visualization Sūtra*. Fourth, in the Northern Wei Dynasty (386–534), Bodhiruci (菩提留支, 5th–6th centuries) translated text 1524, Vasubandhu's treatise *Upadeśa on the Amitāyus Sūtra*. For the following thirteen centuries, devotees of the Pure Land School studied and upheld mainly these four texts.

When Dharma Master Huiyuan (慧遠, 334–416) founded this Pure Land School in 402, only the first two texts had been translated into Chinese. During the development of the Pure Land School, text 417, the *Pratyutpanna Samādhi Sūtra*, has also been a very important sūtra, because earlier patriarchs, including Master Huiyuan, diligently practiced the intense ninety-day meditation taught in this sūtra.

Then, in the 19th century, a layman named Wei Yuan (魏源, 1784–1857) published a book comprising four Pure Land sūtras, the additional one being the last fascicle of text 293, the 40-fascicle version of the *Mahāvaipulya Sūtra of Buddha Adornment*. In the early 20th century, Dharma Master Yinguang (印光, 1861–1940), the thirteenth patriarch of the Pure Land School, proposed to include another sūtra, a subsection titled "Great Might Arrived Bodhisattva's Thinking-of-Buddhas as the Perfect Passage" in text 945, the *Śūraṅgama Sūtra*.

The addition of these two sūtras completes the five Pure Land sūtras. Of these five sūtras, the *Amitāyus Sūtra* is considered the main Pure Land sūtra because it is the most comprehensive one. However, devotees of the Pure Land School regularly recite from memory the *Amitābha Sūtra*, which is like a summary of and an introduction to the *Amitāyus Sūtra*. In this book, the English translations of these five sūtras are listed in the order of their arrival in China, and the English translation of Vasubandhu's treatise is listed as Sūtra 6.

The Place of Pure Land Teachings in Buddhist Doctrine

To help students better understand the scope and depth of His teachings, the Buddha has made certain classifications. For example, in the *Lotus Sūtra*, He summarizes His teachings into the Three Vehicles: the Voice-Hearer Vehicle, the Pratyekabuddha Vehicle, and the Mahāyāna (Great Vehicle), respectively likened to a goat carriage, a deer carriage, and an ox carriage (T09n262, 0012c6–24), all of which are then replaced by the One Vehicle, likened to a great jeweled carriage drawn by a giant white ox. In the *Mahāparinirvāṇa Sūtra*, fascicle 10, the Buddha uses five flavors to describe different spiritual characters, as He likens voice-hearers to milk, Pratyekabuddhas to cream, Bodhisattvas to fresh butter and melted butter, and Buddhas to ghee (T12n0374, 0423b1–4). In the *Sūtra of Immeasurable Meaning*, He classifies His teachings by the time periods in his life, as he states: "The teachings given at the beginning, in the middle, and at the end use the same words but their meanings are different" (Rulu 2012a, 203).

By the time of the Southern and Northern Dynasties (420–589), many Buddhist texts had been translated into Chinese, and organization of the Buddha's teachings was sorely needed. Quite a few Chinese masters, based on their study and understanding, classified the teachings into categories or levels according to certain criteria. Masters of the Tiantai School and the Huayan School, two of the eight Mahāyāna Schools of China, after evaluating earlier classifications, established their own systems, which have since been recognized as models. In order to show where Pure Land teachings are placed in Buddhist doctrine, each of these two systems is summarized below, followed by the classification system established by two masters of the Pure Land School.

Classifications by the Tiantai School

The Tiantai School was founded by Dharma Master Zhiyi (智顗, 538–97) and was named after the Tiantai Mountain (天台山) in Zhejiang Province, where he lived. Zhiyi is honored as the fourth patriarch, succeeding Ācārya Nāgārjuna (龍樹菩薩, circa 150–250) from India, and his Chinese predecessors, Dharma Masters Huiwen (慧文, dates unknown) and Huisi (慧思, 515–77). He taught and promoted Huiwen's theory of the three truths (the doctrine) and the three observations (the training), which is based on Nāgārjuna's *Treatise on the Sūtra of Mahā-Prajñā-Pāramitā* (T25n1509) in 100 fascicles. Through training in observation, one will come to realize the three truths in every dharma. For example, that a name appears through causes and conditions is the worldly truth; that a name is empty by nature is the absolute truth; that the appearance and the nature of a name are not two things is the middle truth. Moreover, seeing each thought clearly appearing in one's mind is the observation of falseness; seeing that, thought after thought, the thinking mind never changes is the observation of emptiness; seeing that the thinking mind as the subject and each thought as the object are neither the same nor different is the observation of the middle truth. When one says a Buddha's name, one should be aware of the presence of all three truths.

Refining and integrating the ideas of three masters in the southern region and seven masters in the northern region, Zhiyi made three classifications, organizing the Buddha's teachings by (A) five time periods, (B) four levels, and (C) four teaching approaches. The following summary is based on the explanation, in text 1939 (T46n1939), of Dharma Master Zhixu (智旭, 1599–1655), the ninth patriarch of the Pure Land School, who also excelled in the Tiantai doctrine.

The Teachings by Time Period

According to the Tiantai School, the five chronological periods in which the Buddha has given teachings are likened to the five flavors mentioned in the *Mahāparinirvāṇa Sūtra.* These five periods are (1) the Buddha adornment period of the first three weeks after His enlightenment, during which the Buddha pronounced the *Mahāvaipulya Sūtra of Buddha Adornment* to inspire advanced Bodhisattvas with what He had realized, giving teachings likened to pure milk; (2) the Āgamas period of the next twelve years, during which the Buddha pronounced the Five Āgamas to guide voice-hearers into the Dharma, giving teachings likened to cream; (3) the vaipulya period of the next eight years, during which the Buddha pronounced the vaipulya (vast and extensive) sūtras, such as the *Vimalakīrti-nirdeśa Sūtra* and the *Śūraṅgama Sūtra,* to reprove voice-hearers and direct them to the Mahāyāna, giving teachings likened to fresh butter; (4) the prajñā period of the next twenty-two years, during which the Buddha, in order to eliminate one's differentiation of dharmas, pronounced the prajñā-pāramitā sūtras to expound emptiness in the Mahāyāna perspective, giving teachings likened to melted butter; (5) the Dharma flower and nirvāṇa period, during which the Buddha pronounced the *Lotus Sūtra* in the last eight years of His life, to reveal the One Vehicle for all, and pronounced the *Mahāparinirvāṇa Sūtra* in the day and night before entering parinirvāṇa, to reveal Buddha nature in all, giving His concluding teachings likened to ghee.

Actually, with inconceivable spiritual power, the Buddha spontaneously gives teachings to sentient beings according to their capacities, at any time. Although Pure Land sūtras were pronounced during the vaipulya period, Pure Land teachings can be found across all five periods. For example, in the 40-fascicle version of the *Mahāvaipulya Sūtra of Buddha Adornment*, the youth Sudhana visits fifty-three beneficent learned teachers. His first teacher, the bhikṣu Auspicious Cloud,[1] who has attained the Thinking-of-Buddhas Samādhi, introduces to him numerous Doors of thinking of Buddhas, i.e., various kinds of the Thinking-of-Buddhas Samādhi (T10n0293, 0679c4–0680b20). His last teacher, Samantabhadra Bodhisattva, teaches him the vow of the ten great actions, which leads everyone to rebirth in Amitābha Buddha's Land of Ultimate Bliss (Sūtra 5). The Thinking-of-Buddhas Samādhi is also mentioned in chapters 37 and 76 in the *of Mahā-prajñā-pāramitā Sūtra* (T08n0223). Moreover, the significance of saying a Buddha's name is revealed in the *Lotus Sūtra,* fascicle 1, as the Buddha states: "If those with turbulent minds enter a temple, by once saying 'namo buddhāya' they all have attained Buddha bodhi" (T09n0262, 0009a24–25).

The Teachings by Level

According to the Tiantai School, to transform sentient beings of different capacities, the Buddha has given teachings at four levels: first, Tripiṭaka teachings (藏教); second, common teachings (通教); third, special teachings (別教); fourth, all-embracing teachings (圓教).

(1) The Tripiṭaka teachings are for people who are not sharp, primarily voice-hearers and Pratyekabuddhas, and secondarily some Bodhisattvas. Through analysis of dharmas considered real, they realize that dharmas are empty. To them, the absolute truth and the relative truth are apart because they must end saṁsāra to realize the nirvāṇa without remnant. Therefore, the emptiness they realize is called the apart-emptiness (但空), and the nirvāṇa they realize is called the exclusive-absolute-truth nirvāṇa.

(2) The common teachings are for riders of all Three Vehicles. Through observation of the illusion of dharmas that appear and disappear through causes and conditions, they realize that dharmas have no birth. Therefore, the two truths are both present because saṁsāra at hand is nirvāṇa. The nirvāṇa they realize is the absolute-truth nirvāṇa. This is the beginning level of the Mahāyāna doctrine. After receiving these common teachings, those with low capacity may still end up with the same attainment as those at the first level; others with high capacity may turn to the teachings at the third or even fourth level. Neither of these first two groups knows about the eternity of nirvāṇa or one's Buddha nature.

(3) The special teachings are for Bodhisattvas only, which are separate from those at the other three levels. Through step-by-step training in observation, Bodhisattvas realize successively the absolute truth, the relative truth, and the middle truth. However, until they ascend to the First Ground, the middle truth they know is called the apart-middle (但中) because it stands apart from the other two truths. The nirvāṇa they realize is called the middle-truth nirvāṇa, which abides in neither the absolute truth nor the relative truth.

(4) The all-embracing teachings are for Bodhisattvas of the highest capacity, but are available to people of any capacity as well. They are all-embracing because they are direct, inclusive, and wondrous. Through observation of a single thought in one's mind, one realizes that each truth includes the other two and that the three truths are perfectly unified into one truth, the true mind. The nirvāṇa they realize is the nirvāṇa with the three inseparable virtues: dharma body, wisdom, and liberation. Realizing that these three virtues are the one mind is the perfect realization. They say neither that the mind creates all dharmas nor that it contains all dharmas because the mind is all dharmas and vice versa.

In the opinion of Buddhist masters, Pure Land teachings belong in the fourth level, i.e., all-embracing teachings. In *An Essential Explanation of the Amitābha Sūtra*, Zhixu says that the Dharma Door of the Pure Land is "the medicine that cures all diseases, such as the diametric view of existence or nonexistence. Inconceivable and all-embracing, it is the abstruse store of the *Mahāvaipulya Sūtra of Buddha Adornment*, the secret gist of the *Lotus Sūtra*, the heart secret of all Buddhas, and the compass for the Bodhisattva Way" (T37n1762, 0365b7–9).

Pure Land teachings are also available to those receiving teachings at the first three levels. For example, Amitāyus Buddha vows that all inhabitants of His Pure Land will attain Buddhahood (vow 11 in Sūtra 1). This means that voice-hearers reborn there will all turn toward the great bodhi fruit of the Mahāyāna.

The Teachings by Approach

According to the Tiantai School, with inconceivable spiritual power, the Buddha transforms sentient beings of different capacities by four teaching approaches, giving them (1) immediate teachings (頓教), through which He directly reveals the highest truth in the *Mahāvaipulya Sūtra of Buddha Adornment,* right after His perfect enlightenment; (2) graduated teachings (漸教), through which He guides students by means of the Three Vehicles, successively pronouncing the Five Āgamas, vaipulya sūtras, and prajñā sūtras; (3) secret teachings (祕密教), through which those in the same assembly hear different teachings and do not know the benefits received by one another; (4) indefinite teachings (不定教), through which one person may achieve a small fruit from hearing a great Dharma while another person may achieve a great fruit from hearing a small Dharma.

Of these four teachings classified by teaching approach, Pure Land teachings are identified as immediate teachings because the Buddha gives a direct instruction for sentient beings to attain Buddhahood via rebirth in the Pure Land. This Dharma Door is also included in the graduated, secret, and indefinite teachings. For example, in Sūtra 1, the *Amitāyus Sūtra*, the Buddha gives graduated teachings, as He admonishes people in the world of the five evils, the five pains, and the five burns, to cultivate the five virtues. An example of His secret and indefinite teachings is found in Sūtra 3, the *Visualization Sūtra.* After hearing the Buddha's teachings, instantly Queen Vaidehī achieves the Endurance in the Realization of the No Birth of Dharmas while her five hundred attendants activate the bodhi mind.

The three classifications of the Tiantai School constitute a rational system for categorizing the Buddha's teachings. Merging the last two classifications, the Tiantai system comprises the five periods and the eight teachings. Based on this system, Pure Land teachings are considered as immediate and all-embracing teachings, likened to the flavor of ghee. Pure Land teachings also encompass and transcend all classifications. To take this great path, students would be well advised to acquire a perfect understanding, then to train in the perfect actions, in order to achieve the perfect fruit.

Classifications by the Huayan School

The first patriarch of the Huayan School is Dharma Master Dushun (杜順, 557–640), who conceived the four dharma realms, based on the *Mahāvaipulya Sūtra of Buddha Adornment* (Buddhāvataṁsaka-mahāvaipulya-sūtra), which is the principal text of this school. The Sanskrit word *avataṁsaka,* meaning garland or adornment, is translated into two Chinese words *huayan* (flower adornment), which are used as the name of this school. In the West, this sūtra is referred to as the *Avataṁsaka Sūtra* or the *Flower Adornment Sūtra*, the word Buddha unfortunately omitted.

The four dharma realms expounded by Dushun are four aspects of the one true dharma realm (一真法界), one's true mind. His theory and terminology have significantly influenced the development of Chinese Buddhism, including the Pure Land doctrine. Therefore, they are introduced below.

(1) The dharma realm of the principle (理法界). The principle refers to the nature of one's mind in the appearance of each thought. It is true suchness, the essence of the dharma realm, or the dharma body. Even in one thought, all dharmas are within one's mind.

(2) The dharma realm of manifestations (事法界). All dharmas are manifestations of one's true mind, like reflections in a clear mirror. Although the principle is formless and timeless, it is revealed through illusory manifestations.

(3) The dharma realm with no hindrance between the principle and manifestations (理事無礙法界). As manifestations are founded on the principle, the principle is implicit in manifestations. Although manifestations appear and disappear like birth and death, the principle is changeless. For example, Amitābha Buddha's reward body and all the splendors of His land are no different from His mind, or His dharma body.

(4) The dharma realm with no hindrance among manifestations (事事無礙法界). As distinct manifestations are in essence true suchness, they do not hinder one another. For example, because space and time are illusory, a dust particle contains all lands; holy Bodhisattvas, who have realized their dharma body, even if only partly, can travel in time and anywhere in space. For an ordinary person who aspires to the land of Amitābha Buddha, he can abandon his human body in

this land and be reborn in a magnificent ethereal body, in a lotus flower in that land, transcending the human conception of space and time.

In the 80-fascicle version of the *Mahāvaipulya Sūtra of Buddha Adornment,* fascicle 50, the Buddha characterizes a Tathāgata by five features, and the fourth feature is wisdom, which shines on all without discrimination. However, because sentient beings have different capacities and preferences, His wisdom is like sunlight shining on Mount Sumeru, the black mountains, plateaus, or plains, at different times of day (T10n0279, 0266b3–19). Inspired by this analogy, Dharma Master Fazang (法藏, 643–712), the third patriarch of the Huayan School, who was honored as the Imperial Teacher under the name Xianshou (賢首), officially established the Huayan system by integrating the ideas of the first two patriarchs. He classified the Buddha's teachings by (A) three time periods and (B) five levels. The summary below is based on the explanation of Dharma Master Ciyun (慈雲, dates unknown) of the Qing Dynasty (1644–1912), in text 1025 in the Extension of the Chinese Canon (X58n1025).

The Teachings by Time Period

According to the Huayan School, the three time periods are (1) the sunrise period, during which the sun at the horizon shines its light onto the mountaintop, just as the Buddha turns the root Dharma wheel, directly revealing in the *Mahāvaipulya Sūtra of Buddha Adornment* His perfect realization to the most advanced Bodhisattvas; (2) the moving sunshine period, during which the Buddha turns the wide-ranging Dharma wheel three times, skillfully giving teachings by divisions: first, He turns the Hīnayāna Dharma wheel for sentient beings of low capacity, revealing in the Āgamas the Four Noble Truths and the Twelve Links of Dependent Arising; second, He turns the Three-Vehicle Dharma wheel for sentient beings of middling capacity, revealing in vaipulya sūtras that dharmas are projections of one's consciousness, to guide riders of the Two Vehicles to the Mahāyāna; third, He turns the Mahāyāna Dharma wheel for sentient beings of high capacity, revealing in Tathāgata-store sūtras the definitive teachings of the One Vehicle; (3) the sunset period, during which the sun at the horizon once again shines its light onto the mountaintop, just as the Buddha turns the return-to-the-root Dharma wheel for His sharpest disciples, confirming the agreement of His all-embracing teachings in the *Mahāvaipulya Sūtra of Buddha Adornment* with those in the *Lotus Sūtra.*

Of these three periods, Pure Land teachings are primarily identified as the highest teachings given in the sunrise period, as evidenced by Sūtra 5, the last fascicle of the 40-fascicle version of the *Mahāvaipulya Sūtra of Buddha Adornment,* in which Samantabhadra Bodhisattva persuades all to come home to Amitābha Buddha's land. Next, in the period of moving sunshine, the Buddha pronounces the three Pure Land sūtras (Sūtras 1–3), giving teachings to sentient beings of high, middling, and low capacities. Finally, in the sunset period, the Buddha again gives His highest teachings in the *Lotus Sūtra*, in which He reveals that He and Amitābha Buddha were prince brothers in a past life.

The Teachings by Level

Taking into consideration not only the eight teachings identified by the Tiantai system but also the tenets of the Chan (dhyāna) School and the Faxiang (dharma appearance) School, both thriving in the Tang Dynasty, the Huayan School classifies the Buddha's teachings into five levels: first, Hīnayāna teachings; second, beginning Mahāyāna teachings; third, mature Mahāyāna teachings; fourth, immediate-realization teachings; fifth, all-embracing teachings.

(1) The Hīnayāna teachings are for those incapable of accepting the Mahāyāna doctrine. These teachings expound that there is no self in a person and expound the emptiness of a person composed of dharmas, such as the five aggregates, but cover little about no self in a dharma and the emptiness of a dharma. Followers of these teachings only recognize one's six consciousnesses and the dependent arising of dharmas from one's karmas. Striving to end their karmic birth and death, they do not know a holy Bodhisattva's changeable birth and death.

(2) The beginning Mahāyāna teachings expound more dharma appearances than dharma nature. These teachings introduce the emptiness of dharmas as taught in prajñā-pāramitā sūtras, and emphasize the dependent arising of dharmas from one's ālaya consciousness (the eighth consciousness) as taught in the *Sandhinirmocana Sūtra* (T16n0676).

(3) The mature Mahāyāna teachings expound more dharma nature than dharma appearances, which all come down to dharma nature. According to sūtras such as the *Laṅkāvatāra Sūtra* (T16n0670) and *Śrīmālādevi Sūtra* (T12n0353), all sentient beings have the Tathāgata store, which is synonymous with true suchness, and they all will attain Buddhahood. These teachings introduce the dependent arising of dharmas from true suchness, which remains changeless.

(4) The immediate-realization teachings are based on dharma nature only. Because dharmas by nature are true suchness, one comes to realization immediately without using words or skillful observations, just as Vimalakīrti Bodhisattva explains non-duality by his silence. According to the inconceivable liberation taught in the *Vimalakīrti-nirdeśa Sūtra* (T14n0475), one's realization of Buddhahood can be immediate, bypassing the stages of the Bodhisattva Way. As proclaimed by the Chan School, if one does not have a single thought, one is called a Buddha.[2] By contrast, the Mahāyāna teachings at levels 2 and 3 are gradual-realization teachings.

(5) The all-embracing teachings expound the inconceivable one dharma realm, where dharma nature is like the ocean that dissolves all into one, and the dependent arising of dharmas is hindrance free. The endless and interactive dependent arising of dharmas is the way of this one dharma realm. All manifestations interpenetrate one another like layers of the god-king Indra's net, as stated by Samantabhadra Bodhisattva. In Sūtra 5, he says, "In the time of one thought, I can enter all kalpas of the past and future . . . On the tips of hairs are worlds in the ten directions, as numerous as dust particles. I enter all these worlds and adorn them with purity. . . ."

Of these five levels of teachings, Pure Land teachings are mainly classified as immediate-realization teachings. Through the Dharma Door of thinking of Amitābha Buddha, one will be reborn in His land and attain Buddhahood in one lifetime, bypassing the graduated stages of the Bodhisattva Way. Furthermore, Pure Land teachings are classified as all-embracing teachings because the tenets of Pure Land sūtras accord with those of the *Mahāvaipulya Sūtra of Buddha Adornment*. In addition, in veiled or explicit statements, Pure Land teachings can also be found in the first three levels of teachings.

Classifications by the Pure Land School

The Difficult Path and the Easy Path

Dharma Master Tanluan (曇鸞, 476–542 or after 554) annotated Vasubandhu's treatise *Upadeśa on the Sūtra of Amitāyus Buddha* (Sūtra 6). In his annotation (T40n1819), he initiates the theory of the two paths and the two powers, based on the words in Nāgārjuna's *Comprehensive Treatise on the Ten Grounds* (T26n1521), Tanluan reiterates Nāgārjuna's statement that those who seek to attain avinivartanīya (the spiritual level of no regress) can take either the Difficult Path or the Easy Path. He gives five reasons why achieving avinivartanīya in this world of the five turbidities is the Difficult Path, the fifth of which is that one must rely on one's self-power alone to perfect observance of precepts, attain samādhi, and unfold wisdom, through repeated birth and death in the Three Realms of Existence. By contrast, achieving rebirth in Amitābha Buddha's land through both the other-power (the power of Amitābha Buddha's vows) and the self-power (one's faith in Him and one's wish for rebirth in His land) is the Easy Path because, in the Pure Land, one will join the group of sentient beings that definitely progress on the right path to bodhi (vow 11 in Sūtra 1), never to regress. He reiterates Nāgārjuna's analogy that the Difficult Path is like taking a land trip on foot, and that the Easy Path is like joyfully sailing down a waterway by boat (T40n1819, 0826a28–b11).

Tanluan, who became a novice monk at age fifteen, lived during the Northern Wei (386–534), the first of the five Northern Dynasties (386–581) established by nomadic ethnic groups. The turning point of his spiritual life came when he encountered Bodhiruci (菩提留支) in 529, who gave him a copy of the *Visualization Sūtra* (Sūtra 3), and told him about one's infinite life in Amitābha Buddha's land. Tanluan dedicated the rest of his life to the study, practice, and dissemination of Pure Land teachings. Through his promotion of his theory and practice in northern China, Pure Land teachings began to be accepted by the masses.

The Holy Door and the Pure Land Door

Dharma Master Daochuo (道綽, 562–645) gives the Difficult Path and the Easy Path new names, calling them the Holy Door and the Pure Land Door. In his work *Peace and Bliss,* he declares that it is just too difficult to achieve holy fruits in this world by going through the Holy Door with one's self-power alone, because one cannot be with the Buddha and because one has inadequate understanding of His profound holy teachings (T47n1958, 0012c4–0013c11). Daochuo is convinced that only the Pure Land Door can lead one to spiritual attainment in this Dharma-ending age. He explains that, through the Pure Land Door, one's resolve to be reborn in the Pure Land and one's training to this end are called the self-power, and that being received at one's death by Amitābha Buddha is called the other-power. He reminds us that, in the Pure Land, one will join the group that definitely progresses on the right path to bodhi, never to regress.

The Pure Land Door is the Easy Path because, after rebirth in the Pure Land, one will attain the spiritual level of no regress, which through the Holy Door (Difficult Path) is achieved by voice-hearers when they enter the holy stream, becoming Srotāpannas, and by Bodhisattvas when they ascend to the First Ground. Furthermore, the Pure Land Door is the Easy Path because one will attain Buddhahood in the Pure Land in one lifetime. Therefore, one's rebirth there means the end of one's cycle of birth and death, which through the Holy Door is achieved by Arhats, Pratyekabuddhas, and Buddhas upon their realization of nirvāṇa after myriad lifetimes of endeavor.

Daochuo brought a sense of urgency to the Pure Land School, as he perceived the arrival of the Dharma-ending age during his life in the turbulent times of dynasty change, from Northern Qi (550–77) to Northern Zhou (557–81), then to Sui (581–618), and then to Tang (618–907). His sense of crisis also arose from the persecution of Buddhist monks and nuns during the Northern Zhou.[3] To Daochuo, it would be impossible for ordinary people in this Dharma-ending age to achieve holy fruits through the Holy Door.

Daochuo, who became a novice monk at age fourteen, upheld the *Mahāparinirvāṇa Sūtra* and expounded it twenty-four times. At age forty-eight, after seeing the words on Tanluan's memorial stele at the Xuanzhong Temple (玄中寺) in Shanxi Province, Daochuo converted from the Nirvāṇa School to the Pure Land School. He expounded the *Visualization Sūtra* (Sūtra 3) two hundred times. However, the Pure Land Door he promoted was the Dharma Door of saying Amitābha Buddha's name. He said "amituo fo" (Amitābha Buddha) 70,000 times a day, and taught people to use a mālā (strand of beads) to count their repetitions. Daochuo was the first master of the Pure Land School to promote saying Amitābha Buddha's name as the main practice of the Easy Path.

Although Tanluan and Daochuo are not recognized in China as patriarchs of the Pure Land School, they have significantly contributed to laying down its foundation. Their work was continued by Daochuo's disciple Dharma Master Shandao (善導, 613–81), the second patriarch of the Pure Land School, who solidified the foundation. Since the early Song Dynasty (960–1279), through the example of and promotion by many masters of the Pure Land School, other Mahāyāna Schools, including the Tiantai School, the Huayan School, the Vinaya School, and the Chan School, have also accepted Pure Land teachings in parallel with their own doctrines. The Tiantai School especially has a close connection with the Pure Land School, as demonstrated by Patriarch Zhiyi, who had auspicious signs of rebirth in the Pure Land. The Pure Land School has gradually become the most widely welcomed Dharma Door in China. Nowadays, almost all Chinese Buddhists say "amituo fo" as a form of greeting.

The Origin of Amitābha Buddha and His Land

The Pure Land Door is provided by Amitābha Buddha and introduced by Śākyamuni Buddha. It is special because it is for sentient beings of all capacities: high, middling, and low. Not only holy Bodhisattvas from worlds in the ten directions choose to be reborn in Amitābha Buddha's land, but those who have done evil karmas have a chance to be reborn there.

His Past Life and His Vows

Stories of Amitābha Buddha's past lives are given in several sūtras. For example, according to the *Mahāyāna Vaipulya Sūtra of Total Retention* (T09n0275), He was once a bhikṣu called Pure Life, who retained fourteen koṭi sūtras and six million Mahāyāna sūtras. Subsequently, he encountered 63 nayuta Buddhas, and he asked each Buddha to turn the true Dharma wheel (Rulu 2012a, 187).

His most significant past life as told in Sūtra 1, the *Amitāyus Sūtra,* was as a bhikṣu named Dharmākara, under the Buddha called Lokeśvararāja, World Sovereign King. He activated the anuttara-samyak-saṁbodhi mind and asked that Buddha how to form the most magnificent Buddha Land for delivering sentient beings after his attainment of Buddhahood. After that Buddha showed him 210 koṭi Buddha Lands, for five kalpas he contemplated and collected the pure actions to adorn his own Buddha Land.

Then he went to that Buddha and made forty-eight great vows before Him, stating in detail his resolve to attain Buddhahood and to deliver sentient beings. Of his forty-eight vows, three vows (12–13 and 17) specify the glory of his Buddhahood, one vow (31) specifies the radiance of his Pure Land; and three vows (27–28 and 32) specify the splendid adornments in his Pure Land. He vowed to benefit sentient beings: gods (1–11, 15–16, 21, and 38–39), Bodhisattvas (22–26, 29–30, 36–37, and 40–48), riders of the Two vehicles (14), and women (35). He also vowed to benefit sentient beings in his land (1–11, 14–16, 21–30, 38–40, and 46), in worlds in the ten directions (18–20 and 33–37), and in other worlds (41–45 and 47–48). They all will be delivered by hearing his name (18, 20, 34–37, 41–45, and 47–48), being touched by his radiance (33), being received by him in person (19), hearing his Dharma (46), or being blessed by his mind (23). Moreover, sentient beings in his land will have their suffering forever uprooted (1–2) and will live in a virtuous community (16), enjoying the magnificence of their body (3–4, 15, 21, 23, 26, 35, 38, and 41), the eloquence of their voice (25 and 29–30), and the power of their mind (5–11, 34, 39–40, 42, and 45–48).

The crucial incentive of those who aspire to the Pure Land comes from vow 11 (one will join the group definitely heading for realization of the great bodhi), vow 18 (one will achieve rebirth in Amitābha Buddha's land by only thinking ten thoughts of His name), vow 19 (at death, one will be received by Him), and vow 20 (one's wish for rebirth there will come true).

His Present Life and His Land

All of his vows have come true, because it has been ten kalpas since Dharmākara attained Buddhahood after his accumulation of merit and virtue for countless kalpas. As a Buddha, He has two names in Sanskrit: Amitābha means infinite light (vow 12), describing His wisdom; and Amitāyus means infinite life (vow 13), describing His dharma body, which is beyond the concept of space and time—two characteristics common to all Buddhas. Based on the texts in the Chinese Canon, in this book, the name Amitābha is used in Sūtras 2, 5, 7, 9, and 10, and the name Amitāyus is used in Sūtras 1, 3, and 6. Chinese Buddhists call Him Amituo, omitting the fourth syllable in either Sanskrit name.

As stated in Sūtra 3, Amitāyus Buddha never abandons sentient beings as His radiance "universally illuminates all worlds in the ten directions, attracting and accepting sentient beings that think of Buddhas, . . ." Out of lovingkindness and compassion for sentient beings, Amitāyus Buddha supports their rebirth in His land with the power of His vows, which to them is the other-power.

His land is called Sukhāvatī, which translates into Chinese as the Land of Ultimate Bliss or as the Land of Peace and Bliss. The splendors of this Pure Land, described in detail in Sūtra 1, are summarized in vows 27, 28, 31, and 32. They are also described in Sūtra 2 and Sūtra 3. Moreover, in Sūtra 6 (the treatise), Vasubandhu describes that land as adorned with the virtues of seventeen achievements.

In text 363, one of the five versions of the *Amitāyus Sūtra,* Ānanda asks the Buddha, "Is Dharmākara a past Buddha, a future Buddha, or a present Buddha?" The Buddha answers him, "That Buddha-Tathāgata comes from nowhere, goes to nowhere, has neither birth nor death, and is beyond past, present, or future. To fulfill His vows to deliver sentient beings, He is now in a world called Ultimate Bliss, west of Jambudvīpa, beyond 100,000 koṭi nayuta Buddha Lands" (T12n0363, 0321c9–15). The first sentence in His answer explains the dharma body of a Buddha, which is the truth body with neither form nor place; the second sentence declares that Amitāyus resides in His Pure Land. In the *Sūtra of a Clear Understanding of the Mahāyāna,* the Buddha explains, "While a Buddha who demonstrates attainment of Buddhahood in a Pure Land appears in His reward body (saṁbhogakāya), a Buddha who demonstrates attainment of Buddhahood in an impure land appears in a response body (nirmāṇakāya)" (T16n0673, 0651c5–18).

Citing this passage, Dharma Master Daochuo determines that Amitāyus Buddha is in His reward body (visualization 9 in Sūtra 3), residing in a splendid environment, His reward land (T47n1958, 0005c12–22).

In Sūtra 10, the *Prophecy Sūtra,* the Buddha prophesies Amitābha Buddha's parinirvāṇa in His land, which will be followed by Avalokiteśvara Bodhisattva's attainment of Buddhahood. One may wonder how the infinite life of His reward body could come to an end. In the same sūtra, the Buddha gives an explanation: "Bodhisattvas who have attained the Thinking-of-Buddhas Samādhi will constantly see Amitābha Buddha." Moreover, in Sūtra 3, the Buddha says, "Therefore, when one visualizes a Buddha, one's mind has a Buddha's thirty-two physical marks and eighty excellent characteristics. The mind forms a Buddha, and the mind is the Buddha. The ocean of Saṁbuddhas is formed by one's thinking mind."

The Internal Elements for One's Rebirth in the Pure Land

Amitābha Buddha's vows are like a ship that can carry sentient beings to the Pure Land where they will definitely attain Buddhahood. The issue is whether they are willing to board this ship and whether they can sail this ship to its destination. For Mahāyāna Buddhists, the bodhi mind is their fundamental motivation to board this ship and sail to its destination.

However, one not only relies on the other-power, the power of Amitābha Buddha's lovingkindness and compassion expressed as His vows, but also relies on one's self-power. This power is generated from one's faith, resolve, and training, which serve as the three essential provisions for one's spiritual journey. Therefore, one's rebirth in the Pure Land is achieved with the other-power and one's self-power in mutual responses.

The Bodhi Mind

The initial step for a Bodhisattva to train through any Dharma Door is to activate the anuttara-samyak-saṁbodhi mind, i.e., the bodhi mind. This is the resolve to attain the unsurpassed perfect enlightenment to benefit self and others, as stated in the Four Vast Vows (Prayer 3). The bodhi mind is the core of the Mahāyāna. One who has activated the bodhi mind will not ride the Small Vehicle.

In Sūtra 1, the Buddha clearly states that those in the high, middle, and low classes who wish to be reborn in Amitāyus Buddha's land must first activate the bodhi mind. Moreover, in Sūtra 3, He says that those who wish to achieve a high rebirth in the high rank must invoke three minds in order to succeed: first, an earnest mind; second, a profound mind; third, a mind wishing for rebirth in the Pure Land as one transfers one's merits to other sentient beings. These can be interpreted as the three aspects of the bodhi mind. In other words, one must earnestly wish to be reborn in the Pure Land with profound faith in Śākyamuni Buddha's words and Amitābha Buddha's vows, and always transfer one's merits to others for all to be reborn in Amitābha Buddha's land in order to attain Buddhahood.

The bodhi mind is also the pure mind of great compassion described in Vasubandhu's treatise (Sūtra 6). It includes (1) the untainted pure mind, because one does not seek one's own happiness; (2) the peaceful pure mind, because one uproots the suffering of all sentient beings; (3) the joyful pure mind, because one draws in all sentient beings for them to be reborn in that Buddha Land, enabling them to attain the great bodhi. These three minds merge into one, the wondrous, joyful, superb true mind, which is the essence of the bodhi mind.

Those who have activated the bodhi mind must then gather, as they would food and water, the three essential provisions: faith, resolve, and training.

Faith, the First Provision

Faith is founded on reverent acceptance: As the teacher speaks truthful words, the student reverently accepts them. Faith is the entrance to the ocean of the Buddha Dharma, and it protects one from the seduction of wrong views and wrong paths. Faith is the roots supporting a tree that will grow to bloom and bear fruit. Only with faith can one gain strength in doing good worldly and supra-worldly dharmas, in order to receive good requitals and eventually to attain the perfect enlightenment. Among the Thirty-seven Elements of Bodhi, faith is the first of the Five Roots and the Five Powers. On the Bodhisattva Way, at the initial stage one cultivates the ten faithful minds, the first of which is the mind of faith. The Buddha has repeatedly taught the importance of faith, as sampled from the following texts.

In the 80-fascicle version of the *Mahāvaipulya Sūtra of Buddha Adornment*, fascicle 14, the Buddha says, "Faith is the mother of bodhi and merit, forever growing all good dharmas. It shatters the web of doubts, leads one out of the stream of love,[4] and indicates the unsurpassed Way to nirvāṇa" (T10n0279, 0072b18–19).

In text 363, fascicle 3, the Buddha says, "If there are good men and good women who, having heard Amitāyus Buddha's name, only think one thought of belief, take refuge in Him, and make obeisance to Him, know that they are not riders of the Small Vehicle. In my Dharma, they are called the foremost disciples" (T12n0363, 0326a15–17).

In Sūtra 1, the *Amitāyus Sūtra*, the bhikṣu Dharmākara states his eighteenth vow: "After I become a Buddha, in worlds in the ten directions, there will be sentient beings that, with earnest faith and delight, wish to be reborn in my land, even if by only thinking ten thoughts. If they should fail to be reborn there—excepting those who have committed any of the five rebellious sins or maligned the true Dharma—I would not attain the perfect enlightenment."

In Sūtra 2, the *Amitābha Sūtra*, Buddhas in worlds in each of the six directions speak these words: "You sentient beings should praise His [Amitābha Buddha's] inconceivable merit and believe in this sūtra, which is protected and remembered by all Buddhas." Then Śākyamuni Buddha says, "You all should believe and accept my words and other Buddhas' words." He advises those who believe His words to resolve to be reborn in that land.

In this impure world, however, eliciting faith is very difficult for people who are conditioned to perceive life experienced through their senses as real and pleasurable. As the fortunate pursue pleasures in their life, the unfortunate struggle to catch up with the fortunate. Engrossed in their pursuits, people do not know that repeated birth and death through the five life-paths is suffering.

Moreover, limited by the capacities of the human mind and body, humans can only experience four-dimensional space and time through human measure. It is hard to believe in the dimensions of space and time of the Pure Land as described by the Buddha, much less one's rebirth there in a lotus flower. Knowing the mentality of this world, in Sūtra 2, the Buddha says, "For the sake of the entire world, I expound the hard-to-believe Dharma. It is extremely difficult."

Even Buddhists who have read Pure Land teachings may have doubts. The foolish and indolent, under the guise of humility, say that their karma hindrances are too severe for them to be reborn in Amitābha Buddha's land, a land too distant to reach. The arrogant contend that His Pure Land is intended for people of low capacity, so they do not need to be reborn there.

Therefore, to go through the Pure Land Door, the first provision one needs to acquire is faith. Dharma Master Zhixu discusses it in six aspects, in his work *An Essential Explanation of the Amitābha Sūtra* (T37n1762, 0364b22–c19). First, one should believe in one's Buddha mind, which has infinite light (amitābha) and infinite life (amitāyus). As all universes are manifestations of one's mind, one can be reborn in the Land of Ultimate Bliss manifested by one's mind. Second, one should believe in Śākyamuni Buddha's words, Amitābha Buddha's vows, and all Buddhas' protection and blessing. Third, one should believe in pure causes and conditions, knowing that one's faith, resolve, and training are the pure internal causes and that Amitābha Buddha's vows are the pure external conditions. Fourth, one should believe in causality, trusting that pure causes and conditions will bring a pure effect, that is, one's rebirth in Amitābha Buddha's land will lead to one's attainment of Buddhahood. Fifth, one should believe in manifestations. Amitābha Buddha's Land of Ultimate Bliss with all its splendors, though beyond human observation, is not a fiction or mirage. Although one has impure karma, one still can be reborn there. Sixth, one should believe in the principle implicit in all manifestations, which is one's true mind, also called true suchness, the dharma body, or the Tathāgata store. One should have faith that one's true mind is Amitābha and that there is no difference between Amitābha in His land and the Amitābha in one's mind. Nor is there any difference between the thinking mind and the Amitābha in one's thoughts. Because Amitabha Buddha's land beyond 100,000 koṭi Buddha Lands is not outside one's mind in the appearance of each thought, all the splendors of that land are reflections in the mirror of one's mind.

To strengthen one's faith in the Pure Land Door, one should regularly recite and study Pure Land texts, such as those in this book. It helps to recite in one's morning and evening lessons the *Amitābha Sūtra* (Sūtra 2) and the mantra for rebirth (Mantra 5 or 6), in addition to the *Heart Sūtra.* One may even recite "Thinking-of-Buddhas Samādhi as the Perfect Passage" (Sūtra 4) and Amitāyus Buddha's forty-eight vows (Sūtra 1). On occasion, one should recite the entire Sūtra 1. Before a picture of Amitābha Buddha, one can offer a cup of water, burning incense, and perhaps a flower and a fruit, and do prostrations.

Resolve, the Second Provision

One's Buddha mind is the wish-fulfilling jewel, and one's wish is the power to drive this jewel. Wishes can be stated as vows to take certain actions. For example, all Mahāyāna Buddhists take the Four Vast Vows (Prayer 3), for they are resolved to attain Buddhahood to benefit themselves and others. Another example is the Universally Worthy Vow of the Ten Great Actions introduced by Samantabhadra Bodhisattvas (Sūtra 5 or Prayer 4), which will lead one to be reborn in Amitābha Buddha's land. Buddhas also make their particular vows before their attainment of Buddhahood. For example, the seventh Medicine Master Buddha originally made twelve vows, and Amitābha Buddha originally made forty-eight vows. By contrast, one's resolve to be reborn in Sukhāvatī, Amitābha Buddha's Pure Land of Ultimate Bliss, may seem simplistic, but it has profound significance.

First, this resolve is an affirmation of one's activation of the bodhi mind. The only difference is that one chooses to live in a splendid environment and to train under Amitābha Buddha and advanced Bodhisattvas. This choice is based on one's faith in Śākyamuni Buddha's words and Amitābha Buddha's vows, especially vow 11 in Sūtra 1, which assures that one will never regress on one's spiritual journey to Buddhahood. Moreover, vow 22 allows one to return to this impure world any time for delivering sentient beings in accordance with one's original vows.

Second, this resolve is a momentous decision to end one's cycle of birth and death in the Three Realms of Existence, because attainment of Buddhahood is a certainty after one's rebirth in Amitābha Buddha's land. However, to sever one's deep-rooted attachment to karmic life is a difficult decision for people in this Sahā World. The Sanskrit word *sahā* means endurance, and the inhabitants of the Sahā World excel in their endurance of suffering and cherish the fleeting pleasures in life. The resigned, who accept their lot, and the fortunate, who enjoy their life and take great pride in their worldly achievements, are deeply attached to their karmic life in the Three Realms. Just as attached to such life are the unfortunate who struggle to achieve the material life of the fortunate. Another form of attachment comes from those who wish to be reborn as gods in a desire heaven because the only life they know of that is more pleasurable than human life is celestial life.

Furthermore, we now live in a decreasing kalpa, a kalpa during which human lifespan is decreasing from 84,000 to 10 years. The collective greed, anger, and ignorance in sentient beings' minds will continue to manifest as famine, epidemics, wars, and natural catastrophes, in increasing severity.

Therefore, it would be wise to seek a solution to one's suffering in this impure world, as did Queen Vaidehī. In Sūtra 3, she says, "I pray only that the World-Honored One will reveal to me a place free from sorrow and distress. I wish to be reborn there. I dislike this turbid evil world of Jambudvīpa." So Śākyamuni Buddha teaches her how to be reborn in Amitāyus Buddha's land. In fact, the Buddha highly recommends that ideal place to everyone. In Sūtra 2, He says, "Therefore, Śāriputra, if, among good men and good women, there are those who believe [my words], they should resolve to be reborn in that land."

One may question whether aversion to our world and aspiration to the Pure Land are the right attitude of a spiritual trainee learning to achieve equability in unfavorable and favorable situations. The answer is that such aversion and aspiration are not a matter of disliking or liking worldly objects. This distinction is not only wise but crucial for one's eventual attainment of Buddhahood. For example, the motivation of those who follow the Four Noble Truths is to end their suffering and, with an understanding of its causes, they take the Eightfold Noble Path in order to attain nirvāṇa. Moreover, in the *Lotus Sūtra*, fascicle 2, the Buddha likens sentient beings transmigrating within the Three Realms to children playing with toys in a house on fire. He persuades them to leave their burning house for the Three Vehicles, likened to better toys, then gives them all the One Vehicle to Buddhahood (T09n0262, 0012c8–11).

Dharma Mater Zhixu reminds us that this Sahā World is a reflection of the impurity of one's mind while the Land of Ultimate Bliss is a reflection of the purity of one's mind. It is sensible to reject impurity and accept purity until one's ultimate realization that there is nothing to reject or accept (T37n1762, 0364c19–26).

Another objection comes from those who offhandedly assert that one's leaving saṁsāra for the Pure Land is an act of uncaring for other sentient beings, and indicates a failure to seek enlightenment in one's present life. These critics need to be reminded that the rebirth of every ordinary being is driven, not by a sense of mission, but by ignorance of the truth and thirsty love (tṛṣṇā) for being. Although there are those who are fortunate to have heard the Dharma in their present life, their spiritual attainment is subject to regress. Besides, one will never know, as one's cycle of birth and death turns, how one's next rebirth will turn out. According to the Mahāyāna doctrine, only a holy being, one who has achieved one of the four voice-hearer fruits or has ascended to the First Bodhisattva Ground or above, will never be reborn in any of the three evil life forms. Ordinary beings and Bodhisattvas below the First Ground are not exempt from these evil life-journeys. Therefore, one's rebirth in the Pure Land, in total likeness of a Buddha, overriding the karmic force of saṁsāra, is itself a great achievement. It takes great faith, resolve, and training to achieve it.

According to Zhixu, one's rebirth in the Pure Land depends on one's faith and resolve, and one's rebirth ranking depends on the strength of one's training in saying Amitābha Buddha's name (T37n1762, 0367nb9–12). As one's faith is the compass that points in the right direction, so one's resolve is the navigator that keeps the ship on the right course. Both mental actions are essential for one's rebirth in the Pure Land.

One can affirm one's resolve by praying (Prayers 7–10), and one can fortify one's resolve through meditation. In Sūtra 6 (the treatise), Vasubandhu teaches five training doors. The third door is to "do the mind karma of wishing, by single-mindedly thinking of one's rebirth in the Land of Peace and Bliss." This training in śamatha (meditative concentration) is in accord with true reality. The fourth door is to train in vipaśyanā (right observation), through which one's visualization of the virtues of that land, the virtues of Amitāyus Buddha, and the virtues of His Bodhisattvas, adorns one's mind that wishes for rebirth in that land. To be more specific, one can do the twelfth visualization in Sūtra 3, picturing one's rebirth in a lotus flower in that land.

Moreover, after finishing meditation or doing good karma, one should always transfer one's merits to others with this foremost wish for all to be reborn in that land. This is a skillful way to fortify one's resolve to be reborn in the Pure Land, as an expression of the bodhi mind.

Training in Meditation, the Third Provision

Having set the goal to be reborn in the Pure Land, one must train in order to change one's habitual thoughts, which blindly perpetuate one's karmic birth and death. One must train in thinking of Amitābha Buddha as taught in Sūtras 1–4 and 6–9, aiming to attain the Thinking-of-Buddhas Samādhi. There are three methods of meditation. One can think of Amitābha Buddha (1) by saying His name, (2) by visualizing Him and His land, or (3) by thinking of Him in true reality.

Saying His Name

Method one, saying Amitābha Buddha's name, is prescribed in seven of the ten sūtras in this book. In Sūtra 1, the eighteenth vow of Amitāyus Buddha promises success to those who wish to be reborn in His land, even if they only think ten thoughts. In Sūtra 2, the Buddha says that if one single-mindedly upholds Amitābha Buddha's name for one to seven days, without being distracted, then upon one's dying, Amitābha Buddha, together with a holy multitude, will appear before one. In Sūtra 3, the Buddha states that even a sinful person can achieve a low rebirth in the low rank by saying "namo Amitāyus Buddha" ten times, because by saying Amitāyus Buddha's name, thought after thought, his sins which would entail 80 koṭi kalpas of birth and death will all be expunged. In Sūtra 4, Mahāsthāmaprāpta (Great Might Arrived) Bodhisattva assists those who think of Buddhas to come home to the Pure Land (Amitābha Buddha's land). In Sūtra 6 (the treatise), Vasubandhu teaches that "one should do the voice karma of praising, by saying that Tathāgata's name." In Sūtra 7, Amitābha Buddha says, "Those who wish to be reborn in my land should think of my name. If they can continue without rest, they will succeed in being reborn here." In Sūtra 8, the Buddha states: "If good men and good women aspire to enter the One Action Samādhi, they should sit properly in an open place, facing the direction of a Buddha, . . . focus their minds on that Buddha, and keep saying His name."

Although most of the thirteen patriarchs of the Pure Land School were accomplished in visualization, they all recommended saying Amitābha Buddha's name with faith and reverence. Chinese Buddhists say "namo amituo fo" in six syllables, which become the English words "namo Amitābha Buddha" in eight syllables. The Sanskrit word *namo* means paying homage to or taking refuge in something. Therefore, saying these words is also an affirmation of one's faith and resolve. When one speaks fast, it is easier to use "amituo fo" in four syllables.

One can practice in a formal session of sitting or walking meditation, chanting in a tune, or saying the words aloud or in a whisper. Or one can think these words, coordinating them with breathing, thinking "amituo fo" on inhalation and on exhalation, or thinking "namo" on inhalation and "amituo fo" on exhalation. While doing walking meditation, one can also coordinate the words with one's footsteps. To achieve concentration, one should listen to one's voice or mind, vigilantly guarding against intervening thoughts. When one hears other sounds, whether from nature, traffic, household activities, or sentient beings, without being disturbed, one can simply recognize them as "amituo fo."

If on a busy schedule, one can say "amituo fo" ten times as a set, and should do one set upon rising and one set before sleeping. One can do a set whenever one takes a one-minute break before and after an activity, e.g., eating a meal.

A distinct advantage of this method is that one can say "amituo fo" throughout one's daily activities anywhere and anytime. When one is using the bathroom, one should think these words, not saying them aloud.

Visualizing Him and His Land

Method two, visualizing Amitābha Buddha and His land, is taught specifically in Sūtra 3. As one practices the first thirteen visualizations in the listed order, one can also take into consideration applicable descriptions in Sūtras 1, 2, and 6. Visualization is also taught in Sūtra 7, the *Pratyutpanna Samādhi Sūtra,* in which the Buddha says, "One should always think of Amitābha Buddha's body with the thirty-two physical marks and the eighty excellent characteristics . . . , radiating vast bright light to illuminate everywhere."

If one succeeds in visualization 9 in Sūtra 3, seeing Amitāyus Buddha in His reward body, one has opened a pure dimension in one's mind, and one's rebirth in His land is assured. The Buddha teaches, "To visualize Amitāyus Buddha, one should begin with one major mark, the white hair between His eyebrows, and should make it vividly clear. One who can see the white hair between His eyebrows should readily see all His 84,000 excellent characteristics." He explains, "Seeing Amitāyus Buddha is seeing all Buddhas [in worlds] in the ten directions. Seeing all Buddhas is called the Thinking-of-Buddhas Samādhi."

For those who have difficulty visualizing Amitāyus Buddha in His reward body, they can visualize Him in human size as described by visualization 13 in Sūtra 3. If this too is difficult, one should first observe a Buddha statue or picture as preliminary training. According to Sūtra 9, the *Sūtra of the Inconceivable State of Tathāgatas,* one should face the object of observation in a given place and memorize its features until one can visualize without such support.

However, the objects of visualization can be overwhelming. For example, in Sūtra 6 (the treatise), Vasubandhu teaches us to visualize the virtues of that Buddha Land's seventeen achievements, the virtues of Amitāyus Buddha's eight achievements, and the virtues of His Bodhisattvas' four achievements.

Method two is good training in meditation in its own right and can also be used to support method one. As one keeps saying Amitābha Buddha's name or recites depictive passages in a sūtra, one can simultaneously engage one's mind in visualization.

Meditation with or without Appearance

Both method one and method two are Meditation Doors that involve thinking of Amitābha Buddha by means of appearance, using His name or His image as the meditation object. This is called dhyāna (meditation) with appearance. Intently thinking of Amitābha Buddha through either Meditation Door is a practice of śamatha (meditative concentration); being vigilant in one's thinking is a practice of vipaśyanā (right observation). In Sūtra 6 (the treatise), Vasubandhu says that visualization is a practice of vipaśyanā. This also makes sense because the mind should clearly see each feature of the object of visualization and vigilantly guard against irrelevant thoughts.

If one is able to think of Amitābha Buddha in the back of one's mind without appearance, not allowing any mental object to emerge as a thought, this is called dhyāna without appearance. This method is used by Chan students to contemplate a Chan question, such as "who is thinking of that Buddha" or "who is saying His name." The objective of Chan contemplation is to see one's Buddha nature, not for one's rebirth in the Pure Land. Some masters of the Pure Land School, with a strong background in meditation, saw their Buddha nature through Chan contemplation, then dedicated the rest of their lives to training for rebirth in the Pure Land and to disseminating Pure Land teachings. Most of them advised against Chan contemplation. It would be an unfortunate detour if one spends one's whole life contemplating a Chan question and fails to get the answer.

Thinking of Him in True Reality

Method three, thinking of Amitābha Buddha in true reality, means penetrating the true reality of dharmas. In the *Diamond Sūtra,* the Buddha gives an indirect explanation of the meaning of a Buddha in true reality: "If a person perceives me as form or seeks me through [his perception of] sounds, this person is walking the wrong path and cannot see the Tathāgata" (T08n0235, 0752a16–18). Then, in the *Buddha Store Sūtra,* the Buddha gives a direct instruction for thinking of Buddhas in true reality: "Śāriputra, what is called thinking of Buddhas? Perceiving nothing is called thinking of Buddhas. . . . Making no differentiation is called thinking of Buddhas. Furthermore, seeing the true reality of dharmas is called thinking of Buddhas. What is called the true reality of dharmas? It means that, ultimately, dharmas are empty. . . . Śāriputra, thinking of Buddhas means interrupting the flow of words and transcending thoughts. Finding no thought to capture is called thinking of Buddhas. . . . Śāriputra, all thoughts are in the appearance of nirvāṇa. Being in accord with nirvāṇa is called learning to think of Buddhas. One should not think of Buddhas as form. That which perceives form, grasps appearances, and covets flavors is one's consciousness. Perceiving no shape, no form, no condition, and no nature [self-essence] is called thinking of Buddhas. Therefore, know that the state of no differentiation, no acceptance, and no rejection is truly thinking of Buddhas" (T15n0653, 0785a25–b9).

Influenced by the Huayan School, masters of the Pure Land School have coined two terms to describe how thinking of Amitābha Buddha in true reality can be achieved through either of the first two methods. If one continues the one pure thought of Amitābha Buddha's name or image uninterrupted, it is called the manifestation of the one mind (事一心), which means a highly concentrated mind, undistracted by other objects. In this state, one may realize that the thinking mind as the subject and a Buddha as the object are but the one true mind, which has no birth.[5] This is called the principle of the one mind (理一心). As one thinks of a Buddha according to this principle, one is thinking of Him in true reality.

In Sūtra 4, Mahāsthāmaprāpta Bodhisattva introduces the Thinking-of-Buddhas Samādhi and reveals his own experience: "It was when I stood on the Cause Ground, with my mind thinking only of a Buddha, that I achieved the Endurance in the Realization of the No Birth of Dharmas." This is his testimony that, through the manifestation of the one mind, he attained the Thinking-of-Buddhas Samādhi, realizing that dharmas have no birth.

Therefore, without using Chan contemplation or other methods, through thinking of Amitābha Buddha by saying His name or visualizing His body, one may even enter the Thinking-of-Buddhas Samādhi, realizing one's Buddha nature and penetrating the true reality of dharmas in one's present life, to be followed by one's rebirth in the Pure Land for advanced training toward Buddhahood—a double accomplishment.

Choosing among the Three Methods

The intent of Pure Land teachings is for one to be reborn in the Pure Land, and the primary method recommended by the Pure Land School is saying Amitābha Buddha's name. In Sūtra 2, the Buddha says that those who single-mindedly uphold Amitābha Buddha's name for one to seven days, without being distracted, will be reborn in His Land of Ultimate Bliss. No mention is made of realizing the principle of the one mind or attaining the Thinking-of-Buddhas Samādhi. Achieving the manifestation of the one mind with faith and resolve would be sufficient for one to be reborn in the Pure Land. Most people would be content with achieving the Endurance in the Realization of the No Birth of Dharmas after their rebirth in the Pure Land.

Training in Doing Good Karmas, a Supplemental Provision

In Sūtra 2, the Buddha says, "No one with the condition of few roots of goodness and a meager store of merits can be reborn in that land." In Sūtra 1, the Buddha reveals that the three classes of people who do good works on different scales are reborn in the Pure Land according to their merit and wisdom. Therefore, in addition to the main training in thinking of Amitābha Buddha, in order to accumulate merit, one should train in doing good karmas, which serves as a supplemental provision for one's rebirth in the Pure Land and for one's attainment of Buddhahood.

Specific instructions are given in Sūtra 3. The Buddha tells Queen Vaidehī, "Those who wish to be reborn in that land should carry out three meritorious works. First, they should honor and support their parents, serve their teachers and elders, cultivate lovingkindness by not killing sentient beings, and do the ten good karmas. Second, they should take and uphold the Three Refuges, and fully observe their precepts without any breach in their conduct. Third, they should activate the bodhi mind, deeply believe in causality, read and recite Mahāyāna sūtras, and persuade others to do the same." In the same sūtra, the Buddha also teaches those who aspire to be reborn in the high or middle rank what they need to do during their life (visualizations 14–15 in Sūtra 3).

In Sūtra 1, for those who live in the five evils, the five pains, and the five burns, the Buddha kindly advises them "to destroy the five evils and uphold the five virtues in order to acquire merit, live a long life, and attain nirvāṇa." He encourages all to do good whether they aspire to be reborn in Amitāyus Buddha's land. He says, "If one observes the precepts with purity for one day and one night in this land, one's merit exceeds that from doing good karmas for 100 years in Amitāyus Buddha's land. . . . If one cultivates virtue for ten days and ten nights in this land, one's merit exceeds that from doing good karmas for 1,000 years in Buddha Lands in other directions."

Those who aspire to the Pure Land should also take the ten vowed actions introduced by Samantabhadra Bodhisattva (Sūtra 5 or Prayer 4), which are the essential training of Bodhisattvas using body, voice, and mind. In particular, the ninth great action is to forever support sentient beings. As one helps sentient beings in accordance with the Dharma, one cultivates one's compassion for all. One should strive to give happiness to sentient beings and establish a virtuous connection with them all. Moreover, from benefiting others even in any small way, one acquires merit for oneself.

Whatever merits are acquired from one's good karmas, it is important to transfer them to sentient beings with a wish for all to be reborn in the Pure Land. Transferring one's merits to others is itself a meritorious action, as taught in Sūtras 3, 5, and 6, and it is a skillful means to fulfill one's wish for rebirth in the Pure Land.

Rebirth and Life in the Pure Land

The Main Requital

In Sūtra 1, gods and humans in worlds in the ten directions who earnestly wish to be reborn in the Pure Land are grouped into three classes: high, middle, and low. They all will be reborn there according to their merit and wisdom. According to Sūtra 3, one can be reborn there in one of the nine grades, which are divided into three ranks: high, middle, and low. Under each rank are three rebirths by level. In the top grade are those who achieve a high rebirth in the high rank because they have an earnest mind, a profound mind, and a mind wishing for rebirth in the Pure Land as they transfer their merits to other sentient beings. They will naturally be reborn in lotus flowers made of the seven treasures, and they will abide in the spiritual level of no regress. In the bottom grade are sinful ones who achieve a low rebirth in the low rank because they have learned at death to say "namo Amitāyus Buddha" ten times in ten thoughts. They will remain in unopened lotus flowers in the Pure Land for twelve large kalpas and will receive teachings after the flowers have opened.

A special group of people reborn through the womb is mentioned in Sūtra 1. The womb is a figure of speech, meaning a confined life after rebirth. It is clarified in text 362 (T12n0362) that some of those in the middle or low class who could be reborn in the Pure Land proper are instead, because of their doubts, reborn in lotus flowers in the ponds of a city on the edge of the Pure Land. They will live there in jeweled palaces for 500 years. During their 500-year lifespan, they will not see Amitāyus Buddha or holy Bodhisattvas, and thus will not receive their teachings, unless they repent of their doubts.

Ordinary beings in the three classes who achieve the nine grades of rebirth in the Pure Land are still ordinary beings because of past impure karma, but no one there will ever assume the form of animal, hungry host, or hell-dweller. Moreover, magnificent will be their bodies as the main requital for their pure karma of faith, resolve, and training. As described in Sūtra 1, "Bodhisattvas, voice-hearers, and gods of that land have higher wisdom and greater transcendental powers. They all appear in the same form, without any difference. To conform to the way of other lands, the name 'gods' is used for them. They have wonderful appearances, with even facial features, extraordinary and unearthly. Being neither gods nor humans, they all are endowed with bodies that are naturally ethereal and boundless." Other great features of their body, voice, and mind are detailed in this sūtra.

According to the absolute truth, dharmas born through causes and conditions are empty and, in true reality, have no birth. However, the absolute truth penetrates but does not nullify the relative truth. With the understanding that birth in the Pure Land is no birth, one should still strive to be reborn there because this is the Easy Path to Buddhahood. This special path will remain open in this Dharma-ending age a little longer than other paths, as promised by the Buddha. In Sūtra 1, He says, "In times to come, the Dharma will be annihilated. Out of lovingkindness and compassion, I will specially save this sūtra and make it stay for a hundred years more. Sentient beings that encounter this sūtra will all be delivered as they wish."

The Reliance Requital

The reliance requital is one's living environment that matches one's main requital. According to one's mind, one lives in a Buddha Land of a certain type. Gods in Amitābha Buddha's land are constantly with holy beings as they receive continuing education in that splendid environment. Many inhabitants there are in the holy position of waiting to attain Buddhahood in their next life (Sūtra 2 and vow 22 in Sūtra 1). Therefore, the reliance requital of the gods there is a Pure Land inhabited by both ordinary beings and holy beings. To holy voice-hearers there, who have remaining ignorance, their reliance requital is a Pure Land in which they will turn toward the Mahāyāna. To holy Bodhisattvas there, who have partly realized the dharma body, their reliance requital is a true reward land. Implicit in all three Pure Lands is the land of eternal silent radiance for anyone's dharma body.

The splendors of the Pure Land for the enjoyment of all inhabitants include jeweled ground, trees, flowers, ponds, waters, and palaces and towers, as detailed in Sūtra 1. Living a blissful life and training themselves in this Pure Land, all inhabitants will attain Buddhahood.

The Final Work for Rebirth in the Pure Land

To be reborn in the Pure Land, one's faith, resolve, and training will meet the final test at one's death. During the final hours of truth, one must rely on one's family and an empowering hospice service by a team of volunteers called Lotus Friends, a service provided by some Chinese Buddhist temples and lay groups. Family members and Lotus Friends will chant Amitābha Buddha's name at one's death bed, invoking over again His blessings and strengthening one's final mindfulness and aspiration, as one's consciousness fades into darkness. Chanting should begin before one's death and continue for eight to twelve hours after death. Departing one's life peacefully in the company of Lotus Friends chanting in unison "amituo fo" is a noble sendoff to a noble rebirth. Although one may not necessarily achieve rebirth in the Pure Land, it is comforting to depart this life with the help and support of Lotus Friends. With lovingkindness and compassion for the deceased and the surviving family, Lotus Friends also serve to bear witness to favorable signs, if any, of one's rebirth in the Pure Land.

Death as the Final Test

When ordinary beings die, karmic forces arise from their minds, driving each to be reborn in a karmic life form and in an environment upon which the new life form relies. In the *Mahāyāna Sūtra of Consciousness Revealed,* the Buddha explains, "A sentient being receives requital according to karma, and the stream of consciousness continuously maintains each requital body. A life ends upon the exhaustion of requital, then [ālaya] consciousness abandons the body. It then moves on to accept [the next body] according to karma" (Rulu 2012a, 136). It is recognized that ālaya consciousness abandons the body within twelve hours after death, and assumes an ethereal interim body until it accepts the next karmic body, usually within forty-nine days.

For those who aspire to the Pure Land, death is the crucial time to override the strong karmic force of rebirth in the Three Realms of Existence. If successful, one's rebirth in the Pure Land will be immediate, bypassing the stage of assuming an interim body. In order to open such a pure dimension in one's mind, it is imperative to sustain the right thought and unwavering aspiration up to the final moment—quite a challenge for the dying one. Although the Pure Land School claims that their Dharma Door is the Hard-to-Believe Easy Path, it really may not be that easy.

Therefore, one needs all the help one can get to cope with this solemn matter of death. Amid the sound of family members and Lotus Friends chanting Amitābha Buddha's name, as one's life force is coming to its end, one must strive to think of Him with faith and resolve. One's last pure thought of Amitābha Buddha is the key to one's rebirth in His land.

Responsibilities of Mindfulness Helpers

Before—or even after—the death of a person, the family can invite Lotus Friends to help. As mindfulness helpers, family members and Lotus Friends should keep incense burning and place a picture of Amitābha Buddha where the person can see, or show it to him (or her) before they begin to chant. According to Master Yinguang (印光, 1861–1940), the thirteen patriarch of the Pure Land School, the leading helper, usually a Buddhist monk or nun, should speak to the person, whether he is on the verge of death or already dead, telling him to drop all concerns, single-mindedly follow the chanting of "amituo fo," and firmly believe in his rebirth in the Pure Land.

Mindfulness helpers always start by chanting the six syllables "namo amituo fo" and, after some time, switch to and stay with the four syllables "amituo fo." They can work in three teams to keep their chanting uninterrupted. As one team is chanting aloud for an hour or two, the other two teams can say His name silently or break for food or chores. They should control their chanting, neither too loud nor too soft, neither too fast nor too slow, gauging the condition of the dying one. It is usual to strike a small bell to keep the tempo and alert the dying one. However, if the pitch of the bell is too high for the nerves, it should not be used. When only a few inexperienced helpers chant, it can be helpful for them to chant along with a chanting machine, which is given away for free at most Chinese Buddhist temples. It does not replace human chanting, because live voices are charged with compassion and power that recorded voices cannot carry.

It is essential that family members not be inspired or persuaded to chant instead Medicine Master Buddha's name or Avalokiteśvara Bodhisattva's name, hoping to avert imminent death. They should honestly and faithfully stay with Amitābha Buddha's name.

Lotus Friends should ask those wearing strong perfume or exuding the odor of alcohol, onion, or garlic not to get near the dying one. Family members should not allow visiting relatives and friends to disrupt the concentration of the dying one by wailing or saying meaningless well-wishes, but may invite them to join in chanting.

As the person nears his last breath, all three teams should chant together for an hour. Then they can resume chanting in shifts for eight to twelve hours. If a person is dying in the hospital, it might be possible to pay for a single room, so that mindfulness helpers can do their chanting without upsetting other patients. Even if a person is found dead, mindfulness helpers should still chant for eight to twelve hours. During these hours, it is common for them to notice that the deceased's face has changed from rigid to serene and that the deceased's limbs remain flexible.

Whether a person has died in bed or is found dead on the floor, it is important not to move the body or adjust its posture. Nor should family members bathe the body. Because ālaya consciousness has not completely abandoned the body, any manipulation of the body will cause pain to the deceased, which in turn can arouse anger that will sabotage his resolve for rebirth in the Pure Land.

Lotus Friends may accept tea or water offered by the family, but not gifts or money. They are fully rewarded by their merit acquired from helping a person be reborn in the Pure Land. Because rebirth in the Pure Land definitely leads to attainment of Buddhahood, the merit acquired from helping someone attain Buddhahood is inconceivable and immeasurable.

After the First Twelve Hours

It is usual in Chinese Buddhist tradition that, seven days after the death of a person, a "farewell ceremony" (funeral-memorial service) is held, with cremation or burial of the body immediately afterward. During the ceremony, it helps to have a qualified person explain to the guests the meaning of one's rebirth in the Pure Land, but all fanfare is avoided.

After the ashes of the body are picked up, their disposal is recommended, a practice that has become more acceptable to the public than before. However, some Chinese Buddhists would rather keep the ashes of a parent in an urn stowed away in a memorial tower that holds thousands of urns. Another reason for their choice is that Buddhist services are regularly held there for the deceased customers though they have long been reborn somewhere.

Whether or not a person is considered reborn in the Pure Land, for forty-nine days after death, family members should continue chanting or saying

Amitābha Buddha's name when they are able, with the chanting machine turned on twenty-four hours a day in the deceased's room; they can do good karmas, such as eating vegetarian meals (most lay Buddhists are not vegetarians), reciting sūtras, donating to charity in the name of the deceased, and transferring their merits to the deceased. As stated in the *Sūtra of the Original vows of Earth Store Bodhisattva,* fascicle 2, chapter 7, six sevenths of the merit acquired from one's holy deeds benefits oneself, and only one seventh is received by the deceased (T13n0412, 0784b10–11). When family members do good works to benefit the deceased, they deliver themselves more than they do the deceased. Still, because the deceased in the interim body has keen senses, upon hearing Amitābha Buddha's name, he has a chance to be reborn in His land.

Mahāyāna Buddhists should take care not to recite the *Tibetan Book of the Dead,* day after day dictating to the deceased what horrifying sights and sounds he "should" perceive during the interim stage. Chanting or saying Amitābha Buddha's name is the purest and simplest way to guide the deceased to a good rebirth in this world, if not in the Pure Land. One's good karma of spiritual and worldly endeavor will always bring a corresponding requital.

Documentation of Rebirth Stories

The earliest documentation of rebirth stories was done during the Zhenyuan years (貞元, 785–804) of Emperor Dezong (唐德宗) of the Tang Dynasty, by Dharma Masters Shaokang (少康, ?–805) and Wenshen (文諗, dates unknown). The forty-eight rebirth stories in their collection were later edited and published by Dharma Master Daoshen (道詵, dates unknown), during the Wu Yue Kingdom (吳越國, 907–78), in a book titled *Wangsheng xifang jingtu ruiyingzhuan* 往生西方淨土瑞應傳 [Auspicious signs of rebirth in the Western Pure Land]. This book and six other documentations of rebirth stories are preserved in three texts in the Chinese Canon (T51n2070–72) and in four texts in the Extension of the Chinese canon (X78n1549–52).

Of these seven texts, text 1549 in the Extension of the Chinese Canon is the largest collection. It comprises 464 subjects (including three parrots), from the Eastern Jin Dynasty (317–420) to the early Qing Dynasty, that died with auspicious signs of rebirth in the Pure Land. It was compiled during the reign of Emperor Qianlong (清乾隆帝, 1735–96) of the Qing Dynasty (1644–1911), by a layman named Peng Xisu (彭希涑, 1761–93), and it was reviewed and proofed by his uncle Peng Jiqing (彭際清, 1740–96). This major compilation was initially published in 1783 as a book titled *Jingtu shengxianlu* 淨土聖賢錄 [Records of holies and sages of the Pure Land].

Text 1550 is an extension of text 1549. Near the end of the reign of Emperor Daoguang (清道光帝, 1821–50), a layman named Hu Ting (胡珽, dates unknown) compiled 159 rebirth stories. His book, *Jingtu shengxianlu xubian* 淨土聖賢錄續編 [Extended records of holies and sages of the Pure Land], is referred to as the second compilation.

The third compilation is not included in the Canon. It was done by Dharma Master Desen (德森, 1883–1962) and reviewed by Dharma Master Yinguang.

Desen published in 1933 a collection of 249 rebirth stories taken from two books, *Zhonglianji* 種蓮集 [Planting the lotus] and *Jindai wangsheng zhuan* 近代往生傳 [Stories of rebirth in modern times], and from the unpublished private records of Yu Huiyu (俞慧郁).

In 1995, Dharma Master Huilu (慧律, 1953–) published his 6-volume book, *Jingtu shengxianlu yijie* 淨土聖賢錄易解 [Easily comprehensible records of holies and sages of the Pure Land]. Volumes 1–4 cover the rebirth stories in the three compilations mentioned above, all of which are rewritten in modern Chinese. Volumes 5–6 include 368 stories of rebirth transpired in the 1900s, which were initially published in 1972 as a fourth compilation by a layman named Mao Lingyun (毛凌雲, 1910–2000). These 1,240 rebirth stories span a period of over 1,500 years after the passing of Dharma Master Huiyuan (慧遠, 334–416), the first patriarch of the Pure Land School.

These stories testify that training in accordance with Pure Land teachings produces results, evidenced by auspicious signs before and at one's death. In addition to having visions of Amitābha Buddha and His Pure Land before or upon dying, many foretold their departure dates and actually died on those dates. Completely in self-command, they passed away lying on their right side, in a seated posture, or in a standing posture. Other signs have included fragrance, radiance, the crown of the head staying warm for hours after death, the body remaining flexible for days after death, and so forth. These stories also testify that rebirth in the Pure Land is not exclusive to a few exalted Buddhist masters, but has been achieved by many faithful aspirers, including monks, nuns, laymen, laywomen, and a few animals. In the 21st century, more rebirth stories are being and will continue to be recorded.

The Pure Land School in the West

It is not the mission of Chinese Buddhist communities in the West to impart Pure Land teachings to Westerners. Financially supported by Chinese immigrants who need to recite texts in Chinese and hear teachings in Chinese, Chinese Buddhist temples are there to serve their needs, and most Chinese monks and nuns feel relieved that they have no need to speak a non-Chinese language. Therefore, it is not surprising that native Westerners are rarely seen at such temples.

Another feature of these temples is that they offer a range of group practices for their Chinese-speaking members. Pure Land practice is but one of such practices. Only the Amida Society, a worldwide Buddhist group, is founded exclusively to promote Pure Land teachings and training, under Dharma Master Jingkong (淨空, 1927–). However, all their members are Chinese speakers and everything is conducted in Chinese.

Fortunately, once the Buddha's teachings have been translated into the language of a country, they take root and grow, as they are studied by native readers and taught by native teachers, in their native language. For example, although the Pure Land School honors Indian masters Nāgārjuna and Vasubandhu as the originating patriarchs, neither of them ever set foot in China. Pure Land teachings, after being translated from Sanskrit into Chinese, have flourished in China since the days of Huiyuan, through the efforts of Chinese masters, teachers, and students. So too, Pure Land teachings have thrived in Japan, but the three Chinese masters Tanluan, Daochuo, and Shandao, who are honored as the originating patriarchs of Japan's Pure Land School, never set foot in Japan. Similarly, in the West the presence and charisma of an illustrious foreign teacher are not crucial for the development of the Pure Land School.[6]

Therefore, if Westerners are inspired to study Pure Land teachings and to train for rebirth in the Pure Land, given the Pure Land texts in this book, they would be well advised to plunge into the mode of self-study and self-training with self-motivation, so that they may become leading teachers to help others. They can generate their self-power as taught by the Pure Land School.

Thus, all readers of this book are potential teachers of the Pure Land School in the West, and the biographies of the thirteen Chinese patriarchs in Part III can be their inspiration. If you wonder why you choose to read the sūtras in this book, the Buddha gives His explanation and advice.

> If one had not accumulated merit and wisdom in one's past, one could not have heard this true Dharma. Because you all have made offerings to Tathāgatas, you now are hearing this meaning [sūtra]. Having heard it, you should accept and uphold it, copy and recite it, praise and expound it, and make offerings to it. If you single-mindedly seek the Pure Land, you will definitely be reborn in the Land of Ultimate Bliss. (T12n0363, 0326b4–7)

Notes

1. The name of this monk is translated into Chinese as Virtue Cloud in texts 278 and 279, the 60-fascicle and 80-fascicle versions of the *Mahāvaipulya Sūtra of Buddha Adornment.*

2. A Buddha defined by the Chan School in this way has not fulfilled merit and wisdom to be called the Two-Footed Honored One or to be called by His ten epithets. The Tiantai School qualifies use of the name Buddha to six levels, from a Buddha in principle (a sentient being) to a Buddha in fulfillment (a perfectly enlightened one).

3. In 574, Emperor Wu (北周武帝) of the Northern Zhou condemned Daoism and Buddhism. After taking the Northern Qi in 577, continuing his persecution, he destroyed 40,000 temples and ordered three million Buddhist monks and nuns to return to secular life.

4. The stream of love refers to one's cycle of birth and death perpetuated through one's karma and thirsty love for being.

5. Dharmas that appear and disappear (arise and perish) through causes conditions are empty. In true reality, they have no birth and, therefore, no death. In the *Middle Treatise,* fascicle 1, Nāgārjuna uses four negations to explain no

birth: "A dharma is born neither from itself nor from another, nor from both itself and another, nor from no cause. So we know that dharmas have no birth" (T30n1564, 0002b6–7).

6. The one exception is Chan Master Bodhidharma (circa ?–535) from India, who went to China to teach and is honored as the first patriarch of the Chan School.

PART I

Five Sūtras and One Treatise

Five Sūtras and One Treatise

1 Buddha Pronounces the Sūtra of Amitāyus Buddha (in 2 fascicles)

There are five Chinese versions of this sūtra, each translated from a different Sanskrit text. Four versions are in texts 360–63 (T12n0360–63), and a fifth version is the fifth sūtra in fascicles 17–18 of text 310, the *Great Treasure Pile Sūtra* (T11n0310), which comprises forty-nine sūtras in 120 fascicles. In the Eastern Han Dynasty (25–220), Lokakṣema (支婁迦讖, or 支讖, 147–?) translated text 361; in the Eastern Wu Kingdom (222–80), Zhiqian (支謙, 2nd–3rd centuries) translated text 362; in the Cao Wei Kingdom (220–65), Saṅghavarman (康僧鎧, 3rd century) translated text 360; in the Tang Dynasty (618–907), Bodhiruci (菩提流志, 562–727) translated the fifth sūtra in text 310, but he was not the Bodhiruci who translated text 1524, Vasubandhu's treatise; in the early Song Dynasty (960–1279), Dharmabhadra (法賢, dates unknown) translated text 363.

The three earlier translations are longer than the later two. Another difference is in the number of Dharmākara's vows included in these texts. The first two texts each include twenty-four vows, the next two texts each include forty-eight vows, and the fifth text includes thirty-six vows. Chinese Buddhists refer to these five texts respectively as the Han translation, the Wu translation, the Wei translation, the Tang translation, and the Song translation. The Pure Land School recognizes text 360, the Wei translation, as the best of the five Chinese translations.

In addition, a Chinese layman named Wang Rixiu (王日休, ?–1173) in the Song Dynasty edited four texts (T12n0360–63) into one text, which is collected into the Chinese Canon as text 364. However, it should not be considered as a sixth version. In the 20th century, another Chinese layman, Xia Lianju (夏蓮居, 1884–1965), edited all five texts into an integrated text. It is the adopted text of the Amida Society, a worldwide Buddhist group dedicated to promoting Pure Land teachings and training, under Dharma Master Jingkong (淨空, 1927–).

F. Max Müller (1894, part 2, 1–75) was the first to translate this sūtra from Sanskrit into English. Another translation is found in *A Treasury of Mahāyāna Sūtras* (Chang 1983, 339–60). This abridged translation is based on the Tang translation, the fifth sūtra in text 310. Then Inagaki and Stewart (1995, 21–89) published their translation of text 360.

Sūtra 1 is also an English translation of text 360. For the ease of the reader, headings and subheadings have been added to this translation.

In fascicle 1 of this sūtra, the Buddha tells the story of the most significant past life of Amitāyus Buddha when he was a monk named Dharmākara. He went to the Buddha called World Sovereign King (Lokeśvararāja) and expressed his resolve to become a Buddha and to form a Buddha Land surpassing all other Buddha Lands in its magnificence. Knowing the immensity of his resolve and his capacity, World Sovereign King Buddha showed him 210 koṭi Buddha Lands and their inhabitants. Then, for five kalpas, Dharmākara collected the pure actions to adorn his own Buddha Land. Having trained himself in this way, he returned to that Buddha and declared forty-eight vows to adorn his own Buddha Land.

His forty-eight vows specify, after his perfect enlightenment, the magnificence of Himself, His people, and His land, including His infinite radiance and infinite life, and the far-reaching power of His name, as well as the joys and transcendental powers of His people, and the splendors of His land.

The crucial incentive of those who aspire to the Pure Land comes from vow 11 (one will join the group heading for realization of the great bodhi), vow 18 (one will achieve rebirth in His land by only thinking ten thoughts of His name), vow 19 (at death, one will be received by Him), and vow 20 (one's wish for rebirth there will come true).

In fascicle 2 the Buddha describes the three classes of people who aspire to Amitāyus Buddha's land. All of them must first activate the bodhi mind in order to be reborn in His land according to their merit and wisdom. After their rebirth in lotus flowers, they will enjoy the splendors of His land, such as jeweled ground, trees, flowers, ponds, waters, and palaces and towers, described in detail in both fascicles.

While those with faith in Buddhas' infinite wisdom will be reborn in that Buddha Land proper, others with doubts will be reborn on the edge of that land, and will live a confined life in a jeweled palace. During their 500-year lifespan, they will not see Amitāyus Buddha or holy Bodhisattvas, and thus will not receive their teachings, unless they repent of their doubts.

The Buddha then describes the suffering in our world because of people's evil ways. Their five evils pertain to the ten evil karmas they do; their five pains pertain to their suffering in their present lives; and their five burns pertain to the dreadful requital in their next lives. He solemnly advises all to cultivate the five virtues and resolve to be reborn in Amitāyus Buddha's land.

The Buddha prophesies the astronomical number of rebirths, in that land, of Bodhisattvas from fourteen lands, including this land. Although the true Dharma will perish in the future, He will specially save this sūtra and make it stay for a hundred years more. Sentient beings that encounter this sūtra will all be delivered as they wish.

2 Buddha Pronounces the Sūtra of Amitābha Buddha

Texts 366–67 (T12n0366–67) are two Chinese versions of this sūtra, each translated from a different Sanskrit text. Kumārajīva (鳩摩羅什, 344–413) translated text 366 in the Later Qin Dynasty (384–417). Xuanzang (玄奘, 600– or 602–64) translated text 367 in the Tang Dynasty (618–907). While text 366 provides a list of Buddhas in worlds in the six directions, text 367 provides a list of Buddhas in worlds in the ten directions. Otherwise, these two texts are quite similar.

F. Max Müller (1894, part 2, 89–103) was the first to translate this sūtra from Sanskrit into English. Then Inagaki and Stewart (1995, 121–26) published their translation of text 366.

Sūtra 2 is also an English translation of text 366, the shorter and more popular version of this sūtra. It is commonly called the *Amitābha Sūtra*. After studying Sūtra 2, one has a better understanding and appreciation of Sūtra 1, the *Amitāyus Sūtra*. Regarded as a concise version of the comprehensive Sūtra 1, it is also called the *Smaller Amitāyus Sūtra*. It is the best-known sūtra of the Pure Land School because its shorter length is conducive to recitation and memorization.

In this sūtra Śākyamuni Buddha introduces a Buddha who resides in the Western Land of Ultimate Bliss. He is called Amitābha (infinite light), also called Amitāyus (infinite life). His land is adorned with virtues, such as jeweled ground, railings, trees, and lotus flowers in jeweled ponds. As magically manifested birds pronounce the Thirty-seven Elements of Bodhi, and bells hanging from jeweled nets play exquisite music, the inhabitants all think of the Buddha, the Dharma, and the Saṅgha. They all have attained the spiritual level of avinivartanīya, and many of them are in the holy position of waiting to attain Buddhahood in their next life. Thus, one may regard Amitābha Buddha's land as a wonderful training ground that readies one for Buddhahood.

Faith and resolve are emphasized in this sūtra. In addition, if one upholds Amitābha Buddha's name for one to seven days undistracted, He and a holy multitude will appear before one at death, and one will be reborn in His land. However, no one with few roots of goodness or a meager store of merits can be reborn there.

Dharma Master Zhixu (智旭, 1599–1655), the ninth patriarch of the Pure Land School, in *An Essential Explanation of the Amitābha Sūtra* (T37n1762), affirms that the best way to uphold Amitābha Buddha's name is to keep saying His name. This meditation technique works for spiritual trainees of all capacities: high, middling, and low. Infinite light and infinite life are not only the virtues of Amitābha Buddha but also the virtues of one's true mind. By thinking of Him and His land, one may not only be reborn in His land but also realize one's true mind.

3 Buddha Pronounces the Sūtra of Visualization of Amitāyus Buddha

In the Liu Song Dynasty (420–79), Kālayaśas (畺良耶舍, 383–442) translated this sūtra from Sanskrit into Chinese. His translation is in text 365 (T12n0365). J. Tasakusu (1894, part 2, 161–201) was the first to translate this sūtra from Chinese into English. His English translation is based on text 198, Kālayaśas's Chinese translation, in Nanjio's Catalogue of Tripiṭaka (Ibid., 161). Then Inagaki and Stewart (1995, 93–118) published their translation of text 365.

Sūtra 3 is an English translation of text 365. For the convenience of the reader, headings and subheadings have been added to this translation.

In this sūtra Queen Vaidehī, disgusted with her life in this world, asks the Buddha how she can be reborn in Sukhāvatī, Amitāyus Buddha's Land of Ultimate Bliss. The Buddha tells her that those who wish to be reborn in that land should carry out three meritorious works. Queen Vaidehī next asks the Buddha how to visualize that land and have the right experience.

The first thirteen of the sixteen visualizations are His instructions in response to her request. One should do these visualizations in the listed order. The ninth visualization, that of Amitāyus Buddha's reward body, is the most important. The Buddha says, "Seeing Amitāyus Buddha is seeing all Buddhas [in worlds] in the ten directions. Seeing all Buddhas is called the Thinking-of-Buddhas Samādhi. Doing this visualization is called visualizing the bodies of all Buddhas. By visualizing the bodies of all Buddhas, one sees the Buddha mind. The

Buddha mind is the mind of great lovingkindness and compassion. With unconditional lovingkindness, Buddhas accept all sentient beings. . . ."

Visualizations 14–16 are teachings given without being asked. They indicate what good karma one should do during one's life and upon dying, in order to be reborn in the Pure Land, in one of the nine grades. Those who wish to achieve a high rebirth in the high rank must invoke three minds in order to succeed. First, an earnest mind; second, a profound mind; and third, a mind wishing for rebirth in the Pure Land as one transfers one's merits to other sentient beings.

In the worse case, even a person who has done evil karma may achieve a low rebirth in the low rank. However, he needs to be fortunate enough to encounter a beneficent friend, who will advise him to take refuge in Amitāyus Buddha and to say "namo Amitāyus Buddha" ten times in ten thoughts. This condition is more lenient than that of vow 18 in Sūtra 1, which excludes those who have committed any of the five rebellious sins or maligned the true Dharma. Gradually, saying the name of Amitāyus Buddha, instead of doing elaborate visualizations, has become the main training of the Pure Land School.

4 Great Might Arrived Bodhisattva's Thinking-of-Buddhas as the Perfect Passage (a subsection in the Śūraṅgama Sūtra)

In the Tang Dynasty (618–907), Pramiti (般剌蜜帝, 7th–8th centuries) translated the *Śūraṅgama Sūtra* from Sanskrit into Chinese. His translation is in text 945 (T19n0945). Charles Luk (1966) was the first to translate text 945 into English. Then the Buddhist Text Translation Society (2009) published a more recent translation of this text.

Sūtra 4 is an English translation of a subsection in fascicle 5 of text 945. In this fascicle, at the Buddha's command, twenty-five Arhats and holy Bodhisattvas reveal their respective perfect passages (圓通). Each passage is a perfect practice of meditation, a Dharma Door, through which one can come to significant realizations. Mahāsthāmaprāpta (Great Might Arrived) Bodhisattva is the twenty-fourth one to report his perfect passage, the Thinking-of-Buddhas Samādhi.

He skillfully likens Buddhas and sentient beings to mother and son. Buddhas remember sentient beings as a mother remembers her son. However, sentient beings need to train themselves to remember Buddhas. He says, "If sentient beings' minds remember and think of Buddhas, in the present or a future life, they will definitely see Buddhas and will never be far from Buddhas. Without using other methods, their minds will spontaneously open."

He testifies, "It was when I stood on the Cause Ground, with my mind thinking only of a Buddha, that I achieved the Endurance in the Realization of the No Birth of Dharmas. In this world, I now assist those who think of Buddhas to come home to the Pure Land."

To attain the Thinking-of-Buddhas Samādhi, he recommends, "The foremost way is to continue the one pure thought to restrain the six faculties."

5 Mahāvaipulya Sūtra of Buddha Adornment, fascicle 40

There are three Chinese versions of the *Mahāvaipulya Sūtra of Buddha Adornment* (Buddhāvataṁsaka-mahāvaipulya-sūtra), each translated from a different Sanskrit text. In the Eastern Jin Dynasty (316–420), Buddhabhadra (佛馱跋陀羅, 359–429) translated text 278 (T09n0278) in 60 fascicles. In the Tang Dynasty (618–907), Śikṣānanda (實叉難陀, 652–710) translated text 279 (T10n0279) in 80 fascicles. Later in the Tang Dynasty, Prajñā (般若, 734–?) translated text 293 (T10n0293) in 40 fascicles.

Sūtra 5 is an English translation of the last fascicle of text 293. The whole text in 40 fascicles is a chapter titled "The Universally Worthy Action Vow to Enter the Inconceivable Liberation State," commonly simplified as "The Universally Worthy Action Vow." The first 39 fascicles of this chapter are a more extensive version of "Entering the Dharma Realm," the last chapter of either the 60-fascicle or the 80-fascicle text. But its 40th and last fascicle is unique, and it is widely circulated and studied in China as a stand-alone sūtra because it is considered the culmination of not only text 293 but also texts 278 and 279.

In Sūtra 5, after visiting fifty-two beneficent learned teachers, the youth Sudhana finally comes to Samantabhadra Bodhisattva, who reveals to him the universally worthy vow of the ten great actions to acquire the immeasurable merit required for Buddhahood. Therefore, this vow is also called Samantabhadra's vow of the ten great actions. Because his Sanskrit name Samantabhadra means universally worthy, he is revered in China as the Great Action Universally Worthy Bodhisattva.

Mahāyāna Buddhists all take this vow of the ten great actions and strive to fulfill this vow as their principal training, using body, voice, and mind. As stated by Samantabhadra Bodhisattva, after a person dies, "only this king of vows will not abandon him. . . . In the time of a kṣaṇa, he will be reborn in the World of Ultimate Bliss. . . . This person will see himself reborn in a lotus flower and have a prophecy [of attaining Buddhahood] bestowed upon him by that Buddha."

As lovingkindness and compassion for all sentient beings are the heart of the Mahāyāna, the ninth great action, to forever support sentient beings, demonstrates the spirit of the Mahāyāna. Samantabhadra Bodhisattva says, "Sentient beings are the tree roots, and Bodhisattvas and Buddhas are respectively the flowers and fruits. If one benefits sentient beings with the water of great compassion, one can develop the flowers and fruits of wisdom, becoming a Bodhisattva then a Buddha. Why? Because if Bodhisattvas benefit sentient beings with the water of great compassion, they can attain anuttara-samyak-saṁbodhi. Therefore, bodhi belongs to sentient beings. Without sentient beings, Bodhisattvas can never attain the unsurpassed saṁbodhi."

Then Samantabhadra Bodhisattva repeats his explanation of the ten vowed actions in verse, ending with an important wish. He says, "I wish that, at the end of my life, all hindrances will be removed. I will instantly be reborn in the Land of Peace and Bliss to behold Amitābha Buddha." Then he takes the tenth vowed action by transferring the superb merit acquired from his universally worthy, great actions to all sentient beings for their rebirth in Amitābha Buddha's land.

6 Upadeśa on the Sūtra of Amitāyus Buddha

In the Northern Wei Dynasty (386–534), Bodhiruci (菩提留支, 5th–6th centuries) translated from Sanskrit into Chinese Vasubandhu's treatise *Upadeśa on the Sūtra of Amitāyus Buddha*. His translation is in text 1524 (T26n1524). Because of this definitive treatise, Vasubandhu (世親, circa 320–80), who is revered in China as the originating patriarch of the Faxiang (dharma appearance) School, is also revered as an originating patriarch of the Pure Land School. This school is founded on five sūtras (Sūtras 1–5) and one treatise, Vasubandhu's treatise (Sūtra 6).

Dharma Master Tanluan (曇鸞, 476–542 or after 554) annotated this treatise. His annotation has contributed greatly to the study of this treatise and to the wide acceptance of the trainings taught in this treatise. For simplicity, Chinese Buddhists generally refer to this upadeśa as the treatise on rebirth, and refer to Tanluan's annotation as the annotation of the treatise on rebirth (T40n1819).

Sūtra 6 is an English translation of text 1524; headings and subheadings have been added to this translation. For those who wish to be reborn in Amitāyus Buddha's land, Vasubandhu introduces five training doors called the five doors of vigilance: making obeisance, praising, wishing, visualizing, and transferring merit.

Elaborating on the fourth training door, Vasubandhu divides the objects of one's visualization into three groups: the virtues of Amitāyus Buddha's land, the virtues of Amitāyus Buddha, and the virtues of the Bodhisattvas in His land. Also emphasized is the fifth training door, through which one transfers one's merits to others with a wish for all to be reborn in the Land of Peace and Bliss.

Through these five trainings, one acquires the pure true mind, and will be reborn in the Land of Peace and Bliss. One's achievements are described by five corresponding achievement doors: the near door, the door to the great assembly, the door to the residence, the door to the house, and the door to the playground in the garden. The first four progressive achievements are for self-benefit, and the fifth achievement is to benefit others.

Vasubandhu says only briefly that the second training door is praising Amitāyus Buddha by saying His name. Over time, this has become the main practice for those who aspire to that Pure Land.

1 佛說無量壽經
Buddha Pronounces the Sūtra of Amitāyus Buddha

Translated from Sanskrit into Chinese in the Cao Wei Dynasty
by
The Tripiṭaka Master Saṅghavarman from India

Fascicle 1 (of 2)

Preface

Thus I have heard:

At one time the Buddha was staying on the Gṛdhrakūṭa Mountain, near the city of Rājagṛha, together with 12,000 great bhikṣus, who all had achieved great transcendental powers. Such venerable ones included Ājñātakauṇḍinya, Aśvajit, Bāṣpa, Mahānāma, Bhadrajit, Yaśodeva, Vimala, Subāhu, Pūrṇa-Maitrayāṇīputra, Uruvilvākāśyapa, Nadīkāśyapa, Gayākāśyapa, Kumārakāśyapa, Mahākāśyapa, Śāriputra, Mahāmaudgalyāyana, Mahākauṣṭhila, Mahākapphiṇa, Mahācunda, Aniruddha, Nandika, Kampila, Subhūti, Revata, Khadiravaṇika, Vakula, Svāgata, Amogharāja, Pārāyaṇika, Patka, Cullapatka, Nanda, Rāhula, and the blessed Ānanda.[1] Holy bhikṣus such as these were at the head of the assembly.

In attendance as well was a multitude of Bodhisattva-Mahāsattvas, such as Samantabhadra Bodhisattva, Mañjuśrī Bodhisattva, and Maitreya Bodhisattva. Also present were all Bodhisattvas of this Worthy Kalpa, including the sixteen Upright Ones: Worthy Protector Bodhisattva, Good Deliberation Bodhisattva, [Wisdom Eloquence Bodhisattva[2]], Faith and Wisdom Bodhisattva, Emptiness Bodhisattva, Transcendental Power Bloom Bodhisattva, Brilliant Hero Bodhisattva, Wisdom Superior Bodhisattva, Knowledge Banner Bodhisattva, Silent Faculty Bodhisattva, Vow and Wisdom Bodhisattva, Fragrant Elephant Bodhisattva, Jewel Hero Bodhisattva, Center Abiding Bodhisattva, Restrained Action Bodhisattva, and Liberation Bodhisattva.

They all cultivate the virtues of Samantabhadra Bodhisattva-Mahāsattva. Equipped with immeasurable Bodhisattva actions and vows, they stand firm in all virtuous ways. They visit worlds in the ten directions, skillfully carrying out suitable missions. They enter into the store of the Buddha Dharma, arrive on the shore of nirvāṇa, and demonstrate the attainment of samyak-saṁbodhi in innumerable worlds.

A Bodhisattva's Attainment of Buddhahood

A Bodhisattva first stays in Tuṣita Heaven to expound the true Dharma. Then he leaves the celestial palace and descends into his mother's womb. He is born from the right side of his mother and walks seven steps as his dazzling radiance illuminates innumerable Buddha Lands in the ten directions. As the earth quakes in six different ways, he declares aloud, "I will be the unsurpassed honored one in this world."

The Bodhisattva is attended by the god-king Śakra and Brahma-kings, and gods and humans take refuge in him. As a demonstration, he learns mathematics, literature, archery, and horsemanship, masters sacred arts, and studies voluminous texts. Playing in the garden, he discusses martial arts and tests his ability. Even as he manifests enjoyment of sense objects in his palace, such as sights and flavors, he perceives old age, illness, and death, and realizes the impermanence of the world. Abandoning his kingdom, riches, and status, he goes into mountain forests, seeking bodhi. He rides off on his white horse then sends it back with his jeweled crown and necklaces.

Shedding his regal garment, the Bodhisattva puts on the Dharma robe and shaves off his hair and beard. He meditates under trees, training arduously as he should for six years. Because he has appeared in the world of the five turbidities, he conforms to the way of the multitudes and displays dirt on his body. He then bathes in [the Nairañjanā] the river of gold. Gods bend the tree branches so that he can hold them to get out of the river. Intelligent birds follow him to his bodhimaṇḍa. The youth who offers him grass is an auspicious sign of the fullness of his merit and endeavor. Out of compassion, the Bodhisattva accepts this offering of grass and makes a seat under the bodhi tree, upon which he sits cross-legged. Alerted by his great radiance, the celestial māra-king leads māra legions to harass and test him. However, he subjugates them all with his wisdom and power.

Then he realizes the wondrous Dharma and attains anuttara-samyak-saṁbodhi. The god-king Śakra and Brahma-kings all beseech Him to turn the Dharma wheel. As a Buddha, He walks the Buddha steps and roars the Buddha roar. He beats the Dharma drum, blows the Dharma conch shell, wields the Dharma sword, and erects the Dharma banner. He rumbles the Dharma thunder, flashes the Dharma lightning, pours down the Dharma rain, and gives the Dharma alms. Sounding the wondrous Dharma tones, he awakens the world. As the Buddha illuminates everywhere in innumerable Buddha Lands with His radiance, the entire world quakes in six different ways, reaching the māra's dominion, and the māra's palace is shaken. The māras in multitudes are intimidated and terrified, and none of them fails to fall under submission. He shatters the web of evils and crushes the wrong views. He expels [sentient beings'] afflictions, which enslave their body and mind, and destroys their pit of desires. He cleanses their impurities to reveal purity. He protects the Dharma fortress and opens Dharma Doors. He illuminates the Buddha Dharma and widely disseminates it to transform all [sentient beings].

The Buddha enters towns to beg for food and receives offerings in abundance. Revealing Himself as a fortune field, He enables the almsgivers to accumulate merit acquired from their planting. He smiles as He expounds the

Dharma. He heals with Dharma medicine the three kinds of suffering. He teaches the immeasurable merit of the resolve to attain bodhi. He bestows upon Bodhisattvas the prophecy that they all will attain Buddhahood. By His demonstration of entering parinirvāṇa, He helps innumerable multitudes to eradicate their afflictions and plant their roots of virtue.

The merit He has acquired is wondrous and immeasurable as he visits Buddha Lands, giving everyone the teachings for attaining bodhi. His actions are pure and untainted. Like a master of illusion who conjures up various images, He manifests Himself as male or female, or in any suitable form. With perfect understanding of what He has learned, He manifests Himself at will.

The Bodhisattva Way

The Bodhisattvas [in this assembly] do the same. To learn all Dharmas [on their Way to Buddhahood], they collect them and train accordingly. The truth they uphold can inspire and transform all sentient beings. Fully equipped with ways to help sentient beings compassionately, they manifest themselves everywhere in innumerable Buddha Lands, never acting arrogant or domineering. They thoroughly understand the essentials of Bodhisattva scriptural texts. As their names spread everywhere, their virtuous ways prevail in the ten directions. They are protected and remembered by innumerable Buddhas. They abide in the truths that Buddhas abide in, and they establish the teachings that great holy ones have established. Under Tathāgatas' guidance, they are Bodhisattvas and great teachers, who each can proclaim the Way. With wisdom arising from profound meditation, they educate and guide multitudes of sentient beings. Penetrating dharma nature, they understand sentient beings' appearances and their lands.

When such Bodhisattvas make offerings to Buddhas, they magically manifest themselves like flashes of lightning. They skillfully learn the way of fearlessness and fully understand that dharmas are illusory. They annihilate the webs of māras and liberate sentient beings from bondage and fetters. Transcending the ground of voice-hearers and Pratyekabuddhas, they attain the Three Samādhis: emptiness, no appearance, and no wish. By skillful means, they present the Three Vehicles. For those of middling or low capacity, they demonstrate parinirvāṇa. Knowing that [in true reality] there is neither action nor existence, neither arising nor ceasing, they realize the truth of equality and fully attain innumerable dhāranīs and hundreds and thousands of samādhis. As their faculties and wisdom remain in boundless silence, they delve into the store of the Bodhisattva Dharma and attain the Samādhi of Buddha Adornment. While they remain inside the profound Samādhi Door, they see Buddhas before them.

Then they promote and expound the Dharma in all the sūtras. In the instant of a thought, they visit everywhere in all Buddha Lands, rescuing those in extreme suffering, both those who do and those who do not find respite from suffering. As they explicate the true reality of dharmas, they acquire a Tathāgata's eloquence. With mastery of the languages of the multitudes, they educate and transform them all. Having transcended the dharmas of the world, their minds abide in ways to deliver the world. With command of all things in the world, they are the unasked friends to multitudes of sentient beings, and they carry the heavy load of sentient beings [to the shore of nirvāṇa].

As such Bodhisattvas accept and uphold Tathāgatas' profound Dharma store, they protect those of the Tathāgata character-type and help them to carry on this character-type. Exuding great compassion for sentient beings, they speak to them with lovingkindness to open their dharma-eye. As they block the three evil life-paths, they open the door to the good life-paths and, unasked, they teach the Dharma to the multitudes. Like a dutiful son who loves and respects his parents, they regard sentient beings as they do themselves. All their roots of goodness contribute to their crossing over to the shore of nirvāṇa, as they acquire the immeasurable merit, inconceivable wisdom, and holy knowledge of Buddhas.

The Request for Teachings

Innumerable such Bodhisattva-Mahāsattvas came to this assembly. At that time the World-Honored One looked vigorous and joyful, His appearance pure, radiant, and majestic. The venerable Ānanda, at the Buddha's unspoken holy command, rose from his seat, bared his right shoulder, and fell on both knees. With palms joined, he said to the Buddha, "World-Honored One, You look vigorous and joyful today, Your appearance pure, radiant, and majestic, like a clear mirror that reflects images inside and is shiny outside. Your sublime visage is resplendent, unparalleled, and indescribable. Never have I beheld such wondrous splendor as You now display. Indeed, Great Holiness, my mind has these thoughts: 'Today the World-Honored One abides in the extraordinary Dharma. Today the Hero of the World abides in the truth in which all Buddhas abide. Today the Eye of the World carries on as the guiding teacher. Today the Victor of the World abides in the supreme bodhi. Today the Heaven-Honored One demonstrates the Tathāgata virtues. As Buddhas of the past, present, and future think of one another, does the present Buddha not think of other Buddhas? Why is His awesome presence so radiant?'"

The World-Honored One asked Ānanda, "Why Ānanda? Did the gods tell you to ask the Buddha? Do you ask about my sublime visage based on your own perception?"

Ānanda replied to the Buddha, "No god told me to. I ask about this meaning based on my own perception."

The Buddha said, "Very good! Ānanda, your question is opportune. You have developed profound wisdom and truly wonderful eloquence and, out of compassion for sentient beings, you wisely ask about this meaning.

"The Tathāgata, out of inexhaustible great compassion for sentient beings in the Three Realms of Existence, has appeared in the world to expound the teachings for attaining bodhi, to rescue sentient beings, and to give them true benefits. Like an udumbara flower, the auspicious, wonderful flower that appears only once in a long while, He is hard to encounter in innumerable koṭis of kalpas. What you ask now will greatly benefit and transform all gods and humans.

"Ānanda, know that immeasurable is the Tathāgata-Saṁbuddha's wisdom, which leads and guides. His knowledge and views are hindrance free and indestructible. With the power of one meal, He can make his life last 100,000 koṭi kalpas or even innumerable, countless kalpas, His faculties undiminished in vigor and His appearance unchanged in radiance. What is the reason? Because the Tathāgata, with His boundless and endless samādhi and wisdom, has command of all dharmas. Hearken, Ānanda, I now will explain to you."

"Indeed, I would be glad to hear," responded Ānanda.

The Teachings

The Fifty-four Buddhas Who Appeared in Succession

The Buddha told Ānanda, "In the distant past, innumerable, countless inconceivable kalpas ago, a Tathāgata called [Dīpaṁkara] Lamp Lighter appeared in the world. He taught and delivered innumerable sentient beings, enabling them to attain bodhi, and then entered parinirvāṇa. After Him, Tathāgatas that appeared in succession included Distant Light, Moonlight, Sandalwood Scent, Fine Mountain King, Sumeru Celestial Crown, Sumeru Equal Brilliance, Moon Color, Right Mindfulness, No Affliction, No Attachment, Dragon God, Nocturnal Light, Peaceful Bright Summit, Immovable Ground, Wonderful Aquamarine Flower, Golden Aquamarine Color, Gold Store, Flaming Light, Flaming Faculty, Earth Seed, Moon Image, Sun Tone, Liberation Flower, Splendid Radiance, Transcendental Power in the Ocean of Enlightenment, Water Light, Great Fragrance, Freedom from Sense Objects, Abandoning Aversion, Jewel Flame, Wonderful Summit, Valiant Stand, Merit Held in Wisdom, Outshining the Sun-Moon Light, Sun-Moon Aquamarine Light, Unsurpassed Aquamarine Light, Foremost Position, Bodhi Flower, Moon Radiance, Sunlight, Flower Color King, Water-Moon light, Removing the Darkness of Delusion, Action to Remove Hindrance, Pure Faith, Fine Constellation, Awesome Spirit, Dharma Wisdom, Bird Tone, Lion Tone, Dragon Tone, and Staying in the World. These Buddhas have all passed away.

"Next appeared a Buddha called [Lokeśvararāja] World Sovereign King, the Tathāgata, Arhat, Samyak-Saṁbuddha, Knowledge and Conduct Perfected, Sugata, Understanding the World, Unsurpassed One, Tamer of Men, Teacher to Gods and Humans, Buddha the World-Honored One.

Dharmākara on the Cause Ground

His Resolve to Form a Splendid Buddha Land

"At that time there was a king who heard that a Buddha was expounding the Dharma. With joy in his heart, he immediately activated the anuttara-samyak-saṁbodhi mind. He abandoned his kingdom and throne and became a śramaṇa named Dharmākara. Exceptionally intelligent and valiant, he was outstanding in the world. He went to World Sovereign King Tathāgata. He made obeisance at that Buddha's feet, then circled Him to the right three times. Kneeling on both knees, he joined his palms and praised in verse:

Sublime is the radiant visage.
Boundless is the awesome spirit.
Such resplendent glow
Is unparalleled!
The sun-moon jewel
That shines with flaming brilliance
Is obscured
Like pooled ink.

The Tathāgata's features are
Unrivaled, beyond the world.
His great tones of true enlightenment
Flow to and resound in the ten directions.
His achievement of precepts, knowledge, energetic progress,
Samādhi, wisdom,
And awesome virtue are
Unequaled, supreme, and rare.
His profound contemplation and deliberation of
The ocean of the Buddha Dharma
Unravel its profound secrets and
Penetrate to its bottom.

Nevermore has the World-Honored One
Ignorance, greed, or anger.
He, the hero and lion among men,
Has immeasurable spiritual virtue,
Immense merit,
And profound, wondrous wisdom.
His radiance and awesome appearance
Shake the Large Thousandfold World.

I resolve to become a Buddha,
Equal to the holy Dharma King,
To deliver others from their cycle of birth and death,
Enabling them all to achieve liberation.
I will give alms and control my mind,
Observe precepts, endure adversities, make energetic progress,
Abide in samādhi,
And unfold wisdom, as the foremost training.
I vow to attain Buddhahood
And completely fulfill this vow
To give great peace to
Those living in fear.

Suppose there are Buddhas
A billion koṭi in number
And great holy beings as
Numerous as the sands of the Ganges.
Making offerings to

Buddhas such as these
Is inferior to seeking bodhi
Resolutely without retreat.
Buddha Lands are as numerous as
The sands of the Ganges.
Although they are countless,
Beyond reckoning,
My radiance will illuminate everywhere
In all these lands.
As I make energetic progress,
My awesome spirit is measureless.

After I become a Buddha,
My land will be foremost in splendor,
Adorned with myriad wonders,
And its bodhimaṇḍa will be supreme.
My land will be like nirvāṇa,
Peaceful beyond comparison.
With compassion,
I will deliver all [sentient beings].
Those from worlds in the ten directions who are reborn in my land
Will have joyful pure minds.
Upon arrival in my land,
They all will have peace and bliss.

May the Buddha's pure trust
Be my true witness.
Before Him, I make my vow
And strive to achieve my goal.
Just as World-Honored Ones [in worlds] in the ten directions
Have hindrance-free wisdom,
So does this World-Honored One know
My mind and actions.
Even if I am in the midst of
Pain and anguish,
I persist in my energetic progress
And endure without regrets.

"Having spoken these stanzas, the bhikṣu Dharmākara said to that Buddha, 'Indeed, World-Honored One, I have activated the anuttara-samyak-saṁbodhi mind, and I pray that the Buddha will fully expound to me the Dharma in the sūtras. I will train myself and collect the pure adornments of innumerable Buddha Lands, so that I will quickly attain the perfect enlightenment and uproot the suffering of repeated birth and death.'"

The Buddha told Ānanda, "Then, World Sovereign King Buddha said to the bhikṣu Dharmākara, 'You should know how to train yourself and adorn your Buddha Land.' The bhikṣu replied to that Buddha, 'This profound significance is beyond my state. World-Honored One, I pray that You will fully expound to me the way Buddha-Tathāgatas form their Pure Lands. Having heard it, I will train according to what You say and fulfill my vow.'

"At that time World Sovereign King Buddha knew this bhikṣu's exceptional capacity, and the profundity and immensity of his resolve. He then said to the bhikṣu Dharmākara, 'As an analogy, a person keeps drawing water from an ocean with a small container. After kalpas of work, he can reach its bottom and obtain the treasures there. Likewise, if a person makes earnest, energetic progress to seek bodhi unceasingly, he will definitely harvest the holy fruit. No wish will fail to come true.'

"Then, World Sovereign King Buddha fully described to him 210 koṭi Buddha Lands. In response to his request, that Buddha also displayed all lands, coarse or fine, and the gods and humans there, good or evil.

"At that time the bhikṣu heard that Buddha's description of magnificent Pure Lands and also beheld them all. He made the unsurpassed supreme resolve. His mind was silent and free from attachment, and no one in the entire world could compare with him. For five kalpas, he contemplated and collected the pure actions to adorn a Buddha Land."

Ānanda asked the Buddha, "What was that Buddha's lifespan?"

The Buddha replied, "That Buddha lived for forty-two kalpas, during which time the bhikṣu Dharmākara collected the pure actions taken to adorn those 210 koṭi wonderful Buddha Lands. Having trained himself in this way, he went to that Buddha. He made obeisance at that Buddha's feet and circled Him three times. Standing properly with his palms joined, he said to that Buddha, 'World-Honored One, I have collected the pure actions to adorn my Buddha Land.'

"That Buddha told the bhikṣu, 'You now may declare your vows. Know that now is the right time to delight all multitudes. After other Bodhisattvas have heard you, they too can train in the way that you have, and fulfill immeasurable great vows.'

His Forty-eight Vows

"The bhikṣu said to that Buddha, 'I pray that you will grant me your attention. I will declare my vows completely:

1. After I become a Buddha, if there should be hell-dwellers, hungry ghosts, or animals in my land, I would not attain the perfect enlightenment.
2. After I become a Buddha, if gods[3] in my land, after their death, should take any of the three evil life-paths, I would not attain the perfect enlightenment.
3. After I become a Buddha, if gods in my land should not be the color of gold, I would not attain the perfect enlightenment.
4. After I become a Buddha, if gods in my land should have varied shapes and forms, beautiful or ugly, I would not attain the perfect enlightenment.
5. After I become a Buddha, if gods in my land should not have the power to know their past lives and the past events in 100,000 koṭi nayuta kalpas, I would not attain the perfect enlightenment.
6. After I become a Buddha, if gods in my land should not have the god-eye to see everything in 100,000 koṭi nayuta Buddha Lands, I would not attain the perfect enlightenment.

7. After I become a Buddha, if gods in my land should not have the god-ear to hear, accept, and uphold the words spoken by 100,000 koṭi nayuta Buddhas, I would not attain the perfect enlightenment.

8. After I become a Buddha, if gods in my land should not have the power to know the thoughts of sentient beings in 100,000 koṭi nayuta Buddha Lands, I would not attain the perfect enlightenment.

9. After I become a Buddha, if gods in my land should not have the power to travel, in the instant of a thought, to 100,000 koṭi nayuta Buddha Lands, I would not attain the perfect enlightenment.

10. After I become a Buddha, if gods in my land should imagine that they have embodied selves, I would not attain the perfect enlightenment.

11. After I become a Buddha, if gods in my land should not belong in the group of sentient beings that definitely progress on the right path to bodhi until their attainment of the great nirvāṇa, I would not attain the perfect enlightenment.

12. After I become a Buddha, if my radiance should have a limit of illuminating 100,000 koṭi nayuta Buddha Lands, I would not attain the perfect enlightenment.

13. After I become a Buddha, if my lifespan should have a limit of 100,000 koṭi nayuta kalpas, I would not attain the perfect enlightenment.

14. After I become a Buddha, if the number of voice-hearers in my land should be known by calculation, and be obtained through calculating for 100,000 kalpas by sentient beings in the Three-Thousand Large Thousandfold World that all have become Pratyekabuddhas, I would not attain the perfect enlightenment.

15. After I become a Buddha, if the lifespan of gods in my land should have a limit, except being shortened by their own wish, I would not attain the perfect enlightenment.

16. After I become a Buddha, if gods in my land should ever hear of any wrongdoings there, I would not attain the perfect enlightenment.

17. After I become a Buddha, if innumerable Buddhas in worlds in the ten directions should not praise my name, I would not attain the perfect enlightenment.

18. After I become a Buddha, in worlds in the ten directions, there will be sentient beings that, with earnest faith and delight, wish to be reborn in my land, even if by only thinking ten thoughts. If they should fail to be reborn there—excepting those who have committed any of the five rebellious sins or maligned the true Dharma—I would not attain the perfect enlightenment.

19. After I become a Buddha, in worlds in the ten directions, there will be sentient beings that activate the bodhi mind, acquire merit, and earnestly wish to be reborn in my land. If I should not appear, surrounded by a holy multitude, before them at their death, I would not attain the perfect enlightenment.

20. After I become a Buddha, in worlds in the ten directions, there will be sentient beings that hear my name, intently think of my land, plant their roots of virtue and, with a wish for rebirth in my land, transfer their merits to others. If they should fail to be reborn in my land, I would not attain the perfect enlightenment.

21. After I become a Buddha, if gods in my land should not be complete with a great man's thirty-two physical marks, I would not attain the perfect enlightenment.

22. After I become a Buddha, if Bodhisattvas from other Buddha Lands who are reborn in my land should eventually fail to be in the holy position of waiting to attain Buddhahood in their next life, I would not attain the perfect enlightenment. Excepted are Bodhisattvas who choose not to be in that position because of their original vows. For the sake of delivering all sentient beings, they don their armor of great vows and develop their roots of virtue. They visit Buddha Lands, train in the Bodhisattva Way, and make offerings to Buddha-Tathāgatas [in worlds] in the ten directions. They develop and transform as many sentient beings as the sands of the Ganges, setting them on the Way to the unsurpassed bodhi. Transcending the regular course through the Bodhisattva Grounds, they currently cultivate the virtues of Samantabhadra Bodhisattva.

23. After I become a Buddha, if Bodhisattvas in my land should fail to arrive, by virtue of my spiritual power, in the time of a meal, in innumerable, countless koṭis of nayutas of Buddha Lands to make offerings to those Buddhas, I would not attain the perfect enlightenment.

24. After I become a Buddha, Bodhisattvas in my land will demonstrate their roots of virtue before Buddhas. If they should fail to manifest at will their intended offerings to their satisfaction, I would not attain the perfect enlightenment.

25. After I become a Buddha, if Bodhisattvas in my land should be unable to expound [sarvajña] the overall wisdom-knowledge, I would not attain the perfect enlightenment.

26. After I become a Buddha, if Bodhisattvas in my land should not have the god Nārāyaṇa's adamantine body, I would not attain the perfect enlightenment.

27. After I become a Buddha, all things in my land will be radiant and splendid in extraordinary forms and colors, beyond description. If sentient beings in my land, including those with the god-eye, should know and distinguish them all by their names and numbers, I would not attain the perfect enlightenment.

28. After I become a Buddha, if Bodhisattvas in my land, including those with a meager store of merits, should fail to know and see in my bodhimaṇḍa the innumerable radiant colors of the [bodhi] tree, which is four million lis tall, I would not attain the perfect enlightenment.

29. After I become a Buddha, if Bodhisattvas in my land who read, recite, uphold, and expound sūtras should fail to acquire eloquence and wisdom, I would not attain the perfect enlightenment.

30. After I become a Buddha, if Bodhisattvas in my land should have a limit in their eloquence and wisdom, I would not attain the perfect enlightenment.

31. After I become a Buddha, my land will be so pure that it illuminates and reflects innumerable, countless inconceivable Buddha Lands in the ten directions, like one's own facial image seen in a clear mirror. If this should not come true, I would not attain the perfect enlightenment.

32. After I become a Buddha, in my land, from the ground to the open sky, there will be palaces, towers, ponds, streams, flowers, and trees. Myriad things in my land will be made of innumerable varieties of treasures and 100,000 kinds of fragrances, and these wonderful adornments will surpass those of gods. As the fragrances suffuse all worlds in the ten directions, Bodhisattvas who smell them will all train in the Buddha Way. If this should not come true, I would not attain the perfect enlightenment.

33. After I become a Buddha, in innumerable inconceivable Buddha Lands in the ten directions, all sentient beings touched by my radiance will become gentle in body and mind, surpassing gods. If this should not come true, I would not attain the perfect enlightenment.

34. After I become a Buddha, in innumerable inconceivable Buddha Lands in the ten directions, if sentient beings that hear my name should fail to achieve the Bodhisattva Endurance in the Realization of the No Birth of Dharmas and to acquire profound dhāranīs, I would not attain the perfect enlightenment.

35. After I become a Buddha, in innumerable inconceivable Buddha Lands in the ten directions, women who hear my name will have faith and delight, activate the bodhi mind, and tire of their female form. If, after their death, they should be reborn in female form, I would not attain the perfect enlightenment.

36. After I become a Buddha, in innumerable inconceivable Buddha Lands in the ten directions, multitudes of Bodhisattvas who hear my name, after their death, will be reborn to train in the Brahma way of life until their attainment of Buddhahood. If this should not come true, I would not attain the perfect enlightenment.

37. After I become a Buddha, in innumerable inconceivable Buddha Lands in the ten directions, Bodhisattvas[4] who hear my name will prostrate themselves in obeisance and, with faith and delight, train in the Bodhisattva Way, and gods and humans will salute them. If this should not come true, I would not attain the perfect enlightenment.

38. After I become a Buddha, gods in my land, by a single thought, will be able to make appear on their bodies garments, which are as wonderful as Buddhas say. If their garments should require sewing, dyeing, or laundering, I would not attain the perfect enlightenment.

39. After I become a Buddha, if the bliss experienced by gods in my land should be inferior to that of bhikṣus with no more afflictions to discharge, I would not attain the perfect enlightenment.

40. After I become a Buddha, Bodhisattvas in my land who wish to see innumerable splendid, pure Buddha Lands in the ten directions will see them all displayed in the jeweled trees as they wish, like one's facial image in a clear mirror. If this should not come true, I would not attain the perfect enlightenment.

41. After I become a Buddha, if multitudes of Bodhisattvas in other lands who hear my name should remain incomplete in their faculties until their attainment of Buddhahood, I would not attain the perfect enlightenment.

42. After I become a Buddha, multitudes of Bodhisattvas in other lands who hear my name will all attain the Samādhi of Pure Liberation and abide in it. By a single thought, they will be able to make offerings to innumerable inconceivable Buddha-Bhagavāns without losing their samādhi state. If this should not come true, I would not attain the perfect enlightenment.

43. After I become a Buddha, multitudes of Bodhisattvas in other lands who hear my name will, after their death, be reborn into a noble family. If this should not come true, I would not attain the perfect enlightenment.

44. After I become a Buddha, multitudes of Bodhisattvas in other lands who hear my name will, with delight and exuberance, train in the Bodhisattva Way and fully develop their roots of virtue. If this should not come true, I would not attain the perfect enlightenment.

45. After I become a Buddha, multitudes of Bodhisattvas in other lands who hear my name will all attain the Samādhi of Universal Equality and abide in it until their attainment of Buddhahood. They will constantly see innumerable inconceivable Buddhas. If this should not come true, I would not attain the perfect enlightenment.

46. After I become a Buddha, Bodhisattvas in my land will hear the Dharma according to their wishes and preferences. If this should not come true, I would not attain the perfect enlightenment.

47. After I become a Buddha, if multitudes of Bodhisattvas in other lands who hear my name should not soon attain [avinivartanīya] the spiritual level of no regress, I would not attain the perfect enlightenment.

48. After I become a Buddha, if multitudes of Bodhisattvas in other lands who hear my name should not achieve the first, second, or third of the Three Endurances in the Dharma, and thus fail to attain the level of no regress from the Buddha Dharma, I would not attain the perfect enlightenment.'"

The Buddha told Ānanda, "After the bhikṣu Dharmākara finished declaring his vows, he spoke in verse:

Making vows to transcend the world,
I will definitely attain the unsurpassed bodhi.
If my vows are not fulfilled,
I swear not to attain samyak-saṁbodhi.
If I am not a great almsgiver who,
For innumerable kalpas,
Universally relieves all those in poverty and suffering,
I vow not to attain samyak-saṁbodhi.
After I attain Buddha bodhi,
My renown will spread [to worlds] in the ten directions.
If there are those who never hear my name,
I vow not to attain samyak-saṁbodhi.

Leaving behind desires and keeping the right mindfulness,
I will train in the Brahma way of life with pure wisdom.
Resolved to attain the unsurpassed bodhi,
I will become the teacher to gods and humans.
I will display vast radiance with my spiritual power,
Universally illuminating innumerable lands,
To dispel the darkness of the three afflictions
And rescue those in tribulations.
I will open their wisdom-eye
And dispel the darkness of their blindness.
I will close the evil life-paths
And open the door to the good life-paths.

When my meritorious work is completed,
My awesome radiance will shine in the ten directions.
The double luminosity of the sun and the moon will be eclipsed
And the light of the skies will be withdrawn.

I open the Dharma store to the multitudes
And lavish upon them the treasure of merits.
In the midst of the multitudes,
I expound the Dharma with the lion's roar.

I make offerings to all Buddhas,
Fully developing my roots of virtue.
I wish to unfold my wisdom in full,
To become the hero in the Three Realms,
Like the Buddha, whose immeasurable wisdom
Penetrates everything everywhere.
I wish that the power of my merit
May equal that of the Supreme Honored One.

If my vows are to bear fruit,
The Thousandfold World will be moved,
And gods in the open sky
Will shower splendid flowers.

"As soon as the bhikṣu spoke these stanzas, the earth quaked in six different ways, and the sky rained wonderful flowers down upon him. Music sprang up in the sky, praising, 'He will definitely attain anuttara-samyak-saṁbodhi.' Then the bhikṣu Dharmākara completely fulfilled these great vows. Truly he transcended the world, for he deeply delighted in nirvāṇa."

His Accumulation of Merits from Virtuous Actions

The Buddha said, "Ānanda, the bhikṣu Dharmākara made these great vows before that Buddha, amid multitudes of celestial māras, Brahma gods, and the eight classes of Dharma protectors, such as gods and dragons. Having made his vows, he intently worked on the adornment of his Buddha Land so that it should be open and vast, superb and uniquely wonderful, as well as everlasting, without decay or change.

"For inconceivable trillions of kalpas, the bhikṣu engaged in immeasurable virtuous Bodhisattva actions. He permitted neither thoughts nor perceptions of greed, anger, or harm to arise in his mind. He was not attached to the sense objects: sights, sounds, scents, flavors, tactile sensations, and mental objects. He was accomplished in endurance, never disheartened by myriad tribulations. With few desires and much contentment, he had no greed, anger, or delusion. Silently abiding in samādhi, his wisdom was hindrance free. Free from the mind of falsehood and sycophancy, he spoke loving words with a kind face and considerately asked the questions for those who hesitated to ask.

"He made boldly energetic progress, never feeling weary. He sought only the pure dharmas to benefit sentient beings. He revered the Three Jewels and served his teachers and elders. With great adornments [his merit and wisdom], he completed many works and enabled sentient beings to acquire merit. He abided in the Three Samādhis: emptiness, no appearance, and no wish. With no act and no arising in his mind, he saw that dharmas are illusory. Keeping far away from abusive speech, which can harm self, others, and both, he trained in speaking virtuous words to benefit self, others, and both.

"He abandoned his kingdom and throne, wealth, and women to practice the six pāramitās and teach others to practice them as well. After countless kalpas of accumulation of merit and virtue, in any place where he was reborn, innumerable treasure stores were spontaneously uncovered at his wish. He taught and transformed innumerable sentient beings, setting them on the Way to the unsurpassed enlightenment. He manifested himself as elders, laypeople, people with a great family name, or dignitaries, as kings in the kṣatriya caste or Wheel-Turning Kings, and as god-kings of the six desire heavens or even god-kings of Brahma heavens. He always reverently offered the four necessities to all Buddhas. Such merit is beyond description and acclaim.

"His breath was fragrant and fresh, like utpala flowers. The pores of his body emitted sandalwood scent, which suffused innumerable worlds. His facial features were even and comely and his appearance superb. Manifested from his hands were inexhaustible treasures, clothing, food and drink, and adornments, such as splendid flowers, incense, and silky canopies and banners. Things such as these surpass those of gods. He achieved command of all dharmas."

Dharmākara as Amitāyus Buddha

Ānanda asked the Buddha, "Has Dharmākara Bodhisattva already attained Buddhahood and entered parinirvāṇa? Has he not yet attained Buddhahood? Is he now somewhere?"

The Buddha replied to Ānanda, "Dharmākara Bodhisattva has already attained Buddhahood. He is now in the west, 100,000 koṭi lands away from here. His Buddha Land is called Peace and Bliss."

Ānanda next asked, "How long has it been since that Buddha attained bodhi?"

The Buddha replied, "It has been ten kalpas since He attained Buddhahood.

The Virtues of His Land

"His Buddha Land naturally has the seven treasures. Its ground is made of gold, silver, aquamarine, coral, amber, conch shell, and emerald, and it is open, vast, and boundless. The treasures intermingle and combine with one another, dazzling and sparkling. They are wonderful, beautiful, pure, and splendid, surpassing those in all worlds in the ten directions. These treasures, the best of all treasures, are like those in the sixth desire heaven.

"His land does not have the four seasons. In spring, autumn, winter, or summer, the temperature is neither cold nor hot, but constantly pleasant and comfortable. By virtue of that Buddha's spiritual power, things manifest at one's wish. Life forms that take grueling life-journeys, i.e., hell-dwellers, hungry ghosts, and animals, do not exist in His land.

"In addition, His land has neither Mount Sumeru nor its surrounding mountain ranges, such as the vajra mountain range. Nor does it have immense oceans, small seas, streams, channels, wells, or valleys."

Then Ānanda asked the Buddha, "If that land does not have Mount Sumeru, upon what do Heaven of the Four God-Kings [the first desire heaven] and Trayastriṁśa Heaven [the second desire heaven] rely?"

The Buddha replied to Ānanda, "Upon what do other heavens, from Yāma Heaven, the third desire heaven, up to [Akaniṣṭha Heaven] the Ultimate Form Heaven, rely?"

Ānanda said to the Buddha, "One's karmas and their corresponding requitals are inconceivable!"

The Buddha told Ānanda, "As karmas and corresponding requitals are inconceivable, so too are Buddha Lands inconceivable. For sentient beings in any land, their merits and powers are grounded in their karmas."

Ānanda said to the Buddha, "I have no doubts regarding this Dharma. It is for removing the doubts of sentient beings of the future that I ask about this meaning."

His Infinite Light

The Buddha told Ānanda, "Amitāyus Buddha's radiance is dignified and supreme, with which other Buddhas' radiance cannot compare. There are Buddhas whose radiance reaches a distance of seven feet, or one, two, three, four, or five yojanas, or to a distance extended to illuminate one Buddha Land. There are Buddhas whose radiance illuminates 100 or 1,000 Buddha Lands.

"As Amitāyus Buddha's radiance illuminates as many Buddha Lands in the east as the sands of the Ganges, so does it illuminate those in the south, west, and north, in the in-between directions, and toward the zenith and the nadir. Therefore, Amitāyus Buddha is also called Infinite Light Buddha, Boundless Light Buddha, Hindrance-Free Light Buddha, Matchless Light Buddha, Flame-King Light Buddha, Pure Light Buddha, Joyful Light Buddha, Wisdom Light Buddha, Ceaseless Light Buddha, Inconceivable Light Buddha, Ineffable Light Buddha, and Outshining the Sun-Moon Light Buddha.

"If sentient beings are touched by His radiance, their three afflictions will be eliminated and their bodies and minds will become gentle. They will be filled with joy and exuberance as benevolence arises in their minds. If those who are in extreme suffering, taking any of the three evil life-journeys, see this radiance, they can rest, no more pain or distress. After their death, they will be saved [from resuming such life-journeys].

"Amitāyus Buddha's radiance gloriously illuminates Buddha Lands in the ten directions, and no one fails to hear of it. As I now praise His radiance, so too do all Buddhas, Bodhisattvas, Pratyekabuddhas, and voice-hearers.

"If sentient beings that have heard of His radiance, awesome spirit, and merit, unceasingly praise Him day and night with an earnest mind, they will be reborn in His land as they wish. There, multitudes of Bodhisattvas and voice-hearers will praise their merit. In addition, Buddhas and Bodhisattvas [in worlds] in the ten directions, just as they now praise [Amitāyus Buddha's radiance], will praise these sentient beings' radiance until their eventual attainment of Buddha bodhi."

The Buddha continued, "I could describe the majesty and wonder of Amitāyus Buddha's radiance and awesome spirit day and night for a kalpa, but still could not finish my narration."

His Infinite Life

The Buddha told Ānanda, "Amitāyus Buddha's lifespan is so long that it is beyond calculation. Do you not know? Suppose innumerable sentient beings in worlds in the ten directions all assume human form and become voice-hearers or Pratyekabuddhas. Suppose they assemble and single-mindedly calculate, for a billion kalpas, with all the power of their intellect, the length of His lifespan in terms of kalpas. They can never find its end or know its limit. The lifespan of the multitude of Bodhisattvas, voice-hearers, and gods there is also not a number that can be known by calculation or analogy.

The Countless Numbers of the Holy Multitudes

"In addition, the numbers of voice-hearers and Bodhisattvas are hard to calculate and describe. They have superb spiritual knowledge and command of awesome powers. They can hold the entire world in their hands."

The Buddha told Ānanda, "The number of voice-hearers and Bodhisattvas who attended that Buddha's first assembly is beyond calculation. Suppose there are innumerable, countless billions of koṭis of people just like Mahāmaudgalyāyana, and they all calculate for asaṁkhyeya nayuta kalpas until they enter parinirvāṇa. They can never find this number, which is like the immeasurable depth of the immense ocean. Suppose someone cuts a hair into a hundred pieces and uses a piece to draw a drop of water from the ocean. What is your opinion? Is this drop more than the water in the immense ocean?"

Ānanda replied to the Buddha, "The quantity of water in the immense ocean can never be gauged by the drop of water taken by the person. It cannot be known by skillful calculation or described by words."

The Buddha told Ānanda, "The number of voice-hearers and Bodhisattvas who attended the first assembly as calculated by Maudgalyāyana for a billion koṭi nayuta kalpas is like a drop of water. The number unknowable to him is like the water in the immense ocean.

The Jeweled Trees

"In addition, all over that land are trees made of the seven treasures, such as gold trees, silver trees, aquamarine trees, crystal trees, coral trees, emerald trees, and conch shell trees. Some trees are made of two, three, or even seven treasures. Some gold trees have silver leaves, flowers, and fruits. Some silver trees have gold leaves, flowers, and fruits. Some aquamarine trees have crystal leaves, flowers, and fruits. Some crystal trees have aquamarine leaves, flowers, and fruits. Some coral trees have emerald leaves, flowers, and fruits. Some emerald trees have aquamarine leaves, flowers, and fruits. Some conch shell trees have leaves, flowers, and fruits made of several treasures.

"Some jeweled trees have purple-tinged gold roots, silver trunks, aquamarine branches, crystal twigs, coral leaves, emerald flowers, and conch shell fruits. Some jeweled trees have silver roots, aquamarine trunks, crystal branches, coral twigs, emerald leaves, conch shell flowers, and purple-tinged gold fruits. Some jeweled trees have aquamarine roots, crystal trunks, coral branches, emerald twigs, conch shell leaves, purple-tinged gold flowers, and silver fruits. Some jeweled trees have crystal roots, coral trunks, emerald branches, conch shell twigs, purple-tinged gold leaves, silver flowers, and aquamarine fruits. Some jeweled trees have coral roots, emerald trunks, conch shell branches, purple-tinged gold twigs, silver leaves, aquamarine flowers, and crystal fruits. Some jeweled trees have emerald roots, conch shell trunks, purple-tinged gold branches, silver twigs, aquamarine leaves, crystal flowers, and coral fruits. Some jeweled trees have conch shell roots, purple-tinged gold trunks, silver branches, aquamarine twigs, crystal leaves, coral flowers, and emerald fruits.

"These trees in lines are matched line to line, trunk to trunk, branch to branch, leaf to leaf, flower to flower, and fruit to fruit. Their splendid colors and radiance are beyond the capacity of one's eyesight. When cool breezes blow, these trees play music in the five tones, and their wonderful melodies are naturally in harmony.

The Bodhi Tree in His Bodhimaṇḍa

"In addition, the bodhi tree in Amitāyus Buddha's bodhimaṇḍa is four million lis tall. The tree trunk is 5,000 yojanas in circumference, with branches and leaves spreading 200,000 lis in the four directions. All are naturally made of various treasures and adorned with the kings of jewels, such as the moonlight jewel and the ocean wheel jewel. Hanging from the twigs are garlands of jewels in a billion changing colors, radiating boundless beams of glowing light. Covering this tree are wonderful jeweled nets that manifest all kinds of adornments at one's wish. They emit wondrous Dharma tones as breezes gently stir. These tones flow to all Buddha Lands in the ten directions. Those who hear them achieve the profound Endurance in Dharmas, abiding in the spiritual level of no regress. Even before they attain Buddhahood, they will not encounter tribulations. Although their eyes see sights, ears hear sounds, noses smell scents, tongues taste flavors, bodies touch the light, and minds perceive mental objects, they acquire purity in their six faculties, which will trouble them no more.

"Ānanda, when gods in that land see this bodhi tree, they achieve the Three Endurances in the Dharma. First, the Endurance in Hearing the Sounds; second, the Endurance in Accord; third, the Endurance in the Realization of the No Birth of Dharmas. They achieve these endurances entirely by virtue of Amitāyus Buddha's awesome spiritual power and by virtue of the power of His original vows, the fulfillment of these vows, the clarity of these vows, the firmness of these vows, and the ultimacy of these vows."

The Musical Trees

The Buddha told Ānanda, "A king in the human world is entertained by 100,000 kinds of music, and music is also played in the palace of a Wheel-Turning King and in each of the six desire heavens. The music in each place is ten million koṭi times superior to that in the preceding place. However, the 10,000 musical tones in the sixth desire heaven are 1,000 koṭi times inferior to even a single tone from the trees made of the seven treasures, in Amitāyus Buddha's land. These trees naturally play 10,000 kinds of instrumental music. The sounds of music are none other than Dharma tones, which are pure and resonant, wonderful and harmonious. They are foremost among all the sounds in worlds in the ten directions.

The Palaces and Towers

"The auditoriums, ashrams, palaces, and towers in that land are made of the seven treasures by magic. Covering them are intermingled multitudinous jewels, such as precious gems and moon jewels.

The Jeweled Ponds

"Inside and outside of these structures are bathing ponds 10, 20, or 30 yojanas, or even 100,000 yojanas in size. Each pond's length, width, and depth are equal. They are filled with water with the eight virtues, pure and fragrant, tasting like sweet nectar. The beds of yellow gold ponds are covered with silver dust. The beds of silver ponds are covered with yellow gold dust. The beds of crystal ponds are covered with aquamarine dust. The beds of aquamarine ponds are covered with crystal dust. The beds of coral ponds are covered with amber dust. The beds of amber ponds are covered with coral dust. The beds of conch shell ponds are covered with emerald dust. The beds of emerald ponds are covered with conch shell dust. The beds of white jade ponds are covered with purple-tinged gold dust. The beds of purple-tinged gold ponds are covered with white jade dust. Some ponds are made of two, three, or even seven treasures.

"On the banks of these ponds stand sandalwood trees covered with leaves and flowers, wafting fragrances everywhere. All over the surfaces of the waters are lotus flowers, such as celestial utpalas, padmas, kumadas, and puṇḍarīkas, all gleaming with colorful light.

"When Bodhisattvas and voice-hearers enter a jeweled pond, if they wish the water to cover their feet, the water will cover their feet. If they wish the water to reach their knees, the water will rise to their knees. If they wish the water to reach their waist, the water will rise to their waist. If they wish the water to reach their chest, the water will rise to their chest. If they wish the water to reach their neck, the water will rise to their neck. If they wish the water to shower on their body, the water will shower on their body. If they wish the water to return to its former level, the water will return to its former level. The water temperature can be adjusted at will to either cool or warm. The water vitalizes the spirit, delights the body, and cleanses the mind of filth. Pure and clean, it is as clear as if invisible, and the treasure dust at the bottom of the pond can be seen at any depth. The ripples merge and separate, vanishing peacefully, neither too slow nor too fast.

"The ripples produce innumerable wonderful sounds. No one fails to hear the sounds suiting his needs, whether the sounds of the Buddha, the Dharma, the Saṅgha, silence, emptiness, no self, great lovingkindness and compassion, the pāramitās, the Ten Powers, the Four Fearlessnesses, the Eighteen Exclusive Dharmas, the overall wisdom-knowledge, no act, no arising or ceasing, the Endurance in the Realization of the No Birth of Dharmas, or even sweet nectar pouring on one's head. Such wonderful Dharma sounds that suit one's needs delight one beyond measure. They accord with the true meaning of purity, freedom from desires, and nirvāṇa; with the power of the Three Jewels, the Fearlessnesses, and the Eighteen Exclusive Dharmas; and with the path and wisdom of Bodhisattvas and voice-hearers. That land does not have even the names of the three evil life-journeys; it has only joyful tones. Therefore, that land is called Peace and Bliss."

The Inhabitants

"Ānanda, those who are reborn in that land are endowed with pure physical bodies, wonderful voices, and the virtue of transcendental powers.

"The palaces in which they live, their clothing, food and drink, and adornments, such as wonderful flowers and incense, are like those in the sixth desire heaven. When they desire to eat, bowls made of the seven treasures spontaneously appear before them. Such bowls, made of gold, silver, aquamarine, conch shell, emerald, coral, amber, or the moonlight jewel, appear at their wish. The bowls are naturally filled with food and drink of one hundred flavors. Although such food is present, there are no eaters. Gentle in body and mind, they are naturally satiated merely by seeing the food and smelling its aroma. They take their intention of eating as food, with no attachment to flavors. The bowls vanish when the meal is over, and reappear in due time. The purity, peace, and wonderful pleasures of that Buddha Land are below only the state of nirvāṇa, which is free from causes and conditions.

"The Bodhisattvas, voice-hearers, and gods of that land have superb wisdom and marvelous transcendental powers. They all appear in the same form, without any difference. To conform to the way of other lands, the name 'gods' is used for them. They have wonderful appearances, with even facial features, extraordinary and unearthly. Being neither gods nor humans, they all are endowed with bodies that are naturally ethereal and boundless."

The Buddha told Ānanda, "As an analogy, when a poor beggar in the world stands beside a king, can you compare his features with those of the king?"

Ānanda replied to the Buddha, "If this person stands beside the king, his features, ugly and sordid beyond analogy, are reckoned as a billion koṭi times inferior to the king's. Why is he so? The poor beggar is lowly, and his clothes can barely cover his body. He can hardly feed himself to stay alive. He is always hungry, cold, and in distress, having lost all human standards. All his tribulations stem from his past lives, during which he did not plant roots of virtue. Wealthy and miserly, he did not give any of his accumulated riches to others. He desired to acquire things unearned, never tiring of his greedy pursuits. He did not believe in cultivation of virtue, and the evil he did piled high, like a mountain. In this way, he died, and his wealth and treasures all dispersed. The wealth amassed by his toiling body, which caused him concern and distress, did not benefit him, but went to others in the end. Without goodness or virtue to depend upon, after death he went down an evil life-path to undergo long suffering. After his sins have been purged, although he is reborn as a human, he is lowly and extremely stupid and sordid.

"A king in the world is honored among men because of the merit he has accumulated in his past lives. Caring and generous, he gave alms to the needy with lovingkindness. He honored his trust and cultivated virtue, never disputative. After his death, supported by his merit, he is reborn to go up a good life-path. He can even be reborn [as a god] in a heaven to enjoy myriad pleasures. With a wealth of accumulated credit, he is reborn as a human into a royal family. Noble by birth, he has even, comely features. Respected and served by the multitudes, he enjoys wonderful garments and choice delicacies served at his command. Supported by the merit acquired in his past lives, a king lives a king's life."

The Buddha told Ānanda, "What you say is true. Although a king is dignified and noble among men, his even, comely features, in comparison with those of a Wheel-Turning King, are lowly and sordid, just like the beggar standing beside the king. The Wheel-Turning King's awesome appearance is the foremost one in the world. However, he is ugly in the presence of the god-king of Trayastriṁśa Heaven, 10,000 koṭi times uglier by comparison. If this god-king is compared with the god-king of the sixth desire heaven, he is 100,000 koṭi times inferior in appearance. If the god-king of the sixth desire heaven is compared with Bodhisattvas and voice-hearers in Amitāyus Buddha's land, his radiant features and colors are a billion koṭi times inferior."

The Splendors of His Land

The Buddha told Ānanda, "Gods in Amitāyus Buddha's land, by a single thought, can instantly manifest clothing, food and drink, flowers and incense, necklaces, silky canopies and banners, and wonderful music, as well as dwellings, palaces, and towers, made of one, two, or even innumerable treasures, in desired shapes, colors, heights, and sizes.

"Spread all over the ground are wonderful garments made with jewels. Gods step on them as they walk. Canopying that Buddha Land are innumerable jeweled nets, made of gold threads and precious gems and adorned with 100,000 varieties of jewels and wonderful treasures. Hanging from the four sides of these nets are jeweled bells, which sparkle with colorful light, extremely beautiful.

"Breezes of virtue naturally stir, and they are gentle and pleasant, neither hot nor cold, but warm or cool. Neither too weakly nor too strongly, they sweep across the jeweled nets and the jeweled trees, which sound innumerable wonderful Dharma tones and waft 10,000 kinds of gentle fragrances of virtue. For those who smell the fragrances, their afflictions, which enslave their body and mind, and their defiling habits will remain inactive. When these winds touch their bodies, they experience bliss like that of a bhikṣu in the Samādhi of Total Suspension of Sensory Reception and Perception.

"Moreover, the breezes carry flowers all over that Buddha Land, which fall orderly, according to their colors, not chaotically. They are soft and lustrous, with a strong perfume. When one steps on them, the foot sinks down four inches. When one lifts one's foot, the flowers spring back to the same height as before. After the flowers have been stepped on, the ground cracks open, and they gradually vanish, leaving no trace behind. According to schedule, the breezes disperse the flowers in this way six times a day.

"Moreover, there are jeweled lotus flowers all over that world, and each jeweled flower has 100,000 koṭi petals. The petals in innumerable colors are radiant. The blue colors gleam with blue light; the white colors, with white light. In black, yellow, red, and purple, the colorful light is striking, radiant, and splendid, outshining the sun and the moon. Each flower emits 3,600,000 koṭi beams of light. Manifested in each beam are 3,600,000 koṭi Buddhas, each with a purple-tinged golden body and an extraordinary, superb appearance. Each Buddha emits 100,000 beams of light as He expounds the wondrous Dharma [in worlds] in the ten directions. These Buddhas each set innumerable sentient beings on the right path to Buddhahood."

Fascicle 2 (of 2)

The Certainty of Buddhahood

The Buddha told Ānanda, "Those who are reborn in that land all belong in the group of sentient beings that definitely progress on the right path to bodhi. Why? Because in that Buddha Land, there is neither the group that definitely is not on the bodhi path nor the group that is indecisive about its paths.

The Three Classes to Be Reborn

"Buddha-Tathāgatas in worlds in the ten directions, who are as numerous as the sands of the Ganges, each praise Amitāyus Buddha's inconceivable awesome spirit and merit. If sentient beings that hear His name elicit faith and joy in but one thought and, with an earnest wish for rebirth in that land, transfer their merits to others, they will be reborn there and attain the spiritual level of no regress. Excepted are those who have committed any of the five rebellious sins or maligned the true Dharma."

The Buddha told Ānanda, "Gods and humans in worlds in the ten directions who earnestly wish to be reborn in that land are grouped into three classes. In the high class are those who have renounced family life, abandoned desires, and become śramaṇas. They should activate the bodhi mind and constantly think only of Amitāyus Buddha. They should accumulate merit and resolve to be reborn in His land.

"When they die, Amitāyus Buddha, together with a holy multitude, will appear before them, and they will follow that Buddha to His land. They will be naturally reborn in lotus flowers made of the seven treasures, and they will abide in the spiritual level of no regress. Their wisdom will be keen, and they will have command of transcendental powers. Therefore, Ānanda, if there are sentient beings that wish to see Amitāyus Buddha in their present life, they should activate the unsurpassed bodhi mind, accumulate merit, and resolve to be reborn in His land."

The Buddha told Ānanda, "In the middle class are gods and humans in worlds in the ten directions who earnestly wish to be reborn in that land, but are unable to become śramaṇas and to accumulate merit on a large scale. They should activate the unsurpassed bodhi mind and constantly think only of Amitāyus Buddha as they cultivate goodness on a smaller scale. They should observe the pure precepts, erect memorial towers, enshrine Buddha images, offer food to śramaṇas, hang silk screens, light lamps, scatter flowers, and burn incense. With a wish for rebirth in that land, they should transfer their merits to others.

"When they die, Amitāyus Buddha will magically manifest a copy of Himself, who is just as radiant and splendid as a real Buddha, to appear, together with a holy multitude, before them. They will follow this magically manifested Buddha to His land, and will abide in the spiritual level of no regress. Their merit and wisdom will be below those in the high class."

The Buddha told Ānanda, "In the low class are gods and humans in worlds in the ten directions who earnestly wish to be reborn in that land. Although they are unable to acquire various merits, they should activate the unsurpassed bodhi mind and, with a wish for rebirth in that land, single-mindedly think ten thoughts of Amitāyus Buddha. If they hear the profound Dharma, they should delight and believe in it without raising doubts. Even if they think only one thought of that Buddha, with utmost sincerity they should resolve to be reborn in His land. When they die, they will dream of that Buddha and will be reborn in His land. Their merit and wisdom are below those in the middle class."

Praises by Buddhas and Homage by Bodhisattvas

The Buddha told Ānanda, "Amitāyus Buddha's awesome spirit is boundless. None of the innumerable, countless inconceivable Buddha-Tathāgatas in worlds in the ten directions fails to praise Him. Innumerable, countless multitudes of Bodhisattvas in Buddha Lands in the east, which are as numerous as the sands of the Ganges, together with multitudes of voice-hearers, all go to Amitāyus Buddha, to make offerings reverently to Him and the Bodhisattvas and voice-hearers there. They hear and accept the Dharma, in order to disseminate the Dharma and transform sentient beings. As they do these things, so too do Bodhisattvas in worlds in the south, west, and north, in the in-between directions, and toward the zenith and the nadir."

At that time the World-Honored One spoke in verse:

Buddha Lands in the east,
Their numbers are like the sands of the Ganges.
Multitudes of Bodhisattvas in those lands
Visit Amitāyus Buddha reverently.
In the south, west, and north, in the four in-between directions,
Toward the zenith, and toward the nadir,
Multitudes of Bodhisattvas in those lands
Also visit Amitāyus Buddha reverently.
Every Bodhisattva
Carries wonderful celestial flowers,
Choice incense, and priceless garments
To make offerings to Amitāyus Buddha.

Celestial music plays harmoniously,
Exquisite tones in concert.
They praise the Supreme Honored One in hymns
As an offering to Amitāyus Buddha,
Who has fully attained wisdom and spiritual power,
Gone through profound Dharma Doors,
And completed His store of merits.
His unparalleled wondrous wisdom-knowledge
Shines on the world like the sun of wisdom,
And removes the clouds of birth and death.
They reverently circle Him three times
And bow down to the Unsurpassed Honored One.
Seeing that His well-adorned Pure Land is
So wondrous and inconceivable,
They hereupon activate the unsurpassed bodhi mind,
Each wishing the land [he will form] to be the same.

Then Amitāyus Buddha is moved,
And he smiles joyfully.
His mouth emits innumerable beams of light,
Illuminating everywhere in worlds in the ten directions.
The returning beams of light circle His body three times
And enter into the crown of His head.
The entire multitude of gods is
Exuberant and exultant.
Avalokiteśvara Bodhisattva-Mahāsattva
Arranges his garment, bows his head, and asks
Why the Buddha is smiling.
To the request for an explanation, that Buddha replies,

"Brahma sounds reverberate like thunders,
The eight tones resonating wonderful melodies,
An accompaniment to my bestowal of prophecies upon Bodhisattvas!
I now explain and you should hearken.
The Upright Ones have come from worlds in the ten directions,
And I know all their wishes.
They resolve to form and adorn their Pure Lands
And to attain Buddhahood.
Realizing that all dharmas are
Like dreams, illusions, and echoes,
They will fulfill their wonderful wishes,
Definitely to form such lands as mine.
Knowing that dharmas are like lightning and reflection,
They will eventually complete the Bodhisattva Way,
Perfect their roots of virtue,
And attain Buddhahood.
Thoroughly understanding dharma nature,
They know that everything is empty and has no self.
Intently seeking pure Buddha Lands,
They definitely will form such lands."

All Buddhas tell Bodhisattvas to visit
That Buddha in the Land of Peace and Bliss,
To hear the Dharma, accept it joyfully and train accordingly,
And quickly attain the state of purity.
Upon arrival in that well-adorned Pure Land,
One will quickly acquire transcendental powers
And will definitely receive from Amitāyus Buddha
The prophecy of attaining Buddhahood.
By virtue of the power of that Buddha's original vows,
Those who hear His name and resolve to be reborn [in His land]
Will all arrive in that land
And attain the spiritual level of no regress.

Bodhisattvas who make earnest vows,
Wishing that their own lands be no different from that land,
Remember and deliver all sentient beings.
Their renown spreads across worlds in the ten directions.
To serve koṭis of Tathāgatas,
They fly to all lands.
After joyfully paying homage to Tathāgatas,
They return to the Land of Peace and Bliss.

Those who do not have roots of goodness
Cannot hear this sūtra.
Only those who are pure and observe their precepts
Will come to hear the true Dharma.
Only those who have seen a World-Honored One before
Will believe this explanation.
Humble and reverent, they hear and carry out the Dharma
With exuberance and great joy.
For those who are arrogant and indolent,
It is difficult to believe in the Dharma.
But those who have seen Buddhas in their past lives
Delight in hearing these teachings.

Voice-hearers and Bodhisattvas are unable
To fathom the mind of the Holiest One,
Just as a person who is born blind
Tries to guide others.
The ocean of the Tathāgata's wisdom is
Deep and vast, without a bottom.
Those riding the Two Vehicles can never measure it.
Only Buddhas themselves can understand.
Suppose that all people
Have attained bodhi [through the Two Vehicles] and
Acquired the pure wisdom that everything is empty.
For koṭis of kalpas, they ponder the wisdom of a Buddha,
Trying to describe it with all their strength.
They still do not know it at the end of their life.
Buddha wisdom is boundless,
And it brings the ultimate state of purity.

As a long lifespan is hard to obtain,
Even harder is to encounter a Buddha appearing in the world.
It is difficult for people to have faith and wisdom.
Those who energetically seek to hear the Dharma
And do not forget the Dharma they have heard
Will face that Buddha and receive great benefits.
Therefore, my good kinfolk and friends,
You should resolve
To hear the Dharma
Even if the world is in flames.

Then you will definitely attain Buddha bodhi
To rescue all those in the flow of birth and death.

The Sublime Bodhisattvas

The Buddha told Ānanda, "All Bodhisattvas in that land will eventually be in the holy position of waiting to attain Buddhahood in their next life, except those whose original vows put sentient beings first. They adorn themselves with the merit of their great vows, hastening to deliver all sentient beings everywhere.

"Ānanda, in that Buddha Land, a voice-hearer's body light is one yojana across, and a Bodhisattva's radiance reaches a distance of one hundred yojanas. There are two foremost Bodhisattvas, who are most honored. Their awesome spiritual radiance shines everywhere in the Three-Thousand Large Thousandfold World."

Ānanda asked the Buddha, "What are these two Bodhisattvas' names?"

The Buddha replied, "One is called Avalokiteśvara and the other [Mahāsthāmaprāpta] Great Might Arrived. These two Bodhisattvas trained in the Bodhisattva Way in this land. After their death, they have been reborn in that Buddha Land.

"Ānanda, sentient beings reborn in that land are all endowed with a great man's thirty-two physical marks. Fulfilled in wisdom, they delve into dharmas and understand their essence. Their transcendental powers are hindrance free, and their faculties are brilliant and keen. Those of inferior capacity achieve the first two of the Three Endurances, and those of superior capacity achieve the asaṁkhyeya Endurance in the Realization of the No Birth of Dharmas.

"In addition, these Bodhisattvas, on their way to Buddhahood, will never again go down the evil life-journeys. They have command of transcendental powers and know the past lives of themselves and others. However, if they choose to be reborn elsewhere, in an evil world with the five turbidities, resembling my world, they will manifest themselves to resemble the inhabitants there."

The Buddha told Ānanda, "Bodhisattvas in that land, by virtue of that Buddha's power, in the time of a meal, can visit innumerable worlds in the ten directions to make offerings to the Buddha-Tathāgatas there. According to their thoughts, innumerable, countless offerings instantly appear like magic, such as flowers, incense, instrumental music, silky canopies, and banners, which are precious and extraordinary, not of this world. These Bodhisattvas offer such objects to the multitude of Buddhas, Bodhisattvas, and voice-hearers there, which then change into flower canopies in the sky. The flower canopies are radiant and colorful, wafting fragrances everywhere. Each flower canopy is 400 lis in circumference, and continues to double in size until it covers the Three-Thousand Large Thousandfold World. These flower canopies then vanish, one after another. Delighted, these Bodhisattvas play celestial music in the sky and, with wonderful tones, they hymn Buddhas' virtues. They hear and accept the Dharma with infinite joy. After making offerings to those Buddhas, before mealtime, they effortlessly lift off and return to their own land."

Pronouncement of the Dharma and Presentation of Offerings

The Buddha told Ānanda, "When Amitāyus Buddha pronounces the Dharma to Bodhisattvas, voice-hearers, and gods, they all assemble in the auditorium made of the seven treasures. As He widely expounds the wondrous Dharma, no one fails to understand and accept with delight the teachings for attaining bodhi.

"Meanwhile, winds arise from the four directions, blowing across trees made of the seven treasures, which sound the five tones. The winds scatter innumerable wonderful flowers everywhere. These natural offerings continue endlessly. All gods take 100,000 celestial flowers and fragrances, and play 10,000 kinds of instrumental music, to make offerings to that Buddha and the multitude of Bodhisattvas and voice-hearers. Scattering flowers and incense, playing music, they walk to and fro and quickly get out of one another's way. During that time, their harmony and delight are beyond words."

The Merit of the Bodhisattvas

The Buddha told Ānanda, "When Bodhisattvas reborn in that Buddha Land speak, they always pronounce the true Dharma in accord with their wisdom, with no contradictions or mistakes. For the myriad things in that land, they hold no concept of belonging or attachment. Without emotional bondage, they come and go, move or stop, completely at ease. Unfettered by endearment or alienation, with no sense of self versus others, neither competitive nor disputative, they have the altruistic mind of great lovingkindness and compassion for sentient beings. Gentle and docile, they have no anger. Free from the mental coverings, they have a pure mind. Never weary or indolent, they retain in their minds equality, excellence, profundity, and concentration, as well as love, appreciation, and joy of the Dharma. Having eradicated afflictions and purified the mind bent on the evil life-journeys, they take all Bodhisattva actions and acquire immeasurable merit.

"Equipped with profound samādhi, transcendental powers, and illuminating wisdom, they practice the Seven Bodhi Factors, training their minds in accordance with the Buddha Dharma. Their physical-eye is pure and perceptive, able to distinguish all things. Their god-eye reaches an immeasurable, boundless distance. Their dharma-eye observes the ultimate Way. Their wisdom-eye sees the truth, which can cross them over to the opposite shore. Their Buddha-eye completely penetrates dharma nature.

"With hindrance-free wisdom, they expound the Dharma to others. Seeing that all things in the Three Realms of Existence are equal in their emptiness, they resolve to seek the Buddha Dharma. Equipped with eloquence, they annihilate the afflictions that trouble all sentient beings. Born from the Tathātaga, they understand the true suchness of dharmas. Equipped with a good understanding of nirvāṇa and with verbal skills, they do not enjoy worldly talks but delight in true discussions [of the Dharma]. They develop their roots of goodness and resolve to attain Buddha bodhi. Knowing that all dharmas are in nirvāṇa, they end both their afflictions and their cycle of birth and death. When they hear the profound Dharma, they have no fears or doubts in their minds and are able to train themselves accordingly. Their great compassion is so profound, far-reaching, and wonderful that it embraces all sentient beings without exception, and they carry them all aboard the ultimate One Vehicle to the opposite shore.

"As they resolutely shatter the web of doubts, wisdom arises in their minds, completely encompassing the Buddha Dharma. Their wisdom is like the immense ocean, and their samādhi is like the king of mountains. The radiance of their wisdom surpasses that of the sun and the moon, as they master the pure ways.

"They are like the snow mountain because they sparkle with merits that are equal in purity; like the great earth because they do not discriminate between purity and impurity, good and evil; like the pure water because they wash away afflictions, like filth; like the fire-king because they burn way afflictions, like firewood; like the powerful wind because they travel across worlds unhindered; like the open sky because they are not attached to anything; like the lotus flower because they live in the world untainted; like the Mahāyāna because they carry sentient beings out of their cycle of birth and death; like the thick clouds because they rumble the great Dharma thunder to awaken those asleep; like the torrential rain because they pour down sweet nectar to water sentient beings; like the vajra mountain because they cannot be moved by māras or non-Buddhists; like the Brahma-kings because they are foremost in upholding virtuous dharmas; like the banyan tree because they shelter all; like the udumbara flower because they are rare to encounter; like the golden-winged garuḍa because they subdue adherents of the wrong views; like the soaring birds because they do not accumulate things; like the ox-king because they are invincible; like the elephant-king because they are skilled tamers; like the lion-king because they are fearless; like the vast sky because their lovingkindness is given equally.

"They annihilate the mind of jealousy, not wanting to overtake others. They delight in seeking the Dharma, never satiated. They widely expound the Dharma, never tiring. They beat the Dharma drum and erect the Dharma banner. They invoke the sun of wisdom to shine and dispel the darkness of delusion. They live by the six elements of harmony and respect. They always give the Dharma as alms. They make boldly energetic progress, never feeling weak or discouraged. They serve as the world-illuminating lamp and as the supreme fortune field. They serve as the guiding teacher who teaches all equally without likes or dislikes. They delight in only the true Way without elation or dejection. They pull out the thorns of desire to give comfort to sentient beings. Their merit is so outstanding that no one fails to respect them. They destroy the hindrances caused by the three afflictions and playfully demonstrate their transcendental powers.

"They have the power of causes, conditions, mind, resolve, skillful means, persistency, virtue, samādhi, wisdom, hearing much of the Dharma, and the six pāramitās—almsgiving, observance of precepts, endurance of adversity, energetic progress, meditation, and wisdom—and the power of right mindfulness, right observation, the six transcendental powers, the Three Clarities, and taming sentient beings in accordance with the Dharma. Such power is complete in them!

"Adorned with merit and eloquence, their physical features are majestic. No one can compare with them. They reverently make offerings to innumerable Buddhas, and they are always praised by Buddhas. They perfect their practice of pāramitās required for Bodhisattvas as they train in the Three Samādhis—emptiness, no appearance, and no wish—and go through Samādhi Doors, such as no birth and no death. They stay far away from the ground of voice-hearers and Pratyekabuddhas.

"Ānanda, those Bodhisattvas are adorned with such immeasurable merit, which I have only briefly described to you. If I elaborate, I cannot finish even in a billion kalpas."

Encouragement to Achieve Rebirth in That Land

The Buddha told Maitreya Bodhisattva, gods, and humans, "The merit and wisdom of the voice-hearers and Bodhisattvas in Amitāyus Buddha's land are beyond description. So peaceful, blissful, and pure is that land! How can one not strive for merit, and not think of bodhi, which transcends the boundless limit, beyond the distinction between high and low? If one makes energetic progress seeking bodhi, one definitely will transcend this world and be reborn in the Land of Peace and Bliss. If one decisively rejects the five evil life-paths,[5] they will be closed to one. However, although the limitless [spiritual] ascension is easy to achieve, no one wants to go that way. Although that land poses no obstructions, people are tethered to their world. Why does one not give up one's worldly matters to walk the virtuous Way in order to acquire an extremely long life and infinite delight?

The Evil Ways of the World

"However, people of the world are shallow and earthly, and they fight over minor matters. In extreme suffering, they toil to support themselves. Noble or base, rich or poor, young or old, male or female, they all are concerned about money. Whether or not they have money, they worry about it just the same. Burdened by their concerns and anxieties, they are in anguish and sorrow. Driven by their minds, they never live in peace.

"If they own farmland, they worry about their farmland. If they own houses, they worry about their houses. In addition, their slaves, riches, clothing, food, sundry goods, and the six kinds of livestock, such as cows and horses, are all their concerns. Thinking and panting, they live in anxiety and fear.

"Unexpectedly, floods, fires, bandits, enemies, and creditors wash, burn, and take away their goods. When the objects of their concern are all destroyed or dispersed, their toxic anxiety and anguish can find no release. Anger stays in their minds, together with concern and distress. Obstinately attached to their belongings, they refuse to let go of them. Some live out the rest of their lives as ruined men. After death, they leave everything behind, and nothing follows them. The dignified and the wealthy have this trouble as well, which causes them myriad concerns and fears. As all toil painfully in cold or hot weather, all live in pain.

"The poor and lowly are constantly in destitution. Those who do not own farmland desire to own farmland; those who do not own houses desire to own houses; those who do not own slaves, riches, clothing, food, sundry goods, or the six kinds of livestock, such as cows and horses, desire to own them. They may have one item, lacking another; they may have some items, lacking others. They think about getting all of them. Even as they get everything, these objects soon are dispersed. With anxiety and pain, they seek but cannot get what they want. Their thinking is futile, which only tires their body and mind. Plagued by their concerns, they are restless in their conduct. They cannot help toiling in cold or hot weather, living in pain. They carry on in this way until they die.

"They refuse to do good, walk the right path, or cultivate virtue. After death, each of them will travel long distances alone, taking the next life-journey, unable to know whether it is good or evil.

"People of the world—parents, children, siblings, spouses, and close or distant relatives—should have love and respect for one another, not hatred. The fortunate should be generous to the unfortunate, not stingy. People should be kind and gentle to one another in their speech and manners, not hostile. However, those who are in dispute harbor anger, and their anger in the present life will become an enormous feud in a future life. Why? Because although mutually harmful acts in one's present life may not immediately result in a deadly fight, the poisonous anger and hardened fury remain in one's [ālaya] consciousness, not going away. Life after life, enemies reciprocate their revenge.

"People live in the loves and desires of the world. However, everyone is born alone, dies alone, comes alone, and goes alone. One must complete one's own life-journey of pain or pleasure, and no one else can take one's place. One's good or evil karmas lead one to fortune or misfortune. As one's past karmas relentlessly await, one must go alone on one's next life-journey to a distant place that cannot be known. Family members, each accompanied by good and evil karmas, which are hidden from them, will be separated by their different life-paths for a long time. It will be extremely difficult for them to meet again. Why do people not give up their worldly pursuits and not strive to cultivate virtue while they are still healthy and strong? If they strive to cultivate virtue and make energetic progress, aiming to transcend the world, they can acquire infinite life. Why do they not seek bodhi? What other delight can they possibly desire?

"However, people of the world do not believe that doing good karmas reaps good requitals or that seeking bodhi leads to attainment of bodhi. They do not believe in rebirth after death. Nor do they believe that generous giving yields good fortune or that requitals match good or evil karmas. They contend that it is not so and that there is no such thing.

"They cling to their wrong views and look to one another for support. From one generation to the next, fathers pass their views down to children. Just like their deceased fathers and forefathers, who neither did good nor recognized morality, these descendants, with their delusions, closed minds, and dark spirits, are of course unable to distinguish between good and evil ways, or to understand the resultant journeys of birth and death. Nor does anyone tell them about these things. Whether good or evil, fortunate or unfortunate, they race to do anything as they please, and no one finds it disturbing.

"In the usual course of karmic life, family members die. Parents weep for the loss of their children; children weep for the loss of their parents. Siblings and spouses weep for their respective losses. Death does not occur according to any order. Under the law of impermanence, nothing can stay forever and all things will pass away. Even when people are told or taught this, few believe it.

"Therefore, one's transmigration through birth and death is endless. But in their ignorance, people still refuse to believe in the Dharma [as explained] in the sūtras. Without any forethought, they each desire instant gratification. Stupefied in their loves and desires, they disregard morality. They are lost in anger and hatred, and greedy for wealth and carnal pleasures. Set in their ways, they do not seek bodhi. They continue to undergo birth and death endlessly, suffering through their evil life-journeys. How agonized and pathetic they are!

"If there is a death in a family, whether a parent, a child, a sibling, or a spouse, the survivors mourn their loss. They think of their loved one, and their thoughts of grief form a knot. Enduring days and years of pain in their hearts, they still cannot release themselves from their attachment. Even when they are given the true teachings, their minds stay closed because their thoughts are not apart from sensual desires. Dazed and blocked, their minds are mired in delusion. They cannot reflect and think straight in order to make a decision about their worldly affairs and to set off on the Way. Before long, their lives come to an end. They cannot help failing to attain bodhi.

"Troubled and confused, people are greedy for loves and desires. The deluded are many while the enlightened are few. In this bustling world, a place upon which one cannot rely, whether dignified or humble, high or low, rich or poor, noble or base, each toils in his work, harboring malice and dark, evil energy. They launch enterprises that are against the heaven and earth and disagreeable to people's hearts. They attract evils to follow them, which let them do as they please until their sins have peaked. Before the end of their natural lifespans, they die sudden deaths. Then they go down the evil life-paths life after life, for thousands of koṭis of kalpas, not knowing when release will come. Their suffering is indescribable. How pathetic they are!"

The Solemn Admonition

The Buddha told Maitreya Bodhisattva, gods, and humans, "I now have described to you the affairs of the world. Those who are involved cannot attain bodhi. One should carefully reflect on one's life, stay far away from evils, and diligently do well-chosen good deeds. Love, desire, rank, and wealth are impossible to preserve. They are not pleasurable, and they all will depart. When one encounters a Buddha in the world, one should make energetic progress. Those who earnestly resolve to be reborn in the Land of Peace and Bliss will acquire illuminating wisdom and excellent merit. One should not allow self-indulgence or fail the teachings and the precepts, thus falling behind others. If you have any doubts about this sūtra, you may ask the Buddha. I will explain to you."

Maitreya Bodhisattva fell on both knees and said, "The Buddha is revered for His awesome spirit. His words are direct and virtuous. Having heard the Buddha's teachings, we each should thoroughly think them over. People of the world act just as described by the Buddha. Out of His lovingkindness and compassion, the Buddha now has indicated the great Way. One's ear and eye are opened and cleared because of one's deliverance. None of those who have heard the Buddha fails to rejoice. By His lovingkindness, gods, humans, and even wriggly insects are all liberated from anxiety and suffering. The Buddha's admonition is profound and virtuous. His wisdom clearly sees all things of the past, present, and future, everywhere [in worlds] in the ten directions, hindrance free. The reason we have deliverance bestowed upon us is that the Buddha in His past lives arduously sought bodhi with humility. His kindness is all-embracing and his merit majestic. His radiance shines through the limitless emptiness [of all dharmas], opening the entrance to nirvāṇa. He ceaselessly teaches, tames, commands, transforms, and inspires all [sentient beings in worlds] in the ten directions. The Buddha is the Dharma King revered above all multitudes of holy beings. As the teacher to all gods and humans, He enables them to attain bodhi as they wish. We now have encountered the Buddha and even heard His introduction of Amitāyus Buddha. No one fails to rejoice and open his mind wide."

The Buddha told Maitreya Bodhisattva, "What you say is true. Reverence for the Buddha is a great virtue. Only once in a long, long time will a Buddha appear in the world. I now have become a Buddha in this world to expound the Dharma, giving the teachings for attaining bodhi, to shatter the web of doubts, to pull out the roots of love and desire, and to destroy the source of evils, as I visit the Three Realms of Existence unhindered. With all-encompassing wisdom, I teach the essentials of the right path and explain its guidelines. I reveal the five life-journeys and deliver those who have not been delivered, enabling them to take the right path that goes from saṁsāra to nirvāṇa.

"Maitreya, know that you have trained in the Bodhisattva Way for innumerable kalpas. It has been a long time since you first resolved to deliver sentient beings. Those whom you will deliver in the time period between your attainment of bodhi and your parinirvāṇa will be innumerable.

"You, gods and humans in worlds in the ten directions, and my four groups of disciples have been transmigrating through the five life-paths since time without a beginning. Your anxiety, suffering, and toil are beyond description. Up to the present life, you have not ended your cycle of birth and death. Nevertheless, you have encountered a Buddha, and have heard and accepted the Dharma. You have even heard about Amitāyus Buddha. This is delightful and excellent. I express my sympathetic joy. You all should be tired of the pain of birth, old age, illness, and death, [a process of] discharging impurities, nothing enjoyable. It would be wise to resolve to organize yourselves for the right actions—to do good karmas, to purify your body and mind, and to speak and act truthfully in accord with your mind.

"One can deliver oneself then help and rescue others. To fulfill one's wish energetically, one should develop one's roots of goodness. Although one has to toil arduously in one's entire life, it would be like an instant in comparison [with one's lifespan in the Pure Land]. One will then enjoy infinite bliss after one's rebirth in Amitāyus Buddha's land. One will always act in accord with virtue and will have forever pulled out the roots of birth and death, freed from the trouble of afflictions, such as greed, anger, and delusion. One's lifespan can last for one kalpa, 100 kalpas, 1,000 kalpas, or 10,000 koṭi kalpas, according to one's wish. The freedom and ease of one's mind are below only the state of nirvāṇa.

"You each should make energetic progress, striving to fulfill your wish. Doubts and regrets would be a blunder, which would cause one's rebirth on the edge of that land. There, one would be confined for 500 years in a palace made of the seven treasures, undergoing tribulations."

Maitreya Bodhisattva said, "Having received the Buddha's solemn admonition, we will intently train and learn, carrying out His teachings. We dare not have any doubts."

The Five Evils and the Five Virtues

The Buddha told Maitreya Bodhisattva, "If you each can rectify your minds and intentions and refrain from doing evil, this is the highest virtue, unparalleled in worlds in the ten directions. Why? Because gods and humans in many Buddha Lands spontaneously do good, not evil, and they easily develop and transform themselves. I now have become a Buddha in this world of the five evils, the five pains, and the five burns,[6] and I teach sentient beings in extreme suffering to discard the five evils, remove the five pains, and stay away from the five burns. I transform their minds, enabling them to uphold the five virtues and acquire merits, so that they will live a long life [in Amitāyus Buddha's land] and eventually attain nirvāṇa."

The Buddha asked, "What are the five evils, the five pains, and the five burns? How does one destroy the five evils and uphold the five virtues in order to acquire merit, live a long life, and attain nirvāṇa?"

The First Evil and the First Virtue

The Buddha explained, "The first evil is this. Sentient beings, from gods and humans down to wriggly insects, do evil without exception. As the strong crush the weak, they harm, kill, and eat one another. They do not know how to cultivate virtue, but do evil without compunction. Evildoers receive punishment as they head for the next life-journey. The evils lodged in their [ālaya] consciousnesses find no pardon. That is why there are those who are poor and lowly, deprived and forlorn, those who are deaf, blind, mute, or stupid, and those who are vicious and violent. Then there are those who are dignified, noble, wealthy, or capable and brilliant, because in their past lives they were kind and dutiful, and acquired merit and cultivated virtue.

"Although the world has its regular systems of law and prison, there are those who do not fear them, and they commit crimes. Then, by law, they receive punishment from which it is hard to escape or to be absolved. This kind of punishment takes place in their present life. The consequence in their next life is even more intense and severe. Each of them enters darkness and assumes a body in a new life to undergo torture, as if enforced by human law.

"Hence, there naturally are the three evil life-journeys with immeasurable suffering and distress. The sinners change bodies, forms, and life-paths. Whether a lifespan is long or short, one's [ālaya] consciousness cannot help heading for it. One goes alone in one's rebirth, timed with enemies' rebirths to continue mutual revenge endlessly. Until the purging of one's horrible sins, one is unable to leave the evil life-journeys. One continues to trudge through them, not knowing when release will come. As liberation is hard to achieve, one's pain is indescribable. Such things do take place between heaven and earth. Although requitals are not always immediate, virtuous and evil ways will be returned in due time. These are the first enormous evil, the first pain, and the first burn.

"As one toils painfully, it is like a huge fire burning one's body. In its midst, if one can control one's mind and harness one's body only to do good, not evil, one will achieve liberation, acquire merit, transcend the world, and attain nirvāṇa. This is the first great virtue."

The Second Evil and the Second Virtue

The Buddha said, "The second evil is this. People of the world—parents, children, siblings, and spouses—neither follow honorable principles nor comply with regulations. They revel in extravagance and dissipation for gratification. Self-centered and self-willed, they deceive one another. Their mouth and mind contradict each other; their words and thoughts are dishonest. Sycophantic and untrustworthy, they flatter others with cunning words. They slander the worthy and the virtuous, incriminating them of wrongdoings.

"Unwise rulers appoint deceitful and conniving ministers, who size up the situations and implement their schemes. Those in a shaky position are deceived by them. Against the law of conscience, they purposely slander the loyal and the upright. Ministers deceive their kings; children deceive their parents. Likewise, siblings, spouses, and close or casual friends deceive one another. Afflicted with greed, anger, and delusion, each desires to benefit himself. Dignified or humble, high or low, people have the same mentality. They disregard the consequences of their actions, bringing about the destruction of their families and their own deaths. Both close and distant relatives may be implicated, and the entire clan may be annihilated.

"Sometimes, they engage in enterprises involving family, friends, villagers, townsfolk, fools, and the uncivilized. They exploit one another, and their anger becomes a grudge. The wealthy are miserly and refuse to give alms. Greedy for and attached to riches, they continue to fatigue their bodies and minds. Yet, at the end of their lives, they have nothing to depend upon. As they each have come alone, they each will go alone, and no one will accompany them. Good or evil, fortune or misfortune, follows them as each begins the next life-journey, pleasant or painful. Their remorse comes too late.

"People of the world are stupid and unwise. Instead of admiring the virtuous, they hate and slander them. They desire to do evil and willfully do unlawful deeds. Thievery is in their minds as they covet others' wealth. After they have squandered their goods, they seek to restock them. Although they fear others' detection of their evil motives, they act without any foresight, and regret after they are caught. The world now has law and prison. Evildoers are punished for their crimes. In their past lives, they did not believe in morality, nor did they develop roots of goodness. In their present life, they do evil. Gods even record their names. After death, they go down the evil life-paths.

"Hence, there naturally are the three evil life-journeys with immeasurable suffering and distress. Sinners transmigrate through them life after life, for kalpas, not knowing when release will come. While liberation is hard to achieve, their pain is indescribable. These are the second enormous evil, the second pain, and the second burn.

"As one toils painfully, it is like a huge fire burning one's body. In its midst, if one can control one's mind and harness one's body only to do good, not evil, one will achieve liberation, acquire merit, transcend the world, and attain nirvāṇa. This is the second great virtue."

The Third Evil and the Third Virtue

The Buddha said, "The third evil is this. People of the world, who have limited lifespans, depend upon one another and the environment as they live together between heaven and earth. At the top are wise elders, the dignified, the noble, and the wealthy. At the bottom are the poor, the lowly, the vile, and the foolish. In the middle are the depraved, who are evil and lustful. Filled with chaotic loves and desires, they are restless in their conduct. Greedy and stingy, they desire unearned things. They leer at objects of lust, displaying their evil manners. They detest their own wives and go out to seek adventures. They squander family assets and perform unlawful deeds. They band together and launch lawless warfare, attacking, killing, and pillaging. Their evil minds target external objects, unconcerned about improving their karmas. They obtain things by robbery or thievery. To evade prosecution by law, they give their loot to their wives. They seek gratification in physical pleasure, abusing even their own relatives. People, whether dignified or humble, loathe them, as they cause trouble and anguish to their families. They do not fear the law or other prohibitions. Touching humans and ghosts, their evils are exposed under the sun and the moon and lodged in their [ālaya] consciousnesses.

"Hence, there naturally are the three evil life-journeys with immeasurable suffering and distress. Sinners transmigrate through them life after life, for kalpas, not knowing when release will come. While liberation is hard to achieve, their pain is indescribable. These are the third enormous evil, the third pain, and the third burn.

"As one toils painfully, it is like a huge fire burning one's body. In its midst, if one can control one's mind and harness one's body only to do good, not evil, one will achieve liberation, acquire merit, transcend the world, and attain nirvāṇa. This is the third great virtue."

The Fourth Evil and the Fourth Virtue

The Buddha said, "The fourth evil is this. People of the world do not think of cultivating virtue. Instead, they teach one another to do evil. With divisive speech, abusive speech, false speech, and suggestive speech, they dispute with and slander others. They hate the virtuous and find pleasure in maligning the worthy. They are neither dutiful nor respectful to their parents, and they disdain their teachers and elders. They betray their friends' trust and find it hard to become honest. Conceited and self-aggrandizing, they claim that they are righteous. Lacking self-knowledge, they brutally assault and terrorize others. Considering themselves tough, they do evil shamelessly, making it impossible to earn others' respect. They have no fear of the law between heaven and earth, under the sun and the moon. Unwilling to do good karmas, they are hard to tame. Obstinate and mentally blocked, they claim that their ways can last. With nothing to worry or fear, they are arrogant. All their evils are noted by gods.

"They rely on the merit they acquired in their past lives and use their little virtue for protection and support. Then, in the present life they do evil and deplete their store of merits. Benign spirits all leave them, and they are left alone without any support. After they die, their evils spontaneously return to them and overpower them. Because their evils are lodged in their [ālaya] consciousnesses, their horrible sins will drag them toward inescapable requitals. They must move forward into a cauldron of fire. When their bodies are consumed and their minds in agony, their remorse at that moment comes too late. The way of karma is swift and infallible.

"Hence, there naturally are the three evil life-journeys with immeasurable suffering and distress. Sinners transmigrate through them life after life, for kalpas, not knowing when release will come. While liberation is hard to achieve, their pain is indescribable. These are the fourth enormous evil, the fourth pain, and the fourth burn.

"As one toils painfully, it is like a huge fire burning one's body. In its midst, if one can control one's mind and harness one's body only to do good, not evil, one will achieve liberation, acquire merit, transcend the world, and attain nirvāṇa. This is the fourth great virtue."

The Fifth Evil and the Fifth Virtue

The Buddha said, "The fifth evil is this. People of the world wander in indolence and negligence. They are unwilling to do good karmas, harness their bodies, and earn a livelihood, though their families are in hardship, hungry and cold. When their parents instruct them, they stare and respond in defiance, and argue and contradict, acting like enemies. Parents are better off without such children. They are takers who know no limit, and people loathe them. They take others' kindness and friendship for granted and have no intention of reciprocating. Unable to alter their poverty and hardship, they resort to thievery and vagrancy, and live on what is not earned. They revel in drinking and debauchery, eating and drinking without moderation. Rude and aggressive, they do not understand human rapport and willfully deny it. When they see virtue in people, they envy and hate them. Without any scruples or manners, they have no misgivings. They do as they please, beyond admonition. They have no concern about the means of their six branches of family, never thinking of the kindness of their parents and teachers, or the fellowship of their friends. Devoid of a single virtue, their minds think evil, their mouths speak evil, and their bodies do evil. They disbelieve the Dharma taught by Buddhas and holy ones. They disbelieve that walking the Way leads to transcendence of the world; that after one's death one's [ālaya] consciousness heads for rebirth; or that good karmas reap fortune and evil karmas reap misfortune. They desire to kill the virtuous, damage the Saṅgha, and harm their parents, siblings, and dependents. Their six branches of family are appalled by them, wishing them dead.

"Thus, many people of the world have the same mentality. Stupid and ignorant, they think that they are wise. They know neither whence they are born nor where they will go after death. Cold-hearted and rebellious, they do evil between heaven and earth. They hope to get lucky and live a long life, but only end in death. If someone kindly teaches them to think of virtue and explains to them the good and evil life-journeys, they refuse to believe him. Painstaking advice cannot benefit them because their minds are entirely blocked and impossible to open. Upon the ending of their life, they are crushed by fear and remorse. They refuse to cultivate virtue, only to regret in the end. What good is their remorse to their next life?

"Between heaven and earth, the five life-paths are distinct, extensive, profound, and vast. One's good and evil requitals, manifested as fortune and misfortune, respond without fail to one's good and evil karmas. One must personally bear them, and no one else can take one's place. The karmic law responds to one's actions, and requitals chase one's life, never relenting. While a virtuous person who does good karmas goes from pleasure to pleasure, from light to light, an evil person who does evil karmas goes from pain to pain, from dark to dark. Who, besides a Buddha, knows all this? However, few believe and carry out the teachings. As one's cycle of birth and death and the evil life-journeys are endless, so too people of the world are endless.

"Hence, there naturally are the three evil life-journeys with immeasurable suffering and distress. Sinners transmigrate through them life after life, for kalpas, not knowing when release will come. While liberation is hard to achieve, their pain is indescribable. These are the fifth enormous evil, the fifth pain, and the fifth burn.

"As one toils painfully, it is like a huge fire burning one's body. In its midst, if one can control one's mind and harness one's body to think the right thoughts, to act according to one's words with utmost sincerity, to keep one's words in accord with one's mind, and to do good, not evil, one will achieve liberation, acquire merit, transcend the world, and attain nirvāṇa. This is the fifth great virtue."

Another Solemn Admonition

The Buddha told Maitreya Bodhisattva, "As I say to you all, people of the world toil painfully in the five evils. As a result, they suffer the five pains and, in turn, the five burns. They do myriad evils but do not develop roots of goodness, so they naturally go down the evil life-journeys. As witnessed by the multitudes, some, even in their present life, suffer prolonged illness brought about by their sins, and are unable either to die or to live. Then, after death, they go down the three evil life-paths to experience immeasurable horrendous suffering, burning in fire.

"These people bear each other grudges that begin small but, after a long time, grow into an enormous evil. Because of their greed for wealth, they cannot give alms. Mired in delusion, they can neither think straight nor liberate themselves from the bondage of afflictions. They fight for self-benefit, never stopping to reflect. As they seek fleeting pleasures in wealth and rank, they can neither endure adversity nor cultivate virtue. The little power they hold is soon spent. Their longtime toil only leads to severe consequences. The law of karma prevails, and the net of requitals is accordingly spread. They each fall into the net, alone and afraid. From ancient times to the present, there are such deplorable pains."

The Buddha told Maitreya Bodhisattva, "All Buddhas are sad over the ways of the world. With their awesome spiritual power, they annihilate evils, enabling people to drop their habitual thoughts, uphold sūtras and precepts, and practice the Dharma without misunderstandings or violations. They will eventually transcend the world and attain nirvāṇa."

The Buddha continued, "You, gods and humans, and people of the future, who have received the Buddha's teachings, should ponder them well. Then all can take the right actions with an upright mind. A ruler who cultivates virtue sets an example for his ministers, who in turn command all subjects to maintain good conduct. All should revere the holy and respect the virtuous, and be kind and loving to others. Do not fail the Buddha's teachings. All should seek to transcend the world and uproot the evils of repeated birth and death, leaving forever the immeasurable anxiety and agony through the three evil life-journeys.

"You all should widely plant roots of virtue and practice the six pāramitās: almsgiving, observance of precepts, endurance of adversity, energetic progress, meditation, and development of wisdom. You each should teach others, who in turn will teach many others, to uphold virtue and to rectify one's mind and intention. If one observes the precepts with purity for one day and one night in this land, one's merit exceeds that from doing good karmas for 100 years in Amitāyus Buddha's land. Why? Because that Buddha Land is pure, and its inhabitants, having no evil even as slight as a hair, spontaneously accumulate good karmas. If one cultivates virtue for ten days and ten nights in this land, one's merit exceeds that from doing good karmas for 1,000 years in Buddha Lands in other directions. Why? Because most inhabitants of other Buddha Lands do good, and few do evil. With no place to do evil, acquiring merit is their natural way of life. However, in this land are many evils, and acquiring merit is not the natural way of life. People toil painfully to satisfy their desires, and they take advantage of one another. Exhausted in body and mind, they eat bitterness and drink poison. Their evils never end.

"I pity you gods and humans, and painstakingly instruct you to cultivate virtue. According to your capacities, I guide you and teach you the Dharma for you to carry out, so that you all will attain bodhi as you wish. Wherever the Buddha visits, in countries or settlements, no one will fail to be transformed. The world will be in harmony, the sun and the moon will be bright, and the winds and rains will be timely. Natural disasters and epidemics will not strike. The country will prosper, and the people will live in peace, rendering weaponry useless. As people admire virtue and appreciate kindness, they will learn to be courteous and to yield to one another."

The Buddha continued, "I pity you gods and humans more than parents are concerned about their children. I now have become a Buddha in this world, and I [teach sentient beings to] destroy the five evils, remove the five pains, and eliminate the five burns. I attack evil with virtue to end the suffering of repeated birth and death, enabling all to acquire the five virtues and ascend to the peace [of nirvāṇa], which is free from causes and conditions. After I have left this world, the Way to bodhi will gradually disappear. People will resume their evil ways of sycophancy and falsehood, and will experience the five pains and the five burns just as before. How severe their condition will become cannot be described in detail. I have only told you briefly about it."

The Buddha told Maitreya Bodhisattva, "You all should ponder and admonish one another in accordance with the Buddha Dharma, not to violate it."

Then Maitreya Bodhisattva joined his palms and said, "What the Buddha has said is true. People of the world are like that. The Tathāgata, out of lovingkindness and compassion, enables us all to be liberated. Having received the Buddha's solemn admonition, we dare not defy or lose it."

The Vision of Amitāyus Buddha and His Land

The Buddha told Ānanda, "Rise, arrange your robe, join your palms reverently, and make obeisance to Amitāyus Buddha. Buddha-Tathāgatas in worlds in the ten directions all praise and acclaim that Buddha, who has neither attachment nor hindrance."

Then Ānanda rose, arranged his robe, and stood properly, facing the west. He joined his palms reverently and prostrated himself on the ground, making obeisance to Amitāyus Buddha. He said, "World-Honored One, I wish to see that Buddha, His Land of Peace and Bliss, and the multitude of Bodhisattvas and voice-hearers there."

As soon as he spoke these words, Amitāyus Buddha emitted great radiance, illuminating all Buddha Lands. The vajra mountain range, Sumeru the king of mountains, and other large and small mountains all became the same color. The radiance was like the water covering the world at the end of a kalpa when everything is submerged, and one sees only an expanse of water. That Buddha's radiance had the same effect. The radiance of voice-hearers and Bodhisattvas was entirely obscured, and one saw only that Buddha's radiance, brilliant and magnificent.

At that time Ānanda saw Amitāyus Buddha, awesome and majestic, like Sumeru the mountain-king, taller than all the worlds. The radiance of his sublime appearance shone on everything. As the four groups of Śākyamuni Buddha's disciples in this assembly all saw Amitāyus Buddha and His land, likewise all inhabitants of the Land of Peace and Bliss saw Śākyamuni Buddha and His people in this Sahā World.[7]

Then the Buddha asked Ānanda and Maitreya Bodhisattva, "Do you not see all the wonderful pure adornments in that land, from its ground up to pure abode heavens?"

Ānanda replied, "Yes, I see them."

"Do you not hear Amitāyus Buddha pronounce [the Dharma] aloud to all worlds to transform their sentient beings?"

Ānanda replied, "Yes, I hear Him."

"People of that land ride a palace 100,000 yojanas in size, made of the seven treasures, to make offerings to Buddhas [in worlds] in the ten directions unhindered. Do you see this?"

"I see this," replied Ānanda.

"Some people of that land are reborn from the womb.[8] Do you see this?"

"I see this," replied Ānanda.

"Those who are reborn from the womb live in palaces 100 or 500 yojanas in size. They each enjoy pleasures as naturally as if they were in Trayastriṁśa Heaven."

Doubts Causing a Rebirth from the Womb

At that time Maitreya Bodhisattva asked the Buddha, "World-Honored One, why are people of that land reborn from the womb or reborn miraculously [in lotus flowers]?"

The Buddha told Maitreya Bodhisattva, "There are sentient beings that wish to be reborn in that land, but they accumulate merit with a mind of doubts. They do not understand Buddha wisdom, including the inconceivable wisdom-knowledge, the indescribable wisdom-knowledge, the vast Mahāyāna wisdom-knowledge, and the unsurpassed supreme wisdom-knowledge. They disbelieve in and doubt such wisdom-knowledge. Nevertheless, they believe in sin and merit, and they develop their roots of goodness, wishing to be reborn in that land. These sentient beings are reborn [on the edge of that land] and live a 500-year lifespan in a palace. They never see that Buddha, nor do they hear the Buddha Dharma, nor do they see the multitude of Bodhisattvas and voice-hearers. Therefore, in that land this is called a rebirth from the womb.

"Then, there are sentient beings that believe in Buddha wisdom, including the unsurpassed supreme wisdom-knowledge. They acquire merits and faithfully transfer their merits to others. These sentient beings are reborn miraculously, seated cross-legged in lotus flowers made of the seven treasures. In an instant, their physical features, radiance, wisdom, and merits are as complete as those of the Bodhisattvas already there.

"Moreover, Maitreya, in Buddha Lands in other directions are great Bodhisattvas who wish to see Amitāyus Buddha and His multitude of Bodhisattvas and voice-hearers, and to make offerings reverently to them. These Bodhisattvas after death will also be reborn miraculously in Amitāyus Buddha's land, in lotus flowers made of the seven treasures.

"Maitreya, know that those reborn miraculously have superior wisdom while those reborn from the womb have little wisdom. For 500 years they do not see that Buddha, nor do they hear the Dharma, nor do they see the multitude of Bodhisattvas and voice-hearers. Unable to make offerings to Buddhas and ignorant of Bodhisattvas' Dharma procedures, they cannot acquire merit. Know that all this is caused by their lacking wisdom and harboring doubts in their past lives."

The Buddha told Maitreya Bodhisattva, "As an analogy, a Wheel-Turning King has a special palace adorned with the seven treasures. It is furnished with beds, curtains, and silky canopies. If young princes have offended the king, they are detained in that palace, chained with gold locks. Just like a Wheel-Turning King, they are provided with food and drink, clothing and bedding, flowers and incense, and instrumental music, without any shortage. What is your opinion? Do these princes enjoy staying there?"

"No," replied Maitreya Bodhisattva, "using various methods, they seek the strength to escape."

The Buddha told Maitreya Bodhisattva, "These sentient beings live in the same way. Because they have doubts about Buddha wisdom, they are reborn in that palace made of the seven treasures. There is no punishment, not even a single thought of evil. However, for 500 years, they do not see the Three Jewels and are unable to make offerings or develop roots of goodness. This is their suffering. Although there are pleasures to spare, they do not enjoy that place. However, if these sentient beings can recognize their initial sins, reproach themselves, and beseech to leave that place, their wish will be fulfilled. Then they can go to the place where Amitāyus Buddha is and can make offerings reverently. They also can go to the places where innumerable, countless Buddhas are, to acquire merit. Maitreya, know that those who harbor doubts will lose great benefits. Therefore, one should recognize and believe in Buddhas' unsurpassed wisdom."

Rebirth of Bodhisattvas from This and Other Worlds

Maitreya Bodhisattva asked the Buddha, "World-Honored One, how many Bodhisattvas in this world who are at the spiritual level of no regress have been reborn in that land?"

The Buddha replied to Maitreya Bodhisattva, "From this world, 67 koṭi Bodhisattvas who never regress have been reborn in that land. Each of these Bodhisattvas has made offerings to innumerable Buddhas, though less so than Maitreya. Innumerable Bodhisattvas with lesser achievement and lesser merit will all be reborn there."

The Buddha told Maitreya Bodhisattva, "Not only from my land, but also from Buddha Lands in other directions, will Bodhisattvas be reborn in that land. The first Buddha is called Shining Far, whose 180 koṭi Bodhisattvas will be reborn there. The second Buddha is called Treasure Store, whose 90 koṭi Bodhisattvas will be reborn there. The third Buddha is called Infinite Tone, whose 220 koṭi Bodhisattvas will be reborn there. The fourth Buddha is called Sweet Nectar Flavor, whose 250 koṭi Bodhisattvas will be reborn there. The fifth Buddha is called Dragon Victory, whose 14 koṭi Bodhisattvas will be reborn there. The sixth Buddha is called Victory Power, whose 14,000 Bodhisattvas will be reborn there. The seventh Buddha is called Lion, whose 500 koṭi[9] Bodhisattvas will be reborn there. The eighth Buddha is called Immaculate Light, whose 80 koṭi Bodhisattvas will be reborn there. The ninth Buddha is called Virtue Leader, whose 60 koṭi Bodhisattvas will be reborn there. The tenth Buddha is called Wonderful Virtue Mountain, whose 60 koṭi Bodhisattvas will be reborn there. The eleventh Buddha is called King of Men, whose 10 koṭi Bodhisattvas will be reborn there. The twelfth Buddha is called Supreme Flower, whose innumerable Bodhisattvas, all at the spiritual level of no regress, all with wisdom and valor, having made offerings to innumerable Buddhas, able to collect in seven days the firm dharmas practiced by great Bodhisattvas for 100,000 koṭi kalpas, will be reborn there. The thirteenth Buddha is called Fearlessness, whose 790 koṭi great Bodhisattvas, and innumerable bhikṣus and novice Bodhisattvas, will be reborn there."

The Buddha told Maitreya Bodhisattva, "Not only will Bodhisattvas from these fourteen Buddha Lands be reborn there, but also countless Bodhisattvas from innumerable Buddha Lands in the ten directions will be reborn there. If I tell day and night only the names of Buddhas [in worlds] in the ten directions and their Bodhisattvas and bhikṣus who will be reborn there, I cannot finish the list in a kalpa. I now have told you only in brief."

Circulation of the Sūtra

The Buddha told Maitreya Bodhisattva, "If there is a person who, having heard that Buddha's name, is joyful and exuberant even for a single thought, know that he has acquired great benefits and unsurpassed merits. Therefore, Maitreya, even if there is an enormous fire filling this entire Three-Thousand Large Thousandfold World, one regardless should cross the fire to hear this sūtra, delight and believe in it, accept and uphold it, read and recite it, and train accordingly. Why? Because there are many Bodhisattvas who wish to hear this sūtra but do not have access. If sentient beings have heard this sūtra, they will never regress from their resolve to attain the unsurpassed bodhi. Therefore, they should deeply believe in this sūtra, accept and uphold it, recite and pronounce it, and carry out its teachings. For the sake of sentient beings, I have pronounced this sūtra and enabled them to see Amitāyus Buddha and everything in His land, so that they can resolve to do what should be done[10] and not allow doubts to arise after my parinirvāṇa.

"In times to come, the Dharma will be annihilated. Out of lovingkindness and compassion, I will specially save this sūtra and make it stay for a hundred years more. Sentient beings that encounter this sūtra will all be delivered as they wish."

The Buddha told Maitreya Bodhisattva, "The appearance of a Tathāgata in the world is hard to encounter and hard to see. The Buddha Dharma is hard to acquire and hard to hear. The excellent Bodhisattva Dharma, including the pāramitās, is hard to hear as well. To practice the Dharma after hearing it from a beneficent learned friend is also very hard. To believe, appreciate, accept, and uphold this sūtra after hearing it, is the hardest of all. Nothing is harder than this.

"Such is my Dharma. This is how it is pronounced and how it is taught. You all should believe and follow, and train accordingly."

When the World-Honored One pronounced this sūtra, innumerable sentient beings activated the anuttara-samyak-saṁbodhi mind. In addition, 12,000 nayuta people acquired the pure dharma-eye, 22 Koṭi gods and humans achieved the third voice-hearer fruit, becoming Anāgāmins, and 80 koṭi bhikṣus eradicated their afflictions and liberated their minds, [becoming Arhats]. Forty koṭi Bodhisattvas achieved the spiritual level of no regress, adorning themselves with their great merits and vows. They would in a future life attain true enlightenment.

Then the Three-Thousand Large Thousandfold World quaked in six different ways. Great radiance illuminated everywhere in worlds in the ten directions. One hundred thousand kinds of music spontaneously played, and innumerable wonderful flowers rained down from the sky.

After the Buddha pronounced this sūtra, the entire assembly—Maitreya Bodhisattva and the multitude of Bodhisattvas who came from worlds in the ten directions, together with the Elder Ānanda and other great voice-hearers—having heard the Buddha's words, greatly rejoiced.

Notes

1. These 34 names are taken from the Sanskrit text of *Sukhāvatīvyūhaḥ* at the website of the Digital Sanskrit Buddhist Canon posted by the University of the West, Rosemead, California. The Chinese text (T12n0360) contains only 31 names. Some names phonetically translated into Chinese can be easily matched with their corresponding Sanskrit names. However, other Chinese names were created by using the reputations of given subjects. For example, on the Chinese list is a name Great Pure Willpower (大淨志). According to the *Buddha's Light Dictionary* (1988, 6313a), it belongs to a monk called Raṣṭrapāla (country protector), who refused to accept the woman his parents sent him. Neither Great Pure Willpower nor Raṣṭrapāla is on the Sanskrit list. Therefore, it would be unproductive to try matching such names in the Chinese text with names in the Sanskrit text.

2. The name Wisdom Eloquence is included in a corresponding passage in text 310 (T11n0310, 0091c16–20). Adding this name to the fifteen Upright Ones named in text 360 brings the total to sixteen.

3. In text 360, the Chinese term 天人 can mean gods or gods and humans. The word *gods* is used here because all inhabitants of the Pure Land are reborn miraculously in lotus flowers, not from the womb. The Buddha explains later that they are neither gods nor humans, so *gods* is a false name.

4. In text 360, the subject of vow 37 is gods. However, for the same vow in text 310 (T11n0310, 0094b21–23), the subject is Bodhisattvas. The latter makes more sense in the context.

5. Five evil life-paths refer to the life-paths of gods, humans, animals, hungry ghosts, and hell dwellers. Asuras are not included here as a sixth life form because they may assume any of the first four life forms and live among sentient beings in these forms. In this human world, only the last three life-paths are considered evil. However, compared with the life of the inhabitants in the Land of Peace and Bliss, all five life-paths are evil.

6. Prohibited by the five precepts are the five evils: (1) killing; (2) stealing; (3) sexual misconduct; (4) false speech, divisive speech, abusive speech, suggestive speech; (5) drinking alcohol. All five evils arise from greed, anger, and delusion (the wrong views). The five pains are an evildoer's suffering in his present life. The five burns are his suffering in his next life in hell. The five virtues are the opposites of the five evils.

7. This sentence is a simplified version of a corresponding passage in text 310 (T11n0310, 0100a2–4).

8. The womb is a figure of speech, meaning a confined life after rebirth. According to texts 361 and 362 (T12n0361, 0292a28–29; T12n0362, 0310b9–10), some of those in the middle class (and very likely in the low class as well) who could be reborn in the Pure Land proper, because of their doubts, are instead reborn in lotus flowers in the ponds of a city on the edge of the Pure Land. There, they live for 500 years in palaces made of the seven jewels. According to text 310 (T11n0310, 0100b17–20), each of them remains for 500 years in an unopened lotus flower, as if in a womb, and thinks that he lives in a palace.

9. Four different figures are found for the number of Bodhisattvas. (1) It is 500 koṭi in text 360. (2) It is 500 in the same text in the Song, Yuan, and Ming

editions of the Chinese Canon, and in text 310. (3) It is 1,800 in text 363. (4) It is 16 koṭi in F. Max Müller's translation (1894, part 2, 66). The first figure is used here though the figure 500 is adopted in the circulation text.

10. They should train for rebirth in Amitāyus Buddha's land.

2 佛說阿彌陀經
Buddha Pronounces the Sūtra of Amitābha Buddha

Translated from Sanskrit into Chinese in the Later Qin Dynasty
by
The Tripiṭaka Master Kumārajīva from Kucha

Thus I have heard:

At one time the Buddha was staying in the Anāthapiṇḍika Garden of Jetavana Park in the city kingdom of Śrāvastī, together with 1,250 great bhikṣus, who all were great Arhats as recognized by the multitudes. Such great disciples included the Elder Śāriputra, Mahāmaudgalyāyana, Mahākāśyapa, Mahākātyāyana, Mahākauṣṭhila, Revata, Śuddhipanthaka, Nanda, Ānanda, Rāhula, Gavāṁpati, Piṇḍola-Bharadvāja, Kālodāyin, Mahākapphiṇa, Vakkula, Aniruddha, and others. Also present were Bodhisattva-Mahāsattvas, such as Mañjuśrī the Dharma Prince, Ajita Bodhisattva, Gandhahastin Bodhisattva, and Persistent Energetic Progress Bodhisattva. Along with great Bodhisattvas such as these, in attendance as well were the god-king Śakro-Devānām-Indra and an innumerable multitude of gods.

At that time the Buddha told the Elder Śāriputra, "West of here, beyond 100,000 koṭi Buddha Lands, is a land called Ultimate Bliss. In that land resides a Buddha called Amitābha, who is now expounding the Dharma. Śāriputra, why is that land called Ultimate Bliss? Sentient beings of that land have no suffering but only experience myriad joys. Therefore, that land is called Ultimate Bliss. Moreover, Śāriputra, the Land of Ultimate Bliss is surrounded by seven rows of railings, seven layers of nets, and seven lines of trees, all made of the four treasures. Therefore, that land is called Ultimate Bliss.

"Also, Śāriputra, in the Land of Ultimate Bliss are ponds made of the seven treasures, filled with water with the eight virtues. Covering the bed of each pond is gold dust. The stairs and walkways on the four sides of each pond are made of gold, silver, aquamarine, and crystal. Standing majestically are lofty towers, all adorned with gold, silver, aquamarine, crystal, conch shell, ruby, and emerald. The lotus flowers in the ponds are as large as carriage wheels. The blue colors gleam with blue light; the yellow colors, yellow light; the red colors, red light; the white colors, white light. They are wonderful, fragrant, and pure. Śāriputra, the Land of Ultimate Bliss is formed with such virtues as its adornments!

"Also, Śāriputra, celestial music is always playing in that Buddha Land, and its ground is made of yellow gold. Day and night in the six periods, the sky rains down celestial māndarāva flowers. At dawn, sentient beings of that land fill their robes with wonderful flowers to make offerings to 100,000 koṭi Buddhas [in worlds] in other directions. At mealtime, they return to their own land to eat and do walking meditation. Śāriputra, the Land of Ultimate Bliss is formed with such virtues as its adornments!

"In addition, Śāriputra, in that land are various kinds of unusual, wonderful birds of diverse colors, such as white cranes, peacocks, parrots, śāris, kalaviṅkas, and jīvajīvas. Day and night in the six periods, these birds sing in harmonious, exquisite tones. These tones pronounce Dharmas, such as the Five Roots, the Five Powers, the Seven Bodhi Factors, and the Eightfold Right Path. Sentient beings that hear these tones all think of the Buddha, think of the Dharma, and think of the Saṅgha. Śāriputra, do not say that these birds are born as a form of requital for sins [in their past lives]. Why not? Because, Śāriputra, that Buddha Land does not have the three evil life-paths. Śāriputra, even the names of the three evil life-paths do not exist in that Buddha Land, much less the actual paths. These birds are all magically manifested by Amitābha Buddha to have the Dharma tones flow everywhere.

"Śāriputra, as breezes blow in that Buddha Land, the jeweled trees in lines and the jeweled nets [with bells[1]] make wonderful music, like 100,000 melodies playing at the same time. Those who hear these tones spontaneously think of the Buddha, think of the Dharma, and think of the Saṅgha. Śāriputra, that Buddha Land is formed with such virtues as its adornments!

"Śāriputra, what is your opinion? Why is that Buddha called Amitābha? Śāriputra, that Buddha's radiance is infinite, illuminating worlds in the ten directions, hindrance free. Therefore, He is called Amitābha. Moreover, Śāriputra, the lifespan of that Buddha and His people is measureless, limitless asaṁkhyeya kalpas. Therefore, He is called Amitāyus. Śāriputra, it has been ten kalpas since Amitābha Buddha attained Buddhahood. In addition, Śāriputra, that Buddha has innumerable, countless voice-hearer disciples. All of them are Arhats, their numbers unknowable by calculation. Equally unknowable is the size of the multitude of Bodhisattvas. Śāriputra, that Buddha Land is formed with such virtues as its adornments!

"Furthermore, Śāriputra, sentient beings reborn in the Land of Ultimate Bliss are at the spiritual level of avinivartanīya. Many among them are in the holy position of waiting to attain Buddhahood in their next life. Their numbers are so large that they are unknowable by calculation, and can be reckoned only in terms of measureless, limitless asaṁkhyeyas. Śāriputra, sentient beings that have heard [of that land] should resolve to be reborn in that land. Why? To be in the same place together with people of superior virtues. Śāriputra, no one with the condition of few roots of goodness and a meager store of merits can be reborn in that land.

"Śāriputra, if, among good men and good women, there are those who, having heard of Amitābha Buddha, single-mindedly uphold His name for one day, two days, three days, four days, five days, six days, or seven days, without being distracted, then upon their dying, Amitābha Buddha, together with a holy multitude, will appear before them. When these people die, their minds will not be demented and they will be reborn in Amitābha Buddha's Land of Ultimate Bliss. Śāriputra, I see this benefit, so I speak these words. If there are sentient beings that hear what I say, they should resolve to be reborn in that land.

"Śāriputra, as I now praise Amitābha Buddha's inconceivable merit, so too do Buddhas in worlds in the east, such as Akṣobhya Buddha, Meru Banner Buddha, Great Meru Buddha, Meru Light Buddha, and Wonderful Tone Buddha. Buddhas such as these are as numerous as the sands of the Ganges. Each Buddha in His own land extends His wide-ranging, far-reaching tongue, completely covering the Three-Thousand Large Thousandfold World, and speaks these truthful words: 'You sentient beings should praise His inconceivable merit and believe in this sūtra, which is protected and remembered by all Buddhas.'

"Śāriputra, in worlds in the south are Sun-Moon Lamp Buddha, Renown Light Buddha, Great Flame Aggregate Buddha,[2] Meru Lamp Buddha, and Infinite Energetic Progress Buddha. Buddhas such as these are as numerous as the sands of the Ganges. Each Buddha in His own land extends His wide-ranging, far-reaching tongue, completely covering the Three-Thousand Large Thousandfold World, and speaks these truthful words: 'You sentient beings should praise His inconceivable merit and believe in this sūtra, which is protected and remembered by all Buddhas.'

"Śāriputra, in worlds in the west are Infinite Life Buddha, Infinite Aggregate Buddha, Infinite Banner Buddha, Great Light Buddha, Great Radiance Buddha, Jewel Brilliance Buddha, and Pure Light Buddha. Buddhas such as these are as numerous as the sands of the Ganges. Each Buddha in His own land extends His wide-ranging, far-reaching tongue, completely covering the Three-Thousand Large Thousandfold World, and speaks these truthful words: 'You sentient beings should praise His inconceivable merit and believe in this sūtra, which is protected and remembered by all Buddhas.'

"Śāriputra, in worlds in the north are Flame Aggregate Buddha, Supreme Tone Buddha, Hard-to-Vanquish Buddha, Sun Birth Buddha, Web-of-Radiance Buddha. Buddhas such as these are as numerous as the sands of the Ganges. Each Buddha in His own land extends His wide-ranging, far-reaching tongue, completely covering the Three-Thousand Large Thousandfold World, and speaks these truthful words: 'You sentient beings should praise His inconceivable merit and believe in this sūtra, which is protected and remembered by all Buddhas.'

"Śāriputra, in worlds toward the nadir are Lion Buddha, Renown Buddha, Renown Light Buddha, Dharma Buddha, Dharma Banner Buddha, and Dharma Upholder Buddha. Buddhas such as these are as numerous as the sands of the Ganges. Each Buddha in His own land extends His wide-ranging, far-reaching tongue, completely covering the Three-Thousand Large Thousandfold World, and speaks these truthful words: 'You sentient beings should praise His inconceivable merit and believe in this sūtra, which is protected and remembered by all Buddhas.'

"Śāriputra, in worlds toward the zenith are Brahma Tone Buddha, Constellation King Buddha, Fragrance Superior Buddha, Fragrant Light Buddha, Great Flame Aggregate Buddha, Adorned with Jeweled Flowers in Diverse Colors Buddha, Salendra King Buddha, Jeweled Lotus Flower Splendor Buddha, Seeing All Meaning Buddha, and Sumeru Likeness Buddha. Buddhas such as these are as numerous as the sands of the Ganges. Each Buddha in His own land extends His wide-ranging, far-reaching tongue, completely covering the Three-Thousand Large Thousandfold World, and speaks these truthful words: 'You sentient beings should praise His inconceivable merit and believe in this sūtra, which is protected and remembered by all Buddhas.'

"Śāriputra, what is your opinion? Why is this sūtra called a sūtra protected and remembered by all Buddhas? Śāriputra, if there are good men and good women who have heard and upheld this sūtra, and have heard Buddhas' names, they are protected and remembered by all Buddhas. They will never regress from their resolve to attain anuttara-samyak-saṁbodhi. Therefore, Śāriputra, you all should believe and accept my words and other Buddhas' words. If there are those who have resolved, are now resolving, or will resolve to be reborn in Amitābha Buddha's land, they will never regress from their resolve to attain anuttara-samyak-saṁbodhi, whether they have already been reborn, are now being reborn, or will be reborn in that land. Therefore, Śāriputra, if, among good men and good women, there are those who believe [my words], they should resolve to be reborn in that land.

"Śāriputra, as I now praise Buddhas' inconceivable merit,[3] likewise those Buddhas praise my inconceivable merit, saying these words: 'Śākyamuni Buddha can do the extremely difficult, extraordinary thing in the Sahā World during the evil times of the five turbidities—the turbidity of a kalpa, the turbidity of views, the turbidity of afflictions, the turbidity of sentient beings, and the turbidity of their lifespan—attaining anuttara-samyak-saṁbodhi. For the sake of sentient beings, He expounds the Dharma, which the entire world finds hard to believe.'

"Śāriputra, know that, in the evil times of the five turbidities, I have done this difficult thing, attaining anuttara-samyak-saṁbodhi. For the sake of the entire world, I expound the hard-to-believe Dharma. It is extremely difficult!"

After the Buddha pronounced this sūtra, Śāriputra and other bhikṣus, as well as gods, humans, asuras, and others in the entire world, having heard the Buddha's words, rejoiced, believed in, and accepted the teachings. They made obeisance and departed.

Notes

1. F. Max Müller footnotes in *Buddhist Mahāyāna Texts* (Cowell et al. 1894, part 2, 92), that he translates the Sanskrit word *kaṅkanījālānām* (bells of nets) as strings of bells. However, bells can hang from a net (jāla), as described in the *Mahāyāna Sūtra of Consciousness Revealed* (Rulu 2012a, 144). So the term is translated as nets with bells.

2. In text 366 (T12n0366), Kumārajīva translates the Sanskrit name Mahārciskandha into Chinese as Great Flame Shoulder. The Sanskrit word *arci* can mean flame or ray, and *skandha* can mean shoulder or aggregate. In text 367 (T12n0367), Xuanzang translates Mahārciskandha as Great Light Aggregate. Here, this name is translated as Great Flame Aggregate.

3. In an earlier passage in this sūtra, the Buddha says, "Śāriputra, as I now praise Amitābha Buddha's inconceivable merit, so too do Buddhas in worlds in the east, . . ." Therefore, for this passage, it seems that Śākyamuni Buddha's praising the inconceivable merit of Amitābha Buddha would confirm the earlier passage and would be more relevant than His praising the merit of Buddhas in general. Support of this comment is found in a corresponding passage in text 367, in which the Buddha states: "Śāriputra, as I now acclaim and praise Amitāyus Buddha's inconceivable merit, who has formed His Buddha Land of Ultimate Bliss,

likewise other Buddha-Tathāgatas [in worlds] in the ten directions praise my inconceivable boundless merit, . . ." (T12n0367, 0351a27–29).

3 佛說觀無量壽佛經
Buddha Pronounces the Sūtra of Visualization of Amitāyus Buddha

Translated into Chinese in the Liu Song Dynasty
by
The Tripiṭaka Master Kālayaśas from India

Preface

Thus I have heard:

At one time the Buddha was staying on the Gṛdhrakūṭa Mountain, near the city of Rājagṛha, together with 1,250 great bhikṣus and 32,000 Bodhisattvas. At the head of this multitude was Mañjuśrī Bodhisattva the Dharma Prince.

At that time, in the great city of Rājagṛha, the crown prince, Ajātaśatru, urged by his evil friend Devadatta, had his father, King Bimbisāra, arrested and locked in a cell behind seven walls. He decreed to all state ministers that no one could visit the king.

Nevertheless, Queen Vaidehī was loyal to the great king. She bathed, smeared her body with honey and roasted flour, and hid [a flask of] grape juice under her necklaces. She secretly offered them to the king [on her visit]. Having eaten the flour and drunk the juice, the great king asked for water to rinse his mouth. After rinsing his mouth, he joined his palms reverently and made obeisance to the World-Honored One, who was on the Gṛdhrakūṭa Mountain in the distance. He said, "Mahāmaudgalyāyana is my kin and friend. I pray that he, out of lovingkindness and compassion, will impart the eight precepts to me."

Maudgalyāyana flew to the king like an eagle. Day after day, he imparted the eight precepts to the king. The World-Honored One also sent the venerable Pūrṇa to expound the Dharma to the king. Time passed this way for twenty-one days. Because each day he ate the honey flour and heard the Dharma, the king looked well and content.

But then Ajātaśatru asked the guard, "Is my father still alive?"

The guard replied, "Your Majesty, each day the queen brings the king honey flour smeared on her body and grape juice concealed under her necklaces. The śramaṇas Maudgalyāyana and Pūrṇa soar across the sky to expound the Dharma to the king. They are unstoppable."

Having heard these words, Ajātaśatru was furious with his mother. He said, "My mother is a traitor, keeping company with traitors. The evil śramaṇas are using magic and spells to stave off death from this evil king for so many days."

He drew his sharp sword to slay his mother. But Moonlight, an intelligent and resourceful minister, and Jīva, another minister, saluted the crown prince and said, "Your Majesty, we have learned from the Vedas that since the beginning of this kalpa, 18,000 evil kings have killed their fathers for the throne.

But never has anyone killed his mother. Your Majesty, if you commit this rebellious sin, it means that you defile the name of the kṣatriya caste and become a caṇḍāla [an outcaste]. As your ministers, we cannot bear to hear of this, so we should remain here no longer."

Having said that, the two great ministers retreated step by step, hands on their swords.

Ajātaśatru was astonished and intimidated. He asked Jīva, "You will not be with me?"

Jīva replied, "Your Majesty, take care not to harm your mother."

So, to save himself, Ajātaśatru relented. He dropped his sword, withdrawing his intent to kill his mother. He then ordered the palace guards to confine his mother in a secluded palace, forbidding her to go out.

While under house arrest, Vaidehī pined. Facing the Gṛdhrakūṭa Mountain in the distance, she made obeisance to the Buddha and said, "In the past, the Tathāgata-Bhagavān often sent Ānanda to greet and comfort me. I now despair because I cannot see the sublime visage of the World-Honored One. I pray that You will send Mahāmaudgalyāyana and the venerable Ānanda to see me."

And with tears of sorrow falling like rain, she made obeisance to the Buddha in the distance. In an instant, even before Vaidehī raised her head, the World-Honored One, on the Gṛdhrakūṭa Mountain, knew the thoughts in her mind. He commanded Mahāmaudgalyāyana and Ānanda to fly there, and He disappeared from the mountain and appeared in the palace. When Vaidehī raised her head from her obeisance, she saw Śākyamuni Buddha the World-Honored One, purple-tinged golden, seated on a lotus flower made of a hundred treasures. He was attended by Mahāmaudgalyāyana on His left and Ānanda on His right. In the sky stood the Brahma-kings, the god-king Śakra, the four god-kings who protect the world, and other gods, and they showered celestial flowers everywhere as an offering to the Buddha.

When Vaidehī saw the Buddha-Bhagavān, she cast off her necklaces and threw herself on the ground. Weeping loudly, she asked the Buddha, "For what sins in my past lives have I given birth to this evil son? Through what causes and conditions does the World-Honored One have Devadatta in His retinue? I pray only that the World-Honored One will reveal to me a place free from sorrow and distress. I wish to be reborn there. I dislike this turbid evil world of Jambudvīpa. This place, teeming with hell-dwellers, hungry ghosts, and animals, is where the evil ones assemble. I wish that, in my next life, I will not hear the evil sounds or see the evil people. I prostrate myself on the ground before the World-Honored One, beseeching You to sympathize with my repentance. I pray only that the Buddha will teach me to visualize a place of pure karma."

The Teachings

Display of All Buddha Lands

Then the World-Honored One sent forth golden beams of light from between His eyebrows. The beams shone everywhere in innumerable worlds in the ten directions. Then they returned to the crown of the Buddha's head and transformed into a golden plateau as immense as Mount Sumeru, in which were displayed pure Buddha Lands in the ten directions. Some lands were made of the seven treasures; some lands were solely lotus flowers; some lands were like the palaces in the sixth desire heaven; some lands were like crystal mirrors. Thus displayed were all lands in the ten directions! And thus Vaidehī could see the splendors of innumerable Buddha Lands.

Then Vaidehī said to the Buddha, "World-Honored One, although these Buddha Lands are all pure and radiant, I now would rather be reborn in Sukhāvatī, Amitāyus Buddha's Land of Ultimate Bliss. I pray only that the World-Honored One will teach me how to visualize that land and have the right experience."

Then the World-Honored One smiled, and beams of light in five colors issued from the Buddha's mouth. Each beam shone on the crown of King Bimbisāra's head. Although the great king was imprisoned, his mind's eye was unhindered as he saw the World-Honored One in the distance. He made obeisance, placing his forehead on the ground, and easily achieved the third voice-hearer fruit, becoming an Anāgāmin.

The Three Meritorious Works

Then the World-Honored One told Vaidehī, "Do you know now? Amitāyus Buddha is not far from here. You should think of and visualize that land formed by pure karma. I now will explicate it to you with analogies and thereby enable those ordinary beings of the future who will do pure karmas to be reborn in the Western Land of Ultimate Bliss.

"Those who wish to be reborn in that land should carry out three meritorious works. First, they should honor and support their parents, serve their teachers and elders, cultivate lovingkindness by not killing sentient beings, and do the ten good karmas. Second, they should take and uphold the Three Refuges, and fully observe their precepts without any breach in their conduct. Third, they should activate the bodhi mind, deeply believe in causality, read and recite Mahāyāna sūtras, and persuade others to do the same. These three works are called the pure karmas."

The Buddha said to Vaidehī, "Do you not know now? These three karmas are the right cause for [all] the pure karmas of Buddhas of the past, present, and future."

Explication of the Sixteen Visualizations

The Buddha told Ānanda and Vaidehī, "Hearken! Hearken! Ponder it well! For the sake of sentient beings of the future that are tormented captives of their own afflictions, which are like bandits, the Tathāgata now will explicate the pure karmas. Very good, Vaidehī, ask your questions at once. Ānanda, accept and uphold the Buddha's words, and pronounce them to the multitudes. The Tathāgata will now teach Vaidehī and all sentient beings of the future how to visualize the Western Land of Ultimate Bliss. By virtue of the power of the

Buddha, you will be able to see that Pure Land, just as you see the reflection of your own face in a clear mirror. Once you see the wonderful and joyful things in that land, you will be delighted and instantly achieve the Endurance in the Realization of the No Birth of Dharmas."

The Buddha told Vaidehī, "You are an ordinary being with coarse perceptions. Without the god-eye, you cannot see far. Nevertheless, Buddha-Tathāgatas have exceptional ways to enable you to see."

At that time Vaidehī asked the Buddha, "By virtue of the Buddha's power, I will be enabled to see that land. However, after the Buddha's parinirvāṇa, how can sentient beings that are impure, wicked, and burdened by the five kinds of suffering see Amitāyus Buddha's Land of Ultimate Bliss?"

1. The Setting Sun

The Buddha told Vaidehī, "You as well as other sentient beings should concentrate your mind and focus on the one place, thinking of the west. How does one visualize? All sentient beings with eyes that are not born blind have seen the setting sun. One should sit properly, facing the west, and visualize that the sun is setting. One should focus one's mind and visualize, with unshakable concentration, the setting sun like a hanging drum. Success in visualizing the setting sun means that one can see it distinctly with eyes open or closed. The vision of the sun is called the first visualization. This visualization is called the right visualization while other visualizations are called the wrong visualization."

2-3. The Water and the Ground

The Buddha told Ānanda and Vaidehī, "Having achieved the first visualization, one should next visualize water. One should visualize that everywhere in the Western Pure Land is an expanse of water, seeing distinctly that the water is pure and clear, not losing this picture.

"Having visualized the water, one then visualizes that it is ice. Seeing the ice as clear and transparent, one then visualizes that it is aquamarine. Having achieved this vision, one can see that the aquamarine ground is completely transparent and that it is supported underneath by golden cylindrical banners made of diamonds and the seven treasures. Each cylindrical banner has eight sides and angles, each side inlaid with 100 gems. Each precious gem emits 1,000 beams of light, and each beam has 84,000 colors, shining through the aquamarine ground like 1,000 koṭi suns, which are too brilliant to be seen in their entirety.

"On the aquamarine ground are crisscrossing golden ropes, which clearly divide the ground into areas for the seven treasures. Each treasure radiates beams of light in 500 colors. These beams are like flowers, also like stars and moons. Gathered in the sky, they form a platform of radiance, on which stand ten million lofty towers, each tower made of 100 treasures. As adornments, on both sides of the platform are 100 koṭi flower banners and innumerable musical instruments. Eight kinds of pure winds flow out of the radiance to stir the musical instruments, which play tones expounding the truths: suffering, emptiness, impermanence, and no self.

"The vision of water is called the second visualization. When one has achieved this vision, one sees each object clearly. One does not lose it, eyes open or closed. Except during sleep,[1] one constantly remembers this picture. This visualization is called the right visualization while other visualizations are called the wrong visualization."

The Buddha told Ānanda and Vaidehī, "The vision of water is called a rough visualization of the ground in the Land of Ultimate Bliss. If one enters samādhi, one will see the ground of that land so clearly that the details are too numerous to be described. The vision of the ground is called the third visualization."

The Buddha told Ānanda, "Uphold the Buddha's words and pronounce this dharma of visualizing the ground to the multitudes of the future who wish to be liberated from their suffering. For those who visualize the ground, their sins which would entail 80 koṭi kalpas of birth and death will all be expunged. After death, they will definitely be reborn, in a future life, in the Pure Land, where they will have no doubts in their minds. This visualization is called the right visualization while other visualizations are called the wrong visualization."

4. The Jeweled Trees

The Buddha told Ānanda and Vaidehī, "After achieving the vision of the ground, one should next visualize the jeweled trees. To visualize the jeweled trees, one should visualize each tree in seven lines of trees. Each jeweled tree is 8,000 yojanas tall, complete with flowers and leaves made of the seven treasures. The flowers and leaves are each of different jewel colors. The aquamarine colors gleam with golden light; the crystal colors, red light; the emerald colors, conch shell light; the conch shell colors, green gem light. Each tree is adorned with coral, amber, and all kinds of treasures.

"Covering the trees are nets of wonderful precious gems. Each tree is covered by seven layers of nets. Between each two layers are 500 koṭi wonderful, splendid palaces, like the palaces of Brahma-gods. Celestial children are in these palaces, and each child is adorned with necklaces of 500 koṭi śakrābhi-lagna jewels. The radiance of these jewels reaches a distance of 100 yojanas, like an assembly of 100 koṭi suns and moons, which are too numerous to be named. So superb are the colors of these intermingled jewels!

"The jeweled trees are matched line to line, leaf to leaf. Among the tree leaves are wonderful flowers, upon which appear fruits made of the seven treasures. Each tree leaf measures 25 yojanas in length and width and has, like celestial necklaces, 1,000 colors and 100 pictures. The wonderful flowers are the colors of the gold from the Jambu River. Like twirling fire wheels, they roll among the leaves, while fruits spring up as if from the god-king Śakra's vase. Their vast radiance is transformed into banners and innumerable jeweled canopies. Displayed in the jeweled canopies is all the Buddha work in the Three-Thousand Large Thousandfold World. Also displayed in them are Buddha Lands in the ten directions.

"Having visualized the trees [as wholes], one should distinctly visualize the tree trunks, branches, leaves, flowers, and fruits, one by one. The vision of the trees is called the fourth visualization. This visualization is called the right visualization while other visualizations are called the wrong visualization."

5. The Pond Waters

The Buddha told Ānanda and Vaidehī, "Having achieved the vision of the trees, one should next visualize the pond waters. To visualize the pond waters, one should visualize the eight ponds in the Land of Ultimate Bliss. The waters in each pond are the liquid form of the seven treasures. The treasure waters are soft, and they issue from the wishing-fulfilling jewel, the king of jewels. They are divided into fourteen tributaries, each in the wonderful colors of the seven treasures. These channels are formed with yellow gold, and their beds are covered with diamond dust. In the waters [of each pond] are 60 koṭi lotus flowers made of the seven treasures. Each lotus flower is perfectly round, 12 yojanas across. As the treasure waters flow up and down the stems of the lotus flowers, they make wonderful sounds expounding the truths—suffering, emptiness, impermanence, and no self—and the pāramitās, and praising Buddhas' sublime appearances.

"Sprung from the wish-fulfilling jewel-king, wonderful golden beams of light transform into birds of 100 jewel colors which, in harmonious, exquisite melodies, constantly praise the merit of thinking of the Buddha, thinking of the Dharma, and thinking of the Saṅgha.

"The vision of waters with the eight virtues is called the fifth visualization. This visualization is called the right visualization while other visualizations are called the wrong visualization."

6. The Towers and the Surroundings

The Buddha told Ānanda and Vaidehī, "In each region of that land of multitudinous treasures are 500 koṭi treasure towers. Inside each tower are innumerable gods, playing celestial music. Musical instruments hover in the sky like celestial jeweled banners, and they sound without being played. Their tones pronounce the thinking of the Buddha, the thinking of the Dharma, and the thinking of the Saṅgha.

"This vision is called a rough visualization of the jeweled ground, jeweled trees, and jeweled ponds in the Land of Ultimate Bliss. This general vision is called the sixth visualization. For those who have achieved this vision, their evil karmas done in innumerable koṭis of kalpas will all be obliterated. After death, they will definitely be reborn in that land. This visualization is called the right visualization while other visualizations are called the wrong visualization."

The Buddha told Ānanda and Vaidehī, "Hearken! Hearken! Ponder it well! I will expound to you this Dharma for removing your suffering. You should remember and uphold it, and widely expound it to the multitudes."

As these words were being said, Amitāyus Buddha appeared. He stood in the sky, attended on His left and His right by the two Great Ones, Avalokiteśvara and Great Might Arrived. Their glowing radiance was too great to be seen in its totality, with which the 100,000 colors of the gold from the Jambu River could never compare.

At that time Vaidehī, upon seeing Amitāyus Buddha, made obeisance at the Buddha's feet and asked, "World-Honored One, by virtue of the Buddha's power, I now have come to see Amitāyus Buddha and the two Bodhisattvas. How should sentient beings of the future visualize Amitāyus Buddha and the two Bodhisattvas?"

7. The Lotus Flower Seat

The Buddha replied to Vaidehī, "To visualize that Buddha, one should first visualize a lotus flower on the ground made of the seven treasures. One should visualize that each petal of the lotus flower has, like celestial pictures, 100 jewel colors and 84,000 veins, and should see clearly that each vein emits 84,000 beams of light. The smaller flower petals each measure 250 yojanas in length and width. Such a lotus flower has 84,000 petals. Between these petals are 100 koṭi jewel-kings serving as adornments. Each jewel emits 1,000 beams of light that are like a blanket made of the seven treasures, covering the ground everywhere.

"On the lotus flower is a platform made of śakrābhi-lagna jewels, and it is adorned with 80,000 diamonds and kiṁśuka-colored gems, jewels from Brahma heavens, and nets of wonderful precious gems. Erected on the platform are jeweled cylindrical banners, each with four posts. Each jeweled banner is as immense as a billion koṭi Sumeru Mountains. The jeweled draperies on each banner are like those in the palaces of Yāma Heaven [the third desire heaven]. They each are adorned with 500 koṭi wonderful precious gems. Each precious gem emits 84,000 beams of light, and each beam has 84,000 distinct colors of gold. Each golden beam spreads all over that treasure land, assuming various forms from place to place—diamond platforms or nets of precious gems or clouds of various flowers—and freely displays Buddha work [in worlds] in the ten directions. The vision of the flower seat is called the seventh visualization."

The Buddha told Ānanda, "Such a wonderful flower is formed by the power of the original vows of the bhikṣu Dharmākara [who is now Amitāyus Buddha]. Those who wish to think of that Buddha should first visualize this wonderful flower seat. When one creates this picture, one should not mix it with other things. One should visualize it item by item, seeing clearly each petal, each gem, each beam, each platform, and each banner. When one visualizes everything so clearly, it is like seeing one's own face in the mirror. For those who have achieved this vision, their sins which would entail 500 koṭi kalpas[2] of birth and death will all be expunged. One will definitely be reborn in the Land of Ultimate Bliss. This visualization is called the right visualization while other visualizations are called the wrong visualization."

8. The Three Holy Ones

The Buddha told Ānanda and Vaidehī, "After achieving this vision, one should next visualize that Buddha. Why? A Buddha-Tathāgata's body is the dharma realm, which pervades the thinking mind of all sentient beings. Therefore, when one visualizes a Buddha, one's mind has a Buddha's thirty-two physical marks and eighty excellent characteristics. The mind forms a Buddha, and the mind is the Buddha. The ocean of Saṁbuddhas is formed by one's thinking mind. Therefore, one should single-mindedly focus on and visualize that Buddha, the Tathāgata, Arhat, Samyak-Saṁbuddha.

"To visualize that Buddha, one should first visualize His image. With eyes open or closed, one should visualize a precious image in the color of the gold from the Jambu River, seated on that lotus flower. Having beheld the image seated there, one's mind's eye is opened and one also sees distinctly all the adornments in the Land of Ultimate Bliss made of the seven treasures, such as the jeweled ground, jeweled ponds, and jeweled trees in lines, as well as the celestial jeweled draperies over the trees and the jeweled nets all over the open sky. The vision of this scene is so clear that it is like seeing it in one's palm.

"Having achieved this vision, one should next visualize on that Buddha's left side a huge lotus flower, which is just like the lotus flower described before, without any difference, and visualize on His right side another such lotus flower. One then visualizes an image of Avalokiteśvara Bodhisattva seated on the left lotus flower seat, golden in color like that Buddha's image. One then visualizes an image of Great Might Arrived Bodhisattva seated on the right lotus flower seat. When this vision is achieved, the images of that Buddha and the two Bodhisattvas all emit wonderful beams of light. Their golden beams of light illuminate all the jeweled trees. Under each tree all across that land are three lotus flowers, seated on which are a Buddha and two Bodhisattvas.

"When this vision is achieved, the meditator should hear radiant flowing waters, jeweled trees, wild ducks, and mandarin ducks expounding the wondrous Dharma. In or out of samādhi, one constantly hears the wondrous Dharma. Even when out of samādhi, one still remembers what one has heard and should verify whether the teachings heard accord with those in the sūtras. If not in accord, they are called false perceptions. If in accord, this vision is called a rough visualization of the Land of Ultimate Bliss. The vision of this scene is called the eighth visualization. For those who do this visualization, their sins which would entail innumerable koṭis of kalpas of birth and death will all be expunged. They will attain the Thinking-of-Buddhas Samādhi in their present life. This visualization is called the right visualization while other visualizations are called the wrong visualization."

9. The Sublime Body of Amitāyus Buddha

The Buddha told Ānanda and Vaidehī, "After achieving this vision, one should next visualize the glory of Amitāyus Buddha's body. Ānanda, know that Amitāyus Buddha's body is in a billion koṭi colors of the superb gold in Yāma Heaven. That Buddha's height measures as many yojanas as the sands of 600,000 koṭi nayuta Ganges Rivers. The white hair between His eyebrows, like five Sumeru Mountains, curls to the right. That Buddha's eyes, with blues and whites distinct, are pure like the water in four great oceans. The pores of His body emit radiance as immense as Mount Sumeru. The halo of that Buddha is as vast as 100 koṭi Three-Thousand Large Thousandfold Worlds. In His halo appear as many magically manifested Buddhas as the sands of a million koṭi nayuta Ganges Rivers. Each Buddha is attended by an innumerable multitude of magically manifested Bodhisattvas.

"Amitāyus Buddha has 84,000 excellent marks; each mark includes 84,000 excellent characteristics; each characteristic emits 84,000 beams of light. Each beam universally illuminates all worlds in the ten directions, attracting and accepting sentient beings that think of Buddhas, never abandoning them. His radiance, excellent characteristics, and magically manifested Buddhas are beyond description. However, one should picture them and make the mind's eye see. Seeing Amitāyus Buddha is seeing all Buddhas [in worlds] in the ten directions. Seeing all Buddhas is called the Thinking-of-Buddhas Samādhi. Doing this visualization is called visualizing the bodies of all Buddhas. By visualizing the bodies of all Buddhas, one sees the Buddha mind. The Buddha mind is [the mind of] great lovingkindness and compassion. With unconditional lovingkindness,

Buddhas accept all sentient beings. Those who do this visualization, after death, will be reborn, in a future life, before Buddhas and will achieve the Endurance in the Realization of the No Birth of Dharmas.

"Therefore, the wise should focus their minds and intently visualize Amitāyus Buddha. To visualize Amitāyus Buddha, one should begin with one excellent mark, the white hair between His eyebrows, and make it vividly clear. One who can see the white hair between His eyebrows should readily see all His 84,000 excellent marks. Seeing Amitāyus Buddha is seeing innumerable Buddhas [in worlds] in the ten directions. Seeing innumerable Buddhas, one will receive in their presence the prophecy [of attaining Buddhahood]. This comprehensive vision of all the features of that Buddha's physical body is called the ninth visualization. This visualization is called the right visualization while other visualizations are called the wrong visualization."

10. The Sublime Body of Avalokiteśvara Bodhisattva

The Buddha told Ānanda and Vaidehī, "Having seen Infinite Light Buddha clearly, one should next visualize Avalokiteśvara Bodhisattva. This Bodhisattva's height measures 800,000 koṭi nayuta yojanas.[3] His body is purple-tinged golden. On the top of his head is a fleshy mound. The light disks in the halo about his neck each measure 100,000 yojanas across. In each light disk are 500 magically manifested Buddhas, who resemble Śākyamuni Buddha. Each magically manifested Buddha is attended by 500 magically manifested Bodhisattvas and innumerable gods. Displayed in the radiance of His entire body are sentient beings in all kinds of physical forms, taking the five life-paths. On the top of his head is a wonderful śakrābhi-lagna jewel, worn as a celestial crown. Standing on his celestial crown is a magically manifested Buddha, 25 yojanas tall.

"Avalokiteśvara Bodhisattva's face is in the colors of the gold from the Jambu River. The hair between his eyebrows has the colors of the seven treasures, and it emits 84,000 beams of light. In each beam are innumerable, countless hundreds of thousands of magically manifested Buddhas. Each Buddha is attended by innumerable magically manifested Bodhisattvas. They all freely manifest themselves everywhere in worlds in the ten directions.

"His arms are red like the color of red lotus flowers, and they gleam with 80 koṭi wonderful beams of light, worn as necklaces. Displayed in these necklaces is the entire majestic Buddha work. His palms have the colors of 500 koṭi diverse lotus flowers. The tips of his ten fingers each display 84,000 pictures, like imprinted markings. Each picture has 84,000 colors, and each color emits 84,000 beams of light, which gently shine on all things. With these precious hands, he accepts and guides sentient beings. When he raises his foot, his sole shows the mark of a thousand-spoked wheel, which readily transforms into 500 koṭi platforms of radiance. Wherever he steps, flowers made of diamonds and jewels spread everywhere and cover everything. His physical characteristics are as perfect as those of a Buddha. Only the fleshy mound on the top of his head and the invisible crown of his head cannot be compared with those of the World-Honored One. The vision of Avalokiteśvara Bodhisattva's physical body is called the tenth visualization."

The Buddha told Ānanda, "Those who wish to see Avalokiteśvara Bodhisattva should do this visualization. Those who visualize him will not encounter disasters. Their karma hindrances will be completely removed, and their sins which would entail innumerable kalpas of birth and death will all be expunged. One will acquire immeasurable merit merely by hearing this Bodhisattva's name, and even more by visualizing him. To visualize Avalokiteśvara Bodhisattva, one should first visualize the fleshy mound on the top of his head, and next visualize his celestial crown. One should visualize other features successively, making each as clear as if seen in one's palm. This visualization is called the right visualization while other visualizations are called the wrong visualization."

11. The Sublime Body of Mahāsthāmaprāpta Bodhisattva

The Buddha told Ānanda and Vaidehī, "One should next visualize [Mahāsthāmaprāpta] Great Might Arrived Bodhisattva. This Bodhisattva's body measurement is the same as Avalokiteśvara's. The light disks in his halo each measure 125 yojanas[4] across and radiate beams of light through a distance of 250 yojanas. The radiance of his entire body illuminates worlds in the ten directions with purple-tinged golden light. Sentient beings with the right conditions all can see it. Seeing the light from even one of this Bodhisattva's pores is seeing the pure radiance of innumerable Buddhas [in worlds] in the ten directions. Therefore, this Bodhisattva is called Boundless Light, who illuminates all sentient beings with the light of wisdom, enabling them to abandon the three evil life-journeys and to gain superb strength. Therefore, this Bodhisattva is called Great Might Arrived.

"This Bodhisattva's celestial crown is adorned with 500 jeweled flowers. On each jeweled flower are 500 jeweled platforms. On each platform are wide-ranging displays of pure Buddha Lands in the ten directions. The fleshy mound on the top of his head is like a red lotus flower. Standing on the fleshy mound is a jeweled vase filled with radiance that displays the entire Buddha work. His other physical marks are equal to Avalokiteśvara Bodhisattva's, without any difference.

"When this Bodhisattva walks, all worlds in the ten directions are shaken. Wherever the earth quakes, 500 koṭi jeweled flowers appear. Each jeweled flower is as splendid and glorious as the Land of Ultimate Bliss. When this Bodhisattva sits down, the land made of the seven treasures is instantly shaken. Magically manifested copies of Amitāyus Buddha, of Avalokiteśvara, and of Great Might Right, as numerous as innumerable dust particles in the space between Golden Light Buddha's land below and Radiance King Buddha's land above, all assemble in the Land of Ultimate Bliss. Jam-packed in the sky, seated on jeweled lotus flower seats, they expound the wondrous Dharma to deliver suffering sentient beings.

"Doing this visualization is called seeing Great Might Arrived Bodhisattva. The vision of Great Might Arrived Bodhisattva's physical body is called the eleventh visualization. For those who do this visualization, their sins which would entail innumerable asaṁkhyeyas of kalpas of birth and death will all be expunged. They will not be reborn through the womb. They will always visit pure Buddha Lands. This visualization is called the complete vision of Bodhisattvas Avalokiteśvara and Great Might Arrived. This visualization is called the right visualization while other visualizations are called the wrong visualization."

12. One's Rebirth in a Lotus Flower

The Buddha told Ānanda and Vaidehī, "Having seen the preceding scenes, one should next visualize oneself reborn in the Western Land of Ultimate Bliss, seated cross-legged in a lotus flower, and imagine the lotus flower closing and opening. One should visualize that, when the lotus flower opens, beams of light in 500 colors come to illuminate one's body. One should visualize that one's eyes are opened to see Buddhas and Bodhisattvas all over the sky. One also hears the wondrous Dharma, expounded by the sounds of the water, birds, trees, and Buddhas, which should accord with the Dharma in sūtras in the twelve categories. One will remember everything without lapse even when one is out of samādhi.

"Seeing this scene is called seeing Amitāyus Buddha's Land of Ultimate Bliss. This comprehensive vision is called the twelfth visualization. Then innumerable magically manifested copies of Amitāyus Buddha, together with those of Avalokiteśvara and Great Might Arrived, will often come to this meditator. This visualization is called the right visualization while other visualizations are called the wrong visualization."

13. The Three Holy Images in Smaller Size

The Buddha told Ānanda and Vaidehī, "If one earnestly wishes to be reborn in the Western Pure Land, one should visualize a Buddha image sixteen feet tall, standing on the surface of pond water. As described earlier, Amitāyus Buddha's body measurement is boundless, beyond the mental power of ordinary beings. However, because of the power of that Tathāgata's original vows, those who visualize Him will succeed. One can acquire immeasurable merit merely by visualizing that Buddha's image, and even more by visualizing all of His physical features. Amitāyus Buddha demonstrates his spiritual powers at will as He freely manifests Himself in worlds in the ten directions, whether as a vast body filling the entire sky or as a small body, only sixteen or eighteen feet tall. The form He manifests is in the color of pure gold. His halo, His magically manifested Buddhas, and His jeweled lotus flower are just as described before.

"The bodies of Bodhisattvas Avalokiteśvara and Great Might Arrived look the same in every aspect. Sentient beings, by observing the appearances of their heads, can know whether it is Avalokiteśvara or Great Might Arrived. These two Bodhisattvas assist Amitāyus Buddha to deliver all sentient beings. The vision of the three images [Amitāyus Buddha and the two Bodhisattvas] is called the thirteenth visualization. This visualization is called the right visualization while other visualizations are called the wrong visualization."

14. The Three Rebirths in the High Rank

The Buddha told Ānanda and Vaidehī, "Sentient beings reborn in the Western Pure Land are classified into nine grades. Those who wish to achieve a high rebirth in the high rank in that land must invoke three minds in order to succeed. What are these three? First, an earnest mind; second, a profound mind; and third, a mind wishing for rebirth in the Pure Land as one transfers one's merits to other sentient beings. Those with these three minds will definitely be reborn in that land.

"Moreover, there are three kinds of sentient beings that will be reborn there. What are those three? First, those who, with the mind of lovingkindness, refrain from killing sentient beings and fully observe the precepts for their conduct. Second, those who read and recite Mahāyāna vaipulya sūtras. Third, those who practice the six remembrances and, with a wish for rebirth in that Buddha Land, transfer their merits to others.

"A person who has acquired such merits in one to seven days will be reborn there. When this person is about to be reborn in that land, because he has made boldly energetic progress, Amitāyus the Tathāgata, together with Bodhisattvas Avalokiteśvara and Great Might Arrived, innumerable magically manifested Buddhas, 100,000 voice-hearer bhikṣus, and innumerable gods riding their palaces made of the seven treasures, will appear to him. Avalokiteśvara Bodhisattva, holding a diamond platform, together with Great Might Arrived Bodhisattva, will come before this person. Amitāyus Buddha, together with Bodhisattvas, will emit great radiance to illuminate his body and extend a welcoming hand to receive him. Avalokiteśvara, Great Might Arrived, and innumerable Bodhisattvas will praise him, encouraging his heart.

"This person, having beheld this scene, will be exultant and exuberant. He will see himself ride the diamond platform, following after that Buddha. In the instant of a finger snap, he will be reborn in that land. After his rebirth in that land, he will see that Buddha and the Bodhisattvas, with all their physical marks, and he will hear radiant jeweled trees expound the wondrous Dharma. Having heard it, he will forthwith achieve the Endurance in the Realization of the No Birth of Dharmas. He can, in a short while, serve Buddhas in all worlds in the ten directions and successively receive before them the prophecy [of attaining Buddhahood]. He will then return to his own land and acquire innumerable hundreds of thousands of Dhāraṇī Doors. This is called a high rebirth in the high rank.

"Those who wish to achieve a middling rebirth in the high rank need not read or recite vaipulya sūtras. However, they should have a good understanding of their tenets, and their minds should not be upset by the highest truth. They should deeply believe in causality, and not malign the Mahāyāna. Then, with a wish for rebirth in the Land of Ultimate Bliss, they can transfer these merits to others. When such a person's life is ending, Amitāyus Buddha, holding a purple-tinged golden platform, together with Bodhisattvas Avalokiteśvara and Great Might Arrived, surrounded by an innumerable multitude and retinue, will come before the person and praise him with these words: 'Dharma-Son, you practice the Mahāyāna teachings and understand the highest truth. Therefore, I now have come to receive you.'

"As Amitāyus Buddha and 1,000 magically manifested Buddhas simultaneously extend their hands, this person will see himself seated on the purple-tinged golden platform, palms joined, praising Buddhas. In the instant of a thought, he will be reborn in that land, in a pond made of the seven treasures. This purple-tinged golden platform is like a huge jeweled flower, which opens after one night.

"The person's body after rebirth will be purple-tinged golden, with a lotus flower made of the seven treasures under his feet. That Buddha and the Bodhisattvas will all emit light to illuminate his body, and his eyes will be opened and bright. Because of his training in his previous life, he will hear sounds that pronounce only the profound highest truth. He will descend the golden platform and make obeisance to that Buddha. Joining his palms, he will praise the World-

Honored One. After seven days, he will achieve [the spiritual level of] no regress from his resolve to attain anuttara-samyak-saṁbodhi. Forthwith, he will fly to worlds in the ten directions to serve Buddhas. He will train in samādhis in the places where Buddhas are. After one small kalpa, he will achieve the Endurance in the Realization of the No Birth of Dharmas and will receive before Buddhas the prophecy [of attaining Buddhahood]. This is called a middling rebirth in the high rank.

"A low rebirth in the high rank can be achieved by those who, though having faith in causality and not maligning the Mahāyāna, mainly activate the unsurpassed bodhi mind and, with a wish for rebirth in the Land of Ultimate Bliss, transfer these merits to others. When such a person's life is ending, Amitāyus Buddha, holding a golden lotus flower, together with Avalokiteśvara, Great Might Arrived, and other Bodhisattvas, will conjure up 500 magically manifested Buddhas to receive him. These 500 magically manifested Buddhas will simultaneously extend their hands, praising, 'Dharma-Son, you are pure, and you have activated the unsurpassed bodhi mind. I have come to receive you.'

"As soon as he beholds this scene, he will find himself seated in the golden lotus flower. Then the lotus flower will close and follow after the World-Honored One. He will be reborn in a pond made of the seven treasures. After one day and one night, the lotus flower will open. He will be able to see that Buddha in seven days. Although he sees that Buddha's body, its features will not clear in his mind. Only after twenty-one days will he be able to see them clearly and hear the wondrous Dharma pronounced by various sounds. He will then travel to worlds in the ten directions and make offerings to Buddhas. Before those Buddhas, he will again hear the profound Dharma. After three small kalpas, he will go through the Illumination Door of the One Hundred Dharmas, ascending to the First Ground, the Ground of Joy. This is called a low rebirth in the high rank.

"The vision of rebirths in the high rank is called the fourteenth visualization. This visualization is called the right visualization while other visualizations are the wrong visualization."

15. The Three Rebirths in the Middle Rank

The Buddha told Ānanda and Vaidehī, "A high rebirth in the middle rank can be achieved by sentient beings that accept and abide by the five precepts and regularly observe the eight precepts. While training in observance of precepts, they commit neither any of the five rebellious sins nor any other wrongdoings. With a wish for rebirth in the Western Land of Ultimate Bliss, they transfer these roots of goodness to others.

"When such a person's life is ending, Amitāyus Buddha, together with bhikṣus, surrounded by His retinue, will radiate golden light as He comes to this person. That Buddha will expound the teachings on suffering, emptiness, impermanence, and no self, praise renunciation of family life, and praise liberation from suffering. Having beheld this scene, this person, with great joy in his heart, will see himself seated on a platform borne by a lotus flower. He will fall on both knees, join his palms, and make obeisance to that Buddha. In the instant before he raises his head, he will be reborn in the Land of Ultimate Bliss. The lotus flower will quickly open. When the flower opens, he will hear various sounds praising the Four Noble Truths, and he will become an Arhat, achieving the Three Clarities, the six transcendental powers, and the eight liberations. This is called a high rebirth in the middle rank.

"A middling rebirth in the middle rank can be achieved by sentient beings that have observed for one day and one night the eight precepts, the śrāmaṇera precepts, or the complete monastic precepts, with no flaw in their conduct. If they, with a wish for rebirth in the Land of Ultimate Bliss, transfer these merits to others, they are infused with the fragrance of the precepts. When such a person's life is ending, he will see Amitāyus Buddha, together with His retinue, radiating golden light and holding a lotus flower made of the seven treasures, come before him. He will hear a voice in the sky, which praises, 'Good man, because a good person such as yourself follows the teachings of Buddhas of the past, present, and future, I have come to receive you.'

"This person will see himself seated in a lotus flower, which then closes. He will be reborn in the Western Land of Ultimate Bliss, in a jeweled pond. After seven days, the lotus flower will open. After the flower has opened, he will open his eyes, join his palms, and praise the World-Honored One. After hearing the Dharma, he will be delighted and become a Srotāpanna [Streamer Enterer]. After half a [small] kalpa, he will become an Arhat. This is called a middling rebirth in the middle rank.

"A low rebirth in the middle rank can be achieved by good men and good women who honor and support their parents and are kind and generous to others. When such a person's life is ending, he may encounter a beneficent learned friend who will expound the joyful things in Amitāyus Buddha's land as well as the bhikṣu Dharmākara's forty-eight great vows. After hearing these things, he will die. In the instant of a strong man extending his arm, this person will be reborn in the Western Land of Ultimate Bliss. Seven days after his rebirth, he will encounter Bodhisattvas Avalokiteśvara and Great Might Arrived. Having heard the Dharma from them, he will be delighted and become a Srotāpanna. After one small kalpa, he will become an Arhat. This is called a low rebirth in the middle rank.

"The vision of rebirths in the middle rank is called the fifteenth visualization. This visualization is the right visualization while other visualizations are called the wrong visualization."

16. The Three Rebirths in the Low Rank

The Buddha told Ānanda and Vaidehī, "A high rebirth in the low rank can be achieved by sentient beings that have done evil karmas. Although they did not malign vaipulya sūtras, these fools have done evils with no sense of shame or dishonor. When such a person's life is ending, however, he may encounter a beneficent learned friend who will pronounce the names of Mahāyāna sūtras in the twelve categories. Because he has heard the names of such sūtras, his evil karmas which would entail 1,000 kalpas of birth and death will be obliterated. The wise friend will also teach him to join his palms and say 'namo Amitāyus Buddha.' By saying Amitāyus Buddha's name, his sins which would entail 50 koṭi kalpas of birth and death will all be expunged. Thereupon, that Buddha will immediately send magically manifested Buddhas and magically manifested Bodhisattvas Avalokiteśvara and Great Might Arrived to come before this person. They will praise him, saying, 'Good man, your sins are expunged because you say the name of a Buddha. I have come to receive you.' These words being said, the person will immediately see the radiance of magically manifested Buddhas entirely filling his room. Having beheld this scene, he will be delighted and then die.

"Riding a jeweled lotus flower, he will follow after the magically manifested Buddhas and will be reborn in a jeweled pond. After forty-nine days, the lotus flower will open. When the flower opens, Great Compassion Avalokiteśvara Bodhisattva and Great Might Arrived Bodhisattva, emitting immense radiance, will stand before this person and pronounce to him profound sūtras in the twelve categories. Having heard these teachings, with faith and understanding, he will activate the unsurpassed bodhi mind. After ten small kalpas, he will go through the Illumination Door of the One Hundred Dharmas, ascending to the First Ground. This called a high rebirth in the low rank.

"There are those who have heard of the words 'Buddha, Dharma, Saṅgha.' By hearing these names of the Three Jewels, they too can be reborn there."[5]

The Buddha told Ānanda and Vaidehī, "A middling rebirth in the low rank can be achieved by sentient beings that have violated any of the five precepts, the eight precepts, or the complete monastic precepts. Such fools have stolen from the Saṅgha and robbed monks. They have made defiling statements with no sense of shame or dishonor. They adorn themselves with their evil ways. These sinners, because of their evil karmas, should fall into hell. When such a person's life is ending, the fires of hell will arrive at once. Nevertheless, he may encounter a beneficent learned friend who will describe the awesome virtues of Amitāyus Buddha's Ten Powers, explain in detail His radiance and spiritual powers, and praise samādhi, wisdom, liberation, and the knowledge and views of liberation. After he has heard these things, his sins which would entail 80 koṭi kalpas of birth and death will all be expunged. The raging fires of hell will be transformed into cool winds, which bring celestial flowers down from the sky. Seated on these flowers will be magically manifested Buddhas and Bodhisattvas who have come to receive this person.

"In the instant of a thought, he will be reborn in a lotus flower in a pond made of the seven treasures. After six [large] kalpas, the lotus flower will open. When it opens, Bodhisattvas Avalokiteśvara and Great Might Arrived will comfort this person with their Brahma tones. They will pronounce to him the profound Mahāyāna sūtras. Having heard the Dharma, he will immediately activate the unsurpassed bodhi mind. This is called a middling rebirth in the low rank."

The Buddha told Ānanda and Vaidehī, "A low rebirth in the low rank can be achieved by sentient beings that have done bad karmas, such as any of the five rebellious acts or the ten evil karmas. Because of their evil karmas, these fools should go down the evil life-paths to undergo endless suffering for many kalpas. But when such a fool's life is ending, he may encounter a beneficent learned friend who will comfort him in many ways, expound the wondrous Dharma, and teach him to think of that Buddha. However, this person, overcome by suffering, will be unable to think of that Buddha. His beneficent friend will then tell him, 'If you are unable to think of that Buddha, you should say that you take refuge in Amitāyus Buddha. Say it earnestly and keep your voice uninterrupted as you say "namo Amitāyus Buddha" ten times in ten thoughts.' By saying Amitāyus Buddha's name, thought after thought, his sins which would entail 80 koṭi kalpas of birth and death will all be expunged. When his life is ending, he will see a golden lotus flower appearing before him like the sun.

"In the instant of a thought, he will be reborn in the Land of Ultimate Bliss. He will remain in the lotus flower for twelve large kalpas. When the lotus flower opens, Bodhisattvas Avalokiteśvara and Great Might Arrived, with tones of great compassion, will expound to him the true reality of dharmas and the Dharma for expunging sins. Having heard the teachings, he will be delighted and immediately activate the bodhi mind. This is called a low rebirth in the low rank.

"The vision of rebirths in the low rank is called the sixteenth visualization."

Benefits Received from the Teachings

When the World-Honored One spoke these words, Vaidehī, together with 500 female attendants, having heard the Buddha's words, immediately saw the wide-ranging features of the Land of Ultimate Bliss and saw that Buddha and the two Bodhisattvas. With such joy, never experienced before, she came to a great realization, achieving the Endurance in the Realization of the No Birth of Dharmas. The 500 female attendants activated the anuttara-samyak-saṁbodhi mind and resolved to be reborn in that land. The World-Honored One bestowed upon them a prophecy that they all would be reborn in that land and that, after their rebirth there, they would attain the Samādhi of All Buddhas Standing before One. Meanwhile, innumerable gods activated the unsurpassed bodhi mind.

Circulation of the Sūtra

At that time Ānanda rose from his seat, came before the Buddha, and asked, "Word-Honored One, what is the name of this sūtra? How does one uphold the tenets of this Dharma?"

The Buddha told Ānanda, "This sūtra is called *Visualization of the Land of Ultimate Bliss, Amitāyus Buddha, Avalokiteśvara Bodhisattva, and Great Might Arrived Bodhisattva*. It is also called *Annihilating Karma Hindrances and Being Reborn before Buddhas*. All of you should accept and uphold it, never forgetting or losing it. Those who train in this samādhi will, in their present life, succeed in seeing Amitāyus Buddha and the two Great Ones. If, among good men and good women, there are those who hear the names of that Buddha and the two Bodhisattvas, their sins which would entail innumerable kalpas of birth and death will all be expunged. Even more will their benefits be if they remember and think of them. Know that, if a person thinks of that Buddha, this person is a puṇḍarīka flower among men. Bodhisattvas Avalokiteśvara and Great Might Arrived will be his beneficent friends, and he will be reborn in Buddha family, to be seated in a bodhimaṇḍa."

The Buddha told Ānanda, "Uphold well these words. To uphold these words is to uphold Amitāyus Buddha's name."

After the Buddha had spoken these words, the venerable Maudgalyāyana, the venerable Ānanda, Vaidehī, and others, having heard the Buddha's words, greatly rejoiced.

The World-Honored One walked across the sky and returned to the Gṛdhrakūṭa Mountain. Then Ānanda proclaimed to the multitudes this event, as described above. Innumerable gods, dragons, and yakṣas, having heard the Buddha's words, greatly rejoiced. They made obeisance to the Buddha and departed.

Notes

1. In text 365 (T12n0365), the exception is allowed for eating. However, in the Ming edition of the Chinese Canon and in the circulation text, the exception is allowed for sleep. The latter makes more sense.

2. Three different figures for the length of time are found. (1) It is 500 koṭi kalpas in text 365. (2) It is 50,000 koṭi kalpas, according to the Song, Yuan, and Ming editions of the Chinese Canon. (3) It is 50,000 kalpas, according to J. Takakusu (1894, part 2, 177). The first of these three figures is used here.

3. Three different figures for the height of Avalokiteśvara are found. (1) It is "as many yojanas as the sands of 80 koṭi nayuta Ganges Rivers" in text 365. (2) It is 800,000 koṭi nayuta yojanas, according to the Song, Yuan, and Ming editions of the Chinese Canon, a figure adopted in the circulation text. (3) It is 800,000 nayuta yojanas in Takakusu's translation (ibid., 181–82). The second of these three figures is used here.

4. Although the figure 225 yojanas is found in text 365, it is 125 yojanas, according to the Song, Yuan, and Ming editions of the Chinese Canon. The latter figure is in agreement with that in Takakusu's translation (ibid., 184).

5. This passage is included in text 365 and in Takakusu's translation (ibid., 196), but not included in the Song, Yuan, and Ming editions of the Chinese Canon.

4 大勢至菩薩念佛圓通章 Great Might Arrived Bodhisattva's Thinking-of-Buddhas as the Perfect Passage

(a subsection in the Śūraṅgama Sūtra)

Translated from Sanskrit into Chinese in the Tang Dynasty
by
The Śramaṇa Pramiti from India

Great Might Arrived Bodhisattva the Dharma Prince, together with his peer group of fifty-two Bodhisattvas, rose from his seat and bowed down at the Buddha's feet. He then said to the Buddha, "As I remember, before past kalpas as numerous as the sands of the Ganges, a Buddha called Infinite Light appeared in the world. Twelve Tathāgatas successively appeared in one kalpa, and the last one was called Outshining the Sun-Moon Light. That Buddha taught me the Thinking-of-Buddhas Samādhi.

"Using two people as an analogy, suppose one person always remembers the other, but the other always forgets the one. These two are this way whether or not they meet each other, whether or not they see each other. However, if two can remember each other, their mutual remembrance will deepen. Then, even from one life to the next, they will be like a form and its shadow, not separating.

"The Tathāgatas [in worlds] in the ten directions pity and think of sentient beings, like a mother remembering her son. If the son runs away, what good can the mother's remembrance be? If the son can remember his mother just as the mother remembers her son, then mother and son will journey together life after life, never alienated from each other.

"If sentient beings' minds remember and think of Buddhas, in the present or a future life, they will definitely see Buddhas and will never be far from Buddhas. Without using other methods, their minds will spontaneously open. Then, like one whose body is fragrant after being suffused with scent, they will be said to be adorned with fragrance and light.

"It was when I stood on the Cause Ground, with my mind thinking only of a Buddha, that I achieved the Endurance in the Realization of the No Birth of Dharmas. In this world, I now assist those who think of Buddhas to come home to the Pure Land. Because the Buddha asks for the Perfect Passage, I must say that the foremost way is to continue the one pure thought to restrain the six faculties, so as to attain samādhi."

5 大方廣佛華嚴經:
入不思議解脫境界普賢行願品卷四十
Mahāvaipulya Sūtra of Buddha Adornment: The Universally Worthy Action Vow to Enter the Inconceivable Liberation State

Translated from Sanskrit into Chinese in the Tang Dynasty
by
The Tripiṭaka Master Prajñā from Kophen

Fascicle 40 (of 40)

At that time Samantabhadra Bodhisattva-Mahāsattva, having praised Tathāgatas' merit, said to the Bodhisattvas and the youth Sudhana: "Good men, if Buddhas [in worlds] in the ten directions expound Tathāgatas' merit continuously for as many kalpas as there are dust particles in innumerable Buddha Lands, they still can never finish their narrations. If one wants to go through this Merit Door, one should train in the ten great vowed actions. What are these ten?

First, make obeisance to Buddhas.
Second, praise Tathāgatas.
Third, make expansive offerings.
Fourth, repent of karma, the cause of hindrances.
Fifth, express sympathetic joy over others' merits.
Sixth, request Buddhas to turn the Dharma wheel.
Seventh, beseech Buddhas to abide in the world.
Eighth, always follow Buddhas to learn.
Ninth, forever support sentient beings.
Tenth, universally transfer all merits to others."

Sudhana asked, "Great Holy One, how does one accomplish these ten, from making obeisance to transferring merit?"

Samantabhadra Bodhisattva told Sudhana, "First, good man, the Buddhas to whom I make obeisance refer to Buddha-Bhagavāns, who are as numerous as dust particles in all Buddha Lands of the past, present, and future, in the ten directions, in the entire dharma realm and the domain of space. Through the power of the universally worthy action vow, I elicit my profound faith and understanding. As if Buddhas are present before me, I ceaselessly make obeisance with the pure karma of my body, voice, and mind. In the place where each Buddha is, I manifest as many copies of myself as there are dust particles in innumerable Buddha Lands. Each copy makes obeisance to Buddhas, who are as numerous as dust particles in innumerable Buddha Lands.

"My obeisances would end only if the domain of space ended. As the domain of space has no end, so my obeisances will have no end. My obeisances would end only if the realm of sentient beings ended, the karmas of sentient beings ended, and the afflictions of sentient beings ended. As the realm of sentient beings and their karmas and afflictions have no end, so my obeisances will have no end. They continue thought after thought without interruption as the karma of my body, voice, and mind knows no tiredness.

"Second, good man, the Tathāgatas I praise refer to Buddhas, who are as numerous as all the dust particles in all the worlds that are contained in every dust particle in all Buddha Lands of the past, present, and future, in the ten directions, in the entire dharma realm and the domain of space. Each Buddha in His place is surrounded by an ocean-like assembly of Bodhisattvas. I will present my knowledge and views with profound understanding. The wonderful tongue [of each of the magically manifested copies of myself], which surpasses the eloquent tongues of goddess-daughters, emits an ocean of endless sounds. Each sound emits an ocean of words in praise of the ocean of all Tathāgatas' merits, continuing ceaselessly into the endless future and reaching everywhere in the entire dharma realm.

"My praises would end only if the domain of space ended, the realm of sentient beings ended, the karmas of sentient beings ended, and the afflictions of sentient beings ended. As these four, from the domain of space to the afflictions of sentient beings, have no end, so my praises will have no end. They continue thought after thought without interruption as the karma of my body, voice, and mind knows no tiredness.

"Third, good man, how does one make expansive offerings? In the entire dharma realm and the domain of space, there are dust particles in all Buddha Lands of the past, present, and future, in the ten directions. In each dust particle are as many Buddhas as there are dust particles in all the worlds. Each Buddha in His place is surrounded by various kinds of ocean-like assemblies of Bodhisattvas. Through the power of the universally worthy action vow, I elicit my profound faith and understanding, and present my knowledge and views. I make superb offerings, such as flower clouds, tiara clouds, celestial music clouds, celestial umbrella clouds, celestial garment clouds, and various kinds of celestial fragrances: solid perfumes, incense for burning, and powdered incense. Clouds [and fragrances] such as these are as immense as Sumeru, king of mountains. I light various kinds of lamps, such as butter lamps, oil lamps, and scented oil lamps. Each lamp wick is like Mount Sumeru, and the oil in each lamp is like the water of the immense ocean. With objects such as these, I ceaselessly make offerings.

"Moreover, good man, among all offerings, supreme are Dharma offerings, such as training according to the teachings as an offering, benefiting sentient beings as an offering, drawing sentient beings into the Dharma as an offering, bearing sentient beings' suffering in their stead as an offering, assiduously developing one's roots of goodness as an offering, never abandoning the Bodhisattva work as an offering, and never losing the bodhi mind as an offering. Good man, the immeasurable merit acquired from making the offerings mentioned earlier is less than one hundredth, one thousandth, one hundred-thousandth, one koṭith, one nayutath, or one kalā of the merit acquired from offering the Dharma even with only one thought, or less than any fraction of it by calculation, mathematics, analogy, or upaniṣad [measure]. Why? Because all Tathāgatas esteem the Dharma and because training according to the teachings gives birth to Buddhas. When Bodhisattvas practice offering the Dharma, they in effect make offerings to Tathāgatas. Training in this way is the true offering.

"My vast superb offerings would end only if the domain of space ended, the realm of sentient beings ended, the karmas of sentient beings ended, and the afflictions of sentient beings ended. As these four, from the domain of space to the afflictions of sentient beings, have no end, so my offering will have no end. It continues thought after thought without interruption as the karma of my body, voice, and mind knows no tiredness.

"Fourth, good man, how does one repent of karma, the cause of hindrances? Bodhisattvas should think: 'Because of greed, anger, and delusion, the evil karma I have done through my body, voice, and mind, in past kalpas without a beginning, is immeasurable and boundless. If this evil karma had substance and appearance, even the entire domain of space could not contain it. I now, with the three pure karmas, earnestly repent before the entire multitude of Buddhas and Bodhisattvas in lands as numerous as dust particles in the dharma realm. I will never do [such evil karma] again, and I will abide by the pure precepts and cultivate all virtues.'

"My repentance would end only if the domain of space ended, the realm of sentient beings ended, the karmas of sentient beings ended, and the afflictions of sentient beings ended. As these four, from the domain of space to the afflictions of sentient beings, have no end, so my repentance will have no end. It continues thought after thought without interruption as the karma of my body, voice, and mind knows no tiredness.

"Fifth, good man, how does one express sympathetic joy over others' merits? In the entire dharma realm and the domain of space, Buddha-Tathāgatas, who are as numerous as dust particles in all Buddha Lands of the past, present, and future, in the ten directions, since their initial resolve to acquire [sarvajña] the overall wisdom-knowledge, have assiduously accumulated merit, never begrudging their bodies and lives. For as many kalpas as there are dust particles in innumerable Buddha Lands, in each kalpa they have generously given their heads, eyes, hands, and feet as many times as there are dust particles in innumerable Buddha Lands. Through such difficult ascetic training, they have gone through various kinds of Pāramitā Doors and ascended through various levels of Bodhisattva Wisdom Ground, and they have attained the unsurpassed Buddha bodhi, entered parinirvāṇa, and had their holy relics distributed. Over all such roots of goodness, I express my sympathetic joy.

"I also express my sympathetic joy over the merits, even one as tiny as a dust particle, of all sentient beings that take the six life-journeys through the four modes of birth in all the worlds in the ten directions. I also express my sympathetic joy over the merits of all voice-hearers, of whom some are still learning and others have nothing more to learn, and of Pratyekabuddhas, of the past, present, and future, [in worlds] in the ten directions. I also express my sympathetic joy over the immense merit of Bodhisattvas who undertake the immeasurable and difficult ascetic training, and resolve to attain anuttara-samyak-saṁbodhi.

"My sympathetic rejoicing would never end even if the domain of space ended, the realm of sentient beings ended, the karmas of sentient beings ended, and the afflictions of sentient beings ended. It continues thought after thought without interruption as the karma of my body, voice, and mind knows no tiredness.

"Sixth, good man, how does one request Buddhas to turn the Dharma wheel? In the entire dharma realm and the domain of space, there are dust particles in all Buddha Lands of the past, present, and future, in the ten directions. Contained in each dust particle are vast Buddha Lands as numerous as dust particles in innumerable Buddha Lands. In each land are Buddhas as numerous as dust particles in innumerable Buddha Lands who, as I think each thought, attain samyak-saṁbodhi and are surrounded by ocean-like assemblies of Bodhisattvas. With the karma of my body, voice, and mind, using various skillful means, I heartily request them to turn the wondrous Dharma wheel.

"Until the domain of space ends, the realm of sentient beings ends, the karmas of sentient beings end, and the afflictions of sentient beings end, I ceaselessly request Buddhas to turn the true Dharma wheel forever. My request continues thought after thought without interruption as the karma of my body, voice, and mind knows no tiredness.

"Seventh, good man, how does one beseech Buddhas to abide in the world? In all Buddha Lands of the past, present, and future, in the ten directions, as Buddha-Tathāgatas, who are as numerous as dust particles, wish to demonstrate entering parinirvāṇa, so too do voice-hearers, of whom some are still learning and others have nothing more to learn, Pratyekabuddhas, Bodhisattvas, and beneficent learned ones. I beseech them all not to enter parinirvāṇa, but to bring benefits and delights to all sentient beings for as many kalpas as there are dust particles in all Buddha Lands.

"My beseeching would never end even if the domain of space ended, the realm of sentient beings ended, the karmas of sentient beings ended, and the afflictions of sentient beings ended. It continues thought after thought without interruption as the karma of my body, voice, and mind knows no tiredness.

"Eighth, good man, how does one always follow Buddhas to learn? For example, Vairocana Tathāgata in this Sahā World, since his initial resolve [to attain Buddhahood], has made energetic progress, never regressing. In innumerable lives, He gave away His body and life as alms. He stripped off His skin for paper, split His bone for pen, and pierced His blood vessels for ink in order to copy sūtras, and the copies He made piled as high as Mount Sumeru. In His veneration for the Dharma, He did not begrudge His body or life, much less all that He owned, such as thrones, cities, towns, palaces, and gardens. He carried out various kinds of difficult ascetic training until he attained the great bodhi under the bodhi tree.

"He has demonstrated various kinds of spiritual powers and has performed various kinds of magical illusions. He has manifested various Buddha bodies to attend various kinds of assemblies: He is present in the bodhimaṇḍa for the assemblies of great Bodhisattvas; in the bodhimaṇḍa for the assemblies of Pratyekabuddhas and voice-hearers; in the bodhimaṇḍa for the assemblies of Wheel-Turning Kings, lesser kings, and their retinues; in the bodhimaṇḍa for the assemblies of kṣatriyas, Brahmins, elders, and laypeople; and even in the bodhimaṇḍa for the assemblies of the eight classes of Dharma protectors, such as gods and dragons, as well as for the assemblies of humans and nonhumans.

"Present in various kinds of assemblies such as these, speaking with the perfect tone like a great thunderclap, He has brought sentient beings to maturity according to their pleasures, and has even demonstrated entering parinirvāṇa. All such things, I follow Buddhas to learn. As Vairocana the World-Honored One in the present world acts in this way, so do all Tathāgatas in all Buddha Lands of the past, present, and future, in the ten directions, which are as numerous as dust particles, in the entire dharma realm and the domain of space. Thought after thought, I follow them to learn.

"My following and learning would never end even if the domain of space ended, the realm of sentient being ended, the karmas of sentient beings ended, and the afflictions of sentient beings ended. My following and learning continue thought after thought without interruption as the karma of my body, voice, and mind knows no tiredness.

"Ninth, good man, how does one support sentient beings forever? In the entire dharma realm and the domain of space, in oceans of worlds in the ten directions, all sentient beings are different in many ways, as they are born through egg, womb, moisture, or miraculous formation. Some depend on earth, water, fire, and wind to be born and to live. Some depend on space and plants to be born and to live.

"There are various living species, various body forms, various shapes, various facial features, various lifespans, various tribes, various names, various mindsets, various kinds of knowledge and views, various kinds of desires and pleasures, various kinds of mental activities, various kinds of behavior, various kinds of attire, various kinds of food and drink. Sentient beings live in various kinds of villages, towns, cities, and palaces. They include even the eight classes of Dharma protectors, such as gods and dragons, as well as humans and nonhumans, whether without feet, with two, four, or multiple feet, with or without form, with or without perception, neither with nor without perception.

"I actively support all such beings, attending to their needs, making various kinds of offerings, in the same way I honor my parents and serve my teachers, as well as Arhats and even Tathāgatas, without any difference. I serve as the good physician to those who are ill or in pain. I indicate the right road to those who have lost their way. I serve as the bright light to those in the dark night. I enable the poor to acquire the hidden treasure.

"Bodhisattvas equally benefit all sentient beings in this way. Why? Because when Bodhisattvas support sentient beings, they in effect serve and make offerings to Buddhas. When they esteem and serve sentient beings, they in effect esteem and serve Tathāgatas. When they enable sentient beings to rejoice, they in effect enable Tathāgatas to rejoice. Why? Because Buddha-Tathāgatas have the mind of great compassion as their essence. Because of sentient beings' suffering, Buddha-Tathāgatas exude great compassion. Because of their great compassion, they activate the bodhi mind. Because of the bodhi mind, they attain samyak-saṁbodhi.

"As an analogy, there is a colossal tree in a wilderness of sand dunes. If its roots receive water, then its branches, leaves, flowers, and fruits will flourish. Likewise is the bodhi tree, the king of trees, in the wilderness of saṁsāra.

Sentient beings are the tree roots, and Bodhisattvas and Buddhas are respectively the flowers and fruits. If one benefits sentient beings with the water of great compassion, one can develop the flowers and fruits of wisdom, becoming a Bodhisattva then a Buddha. Why? Because if Bodhisattvas benefit sentient beings with the water of great compassion, they can attain anuttara-samyak-saṁbodhi. Therefore, bodhi belongs to sentient beings. Without sentient beings, Bodhisattvas can never attain the unsurpassed saṁbodhi. Good man, you should have such an understanding of this meaning. By regarding sentient beings with the mind of equality, one can perfect one's great compassion. By supporting sentient beings with the mind of great compassion, one can complete one's offerings to Tathāgatas.

"As Bodhisattvas support sentient beings in this way, so my support would never end even if the domain of space ended, the realm of sentient beings ended, the karmas of sentient beings ended, and the afflictions of sentient beings ended. It continues thought after thought without interruption as the karma of my body, voice, and mind knows no tiredness.

"Tenth, good man, how does one universally transfer one's merits to others? One transfers all merits, from making obeisance to supporting sentient beings, to all sentient beings in the entire dharma realm and the domain of space, wishing that they always have peace and joy, without illness or suffering; that the evil they desire to do will not be done; that the good they desire to do will quickly be done; that all doors to the evil life-journeys will be closed; and that the right road to human life, celestial life, and nirvāṇa will be revealed. All the bitter fruits produced by sentient beings' evil karmas, one accepts in their stead, so that they will achieve liberation and eventually attain the unsurpassed bodhi.

"As Bodhisattvas transfer their merits in this way, so my merit transferring would never end even if the domain of space ended, the realm of sentient beings ended, the karmas of sentient beings ended, and the afflictions of sentient beings ended. It continues thought after thought without interruption as the karma of my body, voice, and mind knows no tiredness.

"Good man, this is a complete explanation of Bodhisattva-Mahāsattvas' great vow of the ten actions [the king of vows]. If Bodhisattvas progress by fulfilling this great vow, they will be able to bring all sentient beings to maturity, to head for anuttara-samyak-saṁbodhi, and to fulfill Samantabhadra Bodhisattva's ocean of action vows. Therefore, good man, you should have such an understanding of this meaning.

"Suppose, among good men and good women, there are those who, as an offering to all sentient beings in the entire world of yours, and to the Buddha and Bodhisattvas in the entire world of yours, give them the superb seven treasures that fill up all the worlds, which are as numerous as dust particles in innumerable, boundless Buddha Lands in the ten directions, and give them the superb peace and joy in human and celestial worlds, for as many kalpas as there are dust particles in your Buddha Land, and continue [this giving] unceasingly. The merit they have acquired is less than one hundredth, one thousandth, or even one upaniṣadth of that of one who has only once heard this king of vows.

"If there is someone who, with profound faith, accepts and upholds this great vow, reads and recites it, or even copies a four-verse stanza, his karma of the five rebellious acts, which would drive him into [Avīci Hell] the hell of the five no interruptions, will quickly be obliterated. All his physical and mental diseases, various kinds of suffering and distress, and even evil karmas as numerous as dust particles in all Buddha Lands, will all be removed. All māra legions, yakṣas, rakṣasas, kumbhāṇḍas, piśācas, bhūtas, and evil ghosts and spirits that eat flesh and drink blood will either keep far away or be inspired to stay near as his guardians. Therefore, whoever recites this vow walks in the world unhindered, like the moon that emerges from clouds. He is praised by Buddhas and Bodhisattvas. Gods and humans should make obeisance to him, and all sentient beings should make offerings to him. This good person well deserves a human body, and he will acquire all the universally worthy merit. Before long, like Samantabhadra Bodhisattva, he will quickly acquire a wonderful physical body with a great man's thirty-two physical marks. If he is reborn in the human or celestial world, then wherever he is, that is where superior people will live. Like the lion-king that subjugates all other animals, he will be able to destroy all evil life-journeys, keep away from all evil friends, subdue all non-Buddhists, and eradicate all afflictions. He will be worthy of accepting offerings from sentient beings.

"Furthermore, when this person dies, in the final kṣaṇa, all his faculties will perish, all his family members will be abandoned, and all his awesome might will be lost. All things inside or outside the palace, such as attending state ministers, elephants, horses, carriages, precious jewels, and hidden treasures, will no longer follow him. Only this king of vows will not abandon him. At all times, it will guide him forward. In the time of a kṣaṇa, he will be reborn in the Land of Ultimate Bliss. Upon arrival, he will immediately see Amitābha Buddha, Mañjuśrī Bodhisattva, Samantabhadra Bodhisattva, Avalokiteśvara Bodhisattva, and Maitreya Bodhisattva. These Bodhisattvas, surrounded by their retinues, are sublime in their physical appearance and complete in their merit. This person will see himself reborn in a lotus flower and have a prophecy [of attaining Buddhahood] bestowed upon him by that Buddha.

"After receiving the prophecy, in innumerable worlds in the ten directions, through the power of his wisdom, he will benefit sentient beings according to their minds for uncountable hundreds, thousands, tens of thousands, koṭis, and nayutas of kalpas. Before long, he will sit in a bodhimaṇḍa to subjugate the māra legions, attain samyak-saṁbodhi, and turn the wondrous Dharma wheel, enabling sentient beings in worlds as numerous as dust particles in Buddha Lands to activate the bodhi mind. He will teach and transform them and bring them to maturity according to their natures and capacities. Through boundless oceans of kalpas to come, he will widely benefit all sentient beings.

"Good man, if there are sentient beings that, having heard and believed in this great king of vows, accept and uphold it, read and recite it, and widely expound it to others, no one can know their merit, except for Buddha-Bhagavāns. Therefore, all of you, having heard this king of vows, should not entertain thoughts of doubt. You all should accept it earnestly. Having accepted it, you can read it. Having read it, you can recite it. Having recited it, you can uphold it, copy it, and even widely pronounce it to others. People such as these can fulfill in a single thought all their action vows, and acquire immeasurable, boundless merit. They are able to rescue and relieve sentient beings from the immense bitter ocean of afflictions, enabling them to leave it and be reborn in Amitābha Buddha's Land of Ultimate Bliss."

At that time Samantabhadra Bodhisattva, to restate this meaning, looked about everywhere [in worlds] in the ten directions and spoke in verse:

To all Buddhas, the lions among men, of the past, present, and future,
In all worlds in the ten directions,
I make obeisance, omitting none,
With my pure body, voice, and mind.
By the awesome spiritual power of the universally worthy action vow,
I simultaneously appear before all Tathāgatas.
My body is multiplied into as many copies as there are dust particles in all lands,
Each making obeisance to all Buddhas as numerous as dust particles in all lands.

In each dust particle are Buddhas as numerous as dust particles,
And each Buddha attends assemblies of Bodhisattvas.
As dust particles in the boundless dharma realm are the same,
I deeply believe that they all are graced by Buddhas.
Each copy of myself sends forth an ocean of sounds,
Speaking limitless wonderful words endlessly
Through all kalpas to come,
Praising the deep ocean of Buddhas' merits.

Taking superb flowers and tiaras,
Instrumental music, solid perfumes, and canopies,
Such superb adornments as these,
I offer them all to Tathāgatas.
Taking the finest garments, the choicest incense,
Powdered incense, incense for burning, and lamps and candles,
Each and every item in an amazingly lofty pile,
I offer them all to Tathāgatas.
With a mind of vast excellent understanding,
I deeply believe in all Buddhas of the past, present, and future.
Through the power of the universally worthy action vow,
I make offerings to all Tathāgatas.

The evil karmas I have done in the past
With my body, voice, and mind
Were all caused by greed, anger, and delusion, without a beginning in time.
I now repent of them all.
Over the merits of all sentient beings [in worlds] in the ten directions,
Of riders of the Two Vehicles, of whom some are still learning and others have nothing more to learn,
And of all Tathāgatas and Bodhisattvas,
I express my sympathetic joy.

I now request
All Buddhas, the world-illuminating lamps, [in worlds] in the ten directions,

As soon as they attain the great bodhi,
To turn the unsurpassed wondrous Dharma wheel.
If Buddhas wish to demonstrate entering parinirvāṇa,
I beseech them with utmost sincerity
To abide for as many kalpas as there are dust particles in all lands
And to benefit and delight all sentient beings.

The roots of goodness developed from my obeisances, praises, and offerings,
From my repentance and sympathetic joy,
And from my requesting Buddhas to abide in the world and to turn the Dharma wheel,
Are all transferred to sentient beings for [their attainment of] Buddha bodhi.

I follow all Tathāgatas to learn
As I train in the universally worthy, perfect actions.
I make offerings to past Tathāgatas,
Present Buddhas [in worlds] in the ten directions,
And all future teachers to gods and humans,
Bringing delight to all.
I vow to follow all Buddhas of the past, present, and future to learn,
In order to attain the great bodhi quickly.
In all worlds in the ten directions,
Which are vast, pure, and magnificent,
Tathāgatas, each under the bodhi tree, the king of trees,
Are surrounded by assemblies of multitudes.

I wish sentient beings [in worlds] in the ten directions
To leave their anguish and trouble for peace and joy,
To acquire the profound benefits of the true Dharma,
And to eradicate afflictions, omitting none.
Throughout my life-journeys, in training for the great bodhi,
I will acquire the power of past-life knowledge,
And will always renounce family life to observe the pure precepts
Without defilement, violation, or omission.
To gods, dragons, yakṣas, kumbhāṇḍas,
And even humans and nonhumans,
I will expound the Dharma in various tones
In all languages of sentient beings.

As I assiduously practice the pure pāramitās,
I will never lose the bodhi mind.
I will remove hindrances and afflictions, omitting none,
And will accomplish all the wonderful actions.
From afflictions, karmas, and māra states
On the worldly path, I will achieve liberation,
Like the lotus flower, which does not touch the water,
And like the sun and the moon, which do not stay in the sky.

As I remove all the suffering of evil life-journeys,
I will give happiness equally to all sentient beings.
For as many kalpas as there are dust particles in all lands,
My benefits to all [in worlds] in the ten directions will be endless.
I will forever support sentient beings
Through all kalpas to come,
As I persistently train in the universally worthy, great actions
To attain the unsurpassed great bodhi.

All those who walk with me
Congregate with me in assemblies everywhere.
Equal in their karma of body, voice, and mind,
They train together to learn all these vowed actions.
All beneficent learned friends who benefit me
Have indicated to me these universally worthy actions.
They are always willing to congregate with me,
And they always rejoice in appreciating me.

I wish always to behold Tathāgatas
And the multitudes of Buddha-sons surrounding them.
I will make expansive offerings to them all
Tirelessly through all kalpas to come.
I vow to uphold the wondrous Dharma of Buddhas,
To present openly all the training for bodhi,
And to complete the pure, universally worthy path,
Persistently training through all kalpas to come.
Everywhere in the Three Realms of Existence
I will accumulate boundless merit and wisdom.
Through samādhi, wisdom, skillful means, and liberation,
I will acquire a limitless store of merits.

In each dust particle are worlds as numerous as dust particles.
Each and every world has an inconceivable Buddha.
I see each and every Buddha in assemblies of multitudes
Constantly expounding the training for bodhi.
Across oceans of worlds in the ten directions,
Across oceans of the past, present, and future, on the tip of every hair,
Across oceans of Buddhas and oceans of worlds,
I train myself across oceans of kalpas.

The words of all Tathāgatas are pure.
Every word contains an ocean of sounds,
In tune with sentient beings' pleasures,
Flowing one by one from the ocean of Buddhas' eloquence.
All Tathāgatas of the past, present, and future,
By means of oceans of endless words,
Forever turn the wondrous Dharma wheel in accord with the truth,
Which I can penetrate through the power of my profound wisdom.

I can enter into the future,
Merging all kalpas into one thought.
In the time of one thought, I can enter
All kalpas of the past and future.
In one thought, I see all the lions among men,
Of the past, present, and future.
I also frequently enter the Buddha state
Through illusion-like liberation and awesome powers.

In the minuteness of the tip of a hair
Appear magnificent worlds of the past, present, and future.
On the tips of hairs are worlds in the ten directions, as numerous as dust particles.
I enter all these worlds and adorn them with purity.
All future Buddhas, the world-illuminating lamps,
Will attain bodhi, turn the Dharma wheel to awaken sentient beings,
Complete Buddha work, and enter parinirvāṇa as a demonstration.
I will visit and serve them all.

Mastering quickly all transcendental powers,
Acquiring through the universal door the power of the Mahāyāna,
Accumulating through wise actions the power of merit,
Activating with awesome spirit the power of great lovingkindness,
Adorning [myself with] the power of superb blessing,
Unfolding through no attachment and no reliance the power of wisdom,
Achieving the awesome spiritual power of samādhi, wisdom, and skillful means,
Gathering all the power to attain bodhi,
Purifying the power of all good karmas,
Annihilating the power of all afflictions,
Subjugating the power of all māras,
Fulfilling the power of the universally worthy actions,

I universally adorn and purify oceans of worlds
And liberate oceans of sentient beings;
I adeptly differentiate oceans of dharmas
And enter deeply into oceans of wisdom;
I universally purify oceans of actions
And fulfill oceans of vows;
I competently serve and make offerings to oceans of Buddhas
And train tirelessly for oceans of kalpas.
To all Tathāgatas of the past, present, and future,
[Who have] supreme bodhi, and actions and vows,
I make offerings, in perfect training,
In order to attain bodhi through the universally worthy actions.

Every Tathāgata has an eldest son
Called the revered Samantabhadra.

I now transfer my roots of goodness to all,
Wishing that my wisdom and actions will equal his.
I wish that my body, voice, and mind will be forever pure,
As will be my actions and the lands I walk.
Such a wisdom being called Samantabhadra,
I wish to be his equal.

I will accomplish with purity Samantabhadra's great actions
And Mañjuśrī's great vows.
All the work they have completed, I will complete as well,
Tirelessly through all kalpas to come.
My spiritual training having no limit,
I will acquire immeasurable merit.
Persistent in immeasurable actions,
I will master all transcendental powers.
As Mañjuśrī's wisdom is dynamic,
So too are Samantabhadra's wise actions.
I now transfer my roots of goodness,
Wishing always to follow them to train and learn.
As Buddhas of the past, present, and future
Praise such outstanding great wishes,
I now transfer my roots of goodness,
Wishing to accomplish the universally worthy, supreme actions.

I wish that, at the end of my life,
All hindrances will be removed, and that
I will instantly be reborn in the Land of Peace and Bliss
To behold Amitābha Buddha.
Having been reborn in that land,
I will forthwith bring this great vow
Into total fulfillment with no exception,
And bring benefits and delights to the realm of all sentient beings.
As all assemblies of that Buddha are pure,
I will be reborn in a splendid lotus flower.
I will see with my own eye the Tathāgata of infinite light
Bestow upon me the prophecy of attaining bodhi.
Having received the prophecy from that Tathāgata,
I will magically multiply my body countless hundreds of koṭis in number.
With the great power of my wisdom pervading the ten directions,
I will universally benefit the realm of all sentient beings.

[My vow will last] until the domain of space ends,
The realm of sentient beings ends, and their karmas and afflictions end.
As these four have no end,
So my vow will have no end.

People may offer Tathāgatas magnificent treasures
In boundless worlds in the ten directions
And give superb peace and joy to gods and humans,

For as many Kalpas as there are dust particles in all lands.
If someone can elicit faith in this supreme king of vows
After hearing it but once,
And can seek the supreme bodhi with a longing mind,
His merit surpasses that of those benefactors.
He will keep far away from evil philosophers
And forever leave the evil life-paths.
Equipped with the universally worthy, supreme vow,
He will soon behold the Tathāgata of infinite light.

This person well deserves a long life.
This person well deserves to be reborn among humans.
This person will complete before long the Bodhisattva actions
Just as Samantabhadra has.
The extremely evil karmas that would drive him into the hell of the five no interruptions
Were done in the past from lack of wisdom.
They will all be quickly obliterated in one thought
As he recites the universally worthy, great king of vows.

His family name, caste, facial color,
Looks, and wisdom will be perfect.
Māras or non-Buddhists cannot destroy him,
And he is worthy of accepting offerings from the Three Realms of Existence.
He will soon visit the great bodhi tree-king.
Seated under it, he will subjugate the multitude of māras,
Attain samyak-saṁbodhi, turn the Dharma wheel,
And universally benefit all sentient beings.

If someone reads and recites this universally worthy vow,
Accepts, upholds , and expounds it,
Only Buddhas can know the fruition of his requital.
He will definitely be victorious on the bodhi path.
If someone recites this universally worthy vow,
I say that his roots of goodness, no matter how small,
Will fully grow in one thought into
The pure vow to bring sentient beings to accomplishment.

The boundless superb merit acquired from my universally worthy, great actions
Will all be transferred to sentient beings,
Wishing that those who are sinking and drowning
Will go quickly to the land of Infinite Light Buddha.

At that time, before the Tathāgata, Samantabhadra Bodhisattva-Mahāsattva finished speaking these pure stanzas of the universally worthy, great king of vows. The youth Sudhana was exuberant beyond measure, and all Bodhisattvas greatly rejoiced. The Tathāgata praised, "Very good! Very good!"

5 Mahāvaipulya Sūtra of Buddha Adornment, fascicle 40

As the Tathāgata, together with holy Bodhisattva-Mahāsattvas, expounded [through Samantabhadra Bodhisattva] such an excellent Dharma Door to the inconceivable liberation state, Mañjuśrī Bodhisattva was at the head of great Bodhisattvas and the six thousand bhikṣus whom they had brought to spiritual maturity. Maitreya Bodhisattva was at the head of all the great Bodhisattvas of this Worthy Kalpa. The immaculate Samantabhadra Bodhisattva was at the head of Bodhisattvas who had nectar poured on their heads, empowered in the holy position of waiting to attain Buddhahood in their next life, and of Bodhisattva-Mahāsattvas who came from various worlds in the ten directions, in numbers as numerous as dust particles in oceans of worlds. Śāriputra the Great Wisdom and Mahāmaudgalyāyana were at the head of great voice-hearers and multitudes of human and celestial rulers.

All in the huge assembly, including gods, dragons, yakṣas, gandharvas, asuras, garuḍas, kiṁnaras, mahoragas, humans, and nonhumans, having heard the Buddha's words, greatly rejoiced. They all believed in, accepted, and reverently carried out the teachings.

6 無量壽經優波提舍
Upadeśa on the Sūtra of Amitāyus Buddha

Composed by the Indian Master Vasubandhu
Translated from Sanskrit into Chinese in the Northern Wei Dynasty
by
The Tripiṭaka Master Bodhiruci from India

The Stanzas of Wishing for Rebirth

World-Honored One,
I single-mindedly take refuge in
The Tathāgata [Amitāyus], whose hindrance-free light shines in the ten directions,
Wishing to be reborn in His Land of Peace and Bliss.
Following sūtras,
The appearances of true virtue,
I pronounce these all-encompassing stanzas of wishing,
In accordance with the teachings of the Buddha [Śākyamuni].

I visualize the appearance of that land,
Which surpasses that of the path within the Three Realms of Existence.
It is ultimate, like the open sky,
Vast and boundless.
It is born from great lovingkindness and compassion on the right path,
And from supra-worldly roots of goodness.
It is full of pure radiance,
Like a mirror, the disk of the sun or the moon.
It is made of treasures and
Abounds with wonderful adornments.
The immaculate light glows,
Suffusing all lands with radiance and purity.
The grasses of virtue, made of treasures, are soft,
Twirling left and right.
They bring superb joy to those who touch them,
More than the kācalindi grass does.
Tens of millions kinds of jeweled flowers
Cover the ponds and streams.
As breezes stir the flower petals,
Interweaving beams of light freely whirl.
Palaces and towers
Command a hindrance-free view in the ten directions.

Surrounded by jeweled railings,
Diverse trees emit colorful beams of light.
Nets of innumerable interlaced jewels
Hover all across the open sky.
All kinds of bells
Chime wondrous Dharma tones.
As adornments, flowers and garments fall like rain;
Innumerable fragrances waft everywhere.
Like the sun, Buddha wisdom is bright and pure,
And it dispels the darkness of the ignorance of the world.
Brahma tones reach far and wide,
Heard by all [in worlds] in the ten directions.
Amitāyus, the Samyak-Saṁbuddha,
Is the Dharma King who well presides there.
The pure multitudes who accompany that Tathāgata are
Miraculously reborn there from flowers of true enlightenment.
They delight in the flavors of the Buddha Dharma,
Taking dhyāna and samādhi as food.
Having forever left the troubles of body and mind,
They experience uninterrupted bliss.
The roots of goodness in the Mahāyāna domain
Are equal, with no scornful names,
Because no one is reborn there in female form, or with incomplete faculties,
Or as the character-type bent on riding the Two Vehicles.
All wishes and preferences of the sentient beings there
Are fulfilled.
Therefore, I wish to be reborn
In Amitāyus Buddha's land.

Innumerable superb treasures
Adorn [His seat] the wonderful, pure flower-platform.
The radiance of His excellent appearance reaches a distance of one yojana.
His form surpasses those of all sentient beings.
That Tathāgata's wondrous sounds are Brahma tones,
Heard by all [in worlds] in the ten directions.
As earth, water, fire, wind, and space make no differentiations,
So does He not make them.
There, gods and those who cannot be diverted [from the right path]
Are reborn from the ocean of pure wisdom.
Like Sumeru, king of mountains,
Their magnificence is unsurpassed.
Gods and men in multitudes
Reverently surround Him and gaze at Him.
By virtue of the power of that Buddha's original vows,
One's encounter with Him will never be fruitless.
One will be enabled to encompass
The great treasure ocean of virtues.

The Land of Peace and Bliss is pure,
Where the stainless Dharma wheel always turns.
Firm as Mount Sumeru, magically manifested Buddhas and Bodhisattvas
Abide there like the sun.
Their immaculate majestic radiance,
With one thought,
Simultaneously illuminates all Buddha assemblies
And benefits all sentient beings.
As an offering, they rain down
Celestial music, flowers, garments, and wonderful incense.
Without the discriminatory mind,
They praise Buddhas' virtues.
In any land without
The Buddha Dharma, the jewel of virtues,
They wish to be reborn,
To impart the Buddha Dharma as do Buddhas.

I compose this treatise with stanzas,
Wishing to see Amitāyus Buddha and
To be reborn together with all sentient beings
In the Land of Peace and Bliss.

Thus, I have summarized in stanzas the words in the *Sūtra of Amitāyus Buddha*.

The Explanation

What is the meaning of these stanzas of wishing? It indicates [how to] visualize the Land of Peace and Bliss and to visualize Amitāyus Buddha, for those who wish to be reborn in that land.

The Five Training Doors

How does one visualize? How does one elicit belief? If good men and good women come to achievement through the five doors of vigilance, they will ultimately be reborn in the Land of Peace and Bliss, and see Amitāyus Buddha. What are the five doors of vigilance? The first door is making obeisance; the second door is praising; the third door is wishing; the fourth door is visualizing; the fifth door is transferring merit.

Why does one make obeisance? To express the intention to be reborn in that land, one should do the body karma of making obeisance to Amitāyus Tathāgata, the Arhat, Samyak-Saṁbuddha. How does one praise Him? To train in accord with true reality, one should do the voice karma of praising, by saying that Tathāgata's name, because His name and its meaning are like His radiance and wisdom appearance. What does one wish for? To train in śamatha in accord with true reality, one should do the mind karma of wishing, by single-mindedly thinking of one's ultimate rebirth in the Land of Peace and Bliss. How does one visualize? To train in vipaśyanā in accord with true reality, one should visualize with wisdom and right thinking. There are three visualizations. First, one visualizes the virtues of that Buddha Land as its adornments. Second, one visualizes the virtues of Amitāyus Buddha as His adornments. Third, one visualizes the virtues of the Bodhisattvas there as their adornments. How does one transfer one's merits? To invoke the mind of great compassion, one should never abandon any suffering sentient being. One should transfer one's merits to others with this foremost wish for all to be reborn in that land.

The Fourth Training Door

Visualizing the Virtues of That Buddha Land

How does one visualize the virtues of that Buddha Land as its adornments? The virtues adorning that Buddha Land command inconceivable powers, similar to but different from those of the precious wish-fulfilling jewel. One should visualize, as its adornments, the virtues of seventeen achievements of that Buddha Land.

First, the virtues of its purity; second, the virtues of its measure; third, the virtues of its nature; fourth, the virtues of its form; fifth, the virtues of its various things; sixth, the virtues of its wonderful colors; seventh, the virtues of its touch; eighth, the virtues of its adornments; ninth, the virtues of its rain; tenth, the virtues of its radiance; eleventh, the virtues of its wonderful sounds; twelfth, the virtues of its master; thirteen, the virtues of its master's retinue; fourteenth, the virtues of the enjoyment of its inhabitants; fifteenth, the virtues of its no tribulations; sixteenth, the virtues of its door of great meaning; seventeenth, the virtues of its fulfillment of all wishes.

1. The virtues of its purity are described by this stanza: "I visualize the appearance of that land, / Which surpasses that of the path within the Three Realms of Existence."

2. The virtues of its measure are described by this stanza: "It is ultimate, like the open sky, / Vast and boundless."

3. The virtues of its nature are described by this stanza: "It is born from great lovingkindness and compassion on the right path, / And from supra-worldly roots of goodness."

4. The virtues of its form are described by this stanza: "It is full of pure radiance, / Like a mirror, the disk of the sun or the moon."

5. The virtues of its various things are described by this stanza: "It is made of treasures and / Abounds with wonderful adornments."

6. The virtues of its wonderful colors are described by this stanza: "The immaculate light glows, / Suffusing all lands with radiance and purity."

7. The virtues of its touch are described by this stanza: "The grasses of virtue, made of treasures, are soft, / Twirling left and right. / They bring superb joy to those who touch them, / More than the kācalindi grass does."

8. What are the virtues of its adornments? Know the three things that are adorned. What are these three? The first is its water; the second is its ground; the third is its sky. The adornments of its water are described by this stanza: "Tens of millions kinds of jeweled flowers / Cover the ponds and streams. / As breezes stir

the flower petals, / Interweaving beams of light freely whirl." The adornments of its ground are described by this stanza: "Palaces and towers / Command a hindrance-free view in the ten directions. / Surrounded by jeweled railings, / Diverse trees emit colorful beams of light." The adornments of its sky are described by this stanza: "Nets of innumerable interlaced jewels / Hover all across the open sky. / All kinds of bells / Chime wondrous Dharma tones."

9. The virtues of its rain are described by this stanza: "As adornments, flowers and garments fall like rain; / Innumerable fragrances waft everywhere."

10. The virtues of its radiance are described by this stanza: "Like the sun, Buddha wisdom is bright and pure, / And it dispels the darkness of the ignorance of the world."

11. The virtues of its sounds are described by this stanza: "Brahma tones reach far and wide, / Heard by all [in worlds] in the ten directions."

12. The virtues of its master are described by this stanza: "Amitāyus, the Samyak-Saṁbuddha, / Is the Dharma King who well presides there."

13. The virtues of its master's retinue are described by this stanza: "The pure multitudes who accompany that Tathāgata are / Miraculously reborn there from flowers of true enlightenment."

14. The virtues of the enjoyment of its inhabitants are described by this stanza: "They delight in the flavors of the Buddha Dharma, / Taking dhyāna and samādhi as food."

15. The virtues of its no tribulations are described by this stanza: "Having forever left the troubles of body and mind, / They experience uninterrupted bliss."

16. The virtues of its door of great meaning are described by this stanza: "The roots of goodness in the Mahāyāna domain / Are equal, with no scornful names, / Because no one is reborn there in female form, or with incomplete faculties, / Or as the character-type bent on riding the Two Vehicles." One's rebirth in the Pure Land, as one's requital fruit, is free from the faults of two kinds of scorn. One is body, the other is name. There are three kinds of [faulty] bodies: riders of the Two Vehicles, females, and people with incomplete faculties. Freedom from these three faults is called freedom from the scorned bodies. Their three corresponding names are riders of the Two Vehicles, females, and people with incomplete faculties. [In that land] these three kinds of bodies do not even exist, much less have their names heard of. This is called freedom from scornful names. Equality [of roots of goodness] means that all [inhabitants there] are equal in the one appearance.[1]

17. The virtues of its fulfillment of all wishes are described by this stanza: "All wishes and preferences of the sentient beings there / Are fulfilled."

These are brief explanations of the virtues of the seventeen achievements adorning Amitāyus Buddha's land. These virtues indicate that Tathāgata's achievements in benefiting Himself and others. The adornments of Amitāyus Buddha's land are the appearances of the wondrous state of the highest truth. The first achievement [of generality] and its following sixteen achievements [of particulars] have been successively described.

Visualizing the Virtues of That Buddha

How does one visualize the virtues of that Buddha's achievements as His adornments? That Buddha has eight kinds of adornments. What are these eight? First, the adornments of His seat; second, the adornments of His body; third, the adornments of His voice; fourth, the adornments of His mind; fifth, the adornments of His people; sixth, the adornments of the leaders of His retinue; seventh, the adornments of His status as the master; eighth, the adornments of His authority as the presiding teacher.

1. What are the adornments of His seat? This stanza explains, "Innumerable superb treasures / Adorn [His seat] the wonderful, pure flower-platform."
2. What are the adornments of His body? This stanza explains, "The radiance of His excellent appearance reaches a distance of one yojana. / His form surpasses those of all sentient beings."
3. What are the adornments of His voice? This stanza explains, "That Tathāgata's wondrous sounds are Brahma tones, / Heard by all [in worlds] in the ten directions."
4. What are the adornments of His mind? This stanza explains, "As earth, water, fire, wind, and space make no differentiations, / So does He not make them." Making no differentiation means that He does not have the discriminatory mind.
5. What are the adornments of His people? This stanza explains, "There, gods and those who cannot be diverted [from the right path] / Are reborn from the ocean of pure wisdom."
6. What are the adornments of the leaders of His retinue? This stanza explains, "Like Sumeru, king of mountains, / Their magnificence is unsurpassed."
7. What are the adornments of His status as the master? This stanza explains, "Gods and men in multitudes / Reverently surround Him and gaze at Him."
8. What are the adornments of His authority as the presiding teacher? This stanza explains, "By virtue of the power of that Buddha's original vows, / One's encounter with Him will never be fruitless. / One will be enabled to encompass / The great treasure ocean of virtues." Bodhisattvas who have not realized the pure mind, but have seen that Buddha, will ultimately realize the dharma body, which is equal in all, just as Bodhisattvas with the pure mind[2] and Bodhisattvas on higher Grounds will ultimately attain nirvāṇa and realize that it is equal in all.

This is a brief explanation of the eight phrases which successively indicate how that Tathāgata is adorned by the virtues of His achievements in benefiting Himself and others.

Visualizing the Virtues of the Bodhisattvas There

How does one visualize, as their adornments, the virtues of the Bodhisattvas' achievements? Bodhisattvas there have the virtues of four achievements in their right training. What are these four?

1. With their bodies staying put in one Buddha Land, they responsively manifest their bodies everywhere [in worlds] in the ten directions. Training themselves in accord with true reality, they always do Buddha work. They open sentient beings' minds like flowers rising above mud, as described by this stanza:

"The Land of Peace and Bliss is pure, / Where the stainless Dharma wheel always turns. / Firm as Mount Sumeru, magically manifested Buddhas and Bodhisattvas / Abide there like the sun."

2. Their manifested response bodies, with one mind and one thought, emit great radiance, simultaneously reaching everywhere in worlds in the ten directions, teaching and transforming sentient beings. By various skillful means, they train through their work to end the suffering of all sentient beings, as described by this stanza: "Their immaculate majestic radiance, / With one thought, / Simultaneously illuminates all Buddha assemblies / And benefits all sentient beings."

3. They illuminate the multitudes in Buddha assemblies in all lands without exception, make innumerable expansive offerings, and revere and praise Buddha-Tathāgatas, as described by this stanza: "As an offering, they rain down / Celestial music, flowers, garments, and wonderful incense. / Without the discriminatory mind, / They praise Buddhas' virtues."

4. In all worlds in the ten directions, where the Three Jewels are unavailable, they preside over the great ocean of virtues of the Buddha, the Dharma, and the Saṅgha, enabling all to understand [the Buddha Dharma] and to train in accord with true reality, as described by this stanza: "In any land without / The Buddha Dharma, the jewel of virtues, / They wish to be reborn, / To impart the Buddha Dharma as do Buddhas."

Integrating All Virtues into One Word

As stated above, one should visualize, as adornments, the virtues of that Buddha Land's achievements, the virtues of Amitāyus Buddha's achievements, and the virtues of His Bodhisattvas' achievements. Visualization of these three groups of virtues adorns one's mind wishing for rebirth [in that land]. Now I integrate all virtues into one Dharma word. This one Dharma word is *purity*. The word *purity* pertains to true wisdom, the dharma body, which is asaṁskṛta. This purity has two meanings. What are these two? One is the purity of the vessel world; the other is the purity of the sentient beings' world. The virtues of the seventeen achievements of that Buddha Land, as its adornments, are called the purity of the vessel world. The virtues of the eight achievements of that Buddha, as His adornments, and the virtues of the four achievements of Bodhisattvas, as their adornments, are called the purity of the sentient beings' world. Thus, the Dharma word *purity* encompasses these two meanings.

The Fifth Training Door

Bodhisattvas who broadly or simply train in śamatha and vipaśyanā [through the third and fourth doors] will achieve the gentle mind and will truly know dharmas in their broad or simple aspects. Thus, they will achieve skillful transference of their merits.

How does a Bodhisattva skillfully transfer his merits? He transfers all roots of virtue gathered from the five trainings[3] [mentioned above], including making obeisance. Not seeking his own lasting happiness, but for the sake of uprooting the suffering of all sentient beings, he makes a wish to draw in all sentient beings for them to be reborn in that Buddha Land of Peace and Bliss. This is called a Bodhisattva's achievement of skillful transference of his merits.

Bodhisattvas who excel in such skillful transference of their merits will stay far away from dharmas that go against three bodhi doors. What are these three? First, relying on the door of wisdom, one does not seek one's own happiness because one stays far away from the mind captivated by one's own body. Second, relying on the door of lovingkindness and compassion, one uproots the suffering of all sentient beings because one stays far away from the mind indifferent to helping sentient beings. Third, relying on the door of skillful means, one pities all sentient beings because one stays far away from the mind that pampers and worships one's own body. This is called staying far away from dharmas that go against three bodhi doors.

Bodhisattvas who stay far away from dharmas that go against these three bodhi doors will acquire three fulfillments that accord with the Dharma of these doors. What are these three fulfillments? First, the untainted pure mind, because one does not seek one's own happiness. Second, the peaceful pure mind, because one uproots the suffering of all sentient beings. Third, the joyful pure mind, because one draws in all sentient beings for them to be reborn in that Buddha Land, enabling them to attain the great bodhi. These are the three fulfillments that accord with the Dharma of these three bodhi doors.

Achieving Rebirth through the Five Training Doors

The three bodhi doors mentioned above—wisdom, lovingkindness and compassion, and skillful means—lead to prajñā, and prajñā reveals skillful means. The three dharmas mentioned above—staying far away from the mind captivated by one's own body, staying far away from the mind indifferent to helping sentient beings, and staying far away from the mind that pampers and worships one's own body—enable one to stay far way from hindrances to realizing the bodhi mind. The three minds mentioned above—the untainted pure mind, the peaceful pure mind, and the joyful pure mind—merge into one, the wondrous, joyful, superb true mind.

Thus, with the wisdom mind, the skillful-means mind, the hindrance-free mind, and the superb true mind, Bodhisattvas can be reborn in a pure Buddha Land. This is the achievement of Bodhisattvas who go through the five Dharma Doors [making obeisance, praising, wishing, visualizing, and transferring merit] mentioned above. By training through these Dharma Doors, a Bodhisattva's body karmas, voice karmas, mind karmas, visualization-with-wisdom karmas, and skillful merit-transference-with-wisdom karmas are easily accomplished.

The Five Achievement Doors

There are another five doors, though which one can successively achieve five virtues. What are these five [achievement] doors? First, the near door; second, the door to the great assembly; third, the door to the residence; fourth, the door to the house; and fifth, the door to the playground in the garden. Through the first four of these five doors, one achieves the virtue of entrance; through the fifth door, one achieves the virtue of exit.

One enters the first door by making obeisance to Amitāyus Buddha in order to be reborn in His land. One's rebirth in the Land of Peace of Bliss is called entering the near door. One enters the second door by praising Amitāyus Buddha, saying that Tathāgata's name in accordance with the meaning of His name. Through training in thinking of that Tathāgata's radiance, one can join the multitudes in the great assembly. This is called entering the door to the great assembly. One enters the third door by single-mindedly wishing to be reborn there. Through training in śamatha and silent samādhi, one can enter the World of the Lotus Flower Store.[4] This is called entering the door to the residence. One enters the fourth door by intently visualizing the wonderful adornments [of that land, that Buddha, and the Bodhisattvas there]. Through training in vipaśyanā, one arrives there and enjoys the bliss of various Dharma flavors. This is called entering the door to the house.

One exits the fifth door with great lovingkindness and compassion by visualizing all suffering sentient beings, by responsively manifesting one's bodies, by returning to the forest of afflictions in the garden of saṁsāra, and by playfully demonstrating transcendental powers. One's arrival on the teaching ground, because one has transferred one's merits with the power of one's original vows, is called exiting the door to the playground in the garden.

A Bodhisattva's entrance through the first four doors is an achievement for self-benefit. A Bodhisattva's exit through the fifth door to benefit others is an achievement of transferring his merits. Bodhisattvas who train through these five [achievement] doors to benefit themselves and others will quickly attain anuttara-samyak-saṁbodhi.

Thus ends, in this *Upadeśa on the Sūtra of Amitāyus Buddha*, the explanation of the stanzas of wishing for rebirth.

Notes

1. In Sūtra 1, the Buddha says that the inhabitants there "all appear in the same form, without any difference." Furthermore, according to the absolute truth, all appearances are equal in the one appearance of true suchness.

2. Bodhisattvas with the pure mind are those who have ascended to the First Ground (see "stages of the Bodhisattva Way" in the glossary).

3. Perhaps Vasubandhu means the first four of the five trainings.

4. Vasubandhu refers to Amitāyus Buddha's Land of Peace and Bliss as the World of the Lotus Flower Store. This world has different meanings in the *Brahma*

Net Sūtra (T24n1484) and in the 80-fascicle version of the *Mahāvaipulya Sūtra of Buddha Adornment* (T10n0279).

PART II

Four Other Sūtras

Four Other Sūtras

7 Buddha Pronounces the Sūtra of the Pratyutpanna Buddha Sammukhāvasthita Samādhi

Texts 416–19 (T13n0416–19) are four Chinese versions of this sūtra, each translated from a different Sanskrit text. In the Sui Dynasty (581–618), Jñānagupta (闍那崛多, 523–600) translated text 416, the longest version of this sūtra, comprising 17 chapters in 5 fascicles.

In the Eastern Han Dynasty (25–220), Lokakṣema (支婁迦讖, or 支讖, 147–?) translated texts 417 and 418. Text 417, comprising 8 chapters in one fascicle, is shorter than text 418, which comprises 16 chapters in 3 fascicles. Although the eight chapter headings in text 417 match corresponding chapter headings in text 418, the texts in these matching chapters are not identical. So, text 417 is probably not an excerpt of text 418. Text 419 is the shortest version, without the name of a translator, but attributed to Lokakṣema as his earliest translation. Paul Harrison (1998) was the first to translate text 418 from Chinese into English.

Sūtra 7 is an English translation of text 417. Some Chinese wordings in text 417 seem peculiar. However, they are clarified by Jñānagupta's translation in text 416.

In this sūtra the Buddha teaches one to think of Amitābha Buddha and His land for seven days and seven nights. After the seventh day, one will see Amitābha Buddha in a vision, who will teach one to think of His name vigilantly in order to be reborn in His Land of Ultimate Bliss. Moreover, the Buddha teaches a three-month intense-meditation retreat, during which one does walking meditation without rest, except when eating or doing other necessities.

This sūtra is called *Pratyutpanna Buddha Sammukhāvasthita Samādhi,* which means the samādhi in which Buddhas presently stand before one. The word *sammukha* means facing, and *avasthita* means standing near. The word *pratyutpanna* means present or multiplied. Through intense meditation, one sees not only one Buddha but all Buddhas stand before one if one wishes.

Then the meditator will realize this: "The mind forms a Buddha for itself to see; the mind is the Buddha mind. As my mind forms a Buddha, my mind is the Buddha; my mind is the Tathāgata; my mind is my body."

An essential element for people to attain this samādhi is to observe the precepts with purity, whether they are monks, nuns, laymen, or laywomen. They should regard their beneficent teachers as Buddhas and serve them respectfully. Another important element is to have sympathetic joy upon hearing of this samādhi. All Buddhas of the past, present, and future, before attainment of Buddhahood, have sympathetic joy. Because of their sympathetic joy, they attain this samādhi, hear much of the Dharma, and become Buddhas.

8 Sūtra of Mahā-Prajñā-Pāramitā Pronounced by Mañjuśrī Bodhisattva (in 2 fascicles)

Texts 232–33 (T08n0232–33) are two Chinese versions of this sūtra, each translated in the Southern Liang Dynasty (502–57) from a different Sanskrit text. Saṅghapāla (僧伽婆羅, 460–524), also called Saṅghavarman, translated text 233, but he was not the Saṅghavarman who translated text 360, the *Amitāyus Sūtra* (Sūtra 1).

Mandra (曼陀羅仙, 5th–6th centuries) translated text 232, the shorter version of this sūtra. It is also collected into the *Great Treasure Pile Sūtra* (T11n0310) as its 46th sūtra, in fascicles 115–16. An abridged English translation of this text is found in *A Treasury of Mahāyāna Sūtras* (Chang 1985, 100–14).

Sūtra 8 is an unabridged English translation of text 232. In this sūtra the Buddha and Mañjuśrī Bodhisattva jointly teach prajñā-pāramitā, the sixth of the six pāramitās. Mañjuśrī Bodhisattva is revered in China as the Great Wisdom Mañjuśrī Bodhisattva. It is through prajñā (wisdom) that one crosses over to the shore of enlightenment.

Mañjuśrī first teaches the features of true suchness: never changing, never moving, never acting, with neither birth nor death, neither existent nor nonexistent, neither somewhere nor nowhere, neither in the past, present, or future, nor not in the past, present, or future, neither dual nor non-dual, neither pure nor impure. He successively establishes the equivalence of these terms: true reality, true suchness, Tathāgata, bodhi, prajñā-pāramitā, the inconceivable state, and the dharma realm.

Dharmas have neither appearance nor act and are inherently in nirvāṇa. The emptiness of all dharmas is bodhi, which is non-dual and free from differentiation. Not abiding in dharmas is abiding in prajñā-pāramitā, and not abiding in appearances is abiding in prajñā-pāramitā. Bodhisattva-Mahāsattvas who see in the dharma realm neither differentiated appearances nor the one appearance will quickly attain the inconceivable anuttara-samyak-saṁbodhi.

If good men and good women train in the One Action Samādhi, they will quickly attain anuttara-samyak-saṁbodhi. They should focus their minds on one Buddha and keep saying His name. If they can continue, thought after thought, thinking only of one Buddha, they will be able to see, in their thoughts, past, future, and present Buddhas. The merit acquired from thinking of one Buddha is immeasurable and boundless, no different from the merit acquired from thinking of innumerable Buddhas or thinking of the inconceivable Buddha Dharma.

This samādhi is attained through training. Mañjuśrī testifies, “I am always in this samādhi without thinking.” He says, “If one sees appearances, then one can speak of no appearance. I now see neither appearance nor no appearance.”

The Buddha teaches that anuttara-samyak-saṁbodhi is attained through neither causes nor no causes. However, all Bodhisattva-Mahāsattvas who have attained the One Action Samādhi will acquire the Thirty-seven Elements of Bodhi and quickly attain anuttara-samyak-saṁbodhi.

9 Mahāvaipulya Sūtra of the Inconceivable State of Tathāgatas

Texts 300–01 (T10n0300–01) are two Chinese versions of this sūtra, each translated in the Tang Dynasty (618–907) from a different Sanskrit text. Devaprajñā (提雲般若, 7th–8th centuries), who went to China in 689, translated text 300. Śikṣānanda (實叉難陀, 652–710), who went to China in 695, translated text 301.

Sūtra 9 is an English translation of text 301, the shorter version of this sūtra. In this sūtra Samantabhadra Bodhisattva teaches the samādhi called the Inconceivable State of Tathāgatas. All Buddhas are constantly in this samādhi as they each display without effort immeasurable Buddha work in all Buddha Lands in the ten directions, such as being born in heaven, entering parinirvāṇa, or liberating innumerable sentient beings. Such displays will never end for all sentient beings that have not attained the unsurpassed bodhi.

To attain this samādhi, one should first accumulate merit and develop one's roots of goodness by making offerings to the Three Jewels and requite the kindness of one's parents, teachers, and all others. One should next sow a vast seed by making offerings to present Buddhas or their images, with the understanding that making offerings to one Buddha is making offerings to all Buddhas. Then one should water the seed with persistent practice of almsgiving, observing the precepts, making great vows, and developing wisdom.

To develop wisdom, one should observe a Buddha statue meticulously then visualize it in meditation. When one sees a Buddha, one can request His teaching of the Samādhi of the Inconceivable State of Tathāgatas. Or one can ask Him to end one's suffering by shining on one His blue light of compassion. If one knows that the Buddha one sees is imagery, then one understands that all Buddhas and all dharmas are a measure of one's mind, and one achieves the Endurance in Accord. One can even ascend to the First Ground. After death, one will quickly be reborn in either Akṣobhya Buddha's Land of Embracing Joy (abhirati) or Amitābha Buddha's Land of Ultimate Bliss (sukhāvatī).

10 Sūtra of the Prophecy Bestowed upon Avalokiteśvara Bodhisattva

Texts 371–72 (T12n0371–72) are two Chinese versions of this sutra, each translated from a different Sanskrit text. In the Liu Song Dynasty (420–79), Dharmodgata (曇無竭, 4th–5th centuries), a Chinese monk, translated text 371. In the Song Dynasty (960–1279), Dānapāla (施護, ?–1017), an Indian monk from northern India who went to China in 980, translated text 372.

Sūtra 10 is an English translation of text 371, the shorter version of this sūtra. In this sūtra the Buddha teaches that dharmas, born though causes and conditions, are illusory and, in true reality, have no birth. One's realization of the emptiness of dharmas is called the acquiring of the Illusion Samādhi. Then one can transform one's body by skillful means and pronounce the Dharma according to the roots of goodness of various kinds of sentient beings, enabling them to attain anuttara-samyak-saṁbodhi.

At the request of Flower Virtue Store Bodhisattva, the Buddha introduces Amitābha Buddha in the Land of Peace and Bliss, who is attended by Bodhisattvas

Avalokiteśvara and Mahāsthāmaprāpta (Great Might Arrived). Both of them have acquired the Illusion Samādhi. The Buddha encourages all to resolve to be reborn in that land and learn this samādhi from these two holy Bodhisattvas.

In praise of their attainment and merit, the Buddha tells a story of His past life, during the Great King Kalpa, when he was King Awesome Virtue, in Golden Light Lion Frolic Buddha's magnificent land (now Amitābha Buddha's land). While King Awesome Virtue was meditating in his garden, two boys were miraculously born in two lotus flowers. It was in that life that the two boys first activated the anuttara-samyak-saṁbodhi mind before Golden Light Lion Frolic Buddha. They vowed that their Pure Land, after their attainment of Buddhahood, would be even more magnificent and would have no voice-hearers. The two boys are now Bodhisattvas Avalokiteśvara and Mahāsthāmaprāpta.

The Buddha bestows upon these two Bodhisattvas a prophecy of attaining Buddhahood. Immediately after Amitābha Buddha's true Dharma ends in the distant future, Avalokiteśvara Bodhisattva will demonstrate attaining Buddhahood under the bodhi tree. Then, after the end of His true Dharma, Mahāsthāmaprāpta Bodhisattva will attain Buddhahood. However, Bodhisattvas who have attained the Thinking-of-Buddhas Samādhi will constantly see Amitābha Buddha.

7 佛說般舟三昧經
Buddha Pronounces the Sūtra of the Pratyutpanna Buddha Sammukhāvasthita Samādhi

Translated from Sanskrit into Chinese during the Eastern Han Dynasty
by
The Tripiṭaka Master Lokakṣema from the Yuezhi Land

Chapter 1 - The Questions

Thus I have heard:

At one time the Bhagavān was in the Karaṇḍa Bamboo Garden of the city of Rājagṛha, together with an innumerable multitude of great Bodhisattvas, bhikṣus, bhikṣuṇīs, upāsakas, and upāsikās, as well as gods, dragons, asuras, yakṣas, garuḍas, kiṁnaras, and mahoragas. All were seated in the huge assembly.

At that time Bhadrapāla Bodhisattva[1] rose from his seat, arranged his attire, and fell on his knees. He joined his palms and asked the Buddha, "I would like to ask some questions. May I have Your permission to ask them now?"

The Buddha replied, "Very good! Ask any questions as you wish. I will answer them to you."

Bhadrapāla Bodhisattva asked the Buddha, "What dharmas should Bodhisattvas do in order to develop wisdom, like the immense ocean accepting myriad streams? What should they do in order to acquire broad knowledge and understand what they have heard without doubts? What should they do in order to know their past lives and whence they have come to reborn? What should they do in order to live a long life? What should they do in order to be reborn into a family with a great name and to be loved and respected by their parents, siblings, relatives, and friends? What should they do in order to be endowed with even, comely features? What should they do in order to acquire excellent talents, to be outstanding in the multitudes, and to develop superb, all-encompassing wisdom? What should they do in order to acquire the merit and wisdom required for Buddhahood, to achieve immeasurable awesome power, and to adorn their magnificent Buddha Lands? What should they do in order to subjugate hostile māras? What should they do in order to achieve command so that their vows will never fail? What should they do in order to enter the Door of Total Retention? What should they do in order to acquire the transcendental powers to travel to Buddha Lands everywhere? What should they do in order to acquire the bold valor of a lion, with nothing to fear, unmovable by māras? What should they do in order to realize their holy Buddha nature and to accept and uphold the Dharma in the sūtras with understanding, not forgetting anything? What should they do in order to achieve self-fulfillment, free from sycophancy and flattery and unattached to the Three Realms of Existence? What should they do in order to be free from hindrances and to acquire the overall wisdom-knowledge, never deviating from the Buddha's intention? What should they do in order to win people's trust? What should they do in order to acquire the eight tones [of a Buddha] and sound 10,000 koṭi tones? What should they do in order to acquire the sublime appearance [of a Buddha]? What should they do in order to acquire the power of all-hearing? What should they do in order to acquire the bodhi-eye to see into the future? What should they do in order to acquire the Ten Powers and true wisdom? What should they do in order to see, in a single thought, Buddhas from worlds in the ten directions all standing before them? What should they do in order to know that the four appearances of every dharma have no reality? What should they do in order to see in this world innumerable Buddha Lands in the ten directions and to know the good and evil life-journeys of the people, gods, dragons, spirits, and wriggly insects in those lands? These are my questions. I pray that the Buddha will explain to me and resolve all my doubts."

The Buddha told Bhadrapāla, "Very good! Your questions are so comprehensive that they are beyond measure. You can ask these questions because you have acquired merit in your past lives under past Buddhas; because you have made offerings to Buddhas, delighted in the Dharma in the sūtras, observed your precepts, and lived in purity; because you have always begged for food, not accepting meal invitations, convened assemblies of Bodhisattvas, taught people to stop doing evil, and seen the equality of all; and because you have always had great lovingkindness and great compassion. Your merit is beyond measure."

The Buddha told Bhadrapāla, "There is a samādhi called Buddhas from Worlds in the Ten Directions All Standing before One. If you can do this dharma, you will have the answers to all your questions."

Bhadrapāla said to the Buddha, "I pray that You will pronounce it. What the Buddha will now pronounce is all-encompassing. It will give peace to [sentient beings in worlds in] the ten directions and provide great illumination to Bodhisattvas."

The Buddha told Bhadrapāla, "There is a samādhi called Concentrated Mind. Bodhisattvas should constantly guard, learn, and uphold it, never to follow other ways. Of all virtuous ways, this is the foremost one."

Chapter 2 - The Training

The Buddha told Bhadrapāla, "If Bodhisattvas aspire to attain this samādhi quickly, they should stand firm in great faith. Those who train themselves in accordance with the Dharma can attain this samādhi. Do not raise any doubts, even as slight as a hair. This Dharma of Concentrated Mind is also called the Bodhisattva Way Surpassing All Other Ways."

[Then the Buddha spoke in verse:]

With a single thought, believe in this Dharma.
Following the teachings heard, think only of one object.
Keep only one thought, ceasing all other thoughts.
Stand firm in your faith, without any doubts.
Progress energetically, never negligent or indolent.

Think of neither existence nor nonexistence, neither progress nor regress.
Think of neither front nor back, neither left nor right.
Think of neither nonexistence nor existence, neither far nor near.
Think of neither pain nor itch, neither hunger nor thirst.
Think of neither cold nor hot, neither pain nor pleasure.
Think of neither birth nor old age, neither illness nor death.
Think of neither body nor life, nor longevity.
Think of neither wealth nor poverty, neither nobility nor lowliness.
Think of neither sense objects nor desires.
Think of neither large nor small, neither long nor short.
Think of neither beauty nor ugliness.
Think of neither evil nor good, neither anger nor delight.
Think of neither rising nor sitting, neither proceeding nor stopping.
Think of neither the sūtras nor the Dharma.
Think of neither right nor wrong, neither grasping nor abandoning.
Think of neither perception nor consciousness.
Think of neither cessation nor continuation.
Think of neither emptiness nor true reality.
Think of neither heavy nor light, neither hard nor easy.
Think of neither deep nor shallow, neither broad nor narrow.
Think of neither father nor mother, neither wife nor children.
Think of neither friends nor acquaintances, neither love nor hatred.
Think of neither gain nor loss, neither success nor failure.
Think of neither clarity nor turbidity.

Cease all thoughts and be vigilant for a given period of time, never distracted.
Progress energetically, never negligent or indolent.
Do not count the years, nor feel tired in a single day.
Hold one thought, never losing it.
Avoid sleep and keep the mind alert.
Always live alone and avoid gatherings.
Shun evil ones but stay near beneficent friends.
Serve illuminated teachers, regarding them as Buddhas.
Hold firm your resolve, but always be gentle.
Meditate on the equality of all things.
Avoid your hometown and keep away from relatives.
Abandon love and desire and live in purity.
Meditate on that which is asaṁskṛta and cease desires.
Drop distracting thoughts and learn the way of concentration.
Gain wisdom from words in accord with dhyāna.

Remove the three afflictions and purify the six faculties.
Cease lustful pursuits and leave sensory pleasures behind.
Do not be greedy for wealth or accumulate things.
Know contentment in eating and do not covet flavors.
Take care never to eat any sentient being [dead or alive].
Dress in accordance with the Dharma, and do not be ornately adorned.
Do not tease others, nor be proud or arrogant.
Do not be conceited, nor elevate yourself.
Expound sūtras in accordance with the Dharma.
Understand that the body has always been like an illusion.
Do not be engrossed by the [five] aggregates, nor revel in the [twelve] sensory fields.
The five aggregates are like thieves, and the four domains are like snakes.
All are impermanent and all are unstable.
Recognize that there has never been an everlasting ruler in one,
Only convergence and divergence of causes and conditions.
Understand and know that nothing in existence is real.
Bestow lovingkindness and sympathy on all.
Give alms to the poor and relief to the unfortunate.

This is meditative concentration in the Bodhisattva Way, which
Will unfold the fundamental wisdom and elicit myriads of wisdom-knowledge.

The Buddha told Bhadrapāla, "One who trains in this way will attain the samādhi in which present Buddhas all stand before one. If, among bhikṣus, bhikṣuṇīs, upāsakas, and upāsikās, there are those who want to train according to this Dharma, they should fully observe their precepts and live alone in a place to think of Amitābha Buddha, who now is in the west. According to the teachings heard, one should also think of His land called Sukhāvatī, which is ten million koṭi Buddha Lands away from here. One should single-mindedly contemplate for one day and one night, or even seven days and seven nights. After the seventh day, one will see Him. By analogy, one sees things in a dream, not knowing whether it is day or night, indoors or outdoors, and one's sight is impervious to darkness or obstructions.

"Bhadrapāla, Bodhisattvas should do this contemplation. Then huge mountains, Sumeru Mountains, and dark places in the intervening Buddha Lands will all fall away, not posing any obstruction. These Bodhisattvas will see across without having the god-eye, hear across without having the god-ear, and travel to that Buddha Land without possessing transcendental powers. It is not that they have died here and been reborn there, but that they can sit here and see everything there.

"As an analogy, a man hears that in the kingdom of Vaiśālī lives a prostitute named Sumanā; a second man hears of a prostitute called Āmrapālī; and a third man hears that Utpalavarṇā has become a prostitute. These three men have never seen those three women, but they have heard of them and their lust is ignited. They all live in Rājagṛha, and they have lustful thoughts concurrently. Each of them goes, in a dream, to the woman he thinks of and spends the night with her. When they wake up, they all remember their own dreams."

The Buddha told Bhadrapāla, "The three women I have mentioned serve as an analogy. You may use this story to expound the sūtras, enabling others to unfold their wisdom so that they will arrive at the Ground of No Regress on the unsurpassed true Way. When they eventually attain Buddhahood, they all will be called Superb Enlightenment."

The Buddha said, "Bodhisattvas in this land can see Amitābha Buddha by thinking intently only of Him. When they see Him, they can ask, 'What Dharma should I uphold in order to be reborn in Your land?' Amitābha Buddha will reply, 'Those who wish to be reborn in my land should think of my name. If they can continue without rest, they will succeed in being reborn here.'"

The Buddha said, "Because of intent thinking, one will be reborn there. One should always think of Amitābha Buddha's body with the thirty-two physical marks and the eighty excellent characteristics, unequaled in its majesty, radiating vast bright light to illuminate everywhere. He teaches, in the assembly of Bodhisattvas and bhikṣus, that dharmas [in true reality] are empty and, therefore, indestructible. Why? Because indestructible are all dharmas, such as form, pain, itch, thinking, perception, birth, death, consciousness, spirit, earth, water, fire, wind, the human world, and the heaven world, including Great Brahma Heaven. By thinking of a Buddha, one attains the Samādhi of Emptiness."

The Buddha told Bhadrapāla, "Who have attained this Bodhisattva samādhi? My disciple Mahākāśyapa, Indraguṇa Bodhisattva, the god-son Good Virtue, and those who already know this samādhi, have attained it through training. Hence, Bhadrapāla, those who wish to see present Buddhas [in worlds] in the ten directions should think of their lands single-mindedly, without other thoughts. Then they will be able to see them. As an analogy, one travels to a distant land and thinks of family and kin in one's hometown. In a dream, one returns home, sees one's family and relatives, and enjoys talking to them. After waking, one tells one's dream to friends."

The Buddha said, "If Bodhisattvas hear of a Buddha's name and wish to see Him, they will be able to see Him by constantly thinking of Him and His land. For example, a bhikṣu visualizes before him the bones of a corpse, turning blue, white, red, or black. The colors are not brought by anyone, but are imagined by his mind. Likewise, by virtue of Buddhas' awesome spiritual power, Bodhisattvas who skillfully abide in this samādhi can see, as they wish, a Buddha of any land. Why? Because they are able to see Him by virtue of three powers: the power of Buddhas, the power of the samādhi, and the power of their own merit.

"As an analogy, a handsome young man dressed in fine clothes wants to see his own face. He can see his reflection by looking into a hand mirror, pure oil, clear water, or a crystal. Does his reflection come from the outside into the mirror, oil, water, or crystal?"

Bhadrapāla replied, "No, it does not. God of Gods, it is because of the clarity of the mirror, oil, water, or crystal, that the man can see his reflection. His reflection comes from neither the inside [of the medium] nor the outside."

The Buddha said, "Very good, Bhadrapāla. Because the medium is clear, the reflection is clear. Likewise, if one wishes to see a Buddha, one with a pure mind will be able to see. When one sees Him, one can ask questions, and He will give a reply. Having heard the teachings, one will be exultant and think: 'Where does this Buddha come from and where am I going? As I think of this Buddha, He comes from nowhere and I am going nowhere. As I think of the desire realm, the form realm, and the formless realm, these three realms are formed by my mind. I can see what I think of. The mind forms a Buddha for itself to see; the mind is the Buddha mind. As my mind forms a Buddha, my mind is the Buddha; my mind is the Tathāgata; my mind is my body.'

"Although the mind sees a Buddha, the mind neither knows itself nor sees itself. The mind with perceptions is saṁsāra; the mind without perceptions is nirvāṇa. Dharmas as perceived are not something pleasurable. They are empty thoughts, nothing real. This is what Bodhisattvas see as they abide in this samādhi."

Then the Buddha spoke in verse:

> The mind does not know itself; the mind does not see itself.
> The mind that fabricates perceptions is false; the mind without perceptions is nirvāṇa.
> Dharmas are not firm, only founded upon thinking.
> Those who see emptiness with this understanding are free from perceptions and expectations.

Chapter 3 - Four Things to Do

The Buddha continued, "There are four things through which Bodhisattvas can quickly attain this samādhi. First, have faith that no one can destroy. Second, make energetic progress that nothing can deter. Third, have wisdom-knowledge with which no one else's can compare. Fourth, always work under a beneficent teacher. These are the four things.

"There are another four things which will enable one to attain this samādhi quickly. First, do not engage in worldly thinking for three months, not even during a finger snap. Second, do not sleep for three months, not even during a finger snap. Third, do walking meditation for three months without any rest, except when eating and so forth. Fourth, expound sūtras to others, not expecting their offerings. These are the four things.

"There are another four things which will enable one to attain this samādhi quickly. First, take people to the Buddha. Second, gather people to have them hear the teachings. Third, have no jealousy. Fourth, have people learn the Buddha Way. These are the four things.

"There are another four things which will enable one to attain this samādhi quickly. First, construct Buddhas' images. Second, copy this sūtra on fine fabric. Third, teach the conceited ones to enter the Buddha Way. Fourth, always protect and uphold the Buddha Dharma. These are the four things."

Then the Buddha spoke in verse:

> Always believe and delight in the Buddha Dharma.
> Progress energetically to unfold profound wisdom.
> Disseminate and pronounce the Dharma to others.
> Guard against greed for offerings.
> Discard desires with good understanding.

Always think of Buddhas, who have awesome virtue,
And see and know dharmas in limitless diversity.
Past Buddhas, future Buddhas,
And present Buddhas, revered among men,
With no more afflictions to discharge,
Are golden in color and have superb physical marks.
They give firm teachings with wisdom beyond the ultimate.
Listen to this Dharma with an undistracted mind.
Forever discard the way of negligence and indolence.
Never bear malice toward others.
Respect teachers as you do Buddhas.
Take care not to have doubts about this sūtra,
Which is praised by all Buddhas.
Always construct and enshrine Buddhas' images.
Always persuade others to learn this Dharma
And practice it to attain this samādhi.

The Buddha told Bhadrapāla, "Those who want to learn this samādhi should respect their teachers, serve them, and make offerings to them, regarding them as Buddhas. Those who see their teachers as less than Buddhas will have difficulty attaining this samādhi. Bodhisattvas who respect beneficent teachers from whom they have learned this samādhi can advance. By virtue of Buddhas' awesome spiritual power, when they face the east, they will see a billion koṭi Buddhas. In the same way, they will see Buddhas [in worlds] in the ten directions. By analogy, one observes the night sky and sees myriads of stars. Bodhisattvas who wish to see present Buddhas all standing before them should respect beneficent teachers, not looking for their faults. Never negligent or indolent, they should fully train in giving alms, observing precepts, enduring adversity, and making energetic progress single-mindedly."

Chapter 4 - The Analogies

The Buddha told Bhadrapāla, "Bodhisattvas who have attained this samādhi but do not progress energetically are like those who are shipwrecked midway while crossing an immense ocean on a ship fully loaded with treasures. People in Jambudvīpa will all be in tremendous anguish, concerned about the loss of their treasures. If Bodhisattvas have heard this samādhi but do not learn it, gods will all sadly say, 'Our sūtra treasure is lost.'"

The Buddha said, "This samādhi is taught and praised by all Buddhas. Those who have heard this profound samādhi sūtra but do not copy, study, recite, or uphold it in accordance with the Dharma, are foolish. As an analogy, someone gives sandalwood incense to a fool, but he refuses to accept it, saying that the incense is impure. The giver says, 'This is sandalwood incense. Do not say that it is impure. If you smell it, you will know that it is fragrant. If you look at it, you will know that it is pure.' That fool closes his eyes, refusing to see or smell it."

The Buddha said, "Those who have heard this samādhi sūtra but refuse to accept it are as ignorant as that fool. They defiantly argue that everything in the world exists. Not having realized emptiness, they do not know nonexistence. Alleging that their views accord with the Dharma, they say in mockery, 'Does the Buddha have profound sūtras, as well as awesome spiritual powers?' They say these contradictory words: 'Are there bhikṣus in the world who are like Ānanda?'"

The Buddha said, "Those people walk away from the ones who uphold this samādhi sūtra. In twos and threes, they say to one another, 'What do these words mean? Where did they get these words? They must have gathered together to forge this sūtra. It is not pronounced by the Buddha.'"

The Buddha told Bhadrapāla, "As an analogy, a merchant shows a precious gem to a foolish farm boy. The boy asks, 'How much is it worth?' The merchant replies, 'If you place this gem in the dark, its light shines on the treasures that fill up that area.'"

The Buddha said, "The foolish boy still does not know that this gem is precious. He asks, 'Can its value be compared with that of a cow? I would rather trade it for a cow. If you agree, it is fine. If you disagree, forget it.' Bhadrapāla, Bodhisattvas who, having heard this samādhi, do not believe it and make contradictory remarks are like that foolish boy."

The Buddha said, "Bodhisattvas who, having heard this samādhi sūtra, believe, accept, and uphold it, and train accordingly, are supported by those around them, and have nothing to fear. Fully observing their precepts, they are brilliant, and their wisdom is profound. They disseminate the Dharma and tell people to teach others, who in turn teach others, enabling this samādhi sūtra to remain in the world for a long time."

The Buddha said, "Those fools have not made offerings or acquired merits in their past lives. They have instead elevated themselves, carrying on their slanderous and jealous ways. Greedy for wealth and benefits, they seek fame and reputation. They only want to make noisy remarks because they do not believe in profound sūtras. Having heard this samādhi sūtra, they neither believe nor appreciate it, nor learn it. Instead, they malign this sūtra, alleging that it is not pronounced by the Buddha."

The Buddha told Bhadrapāla, "Now I tell you this. If good men and good women give, as alms, treasures that fill up the Three-Thousand Large Thousandfold World, their merit is less than that of those who hear this samādhi sūtra and believe and delight in it. Their merit surpasses that of the almsgivers."

The Buddha told Bhadrapāla, "I now say these words, which will never change. Setting aside those who in future lives will follow evil teachers, if there are those who now have doubts about this samādhi I have pronounced, their merit is not worth mentioning even if in future lives they follow good teachers. These people will nevertheless defect [from good teachers] to work under evil teachers. Why is that they, having heard this samādhi, neither believe nor appreciate it, and choose not to learn it? They disbelieve because they have seen few Buddhas in the past and have little wisdom."

The Buddha told Bhadrapāla, "I have the foresight and foreknowledge of those who, having heard this samādhi sūtra, will not laugh in contempt, malign, doubt, or suddenly believe and suddenly disbelieve, but will delight in copying, learning, reciting, and upholding it. They not only have accumulated merit under one or two Buddhas, but have heard this samādhi sūtra from one hundred Buddhas. When they hear this samādhi sūtra in their future lives, if they copy, learn, recite, and uphold it even for only one day and one night, their merit will be beyond calculation. They will arrive at the spiritual level of avinivartanīya on their own as they wish."

The Buddha told Bhadrapāla, "Hear this analogy. Suppose someone crushes a Buddha Land into dust, then further pulverizes each dust particle into more particles. Is the number of dust particles produced from a Buddha Land very huge?"

Bhadrapāla replied, "Very huge, God of Gods."

The Buddha said, "Suppose a Bodhisattva takes all these dust particles and places each in a Buddha Land. He then takes treasures that fill up all these Buddha Lands to make an offering to Buddhas. His merit is very little in comparison with that of those who have heard this samādhi sūtra and have learned, copied, recited, and upheld it. Even if they explain this sūtra to others only for a short while, this merit is beyond calculation. Even greater is the merit of those who have fully attained this samādhi."

Then the Buddha spoke in verse:

If there are Bodhisattvas who seek merit,
They should pronounce and train in this samādhi.
Those who believe, delight in, and recite [this sūtra] without doubts
Have immeasurable merit.
Crushing one Buddha Land
Into dust particles,
One can give, as alms, treasures filling Buddha Lands that are
As numerous as dust particles.
Those who have heard this samādhi
Have merit greater than that of the almsgiver.
Their merit is beyond analogy.

I entrust you all to teach others
To progress energetically without negligence or indolence.
Those who recite and uphold this samādhi sūtra
Have already beheld 100,000 Buddhas.
As for the huge dread at the final moment of life,
Those abiding in this samādhi will have no fear.
Bhikṣus who train in this way have already seen me.
They will always follow the Buddha, never far from Him.
As the Buddha's words never change,
Bodhisattvas should always follow His teachings
To attain quickly samyak-saṁbodhi, the ocean of wisdom.

Chapter 5 - The Four Groups of Disciples

Bhadrapāla asked the Buddha, "Unrivaled God of Gods, if there are those who, after abandoning loves and desires to become bhikṣus, have heard of this samādhi, how should they learn, uphold, and practice it?"

The Buddha replied, "Those who, having abandoned loves and desires and become bhikṣus, aspire to learn this samādhi should observe their precepts with purity, without any flaw even as slight as a hair. To remain pure, they should dread the suffering of hell and refrain from sycophancy."

"What is a flaw in observing the precepts?"

The Buddha replied, "Seeking form."

"What is meant by seeking form?"

The Buddha replied, "If a person's motive of observing the precepts for self-restraint is to be reborn in the next life as a god or a Wheel-Turning King, such a wish for pleasures, loves, and desires is called a flaw in observing the precepts."

The Buddha told Bhadrapāla, "Those who protect their purity, fully observe their precepts, and do not adulate others, are always praised by the wise. They should give alms and progress energetically in accordance with the sūtras. Their resolve should be strong, and they should have great faith and sympathetic joy. Those who serve their teachers as they do Buddhas will attain this samādhi quickly. Those who are disrespectful and readily deceitful to their teachers will quickly lose this samādhi, though they have been training for a long time."

The Buddha told Bhadrapāla, "Bodhisattvas who have heard this samādhi from bhikṣus, bhikṣuṇīs, upāsakas, or upāsikās should regard them as Buddhas and respect them without intending sycophancy. Bodhisattvas should never be sycophantic but always be earnest. They should always delight in living alone. Though not begrudging even their lives, they should not hope for others to make requests of them. They should always beg for food, not accepting meal invitations. They should guard their moral integrity and be content with what they have. They should do walking meditation, not lying down to relax. Those who are learning this samādhi should abide by the teachings in the sūtras."

Bhadrapāla said to the Buddha, "Unrivaled God of Gods, it cannot be helped that, in future times, there will be negligent and indolent Bodhisattvas who, after hearing this samādhi, will not learn it diligently. However, there will be Bodhisattvas who aspire to learn this samādhi and progress energetically, and we will teach them to follow the Dharma in this sūtra."

The Buddha said, "Very good, Bhadrapāla, as I express my sympathetic joy,[2] so too Buddhas of the past, future, and present all express their sympathetic joy."

Then the Buddha spoke in verse:

Accept and uphold all that I say.
Always live alone and accumulate merit.
Guarding your moral integrity, do not join crowds.
Always beg for food, not accepting meal invitations.
Respect Dharma masters and regard them as Buddhas.
Avoid sleep and strengthen willpower.
Always progress energetically, without negligence or indolence.
Those who train in this way will attain this samādhi.

Bhadrapāla asked the Buddha, "If bhikṣuṇīs who seek the Bodhisattva Way aspire to learn this samādhi, what should they do?"

The Buddha replied, "Bhikṣuṇīs who seek this samādhi should not elevate themselves. They should be humble, neither self-dignifying nor self-aggrandizing. They should harbor neither jealousy nor anger, nor greed for wealth, benefits, or sense objects. They should protect their purity, even at the cost of their lives. They should always delight in the Dharma in the sūtras and learn as much as possible. They should discard greed, anger, and delusion, and they should not be greedy for fine clothing or adornments, such as necklaces of gems. Then they will be praised by the wise. They should respect beneficent teachers and regard them as Buddhas, without intending sycophancy."

Then the Buddha spoke in verse:

> If bhikṣuṇīs seek this samādhi,
> They should progress energetically, never negligent or indolent.
> Do not follow the mind of greed.
> Remove anger and self-glorification.
> Do not be arrogant, deceitful, or playful.
> Always act in earnest, standing firm in the one faith.
> Respect beneficent teachers and regard them as Buddhas.
> Those who train in this way will attain this samādhi.

Bhadrapāla asked the Buddha, "If upāsakas who are training for bodhi have heard of this samādhi and aspire to learn it, what should they do?"

The Buddha replied, "Upāsakas who aspire to learn this samādhi should faithfully observe the five precepts. They should neither drink alcohol nor have others drink alcohol. They should not be intimate with women or advise others to be intimate with women. They should not be attached to their wives, nor to men or other women. They should not have greed for wealth. They should constantly think of renouncing family life to become śramaṇas. They should regularly observe the eight precepts in a Buddhist temple. They should always remember to give alms. Because alms are given to benefit others, after giving alms, they should not think: 'I have gained merit.' They should have great lovingkindness and respect for their beneficent teachers. When they see bhikṣus who observe their precepts, they should not readily talk about their faults. Having carried out these actions, they should learn to abide in this samādhi."

Then the Buddha spoke in verse:

> Upāsakas who aspire to learn this samādhi
> Should observe the five precepts without breach or flaw.
> They should always think of becoming śramaṇas,
> Not greedy for wives, riches, or sense objects.
> They should regularly observe the eight precepts in a Buddhist temple.
> Neither conceited nor contemptuous of others,
> Their minds do not expect glory, nor think of wants.
> They should carry out the Dharma in the sūtras, without a sycophantic mind.
> Abandoning stinginess and greed, they should give generous alms.

They should always respect bhikṣus and make offerings to them.
They should resolve to take the one training without being negligent or indolent.
Those who are learning this samādhi should act in this way.

Bhadrapāla asked the Buddha, "If upāsikās who have heard of this samādhi aspire to learn it, what should they do?"

The Buddha replied, "If upāsikās aspire to learn this samādhi, they should observe the five precepts and willingly take refuge in the Three Jewels. What are these three? They should take refuge in the Buddha, the Dharma, and the Saṅgha, never to follow other paths. They should not make obeisance to gods, nor worship spirits. They should not select auspicious dates. They should not be playful or indulgent, or think of sensory pleasures. Subjugating the mind of greed, they should remember to give alms. Delighting in hearing the sūtras, they should remember to study hard and respect beneficent teachers. Their minds should be vigilant, never negligent or indolent. They should offer a sitting-down meal to bhikṣus or bhikṣuṇīs who pass by."

Then the Buddha spoke in verse:

Upāsikās who aspire to learn this samādhi
Should observe the five precepts without breach or flaw.
They should serve beneficent teachers and regard them as Buddhas.
They should not worship gods, nor idolize spirits.
They should stop killing, stealing, and feeling jealous.
They should never say divisive words to incite conflict among people.
They should be neither stingy nor greedy, but always remember to give alms.
They should not publicize the evil, but always praise the good.
They should refrain from sycophancy and sexual misconduct.
They should be humble, not self-aggrandizing.
They should respectfully serve bhikṣus and bhikṣuṇīs.
Those who train in this way will attain this samādhi.

Chapter 6 - Support and Protection

The eight Bodhisattvas—Bhadrapāla, Ralinnāga, Gaujata, Naradatta, Suṣama, Mahāsusaha, Indrada, and Harandha—having heard the Buddha's words, greatly rejoiced. They offered the Buddha 500 fine cotton garments and precious gems, and joyfully served the Buddha.

The Buddha told Ānanda, "Bhadrapāla and seven others are teachers to the 500 people who are with them. They will uphold the true Dharma, and teach and transform these people accordingly. Then these people will all be joyful, and their minds will be free from desires."

At that time these 500 people joined their palms, standing before the Buddha. Bhadrapāla asked the Buddha, "How many things should Bodhisattvas do in order to attain this samādhi quickly?"

The Buddha replied, "There are four things. First, do not believe in other paths. Second, cease love and desire. Third, carry out the pure ways. Fourth, have no greed. These are the four. Those who do them will acquire 500 benefits in their present lives. For example, bhikṣus with the mind of lovingkindness will never be killed or harmed by poison, knives or other weapons, fire, or water. Even when a kalpa is ending with the world in flames, if they fall into that fire, it will extinguish, just like a small fire put out by a massive amount of water. Whether kings, thieves, water, or fire, whether dragons, yakṣas, serpents, lions, tigers, or wolves, whether forest phantoms, hungry ghosts, or kumbhāṇḍas, those who, targeting Bodhisattvas abiding in this samādhi, desire to bewitch them, kill them, rob them of their robes and bowls, or destroy their meditation and mindfulness, will never succeed. Unless such misfortune is brought about by their past karmas, things will be as I say, not different."

The Buddha said, "Those who uphold this samādhi will not have ailments of the eye, ear, nose, mouth, or body, nor will they have anxiety in their minds, except for misfortune in response to karmas in their past lives."

The Buddha said, "All gods, dragons, asuras, yakṣas, garuḍas, kiṁnaras, and mahoragas, as well as humans and nonhumans, will acclaim these Bodhisattvas. They all will support, protect, and serve these Bodhisattvas, and make offering to them. As they regard these Bodhisattvas with respect and wish to see them, so too will Buddha-Bhagavāns. If there are sūtras that these Bodhisattvas did not hear or uphold before, they will obtain them because of the awesome power of this samādhi. If they do not obtain them during the day, they will receive them in a night dream."

The Buddha told Bhadrapāla, "I can describe, for one kalpa after another, the merit of those who abide in this samādhi, but still cannot cover them all. I have only briefly mentioned a few essential ones."

Chapter 7 - Sympathetic Joy

The Buddha told Bhadrapāla, "Bodhisattvas can think four thoughts to kindle their sympathetic joy in order to attain this samādhi. First, past Buddhas [when they were Bodhisattvas] attained this samādhi because of their sympathetic joy, who then attained, through self-realization, anuttara-samyak-saṁbodhi, with full wisdom-knowledge. Second, innumerable present Buddhas [in worlds] in the ten directions [when they were Bodhisattvas] have attained this samādhi because of their sympathetic joy kindled by thinking these four thoughts. Third, future Buddhas [as present Bodhisattvas] will attain this samādhi because they also think these four thoughts to kindle their sympathetic joy. Fourth, I too have sympathetic joy.[3]"

The Buddha told Bhadrapāla, "In regard to the four thoughts to kindle one's sympathetic joy, I will use a few analogies. A person walks during his 100-year lifespan without rest, and he walks faster than the wind. Can you figure out the area he has covered?"

Bhadrapāla replied, "No one can calculate this. Only the Buddha's disciple Śāriputra and Bodhisattvas at the spiritual level of avinivartanīya can figure this out."

The Buddha said, "Therefore, as I say to Bodhisattvas, if there are good men and good women who give away, as alms, treasures that fill up the area traversed by that person, their merit is less than that from hearing this samādhi and thinking the four thoughts to kindle sympathetic joy. This merit is a billion koṭi times more than that from giving alms. Know that the merit acquired from having sympathetic joy is great."

The Buddha told Bhadrapāla, "Far back, incalculable asaṁkhyeya kalpas ago, in a remote place lived a Buddha called Siṁhamati, the Tathāgata, Arhat, Samyak-Saṁbuddha, Unsurpassed One, Tamer of Men, Teacher to Gods and Men, Buddha the World-Honored One. At that time the continent of Jambudvīpa was 180,000 koṭi lis in length and width. There were 6,400,000 kingdoms, prosperous and densely populated. There was a great kingdom called Bhadrakara, ruled by a Wheel-Turning King named Vaiścin. He went to that Buddha, made obeisance, and stepped back to sit on one side. That Buddha knew his intention and pronounced this samādhi sūtra to him. Having heard it, the king, with sympathetic joy, showered jewels upon that Buddha as he thought: 'I should transfer this merit to people [in worlds] in the ten directions to give them peace.'

"After Siṁhamati Buddha entered parinirvāṇa, the king Vaiścin died. He was reborn in his own family and became the crown prince called Brahmada. At that time there was a bhikṣu called Jewel, who was pronouncing this samādhi sūtra to his four groups of disciples. Brahmada heard of it, and sympathetic joy arose in him. Exuberantly he took jewels worth hundreds of koṭis of great price and showered them upon that bhikṣu, and also offered him fine clothing. Resolved to seek the Buddha Way, together with 1,000 people, Brahmada became a śramaṇa under that bhikṣu. To hear this samādhi sūtra, he and the 1,000 people served their teacher tirelessly for 8,000 years. Because of hearing this samādhi sūtra, though only once, and thinking the four thoughts that kindled his sympathetic joy, he acquired excellent knowledge. For this reason, he subsequently saw 68,000 Buddhas. From each of these Buddhas, he heard this samādhi sūtra again. Through self-realization, he has become a Buddha called Tilavida, the Samyak-Saṁbuddha, Unsurpassed One, Tamer of Men, Teacher to Gods and Humans, Buddha the World-Honored One. Those 1,000 bhikṣus have also attained samyak-saṁbodhi, and all of them are called Tilajuṣa. They have taught innumerable people to seek Buddha bodhi."

The Buddha asked Bhadrapāla, "After hearing this samādhi sūtra, who would not have sympathetic joy? Who would rather not learn, uphold, and recite it, and explain it to others?"

The Buddha said, "Those who abide in this samādhi will quickly attain Buddhahood. The merit acquired from only hearing it is incalculable. Much greater is the merit acquired from learning and upholding it. One should seek this samādhi teaching even if it is 100 or 1,000 lis away. How can one not seek to learn it when it is close by? Those who, having heard of this samādhi, aspire to learn and uphold it, should serve their teachers for ten years, paying visits and making offerings, which they dare not use for themselves. They should follow their teachers' teachings and always remember their kindness."

The Buddha said, "Therefore, I tell you this. If one travels 4,000 lis to hear this samādhi sūtra, one's merit is incalculable even if one fails to hear it. Why? Because, with such motivation to make energetic progress, one will attain Buddhahood through self-realization."

Chapter 8 - Utmost Sincerity

The Buddha said, "In the distant past, there was a Buddha called Sacanama, the Samyak-Saṁbuddha, Unsurpassed One, Teacher to Gods and Men, Buddha the World-Honored One. At that time there lived a bhikṣu named Halan. After that Buddha entered parinirvāṇa, that bhikṣu upheld this samādhi sūtra. At that time I was a king, in the kṣatriya caste, and I heard of this samādhi sūtra in a dream. Upon waking, I immediately went to that bhikṣu and became a śramaṇa under him. For the sake of hearing this samādhi sūtra, I served that teacher for 36,000 years. However, I was unable to hear it because time and again māra matters arose."

The Buddha told the bhikṣus, bhikṣuṇīs, upāsakas, and upāsikās: "Hence I tell you all to learn this samādhi as soon as possible, never to lose it. You should properly serve your teacher and uphold this samādhi sūtra for one kalpa, 100 kalpas, or even 100,000 kalpas, never negligent or indolent. You should stay with a beneficent teacher and never leave him. Do not begrudge food, drink, life-supporting goods, clothing, bedding, beds, or precious jewels. If you do not have any, you should beg for food and offer it to your teacher. Work tirelessly to attain this samādhi. You should even cut off your own flesh to offer to your beneficent teacher, not to mention giving precious things. Serve your beneficent teacher, like a slave serving a great family. Those who seek this samādhi should act in this way.

"Having attained this samādhi, one should abide in it and always remember the kindness of one's teacher. This samādhi sūtra is hard to encounter. There are those who seek for 100,000 kalpas but cannot even hear the name of this samādhi. How could anyone who has learned it not progress diligently? If there are those who give, as alms, treasures filling Buddha Lands as numerous as the sands of the Ganges, they cannot be compared with one who is learning this samādhi or one who has attained it, is progressing energetically, and is teaching it to others."

The Buddha told Bhadrapāla, "If there are those who aspire to learn this samādhi, they need to have sympathetic joy in order to succeed. Students are enabled to learn it by virtue of Buddhas' awesome spiritual power. They should copy this samādhi sūtra on fine fabric, consecrate the copies with the Buddha Seal, and make offerings. What is the Buddha Seal? It refers to freedom from deluded states—no greed, no quest, no perception, no attachment, no wish for rebirth, no intended life form for rebirth, no grasping, no concern, no abiding, no obstruction, no bondage, no existence, no desire, no birth, no death, no destruction, and no decay. This seal is the essence and the root of bodhi. It is beyond Arhats and Pratyekabuddhas, not to mention fools. This seal is the Buddha Seal."

The Buddha said, "As I now pronounce this samādhi, 1,800 koṭi gods, asuras, spirits, dragons, and their retinues have entered the holy stream, becoming Srotāpannas, and 800 bhikṣus and 500 bhikṣuṇīs have become Arhats. Ten thousand Bodhisattvas have attained this samādhi, realizing that dharmas have no birth. Twelve thousand Bodhisattvas have attained the spiritual level of no regress."

The Buddha told the bhikṣus Śāriputra and Maudgalyāyana, as well as Bhadrapāla Bodhisattva and others: "I sought bodhi for uncountable kalpas, and I now have attained Buddhahood. I uphold this sūtra and entrust it to you all. Study and recite it, uphold and guard it, and do not forget or lose it. If there are those who aspire to learn it, you should teach them completely in accordance with the Dharma. You should pronounce it fully to those who wish to hear it."

After the Buddha pronounced this sūtra, Bhadrapāla Bodhisattva and the bhikṣus Śāriputra, Maudgalyāyana, and Ānanda, as well as gods, asuras, dragons, spirits, and their retinues, greatly rejoiced. They made obeisance to the Buddha and departed.

Notes

1. Bhadrapāla Bodhisattva, the interlocutor in this sūtra, is the first of the sixteen Upright Ones in the *Amitāyus Sūtra* (Sūtra 1). He also appears in the *Mahāyāna Sūtra of Consciousness Revealed* and the *Sūtra of the Great Dharma Drum* (Rulu 2012a, Sūtras 13 and 14), in which his Sanskrit name is translated by meaning as Worthy Protector.

2. Here, the Chinese phrase is actually "zhuqi huanxi" (助其歡喜), which means "aid them to rejoice." This phrase is found in another version of this sūtra (T13n0418), also translated by Lokakṣema (支婁迦讖, or 支讖, 147–?). However, in the later version of this sūtra (T13n0416), translated by Jñānagupta (闍那崛多, 523–600), used instead is the phrase "suixi" (隨喜), which means "express sympathetic joy." This is the fifth of the ten great actions taught by Samantabhadra Bodhisattva (Sūtra 5), and it appears in many other sūtras. For consistency, all cases of "aid them to rejoice" are translated as "express sympathetic joy."

3. The corresponding passage in text 416, fascicle 5, chapter 15, better explains the fourth thought: "I now share the merit acquired from my sympathetic joy with all sentient beings so that we all have sympathetic joy and will acquire this samādhi, hear much of the Dharma, and attain anuttara-samyak-saṁbodhi" (T13n0416, 0894b22–24).

8 文殊師利所說摩訶般若波羅蜜經
Sūtra of Mahā-Prajñā-Pāramitā Pronounced by Mañjuśrī Bodhisattva

Translated from Sanskrit into Chinese in the Southern Liang Dynasty
by
The Tripiṭaka Master Mandra from Funan

Fascicle 1 (of 2)

Thus I have heard:

At one time the Buddha was staying in the Anāthapiṇḍika Garden of Jetavana Park in the city kingdom of Śrāvastī, together with 1,000 great bhikṣus and 10,000 Bodhisattva-Mahāsattvas. These great Bodhisattvas are all majestically adorned [with merit and wisdom] and standing on the Ground of No Regress. Among them were Maitreya Bodhisattva, Mañjuśrī Bodhisattva, Unimpeded Eloquence Bodhisattva, and Never Abandoning the Mission Bodhisattva.

Bodhisattva-Mahāsattva Mañjuśrī the Youth came at dawn from his place to the place where the Buddha was and stood outside. Then great voice-hearers, such as the venerable Śāriputra, Pūrṇa-Maitrāyaṇīputra, Mahāmaudgalyāyana, Mahākāśyapa, Mahākātyāyana, and Mahākauṣṭhila, also came from their respective places to the place where the Buddha was and stood outside.

The Buddha knew that the assembly had convened. The Tathāgata came out of His dwelling, arranged His seat, and sat down. He asked Śāriputra, "Why are you standing outside this morning?"

Śāriputra replied to the Buddha, "World-Honored One, Bodhisattva Mañjuśrī the Youth arrived first and stood outside the door. I actually arrived later."

Then the World-Honored One asked Mañjuśrī, "You were the first to arrive here. Did you wish to see the Tathāgata?"

Mañjuśrī replied to the Buddha, "Indeed, World-Honored One, I did come here to see the Tathāgata. Why? Because I delight in making the right observation to benefit sentient beings. I observe the Tathāgata by the appearances of true suchness: never changing, never moving, never acting, no birth, no death, neither existent nor nonexistent, neither somewhere nor nowhere, neither in the past, present, or future, nor not in the past, present, or future, neither dual nor non-dual, neither pure nor impure. Through appearances such as these, I correctly observe the Tathāgata to benefit sentient beings."

The Buddha told Mañjuśrī, "If one can see the Tathāgata as such, one's mind will neither grasp nor not grasp, neither accumulate nor not accumulate."

Śāriputra said to Mañjuśrī, "It is rare for anyone to see the Tathāgata in the way you describe. As you observe the Tathāgata for the sake of all sentient beings, your mind does not grasp the appearances of sentient beings. As you teach all sentient beings to head for nirvāṇa, [your mind] does not grasp the appearance of nirvāṇa. As you manifest such great majesty for all sentient beings, your mind does not see the appearance of majesty."

Then Bodhisattva-Mahāsattva Mañjuśrī the Youth said to Śāriputra, "Indeed, indeed, it is just as you say. Although I activate the mind of great majesty for all sentient beings, I never see the appearances of sentient beings. Although I am adorned with great majesty for all sentient beings, their realm neither increases nor decreases. Suppose a Buddha stays in a world for a kalpa or over a kalpa. Although each world has only one Buddha, there are as many Buddhas as the innumerable, boundless sands of the Ganges. Suppose they all pronounce the Dharma day and night for a kalpa or over a kalpa, never resting their minds. Suppose each of them delivers as many sentient beings as the innumerable sands of the Ganges, enabling them to enter nirvāṇa. Yet the realm of sentient beings neither increases nor decreases. This applies to all Buddha Lands in the ten directions. All Buddhas pronounce the Dharma to teach and transform sentient beings, each delivering as many sentient beings as the innumerable sands of the Ganges, enabling them to enter nirvāṇa. Yet the realm of sentient beings neither increases nor decreases. Why not? Because the definite appearances of sentient beings can never be captured. Hence, the realm of sentient beings neither increases nor decreases."

Śāriputra then asked Mañjuśrī, "Given that the realm of sentient beings neither increases nor decreases, why do Bodhisattvas always pronounce the Dharma to sentient beings, as they seek anuttara-samyak-saṁbodhi?"

Mañjuśrī replied, "Because the appearances of sentient beings are empty, there are neither Bodhisattvas seeking anuttara-samyak-saṁbodhi nor sentient beings to whom they pronounce the Dharma. Why not? Because I say that, in all dharmas, not a single dharma can be captured."

The Buddha asked Mañjuśrī, "If sentient beings do not truly exist, why do you speak of sentient beings and their realm?"

Mañjuśrī replied, "The appearance of the realm of sentient beings is just like that of the realm of Buddhas."

"Is there a measure for the realm of sentient beings?"

"The measure for the realm of sentient beings is just like that for the realm of Buddhas," he replied.

The Buddha next asked, "Is there a place for the measure of the realm of sentient beings?"

He replied, "The measure of the realm of sentient beings is inconceivable."

The Buddha next asked, "Does the appearance of the realm of sentient beings abide [in something]?"

He replied, "Open sky does not abide, nor do sentient beings."

The Buddha asked Mañjuśrī, "If one practices prajñā-pāramitā in this way, how does one abide in prajñā-pāramitā?"

Mañjuśrī replied, "Not abiding in dharmas is abiding in prajñā-pāramitā."

The Buddha next asked Mañjuśrī, "Why is not abiding in dharmas called abiding in prajñā-pāramitā?"

Mañjuśrī replied, "Not abiding in appearances is abiding in prajñā-pāramitā."

The Buddha next asked Mañjuśrī, "As one abides in prajñā-pāramitā in this way, do one's roots of goodness increase or decrease?"

Mañjuśrī replied, "As one abides in prajñā-pāramitā in this way, one's roots of goodness neither increase nor decrease, all dharmas neither increase nor decrease, and the nature and appearance of prajñā-pāramitā neither increase nor decrease. World-Honored One, practicing prajñā-pāramitā in this way, one neither abandons the dharma of ordinary beings nor grasps the dharma of sages and holy beings. Why not? Because as one practices prajñā-pāramitā, one does not see any dharma that can be grasped or abandoned. Moreover, practicing prajñā-pāramitā in this way, one sees neither saṁsāra to dislike nor nirvāṇa to like. Why not? Because one does not even see saṁsāra, much less dislike it, and because one does not even see nirvāṇa, much less like it. Practicing prajñā-pāramitā in this way, one sees neither afflictions to abandon nor merits to grasp. One's mind neither increases nor decreases with respect to all dharmas. Why not? Because one sees neither increase nor decrease in the dharma realm. World-Honored One, training in this way is called practicing prajñā-pāramitā.

"World-Honored One, seeing neither birth nor death of dharmas is practicing prajñā-pāramitā. World-Honored One, seeing neither increase nor decrease of dharmas is practicing prajñā-pāramitā. World-Honored One, wishing for nothing and seeing no dharma appearance to seek are practicing prajñā-pāramitā.

"World-Honored One, one sees nothing beautiful or ugly, high or low, to grasp or abandon. Why? Dharmas are neither beautiful nor ugly because they are free from appearances. Dharmas are neither high nor low because they are equal in dharma nature. Dharmas are beyond being grasped or abandoned because they abide in true reality. This is the way to practice prajñā-pāramitā."

The Buddha asked Mañjuśrī, "Is the Buddha Dharma not superb?"

Mañjuśrī replied, "I do not see any superb appearance in dharmas. It can be verified, as through the Tathāgata's self-realization, that all dharmas are empty."

The Buddha told Mañjuśrī, "Indeed! Indeed! The Tathāgata has attained the perfect enlightenment through self-realization of the emptiness of dharmas."

Mañjuśrī responded to the Buddha, "World-Honored One, in the dharma of emptiness, is there superbness that can be captured?"

The Buddha praised, "Very good! Very good! Mañjuśrī, what you say is the true Dharma!"

The Buddha next asked Mañjuśrī, "Is *anuttara* called the Buddha Dharma?"

Mañjuśrī replied, "As the Buddha says, *anuttara* is called the Buddha Dharma. Why? Because that no dharma can be captured is called *anuttara*."

Mañjuśrī continued, "Whoever practices prajñā-pāramitā in this way is not called a Dharma vessel [which is intended to capture things]. Not seeing dharmas that can transform ordinary beings, not seeing the Buddha Dharma, and not seeing enhancing dharmas, are practicing prajñā-pāramitā. Furthermore, World-Honored One, while practicing prajñā-pāramitā, one does not see any dharma that can be differentiated or contemplated."

The Buddha asked Mañjuśrī, "Do you not contemplate the Buddha Dharma?"

Mañjuśrī replied, "No, World-Honored One, in my contemplation, I do not see the Buddha Dharma. Nor do I differentiate dharmas into ordinary beings, voice-hearers, and Pratyekabuddhas. Hence it is called the unsurpassed Buddha Dharma. Moreover, seeing neither the appearances of ordinary beings nor the appearances of the Buddha Dharma, nor the definite appearances of dharmas, is practicing prajñā-pāramitā. While practicing prajñā-pāramitā, one does not see the desire realm, the form realm, the formless realm, or the nirvāṇa realm. Why not? Because not seeing dharmas with the appearance of extinction is practicing prajñā-pāramitā. Seeing neither the one giving kindness nor the other requiting kindness is practicing prajñā-pāramitā. Contemplating the appearances of subject and object without differentiation is practicing prajñā-pāramitā. Seeing neither the Buddha Dharma to grasp nor the dharma of ordinary beings to abandon is practicing prajñā-pāramitā. Seeing neither the dharma of ordinary beings to end nor the Buddha Dharma to grasp, yet still coming to know it in one's mind, is practicing prajñā-pāramitā."

The Buddha praised Mañjuśrī, "Very good! Very good! You can describe so well the appearances of the profound prajñā-pāramitā, which is the Dharma Seal that Bodhisattva-Mahāsattvas are learning. Even voice-hearers, of whom some are still learning and others have nothing more to learn, and Pratyekabuddhas should train for their bodhi fruit without separating from this Dharma Seal."

The Buddha told Mañjuśrī, "If those who have heard this Dharma are not shocked or terrified, they must have already planted their roots of goodness not just under thousands of Buddhas, but even under billions of koṭis of Buddhas. Then they are able not to be shocked or terrified by this profound prajñā-pāramitā."

Mañjuśrī said to the Buddha, "I now will further explain the meaning of prajñā-pāramitā."

The Buddha said, "Speak, then."

[Mañjuśrī said] "World-Honored One, while practicing prajñā-pāramitā, one should not see whether one should abide in a dharma, nor should one see whether an object has an appearance that can be grasped or abandoned. Why not? Because Tathāgatas do not see the states of dharmas. They do not even see the states of Buddhas, much less those of voice-hearers, Pratyekabuddhas, or ordinary beings. One should not grasp appearances, whether conceivable or inconceivable. By not seeing various dharma appearances, one will realize, on one's own, the inconceivable dharma of emptiness. All Bodhisattvas who train in this way must have made offerings to innumerable billions of koṭis of Buddhas, under whom [they must have] planted their roots of goodness. Consequently, they are able not to be shocked or terrified by this profound prajñā-pāramitā. Moreover, as one practices prajñā-pāramitā, seeing neither bondage nor liberation, nor distinctions among ordinary beings or even among the Three Vehicles, is practicing prajñā-pāramitā."

The Buddha asked Mañjuśrī, "To how many Buddhas have you made offerings?"

Mañjuśrī replied, "Buddhas and I have illusory appearances, which are neither recipients nor givers."

The Buddha asked Mañjuśrī, "Can you not now abide in the Buddha Vehicle?"

Mañjuśrī replied, "I do not see a single dharma in my contemplation. How should I abide in the Buddha Vehicle?"

The Buddha asked, "Mañjuśrī, have you not acquired the Buddha Vehicle?"

Mañjuśrī replied, "The Buddha Vehicle is only a name, which can be neither captured nor seen. How can I acquire it?"

The Buddha asked, "Mañjuśrī, have you acquired the unimpeded wisdom-knowledge?"

Mañjuśrī replied, "I am the unimpeded. How can the unimpeded acquire the unimpeded?"

The Buddha asked, "Do you sit in a bodhimaṇḍa?"

Mañjuśrī replied, "None of the Tathāgatas sits in a bodhimaṇḍa. How should I alone sit in a bodhimaṇḍa? I presently see that dharmas abide in true reality."

The Buddha asked, "What is called true reality?"

Mañjuśrī replied, "The view that one has a self is true reality." [1]

The Buddha asked, "Why is the view that one has a self true reality?"

Mañjuśrī replied, "Taking this view as an appearance of true suchness, which is neither real nor unreal, neither coming nor going, with neither a self nor no self, is called true reality."

Śāriputra said to the Buddha, "World-Honored One, those who can come to a definite understanding of this meaning are called Bodhisattvas. Why? Because they have learned the appearances of this profound prajñā-pāramitā, and their minds are not shocked, not terrified, not baffled, and not regretful."

Maitreya Bodhisattva said to the Buddha, "World-Honored One, those who have learned all the dharma appearances of prajñā-pāramitā are near a Buddha's seat. Why? Because Tathāgatas are presently aware of these dharma appearances."

Mañjuśrī Bodhisattva said to the Buddha, "World-Honored One, if those who have heard this profound prajñā-pāramitā can be not shocked, not terrified, not baffled, and not regretful, we should know that they in effect see Buddhas."

Then the upāsikā No Appearance said to the Buddha, "World-Honored One, dharmas, such as ordinary beings, voice-hearers, Pratyekabuddhas, Bodhisattvas, and Buddhas, have no appearances. Therefore, upon hearing prajñā-pāramitā, we are not astonished, not terrified, not baffled, and not regretful. Why not? Because dharmas have never had any appearances."

The Buddha told Śāriputra, "If good men and good women, having heard this profound prajñā-pāramitā, can come to resoluteness in their minds, not shocked, not terrified, not baffled, and not regretful, know that they stand on the Ground of No Regress. If those who have heard this profound prajñā-pāramitā are not shocked, not terrified, not baffled, and not regretful, but believe, accept, appreciate, and listen tirelessly, they have in effect achieved dāna-pāramitā, śīla-pāramitā, kṣānti-pāramitā, vīrya-pāramitā, dhyāna-pāramitā, and prajñā-pāramitā. Moreover, they can reveal and explicate [the teachings] to others and can have them train accordingly."

The Buddha asked Mañjuśrī, "In your opinion, what is meant by attaining anuttara-samyak-saṁbodhi and by abiding in anuttara-samyak-saṁbodhi?"

Mañjuśrī replied, "I have no anuttara-samyak-saṁbodhi to attain, nor do I abide in the Buddha Vehicle. Then how should I attain anuttara-samyak-saṁbodhi? What I describe is only the appearance of bodhi."

The Buddha praised Mañjuśrī, "Very good! Very good! You have so skillfully explained the meaning of this profound Dharma. You have long planted your roots of goodness under past Buddhas, training with purity in the Brahma way of life according to the dharma of no appearance."

Mañjuśrī replied, "If one sees appearances, then one can speak of no appearance. I now see neither appearance nor no appearance. How can I be said to train in the Brahma way of life according to the dharma of no appearance?"

The Buddha asked Mañjuśrī, "Do you see voice-hearer precepts?"

"Yes, I see them."

The Buddha asked, "How do you see them?"

Mañjuśrī replied, "I do not hold the view of ordinary beings, the view of holy beings, the view of those who are still learning, or the view of those who have nothing more to learn. Nor do I hold the great view, the small view, the view to overcome, or the view not to overcome. I hold neither a view nor its opposite view."

Śāriputra said to Mañjuśrī, "This is how you view the Voice-Hearer Vehicle. How do you view the Buddha Vehicle?"

Mañjuśrī said, "I do not see the dharma of bodhi. Nor do I see anyone training for bodhi or attaining bodhi."

Śāriputra asked Mañjuśrī, "What is called Buddha? How does one observe a Buddha?"

Mañjuśrī asked, "What is self?"

Śāriputra replied, "Self is only a name, and the appearance of a name is empty."

Mañjuśrī said, "Indeed! Indeed! Just as self is only a name, so too Buddha is only a name. Realizing the emptiness of a name is bodhi. One should seek bodhi without using names. The appearance of bodhi is free from words. Why? Because words and bodhi are both empty.

"Furthermore, Śāriputra, you ask me what is called Buddha and how one should observe a Buddha. That which has neither birth nor death, neither names nor appearances, and is neither coming nor going, is called Buddha. As one observes the true reality of one's own body, in the same way one observes a Buddha. Only the wise can understand that this is called observing a Buddha."

Then Śāriputra said to the Buddha, "World-Honored One, prajñā-pāramitā as pronounced by Mañjuśrī is not understandable or knowable to novice Bodhisattvas."

Mañjuśrī said, "Not only novice Bodhisattvas cannot know it, but even riders of the Two Vehicles who have accomplished their undertaking [for Arhatship or Pratyekabuddhahood] cannot understand or know it. No one can know the Dharma expounded in this way. Why not? Because the appearance of bodhi cannot be known through such dharmas as seeing, hearing, capturing, thinking, speaking, or listening. Bodhi is empty and silent in nature and appearance, with no birth, no death, no attaining, no knowing, no shape, and no form. How can there be an attainer of bodhi?"

Śāriputra asked Mañjuśrī, "Has not the Buddha, in the dharma realm, attained anuttara-samyak-saṁbodhi?"

Mañjuśrī replied, "No, Śāriputra. Why not? Because the World-Honored One is the dharma realm. Verifying the dharma realm by means of the dharma realm would be a contradiction. Śāriputra, the appearance of the dharma realm is bodhi. Why? Because in the dharma realm sentient beings have no appearances, as all dharmas are empty. The emptiness of all dharmas is bodhi, which is non-dual and free from differentiation. Śāriputra, without differentiation, there is no knower. Without a knower, there are no words. Without words, there is neither existence nor nonexistence, neither knowing nor not knowing. This is true for all dharmas. Why? Because dharmas cannot be identified by places, which imply a definite nature. For example, the sinful appearance of the [five] rebellious acts is inconceivable. Why? Because the true reality of dharmas is indestructible. Thus, the sin of committing a rebellious act has no self-essence. True reality neither is reborn in heaven nor falls into hell, nor does it enter nirvāṇa. Why not? Because all karmic conditions abide in true reality, which is neither coming nor going, neither cause nor effect. Why? Because the dharma realm has no edge, neither front nor back. Therefore, Śāriputra, [in true reality] pure spiritual trainees do not enter nirvāṇa, and bhikṣus with grave sins do not fall into hell. They are neither worthy nor unworthy of offerings, neither ending nor not ending their afflictions. Why not? Because [in emptiness] all dharmas abide in equality."

Śāriputra asked, "What is called the unwavering Endurance in the Realization of the No Birth of Dharmas?"

Mañjuśrī replied, "Not seeing the appearance of birth or death in even a speck of dharma is called the unwavering Endurance in the Realization of the No Birth of Dharmas."

Śāriputra asked, "Who is called a bhikṣu who does not overcome?"

Mañjuśrī replied, "An Arhat, who has no more afflictions to discharge, is the one who does not overcome. Why? Because, having eradicated all of his afflictions, an Arhat has nothing to overcome. Those who take fallible mental actions are called ordinary beings. Why? Because ordinary beings do not act in accord with the dharma realm and are therefore called the fallible ones."

Śāriputra said, "Very good! Very good! You now have well explained to me the meaning of an Arhat, who has ended his afflictions and the discharges thereof."

Mañjuśrī said, "Indeed! Indeed! I am a true Arhat, who has ended his afflictions. Why? Because I have crushed the desire for the Voice-Hearer Vehicle and the desire for the Pratyekabuddha Vehicle. For this reason, I am called an Arhat, who has ended his afflictions."

The Buddha asked Mañjuśrī, "When a Bodhisattva sits in a bodhimaṇḍa, does he attain anuttara-samyak-saṁbodhi?"

Mañjuśrī replied, "When a Bodhisattva sits in a bodhimaṇḍa, he does not attain anuttara-samyak-saṁbodhi. Why not? Because the appearance of bodhi is true suchness. Not finding a speck of dharma to capture is called anuttara-samyak-saṁbodhi. Because bodhi has no appearance, who can sit and who can rise? For this reason, I see neither a Bodhisattva sitting in a bodhimaṇḍa nor anyone realizing anuttara-samyak-saṁbodhi."

Mañjuśrī said to the Buddha, "World-Honored One, bodhi is the five rebellious acts, and the five rebellious acts are bodhi. Why? Because bodhi and the five rebellious acts are free from duality. Hence there is neither learning nor learner, neither perceiving nor perceiver, neither knowing nor knower, neither differentiating nor differentiator. Such appearances are called bodhi. In the same way one should view the appearances of the five rebellious acts. If there are those who say that they see bodhi and have attained it, we should know that they are the ones with exceeding arrogance."

The World-Honored One asked Mañjuśrī, "Would you say that I am the Thus-Come One, and address me as the Tathāgata?"

Mañjuśrī responded, "No, World-Honored One, I would not say that [the name] Tathāgata is the Thus-Come One. Suchness does not have an appearance that can be called suchness. Nor is there Tathāgata wisdom that can know suchness. Why not? Because the Tathāgata and His wisdom are free from duality.

Because emptiness is Tathāgata, which is only a name, what should I say is the Tathāgata?"

The Buddha asked Mañjuśrī, "Do you doubt the Tathāgata?"

Mañjuśrī replied, "No, World-Honored One, I have no doubt because, in my observation, the Tathāgata, with neither birth nor death, does not have a definite nature."

The Buddha asked Mañjuśrī, "Would you say that the Tathāgata has appeared in the world?"

Mañjuśrī replied, "If the Tathāgata appeared in the world, the entire dharma realm would also appear."

The Buddha asked Mañjuśrī, "Would you say that Buddhas as numerous as the sands of the Ganges have entered parinirvāṇa?"

Mañjuśrī replied, "Buddhas have the one appearance, the inconceivable appearance."

The Buddha agreed with Mañjuśrī, "Indeed! Indeed! Buddhas have the one appearance, the inconceivable appearance."

Mañjuśrī asked the Buddha, "World-Honored One, is the Buddha now staying in this world?"

The Buddha answered Mañjuśrī, "Indeed! Indeed!"

Mañjuśrī said, "If the Buddha were staying in this world, then Buddhas as numerous as the sands of the Ganges would also stay in their worlds. Why? Because all Buddhas have the same one appearance, the inconceivable appearance. The inconceivable appearance has neither birth nor death. If future Buddhas were to appear in their worlds, then all Buddhas [of the past, present, and future] would also appear in their worlds. Why? Because in what is inconceivable, there is no appearance of past, future, or present. However, sentient beings are attached to their perceptions, and they say that there are Buddhas who appear in the world and Buddhas who enter nirvāṇa."

The Buddha told Mañjuśrī, "This is the understanding of Tathāgatas, Arhats, and Bodhisattvas at the level of avinivartanīya. Why? Because these three types of beings, having heard the profound Dharma, are able neither to criticize nor to praise it."

Mañjuśrī agreed with the Buddha, "World-Honored One, who could criticize and who could praise the inconceivable Dharma?"

The Buddha told Mañjuśrī, "Tathāgatas are inconceivable, and ordinary beings are inconceivable as well."

Mañjuśrī asked the Buddha, "Are ordinary beings also inconceivable?"

The Buddha replied, "They too are inconceivable. Why? Because all mental appearances are inconceivable."

Mañjuśrī said, "If you say that Tathāgatas are inconceivable and that ordinary beings are also inconceivable, then innumerable Buddhas are just fatiguing themselves seeking nirvāṇa. Why? Because inconceivable dharmas are nirvāṇa and therefore have no differences."

Mañjuśrī said, "Such inconceivability of ordinary beings and Buddhas can be understood only by good men and good women who have long developed their roots of goodness and stayed near beneficent learned friends."

The Buddha asked Mañjuśrī, "Do you want the Tathāgata to be the superb one among sentient beings?"

Mañjuśrī replied, "I want the Tathāgata to be the foremost one among sentient beings. However, sentient beings' appearances cannot be captured"

The Buddha asked, "Do you want the Tathāgata to acquire the inconceivable Dharma?"

Mañjuśrī replied, "I want the Tathāgata to acquire the inconceivable Dharma without constructing anything."

The Buddha asked Mañjuśrī, "Do you want the Tathāgata to expound the Dharma and to teach and transform sentient beings?"

Mañjuśrī replied to the Buddha, "I want the Tathāgata to expound the Dharma and to teach and transform sentient beings. Yet neither the speaker nor the listener can be captured. Why not? Because they abide in the dharma realm. Sentient beings in the dharma realm have no differentiated appearances."

The Buddha asked Mañjuśrī, "Do you want the Tathāgata to be the unexcelled fortune field?"

Mañjuśrī replied, "The Tathāgata, with the appearance of endlessness, is the endless fortune field. The appearance of endlessness is the unexcelled fortune field. Because [the Tathāgata] is neither a fortune field nor not a fortune field, He is called the fortune field. Because He has no appearances, such as light or dark, birth or death, He is called the fortune field. If one can understand the appearances of the fortune field in this way, the seeds of goodness one plants deeply will neither increase nor decrease."

The Buddha asked Mañjuśrī, "Why do the planted seeds neither increase nor decrease?"

Mañjuśrī replied, "The appearances of the fortune field are inconceivable. Cultivating goodness in the field in accordance with the Dharma is also inconceivable. Planting seeds in this way is called no increase and no decrease, and it is also the unexcelled, superb fortune field."

Then, by virtue of the Buddha's spiritual power, the great earth quaked in six different ways, manifesting the appearances of impermanence. Sixteen thousand people achieved the Endurance in the Realization of the No Birth of Dharmas. Moreover, 700 bhikṣus, 3,000 upāsakas, 40,000 upāsikās, and 60 koṭi nayuta gods of the six desire heavens, in the midst of dharmas, shunned dust and filth [their afflictions], and acquired the pure dharma-eye.

Fascicle 2 (of 2)

At that time Ānanda rose from his seat, bared his right shoulder, and knelt on his right knee. He asked the Buddha, "World-Honored One, why did this great earth quake in six different ways?"

The Buddha answered Ānanda, "It displayed this auspicious sign because I said that the fortune field had no differentiated appearances. When past Buddhas pronounced in this place the appearances of the fortune field to benefit sentient beings, the entire world also quaked in six different ways."

Śāriputra said to the Buddha, "World-Honored One, Mañjuśrī is inconceivable. Why? Because the dharma appearances he has explained are inconceivable."

The Buddha praised Mañjuśrī, "Indeed! Indeed! Just as Śāriputra says, what you have said is truly inconceivable."

Mañjuśrī said to the Buddha, "World-Honored One, the inconceivable is ineffable, and the conceivable is also ineffable. Conceivable and inconceivable natures are both ineffable. All appearances of sound are neither conceivable nor inconceivable."

The Buddha asked, "You have entered the inconceivable samādhi?"

Mañjuśrī replied, "No, World-Honored One, I am the inconceivable. Not seeing a mind that can conceive, how can I be said to enter the inconceivable samādhi? When I first activated the bodhi mind, I resolved to enter this samādhi. Now I think that I have entered this samādhi without any mental appearances. To learn archery, a student has to practice for a long time to acquire the skill. Because of his longtime practice, he now shoots without using his mind, and all his arrows hit the target. I have trained in the same way. When I started learning the inconceivable samādhi, I had to focus my mind on one object. After practicing for a long time, I have come to accomplishment. I now am constantly in this samādhi without thinking."

Śāriputra asked Mañjuśrī, "Is there a silent samādhi that is more wonderful?"

Mañjuśrī replied, "If there were actually an inconceivable samādhi, you could then ask for a silent samādhi. According to my understanding, even the inconceivable samādhi cannot be captured, so how can you ask for a silent samādhi?"

Śāriputra asked, "The inconceivable samādhi cannot be attained?"

Mañjuśrī replied, "The conceivable samādhi has an appearance that can be captured while the inconceivable samādhi has no appearance to be captured. All sentient beings have attained the inconceivable samādhi. Why? Because all mental appearances are not the [true] mind. Therefore, the [mental] appearances of all sentient beings and the appearance of the inconceivable samādhi are the same, not different."

The Buddha praised Mañjuśrī, "Very good! Very good! You have long planted your roots of goodness under Buddhas and trained with purity in the Brahma way of life. So you are able to expound such a profound samādhi. Are you now settled in prajñā-pāramitā?"

Mañjuśrī said, "If I could say that I abide in prajñā-pāramitā, this would be a perception founded on the view that one has a self. Abiding in a perception founded on the view that one has a self means that prajñā-pāramitā has a place. That I do not abide in prajñā-pāramitā is also [a perception] founded on the view that one has a self, and is a place as well. Free from these two places [subject and object], I abide in not abiding, like Buddhas abiding in the inconceivable state of peace and silence. Such an inconceivable state is called the dwelling of prajñā-pāramitā. In the dwelling of prajñā-pāramitā, all dharmas have neither appearance nor act.

"Prajñā-pāramitā is inconceivable. The inconceivable state is the dharma realm, which has no appearance. Having no appearance is the inconceivable state; the inconceivable state is prajñā-pāramitā. Prajñā-pāramitā and the dharma realm are the same, not distinct. Having neither differentiation nor appearance is the dharma realm; the dharma realm is the realm of prajñā-pāramitā. The realm of prajñā-pāramitā is the inconceivable state; the inconceivable state is the realm of no birth and no death."

Mañjuśrī continued, "The realm of a Tathāgata and the realm of a self are the appearance of non-duality. Those who practice prajñā-pāramitā in this way do not seek bodhi. Why not? Because bodhi, which is free from appearances, is prajñā-pāramitā.

"World-Honored One, to know the appearances of a self means not to be captivated by it. Not knowing and not being captivated by anything is what Buddhas know. The inconceivable [state of] not knowing and not being captivated by anything is what Buddhas know. Why? Because they know that the true nature of everything has no appearance. Then what drives the dharma realm? What in its true nature has neither self-essence nor attachment is called no thing[2] and is free from place, dependency, and fixity. Freedom from place, dependency, and fixity means having neither birth nor death. Having neither birth nor death is the virtue of any saṁskṛta or asaṁskṛta dharma. With this knowledge, one will not elicit perception. Without perception, how can one know the virtue of any saṁskṛta or asaṁskṛta dharma? Not knowing is the inconceivable state.[3] The inconceivable state is what Buddhas know, such as neither grasping nor not grasping, seeing neither the appearance of past, present, or future, nor the appearance of coming or going, and grasping neither birth nor death, neither cessation nor perpetuity, neither arising nor acting. This knowledge is called the true wisdom-knowledge, the inconceivable wisdom-knowledge. Like the open sky, with neither appearances nor features, in unequaled equality, it makes no comparison, neither this against that nor good against evil."

The Buddha told Mañjuśrī, "This knowledge is called the wisdom-knowledge that never fades."

Mañjuśrī said, "The wisdom-knowledge of no act is also called the wisdom knowledge that never fades, but it is like gold ore, which has to be processed in order to know whether it is good or bad. If gold is not refined, there is no way to know [its quality]. The same is true for the appearance of the wisdom-knowledge that never fades. One needs to go through the experience in not thinking, not being captivated, not arising, and not acting. When one's mind is completely quiet, neither rising nor falling, then it will be revealed."

Then the Buddha said to Mañjuśrī, "When Tathāgatas speak of their own wisdom-knowledge, who can believe it?"

Mañjuśrī said, "Such wisdom-knowledge is neither the dharma of nirvāṇa nor the dharma of saṁsāra. It is the way of silence and the way of stillness, neither annihilating greed, anger, and delusion, nor not annihilating them. Why? Because [wisdom-knowledge] is endless and indestructible, neither apart from saṁsāra nor together with it. It is acquired through neither training nor not training for bodhi. This understanding is called the right belief."

The Buddha praised Mañjuśrī, "Very good! Very good! What you say is a profound understanding of its meaning."

Then Mahākāśyapa asked the Buddha, "World-Honored One, if such profound true Dharma is pronounced in future times, who will be able to believe, understand, and accept it, and to practice it accordingly?"

The Buddha replied to Mahākāśyapa, "If bhikṣus, bhikṣuṇīs, upāsakas, and upāsikās who have heard this sūtra in this assembly hear this Dharma in future times, they definitely will believe and understand it. They will be able to read and recite this [sūtra of] profound prajñā-pāramitā, to accept and uphold it, and to expound it to others. As an analogy, an elder who has lost his precious jewel feels sad and distressed. If he retrieves it later, he will be very joyous. Therefore, Kāśyapa, likewise will be the bhikṣus, bhikṣuṇīs, upāsakas, and upāsikās in this assembly. They have the mind of faith and delight. If they do not hear the Dharma, they will feel distressed. If they come to hear it, they will, with great joy, believe and understand it, accept and uphold it, and always delight in reading and reciting it. Know that these people in effect see Buddhas and that they in effect serve and make offerings to Buddhas."

The Buddha told Mahākāśyapa, "As an analogy, when gods in Trayastriṁśa Heaven see the buds of the celestial pārijāta tree emerge, they are elated. They know that this tree's buds will soon open into full bloom. Likewise, if, among bhikṣus, bhikṣuṇīs, upāsakas, and upāsikās, there are those who can believe and understand the prajñā-pāramitā they have heard, they too will soon bring the entire Buddha Dharma to bloom. If in future times, among bhikṣus, bhikṣuṇīs, upāsakas, and upāsikās, there are those who, after hearing this [sūtra of] prajñā-pāramitā, can believe and accept it, and read and recite it, without regret or bafflement, know that they have already heard and accepted this sūtra in this assembly. They will also be able to pronounce and circulate it widely to the public in towns and cities. Know that they will be protected and remembered by Buddhas. If, among good men and good women, there are those who can believe and delight in this profound prajñā-pāramitā without doubts, they must have long trained and learned under past Buddhas, and planted their roots of goodness.

"As an analogy, a man stringing beads with his hands suddenly comes across an unexcelled genuine jewel. His heart is filled with great joy. Know that this person must have seen [such a jewel before]. Therefore, Kāśyapa, when good men and good women who are learning other dharmas suddenly come across this profound prajñā-pāramitā, if they rejoice in the same way, know that they must have heard it before. Suppose there are sentient beings that, after hearing this profound prajñā-pāramitā, can believe and accept it with great joy in their hearts. They too must have served innumerable Buddhas, from whom they must have heard prajñā-pāramitā, which they must have studied and practiced.

"As an analogy, a person has passed and seen a city or a town. Later on, he hears others praise how lovely in this city are the gardens, ponds, fountains, flowers, fruits, and trees, as well as the male and female residents, and he is very happy to hear these things. He even asks them to describe this city with its gardens, beautiful decorations, various flowers, ponds and fountains, an abundance of sweet fruits, various kinds of wonders, and all the lovely things. After hearing these descriptions again, this person will be even happier. Those who react in the same way as this person must have seen it before. If, among good men and good women, there are those who, upon hearing prajñā-pāramitā, are able to listen and accept it with faith, to feel joy, to delight in hearing it tirelessly, and even to ask for repetitions, know that they have already heard prajñā-pāramitā from Mañjuśrī."

Mahākāśyapa said to the Buddha, "World-Honored One, if in future times, among good men and good women, there are those who, having heard this profound prajñā-pāramitā, listen and accept it with faith and delight, we should know by this indication that they too have heard it from past Buddhas, and have studied and practiced it."

Mañjuśrī said to the Buddha, "World-Honored One, the Buddha says that dharmas have neither appearance nor act and are inherently in nirvāṇa. If good men and good women can truly understand this meaning and pronounce it as heard, they will be praised by Tathāgatas. Their statement, consistent with dharma appearances, in effect is the pronouncement of Buddhas. It is called the glowing appearance of prajñā-pāramitā, also called the glowing totality of the Buddha Dharma, and it reveals true reality in an inconceivable way."

The Buddha told Mañjuśrī, "When I was walking the Bodhisattva Way, I developed my roots of goodness. Those who aspire to stand on the Ground of Avinivartanīya should learn prajñā-pāramitā. Those who aspire to attain anuttara-samyak-saṁbodhi should learn prajñā-pāramitā. If good men and good women aspire to understand all dharma appearances and to know the equality in sentient beings' mental realm, they should learn prajñā-pāramitā. Mañjuśrī, those who aspire to learn the entire Buddha Dharma without obstructions should learn prajñā-pāramitā. Those who aspire to understand, upon Buddhas' attainment of anuttara-samyak-saṁbodhi, their sublime appearance, majestic deportment, and innumerable Dharma procedures should learn prajñā-pāramitā. Those who aspire to know, before Buddhas' attainment of anuttara-samyak-saṁbodhi, their appearance, deportment, and Dharma procedures should also learn prajñā-pāramitā. Why? Because in the dharma of emptiness, one does not perceive Buddhas, bodhi, and so forth. If, among good men and good women, there are those who aspire to know such appearances without doubts, they should learn prajñā-pāramitā. Why? Because in practicing prajñā-pāramitā, one does not see dharmas as born or dead, pure or impure. Therefore, good men and good women should learn prajñā-pāramitā in this way. Those who aspire to know that all dharmas have no such appearance as past, present, or future should learn prajñā-pāramitā. Why? Because in nature and appearance, the dharma realm does not have past, present, or future. Those who aspire to know, without hindrances in their minds, that all dharmas constitute the dharma realm should learn prajñā-pāramitā. Those who aspire to hear the three turnings of the Dharma wheel in the twelve appearances, and to know them through self-realization, without grasping them or being captivated by them, should learn prajñā-pāramitā. Those who aspire to invoke the mind of lovingkindness for sheltering all sentient beings everywhere without a limit, without thinking of sentient beings' appearances, should learn prajñā-pāramitā. Those who aspire neither to dispute with sentient beings nor to grasp the appearance of no dispute should learn prajñā-pāramitā. Those who aspire to know a Buddha's Ten Powers, such as knowing right or wrong in any situation, to know His Four Fearlessnesses, to abide in His wisdom-knowledge, and to acquire unimpeded eloquence, should learn prajñā-pāramitā."

Mañjuśrī said to the Buddha, "World-Honored One, I correctly observe dharmas and find them to be asaṁskṛta, with no appearance, no attainment, no benefit, no birth, no death, no coming, no going, no knower, no perceiver, and no doer. I see neither prajñā-pāramitā nor the state of prajñā-pāramitā, neither realization nor no realization. I make no differentiation, nor any ludicrous statement. All dharmas are endless, apart from ending. There is no dharma of ordinary beings, no dharma of voice-hearers, no dharma of Pratyekabuddhas, and no dharma of Buddhas. There is neither attainment nor no attainment, neither saṁsāra to abandon nor nirvāṇa to realize, neither the conceivable nor the inconceivable, neither acting nor not acting. Such are dharma appearances! Then how does one learn prajñā-pāramitā?"

The Buddha told Mañjuśrī, "Knowing such dharma appearances is called learning prajñā-pāramitā. If Bodhisattva-Mahāsattvas aspire to learn the Samādhi of Bodhi Command because, after learning it, they can illuminate the entire profound Buddha Dharma, know the names of all Buddhas, and understand their worlds, without obstructions, they should learn prajñā-pāramitā as explained by Mañjuśrī."

Mañjuśrī asked the Buddha, "Why is it called prajñā-pāramitā?"

The Buddha replied, "Prajñā-pāramitā is boundless, limitless, nameless, and with neither appearance nor conception. Like the dharma realm, which has no divisions or limits, it has neither refuge nor [safe] island, neither merit nor demerit, neither light nor dark. It is called prajñā-pāramitā, also called the action range of Bodhisattva-Mahāsattvas. Although neither the action range nor the no-action range, in the One Vehicle, it is called the no-action range. Why? Because there is neither perception nor action."

Mañjuśrī asked the Buddha, "World-Honored One, what actions can one take to attain anuttara-samyak-saṁbodhi quickly?"

The Buddha replied, "Mañjuśrī, those who practice prajñā-pāramitā as explained will quickly attain anuttara-samyak-saṁbodhi. Furthermore, there is the Samādhi of the One Action. If good men and good women train in this samādhi, they will also quickly attain anuttara-samyak-saṁbodhi."

Mañjuśrī asked, "World-Honored One, what is called the One Action Samādhi?"

The Buddha replied, "The dharma realm has the one appearance. Focusing one's mind on the dharma realm is called the One Action Samādhi. If, among good men and good women, there are those who aspire to enter the One Action Samādhi, they should first hear prajñā-pāramitā and next train and learn it accordingly. Then they will be able to enter the One Action Samādhi, which fits the conditions of the dharma realm: indestructible, inconceivable, with no regress, no hindrance, and no appearance. If good men and good women aspire to enter the One Action Samādhi, they should sit properly in an open place, facing the direction of a Buddha, abandon distracting thoughts and appearances, focus their minds on that Buddha, and keep saying His name. If they can continue, thought after thought, thinking of one Buddha, they will be able to see, in their thinking, past, future, and present Buddhas. Why? Because the merit acquired from thinking of one Buddha is immeasurable and boundless, no different from the merit acquired from thinking of innumerable Buddhas or thinking of the inconceivable Buddha Dharma. They all will realize true suchness and attain the perfect enlightenment, acquiring immeasurable merit and eloquence. Those who enter the One Action Samādhi in this way will know that there are no differentiated appearances in the dharma realm of Buddhas, who are as numerous as the sands of the Ganges. Although among voice-hearers Ānanda is foremost in the Buddha Dharma he has heard, in his total retention of memory, and in his eloquence and wisdom, his attainment has a measure and a limit. If one has attained the One Action Samādhi, one will be able to differentiate one by one the Dharma Doors in the sūtras and to know them all, without obstructions. One will be able to expound them day and night unceasingly with wisdom and eloquence. By comparison, Ānanda's eloquence and hearing much [of the Dharma] are not even one hundred-thousandth thereof. Bodhisattva-Mahāsattvas should think: 'How should I attain this One Action Samādhi, which will bring inconceivable merit and innumerable [good] names?'"

The Buddha continued, "Bodhisattva-Mahāsattvas should always think of the One Action Samādhi and assiduously make energetic progress, never negligent or indolent. Through step-by-step gradual training and learning, they will enter the One Action Samādhi, as evidenced by their inconceivable merit. However, those who malign the true Dharma or disbelieve that hindrances are caused by evil karmas will not be able to enter it.

"Moreover, Mañjuśrī, as an analogy, a person has acquired a precious bead, and he shows it to the jeweler. The jeweler says that it is a priceless genuine jewel. He then asks the jeweler, 'Polish it for me. Do not let it lose its luster and color.' After the jeweler has polished it, this precious bead becomes brilliant and transparent throughout. Mañjuśrī, if good men and good women train in the One Action Samādhi in order to acquire inconceivable merit and innumerable [good] names, in the course of their training, they will know dharma appearances with clear understanding, without obstructions. Their merit will grow in the same way. Mañjuśrī, using the sun as an example, its light is pervasive and not diminishing. Likewise, if one attains the One Action Samādhi, one will acquire all merits without any shortfall, like the sunlight illuminating the Buddha Dharma. Mañjuśrī, the Dharma I have pronounced is in the one flavor apart from flavors, which is the flavor of liberation, the flavor of silence and stillness. If good men and good women have attained this One Action Samādhi, what they expound will also be in the one flavor apart from flavors, which is the flavor of liberation, the flavor of silence and stillness, completely in accordance with the true Dharma, without any error or mistake. Mañjuśrī, Bodhisattva-Mahāsattvas who have attained this One Action Samādhi will complete the [Thirty-seven] Elements of Bodhi and quickly attain anuttara-samyak-saṁbodhi.

"Furthermore, Mañjuśrī, Bodhisattva-Mahāsattvas who see in the dharma realm neither differentiated appearances nor the one appearance will quickly attain the inconceivable anuttara-samyak-saṁbodhi. Those who know that in bodhi there is no attainment of Buddhahood will quickly attain anuttara-samyak-saṁbodhi. Those who can endure, without shock, fear, or doubt, their belief that all dharmas are the Buddha Dharma will quickly attain anuttara-samyak-saṁbodhi."

Mañjuśrī asked the Buddha, "World-Honored One, can one quickly attain anuttara-samyak-saṁbodhi through such causes?"

The Buddha replied, "Anuttara-samyak-saṁbodhi is attained through neither causes nor no causes. Why? Because the inconceivable state is realized through neither causes nor no causes. If good men and good women who have heard these words do not become negligent or indolent, know that they have already planted their roots of goodness under past Buddhas. Therefore, if bhikṣus and bhikṣuṇīs who have heard this profound prajñā-pāramitā are not shocked or terrified, they have truly renounced family life to follow the Buddha. If upāsakas and upāsikās who have heard this profound prajñā-pāramitā are not shocked or terrified, they have truly taken refuge [in the Buddha].

"Mañjuśrī, good men and good women who do not study the profound prajñā-pāramitā are not training by means of the Buddha Vehicle. Taking the great earth as an example, all medicinal plants must grow from the earth.

Mañjuśrī, likewise the roots of goodness of Bodhisattva-Mahāsattvas must depend on prajñā-pāramitā to develop, so that their attainment of anuttara-samyak-saṁbodhi will not be obstructed."

Mañjuśrī asked the Buddha, "World-Honored One, in Jambudvīpa's cities and towns, where should we pronounce this profound prajñā-pāramitā?"

The Buddha told Mañjuśrī, "Suppose those who have heard prajñā-pāramitā in this assembly vow that in future lives they will always respond to prajñā-pāramitā in order to strengthen their faith and understanding, and that they will be able to hear this sūtra again. Know that those people did not come with small roots of goodness because they are capable of accepting and appreciating what they hear. Mañjuśrī, if there are those who have heard prajñā-pāramitā from you, they should say this: 'In prajñā-pāramitā, there is no dharma of voice-hearers, no dharma of Pratyekabuddhas, no dharma of Bodhisattvas, and no dharma of Buddhas. Nor is there the dharma of ordinary beings or the dharma of saṁsāra.'"

Mañjuśrī said to the Buddha, "World-Honored One, if bhikṣus, bhikṣuṇīs, upāsakas, and upāsikās ask me, 'How does the Tathāgata pronounce prajñā-pāramitā?' I should reply, 'Given that dharmas do not have the appearance of dispute, how should the Tathāgata pronounce prajñā-pāramitā? He does not see dharmas to dispute over, nor does he see that the minds and consciousnesses of sentient beings can know [dharmas].'

"Moreover, World-Honored One, I should also pronounce the ultimate reality. Why? Because all dharma appearances equally abide in true reality. Arhatship is not a particularly superb dharma. Why not? Because the dharma of Arhats and the dharma of ordinary beings are neither the same nor different. Furthermore, World-Honored One, according to the Dharma explained in this way, no sentient being has already realized nirvāṇa, is realizing it, or will realize it. Why not? Because sentient beings do not have definite appearances."

Mañjuśrī continued, "If there are those who wish to hear prajñā-pāramitā. I will tell them that listeners do not think of, hear, or capture anything, nor are they captivated by anything, just like a magically conjured person who never differentiates. This statement is a true teaching of the Dharma. Therefore, listeners should not construct dual appearances [subject and object]. They should train in the Buddha Dharma without abandoning other views, and they should neither grasp the Buddha Dharma nor abandon the dharma of ordinary beings. Why? Because Buddhas and ordinary beings as two dharmas have empty appearances, beyond grasping or abandoning. When someone asks me, I give these answers, thus comforting him and setting him [on the right path]. Good men and good women should ask such questions and abide in this way, with their minds not regressing or baffled. They should speak of dharma appearances in accord with prajñā-pāramitā."

Then the World-Honored One praised Mañjuśrī, "Very good! Very good! Just as you say, if good men and good women wish to see Buddhas, they should learn prajñā-pāramitā. If they wish to serve Buddhas and to make offerings to them in accordance with the Dharma, they should learn prajñā-pāramitā. If they wish to say that the Tathāgata is the World-Honored One to them, they should learn prajñā-pāramitā. Even if they wish to say that the Tathāgata is not the World-Honored One to them, they should learn prajñā-pāramitā. If they wish to attain anuttara-samyak-saṁbodhi, they should learn prajñā-pāramitā. Even if they do not wish to attain anuttara-samyak-saṁbodhi, they should learn prajñā-pāramitā. If they wish to attain all samādhis, they should learn prajñā-pāramitā. Even if they do not wish to attain all samādhis, they should learn prajñā-pāramitā. Why? Because the Samādhi of No Act has no varied appearances and because dharmas have neither birth nor death. If there are those who wish to know that all dharmas are false names, they should learn prajñā-pāramitā. If those who wish to know, with their minds not regressing or baffled, that all sentient beings that train in the Bodhi Way do not seek the appearance of bodhi, they should learn prajñā-pāramitā. Why? Because all dharmas are the appearance of bodhi. If there are those who wish, with their minds not regressing or baffled, to know the appearances of sentient beings' actions and no actions and to know that not acting is bodhi, that bodhi is the dharma realm, and that the dharma realm is true reality, they should learn prajñā-pāramitā. If there are those who wish to know that Tathāgatas' transcendental powers and magical displays have neither appearances nor obstructions, nor places, they should learn prajñā-pāramitā."

The Buddha told Mañjuśrī, "If bhikṣus, bhikṣuṇīs, upāsakas, and upāsikās do not wish to go down the evil life-paths, they should learn a four-verse stanza on prajñā-pāramitā, accept and uphold it, read and recite it, and explain it to others in accord with true reality. Know that these good men and good women will definitely attain anuttara-samyak-saṁbodhi and reside in Buddha Lands. If there are those who, upon hearing this prajñā-pāramitā, are not shocked or terrified, but elicit faith and understanding from their minds, know that they are sanctified by Buddhas with a seal, the Mahāyāna Dharma Seal held only by Buddhas. If good men and good women learn this Dharma Seal, they will transcend not only the evil life-journeys but also the paths of voice-hearers and Pratyekabuddhas."

At that time the god-king of the Thirty-three Heavens, as an offering to prajñā-pāramitā, the Tathāgata, and Mañjuśrī, brought wonderful celestial flowers of utpala, kumuda, puṇḍarīka, and māndarāva, as well as celestial sandalwood incense, powdered incense, various kinds of golden jewelry, and celestial music. After showering such offerings upon them, he said, "I wish always to learn the Prajñā-Pāramitā Dharma Seal."

The god-king Śakro-Devānām-Indra then made this vow: "I pray that the good men and good women in Jambudvīpa can always hear this sūtra, the definitive Buddha Dharma, and that they will believe and understand it, accept and uphold it, read and recite it, and expound it to others. Let all the gods protect and support them."

At that time the Buddha told Śakro-Devānām-Indra, "Kauśika, indeed, indeed, these good men and good women will definitely attain Buddha bodhi."

Mañjuśrī said to the Buddha, "World-Honored One, good men and good women who accept and uphold [this sūtra] in this way will acquire great benefits and immeasurable merit."

Then, by virtue of the Buddha's spiritual power, the entire great earth quaked in six different ways. The Buddha smiled as He emitted great radiance, illuminating everywhere in the Three-Thousand Large Thousandfold World. Mañjuśrī said to the Buddha, "World-Honored One, this is the appearance of the Tathāgata's sanctifying of prajñā-pāramitā."

The Buddha said, "Mañjuśrī, indeed, indeed. This auspicious sign always appears after prajñā-pāramitā is pronounced. It is for sanctifying prajñā-pāramitā and for enabling people to accept and uphold it, not to praise or criticize it. Why? Because the appearance-free Dharma Seal is beyond praise or criticism. I now, with this Dharma Seal, keep celestial māras from making trouble."

After the Buddha finished these words, great Bodhisattvas and the four groups of disciples, having heard the explanation of prajñā-pāramitā, greatly rejoiced. They all believed in, accepted, and reverently carried out the teachings.

Notes

1. All dharmas as perceived arise and perish through causes and conditions, and in true reality are empty. According to the absolute truth, as the wrong view that one has an autonomous self is empty, so too is the right view that one does not have such a self. Not abandoning the relative truth, a student should hold the right view in order to walk the holy path and realize the absolute truth.

2. The name "no thing" means that everything is empty and is not a thing as perceived. For example, walls obstruct humans, but not ghosts. However, the emptiness of a thing does not mean nothingness because something is vividly perceived by sentient beings according to their karmic faculties. Therefore, this name is not translated as no-thing because in English *no-thing* is the predecessor of the word *nothing*.

3. Knowing means perceiving subject and object.

9 大方廣如來不思議境界經
Mahāvaipulya Sūtra of the Inconceivable State of Tathāgatas

Translated from Sanskrit into Chinese in the Tang Dynasty
by
The Tripiṭaka Master Śikṣānanda from Yutian

Thus I have heard:

At one time the Buddha attained samyak-saṁbodhi under the bodhi tree in the kingdom of Magadha. This bodhi tree was called Aśvattha. It had firm deep roots, and its trunk was straight, rounded, and without joints, like a sandalwood column. Birds circled this tree, but none were able to fly over it. The tree bark was fine and lustrous, with various colors, like beautiful silk. The dense foliage was bright green, spreading over multitudinous branches. In full bloom and emitting fragrances, wonderful and lovely flowers surrounded this tree. Except for the celestial kovidāra tree and pārijāta tree, no other trees could compare. Furthermore, surrounded by innumerable small trees, this king of trees was majestic and graceful, like a wonderful high mountain overlooking other mountains. All could see it from one yojana away. In the midst of fragrances wafting everywhere, it radiated glorious light. This tree seen from a distance at night might be taken as a bunch of fireworks. Under this tree was beautiful landscaping open to the four directions, like a joyous garden carpeted with lush grass as beautiful as peacock feathers. People never tired of beholding it.

In this place sat majestically the Tathāgata, surrounded by the multitudes, like the moon in the midst of stars. Meanwhile, Buddhas from elsewhere, as numerous as dust particles in ten Buddha Lands, for the purpose of adorning the multitudes in Vairocana's bodhimaṇḍa, assumed the form of Bodhisattvas and came to be seated in this assembly. Among them were Avalokiteśvara Bodhisattva, Mañjuśrī Bodhisattva, Earth Store Bodhisattva, Space Store Bodhisattva, Vajra Store Bodhisattva, Vimalakīrti Bodhisattva, Excellent awesome Light Bodhisattva, Removing Coverings Bodhisattva, Jewel Hand Bodhisattva, Great Wisdom Bodhisattva, and Samantabhadra Bodhisattva. Bodhisattva-Mahāsattvas such as these were at the head of this assembly.

In addition, innumerable thousands of koṭis of Bodhisattvas, appearing as voice-hearers, also came to be seated in this assembly. At the head of this group were Śāriputra, Mahāmaudgalyāyana, Subhūti, Rāhula, Ājñātakauṇḍinya, Mahākāśyapa, Upāli, Aniruddha, Revata, Ānanda, Devadatta, Upananda, and others. Having long practiced the six pāramitās, they were getting near attainment of Buddha bodhi. In order to deliver sentient beings in this impure land, they appeared as voice-hearers. Also present, led by Mahāprajāpatī, were innumerable thousands of bhikṣuṇīs. All these bhikṣuṇīs had accomplished the deeds of great men. In order to tame headstrong sentient beings, they appeared in female form. In attendance as well were innumerable Brahma-kings, Śakras, and world protectors, as well as gods, dragons, gandharvas, asuras, garuḍas, Kiṁnaras, mahoragas, humans, nonhumans, and others. They all were great Bodhisattvas, and none were ordinary beings.

At that time the World-Honored One, seated under the bodhi tree, was sublime, pure, and wondrous, like a wish-fulfilling jewel under the pārijāta tree. His right mindfulness was unwavering, like Mount Sumeru. To make Bodhisattvas and sentient beings understand the awesome spiritual power of Buddhas' profound and secret dhyāna, He entered the samādhi called the Inconceivable State of Tathāgatas. Immediately, the World-Honored One's thirty-two physical marks each manifested innumerable Buddha Lands in the ten directions and their Buddhas, like images reflected in a clear mirror. Moreover, the Buddha's eighty excellent characteristics each displayed His training in the Bodhisattva Way in the past, from the time when He had been King Radiance to the time [when He had been training] under Dīpaṁkara Buddha. Also displayed were all His difficult actions and ascetic practices, such as giving away His head, eyes, body, skin, flesh, hands, and feet, as well as wives, servants, thrones, palaces, and so forth.

Great mighty power arises from this samādhi. All Buddhas are constantly in this samādhi as they eat, walk, expound the Dharma, or enter parinirvāṇa. Why? Because all Tathāgatas rely on this samādhi to achieve immeasurable great spiritual power, to verify that all dharmas are empty, and to manifest at will various kinds of things in all Buddha Lands in the ten directions. For example, a person sees various kinds of magical things in a dream. When he wakes up, what he has seen is gone. Thus, ordinary beings, living in dreams fabricated by ignorance [of the truth], mistakenly perceive dharmas as real. By contrast, Buddhas, after enlightenment, are not captivated by anything. Hence, they can manifest at will, in a single thought, immeasurable Buddha work in all worlds in the ten directions, to benefit sentient beings and to bring them to accomplishment, enabling them all to enter the immeasurable, profound, wondrous Liberation Door.

Then Virtue Store Bodhisattva, who had not yet completed his training in the Bodhi Way, asked Samantabhadra Bodhisattva-Mahāsattva, "What is the name of the samādhi that the Tathāgata has just entered? How can it be acquired? Why can He manifest at will various kinds of Buddha work in all worlds in the ten directions, in order to deliver sentient beings?"

Samantabhadra Bodhisattva said to Virtue Store Bodhisattva, "Hearken! Hearken! I will explain to you."

Meanwhile, all other Bodhisattvas single-mindedly gazed at him with respect, praising with one voice: "What a good question! It is profound and wonderful. Holy Samantabhadra, who knows and sees all, is now going to speak."

Forthwith, the earth quaked in six different ways, the sky rained down wonderful flowers, and all sentient beings with afflictions and in pain found respite.

Samantabhadra Bodhisattva said, "Buddha-Son, this samādhi is called the Inconceivable State of Tathāgatas. It is the bodhi of all Buddhas because they constantly stay in it. As soon as the World-Honored One received from Dīpaṁkara Buddha the prophecy of attaining Buddhahood, He immediately entered this samādhi. Without effort, He has since responsively manifested immeasurable Buddha work. As on the tip of a hair in space lie Buddha Lands as numerous as the dust particles in all Buddha Lands, He demonstrates in each land such events: whether He is born in Tuṣita Heaven; whether He descends from that heaven and enters His mother's womb; whether He becomes a newborn child and walks seven steps, announcing, 'I now am at the edge of repeated birth and death'; whether he stays in the palace then renounces family life to undertake ascetic training; whether he subjugates māras, attains samyak-saṁbodhi, and turns the wondrous Dharma wheel; whether He abides in the world and delivers sentient beings for innumerable kalpas, enabling them to leave their suffering; whether He enters parinirvāṇa. He manifests that all kalpas equal one kṣaṇa or that one kṣaṇa equals all kalpas, while each kalpa and each kṣaṇa neither decreases nor increases. As long as sentient beings have not all been liberated, kṣaṇa after kṣaṇa, He constantly does these various kinds of Buddha work everywhere in these worlds, never taking rest, nor making any effort.

"Without effort, thought after thought, He not only manifests Buddhas' various guidelines and majestic deportment, in innumerable worlds on the tip of one hair in space, but also manifests them even [in worlds] on the tips of innumerable hairs throughout space. Moreover, each dust particle in these worlds contains lands greater in number than the dust particles in all Buddha Lands. In one kṣaṇa, everywhere in each of these lands, spontaneously displayed is Buddhas' majestic deportment, such as being born in heaven, entering parinirvāṇa, or liberating innumerable asaṁkhyeyas of sentient beings. Thus, thought after thought into the endless future, Buddhas are constantly doing Buddha work to benefit sentient beings. They will never rest, even if the domain of space and the realm of sentient beings come to an end. However, Buddha Lands never decrease, and dust particles never increase. Why? Because all dharmas are like mirages and are not firm.

"For example, in the kingdom of Magadha, only twelve yojanas across, in this assembly great Bodhisattvas, as numerous as dust particles in ten Buddha Lands, stay together without crowding one another. Likewise, each of those dust particles contains innumerable Buddha Lands. Some of these worlds face upward, and others face downward. Some face each other, and others face outward. Some are alongside one another, and others interpenetrate without obstructing one another. By analogy, one may see in a dream various kinds of things in the same place. Because they are unreal, they do not exclude one another.

"All these worlds are nothing but manifestations of one's mind: whether a world burning at the ending of a kalpa, or the fire already burnt out; whether a world being formed by wind; whether clean or filthy things; whether the absence of a Buddha. Sentient beings perceive various kinds of distinctions according to their karmas. For example, driven by hunger and thirst, hungry ghosts go to the Ganges. Some of them see water, but others see the river filled with impure things, such as ash, pus, blood, and feces.

"Thus, sentient beings each follow their karmas. Some may see their own Buddha Land as pure or impure. Some may see a Buddha living or entering parinirvāṇa. Some may see Him in a bodhimaṇḍa, pronouncing the Dharma to the multitudes. Some may hear Him pronouncing the highest truth. Some may hear Him pronouncing and praising the dharma of almsgiving. Some may see Him standing still or walking. Some may see Him sitting or eating. Some may see His body twice or even seven times the size of a human, or one, one hundred, or one thousand yojanas in height. Some may see His awesome radiance like that of a rising sun or a full moon. Some may see Buddhas, assuming the form of great Bodhisattvas of awesome virtue, come to this assembly from their own lands.

"By contrast, because of karma hindrances, some may happen to live long after a Buddha-Tathāgata has entered parinirvāṇa. Some may never hear Buddhas' names, like those hungry ghosts that cannot see water in the Ganges but can see only various kinds of filthy things.

"Sentient beings in one land may only see their world burning at the ending of a kalpa; sentient beings crowding another land may all see a Buddha. Some may see the Tathāgata put all lands into one Buddha Land; others may see Him put one Buddha Land into every land.

"People with diseased eyes see things in the same place differently, without hindering one another. Because of the eye disease, they are unable to see the true form. This is true for all sentient beings. Although the true nature of form is unobstructed, their mental conditions are different. Ignorant of the right views, they do not understand true reality.

"Buddha-Son, I now will tell you in brief the dharma for staying in this samādhi. As a Buddha-Bhagavān abides in this samādhi, in one thought He is everywhere in innumerable Buddha Lands on the tips of hairs throughout space. Moreover, contained in each of the dust particles in these Buddha Lands are lands as numerous as the dust particles in the dharma realm. For benefiting sentient beings, kṣaṇa after kṣaṇa, everywhere in one and all lands are displayed the skillful ways and the majestic deportment of Buddhas, who are as numerous as the dust particles in ten Buddha Lands. Such displays will never end for all sentient beings that have not attained the unsurpassed bodhi. Thus, not only one Buddha, but also another, and another, and even all the Buddhas [in worlds] in the ten directions each display the great powers of their awesome virtues."

Having heard these words, then and there Virtue Store Bodhisattva acquired this samādhi. Forthwith, he saw innumerable Buddhas and knew their awesome virtues and skillful ways. With the power of this samādhi, he was able to tame sentient beings in the same way. Moreover, Bodhisattvas, as numerous as the sands of one hundred Ganges Rivers, each achieved various kinds of endurance in samādhis and attained various [Bodhisattva] Grounds.

Avalokiteśvara Bodhisattva and other great Bodhisattvas on the Tenth Ground are already complete in their merits and wonderful actions. Having acquired this samādhi far back in the past, they have been able to include innumerable kalpas within one kṣaṇa, to store innumerable lands in one dust particle, and to be everywhere in all lands with one thought. They have been delivering innumerable sentient beings without effort because they can manifest Buddha work at will. Although they heard this Dharma just now, they made no further progress. Like a full bottle of water placed in the rain, with no room for a single raindrop, such are these Bodhisattvas.

At that time the World-Honored One, in this samādhi, emitted from between His eyebrows the light called the great display. All the Bodhisattvas who had to do things with effort because they had not yet attained the Tenth Ground on the Bodhisattva Way, once touched by that light, immediately saw innumerable Buddha Lands on the tips of hairs in space, as well as Buddha Lands in dust particles. As one can see the white mustard seeds in an aquamarine jar, likewise these Bodhisattvas clearly saw all the Buddha Lands in dust particles. They also saw all the Buddhas in those lands. In one Buddha's body, they saw all Buddhas.

Each and every Buddha has innumerable names for benefiting each and every sentient being. Thought after thought, He spontaneously and responsively appears in every Buddha Land and attains anuttara-samyak-saṁbodhi. By analogy, a wish-fulfilling jewel placed on the top of a high cylindrical banner naturally rains down various kinds of treasures according to sentient beings' wishes, to satisfy them. Likewise, Tathāgatas demonstrate their attainment of anuttara-samyak-saṁbodhi and naturally deliver innumerable sentient beings.

In any land, sentient beings are all different, but they do not get in one another's way. Each is like someone traveling across space through transcendental powers, unobstructed by mountains, rivers, and cliffs. Why? Because all life-journeys are like mirages. They are not solid.

Having seen such displays, all the Bodhisattvas saw themselves physically present everywhere in all lands. In one thought, they came before each and every Buddha and made offerings respectfully for one kalpa, two kalpas, three kalpas, or even 100,000 kalpas, or for the duration of one thought, or for a kṣaṇa. They heard each Buddha pronounce the Dhāraṇī Door of Pāramitās or explain various [Bodhisattva] Grounds. Or they saw Him demonstrate spiritual powers, such as including all kalpas within one thought. Perceiving such displays as extraordinary and rare to encounter, they each thought: "How did the World-Honored One, with commanding awesome virtue, have me acquire in one kṣaṇa merit and roots of goodness, which need innumerable kalpas to acquire, and enable me to master so quickly the great, awesome spiritual power of the Samādhi of the Inconceivable State of Tathāgatas?"

Then Virtue Store Bodhisattva, in order to benefit sentient beings, further asked Samantabhadra Bodhisattva, "For those who wish to attain this samādhi, what kind of merit, almsgiving, and wisdom should they accumulate?"

Then Samantabhadra Bodhisattva, who, everywhere in all Pure Lands in the ten directions, demonstrates attaining the perfect enlightenment and transforming sentient beings, told Virtue Store Bodhisattva, "Buddha-Son, to attain this samādhi, one should first accumulate merit and develop one's roots of goodness, that is, one should persistently make offerings to the Buddha, the Dharma, and the Saṅgha, as well as one's parents. One should draw in all who are poor, wretched, helpless, homeless, and pitiable, never abandoning them. One should not begrudge even one's own body or flesh. Why? Because those who make offerings to the Buddha will acquire great merit. They will quickly attain anuttara-samyak-saṁbodhi and enable sentient beings to gain peace and happiness. Those who make offerings to the Dharma can enhance their wisdom and verify the Dharma with ease. They will have the right understanding of the true nature of dharmas. Those who make offerings to the Saṅgha will acquire immeasurable merit and wisdom as provisions required for attaining Buddha bodhi.

"Those who make offerings to parents, monks, teachers, and others in the world, from whom they have received benefits and upon whose kindness they have depended, should remember to requite such kindness with doubled offerings. Why? Because those who know gratitude, though still in the cycle of birth and death, will keep their roots of goodness intact. Those who do not know gratitude have ruined their roots of goodness and will do evil karmas. Therefore,

Tathāgatas commend the grateful and reprove the ungrateful, and they always sympathetically rescue suffering sentient beings. Furthermore, Bodhisattvas will never regress because of their strong roots of goodness. If there are those who can diligently accumulate merit, constantly remember to requite kindness, and have compassion for sentient beings, then bodhi is readily in their hands. We should know that the Buddha says, 'Those who can cultivate these three fortune fields with offerings will develop immeasurable roots of goodness.'

"Virtue Store, know that Bodhisattvas should next sow a vast seed, which will germinate the sprouts of this samādhi and will in time bear the bodhi fruit. How does one sow this seed? Specifically, one should respectfully make offerings of various kinds of wonderful garlands, solid perfumes, powdered incense, and instrumental music to present Buddhas or Buddha images. One should think: 'As said before, everywhere in the innumerable worlds on the tips of hairs throughout space as well as in the innumerable worlds contained in dust particles, one should see Buddhas, with their awesome powers and multitudes of Bodhisattvas. To all Buddhas in all their assemblies, I now, with the right intent, single-mindedly make expansive offerings. If I make offerings to one Buddha's dharma nature, I in effect make offerings to all Buddhas' dharma nature. If I make offerings to one Tathāgata, I in effect make offerings to all Tathāgatas. By virtue of the spiritual power of each of those Buddhas, I too can include several kalpas within one thought. Then, I have in effect made offerings to Tathāgatas for those kalpas.' If sentient beings believe and understand this dharma for sowing the vast seed, they will be able to acquire this immeasurable Samādhi of the Inconceivable State of Tathāgatas. Therefore, good man, one should carry out this dharma by making offerings every day.

"Also, one should make obeisance to Buddhas, because even making only one obeisance will cause the seed to germinate the sprouts of this samādhi. Moreover, one should water the seed with the persistent practice of almsgiving, observing the precepts, making great vows, and developing wisdom.

"[First] when Bodhisattvas practice almsgiving, for the purpose of watering this samādhi seed, they should not discriminate between the fortune fields, whether they are kin or foe, good or evil, rich or poor, observing or breaching the precepts. He should also think: 'Although my alms given to the wealthy are useless to them, I should still practice generosity.'

"[Second] Bodhisattvas should observe the precepts with purity. When they see those who violate the precepts, they should feel great compassion for them, rather than become disgusted or angry.

"[Third] Bodhisattvas should earnestly make great bodhi vows, saying, 'With one thought after another, across the worlds on the tips of hairs throughout space, and even across the innumerable worlds contained in dust particles in all Buddha Lands, I resolve to attain samyak-saṁbodhi and to turn the wondrous Dharma wheel in order to deliver sentient beings. I will be no different from the present World-Honored One, Vairocana Buddha. Without effort, I will include innumerable kalpas within one thought. I will display in each of these lands the majestic deportment of Buddhas, who are as numerous as dust particles in Buddha Lands. Each of my awesome acts will deliver sentient beings as numerous as the sands of the Ganges, enabling them to leave their suffering behind. I will never rest, even if the domain of space and the realm of sentient beings come to an end.'

"[Fourth] Buddha-Son, what is meant by cultivating wisdom? Hearken single-mindedly! I now explain it to you. If, among good men and good women, there are those who, seeking the unsurpassed bodhi, resolve to attain this samādhi, they should first cultivate wisdom because this samādhi arises from wisdom. To cultivate wisdom, one should keep away from false speech, suggestive speech, and distractive, useless matters. As one invokes one's great compassion for sentient beings, one should always restrain one's mind, not letting it be tainted or distracted.

"One should go to an ashram to view a Buddha statue, adorned in golden color or cast in pure gold, complete with a Buddha's physical marks. In its halo one should see innumerable magically manifested Buddhas, who sit in order and are in samādhi. Before this Buddha statue, one should bow down at its feet and think: 'I have heard that innumerable Buddhas are now present in worlds in the ten directions, such as All Meaning Accomplished Buddha, Amitābha Buddha, Jewel Banner Buddha, Akṣobhya Buddha, Vairocana Buddha, Jewel Moon Buddha, Jewel Light Buddha, and other Buddhas.' Following the heart's devotion and esteem for these Buddhas, one elicits great pure faith. One should regard the Buddha statue as the real body of a Tathāgata appearing before one. With esteem and reverence, one should single-mindedly observe the statue up and down, without being distracted.

"Then one should go to a remote open place, sit properly, and visualize that Buddha facing one at an elbow's length. One should focus one's mind on the imagery, not losing it. If it is lost, one should [go back to the ashram and] observe the Buddha statue again. As one is observing it, esteem and reverence arise in one's mind, as if a live Buddha were physically present before one. The sight is so vivid that one no longer understands that it is just a statue. After observing it, there one should make various kinds of offerings, such as wonderful garlands, powdered incense, and solid perfumes, and should circle it to the right. One should single-mindedly hold the image of that World-Honored One standing before one and think: 'Buddha the World-Honored One, who sees all, hears all, and knows all, fully knows my mind.' One should repeatedly ponder in this way.

"Having succeeded in visualizing that Buddha, one should return to the remote open place and hold the image before one, not losing it. With a single mind, one should practice diligently for twenty-one days. Those with merit will then see that Tathāgata appearing before them. Those with hindrances caused by evil karmas from past lives will not be able to see Him. However, if they can single-mindedly apply themselves without regressing or following other thoughts, they should soon see that Buddha. Why? Because nothing will be impossible to accomplish if, seeking the unsurpassed bodhi, one focuses one's mind on a single object. Conversely, if one timidly withdraws from one's training time and again, one will not be able to liberate even oneself, much less to deliver suffering sentient beings. If one encounters such a true Way to attain bodhi quickly but cannot train diligently, one is only a heavy burden to the earth.

"By analogy, if one drinks a handful of water from the massive ocean, one has in effect drunk the water of all the rivers in Jambudvīpa. The same is true for Bodhisattvas. If they can train in this bodhi ocean, they have in effect already trained in all samādhis, endurances, Grounds, and dhāraṇīs. Therefore, one should persistently train with diligence, keeping away from laziness and distractions. One should focus one's mind on a single thought in order to see a Buddha appearing before one.

"During this training, when one sees a Buddha for the first time, one might wonder, 'Is this a real Buddha or just imagery?' If one knows that one is seeing a real Buddha, then one should fall on both knees before the Buddha and join one's palms reverently. One should remember the immeasurable awesome virtue of all the Buddhas [in worlds] on the tips of hairs throughout space and of all the Buddhas [in worlds] in dust particles, and should say, 'Out of great lovingkindness and compassion, the Buddha has come before me. I pray only that the World-Honored One will expound to me the Dharma of the Samādhi of the Inconceivable State of Tathāgatas.' If one hears all that is said by that Tathāgata, one should believe it with conviction, not raising doubts. Right then, one acquires this samādhi.

"If one is unable to ask for teachings because of the hindrance of past karmas, one should ponder that all dharmas are like illusions, mirages, distorted visions, reflections, images, and dreams. Through contemplating the emptiness of dharma nature, one will come to this understanding: 'The Tathāgata knows that all dharmas are like illusions and dreams. The true nature of the Tathāgata is neither an illusion nor a dream, but is like the open sky. However, with wisdom and compassion, He can appear before me. I wish that He will emit for me the blue light of great compassion to end my suffering.' Thereupon, that Buddha will emit from between His eyebrows a beam of light called the blue flame. As soon as the light shines on one, one's suffering will all be ended. One will immediately acquire the Radiant Endurance in Dharmas, and then one will attain innumerable samādhis. On the seventh night, one will dream of that Tathāgata bestowing upon one the prophecy of attaining anuttara-samyak-saṁbodhi.

"If one knows that one is seeing imagery, one should ponder that Buddhas and sentient beings are all like imagery, without real substance. They are seen according to one's perceptions. With the understanding that Tathāgatas are like illusions, conjurations, dreams, and mirages, one then sees a Buddha naturally appearing before one as a dream, not something that can be captured.

"A Tathāgata has no birth yet may appear as born. He has no death yet may disappear. He never departs yet may seem gone. He is not consciousness yet manifests cognition. He is not governed by causality yet manifests processes dependent upon causes and conditions. He is beyond words yet expounds the Dharma. He is neither a self nor a living being. He is neither a sentient being nor a being reared by nurturing. He never transmigrates in saṁsāra. He neither perceives anything nor acts. He is not a knower, nor does he rely on nourishment. He is neither the five aggregates nor something inside them, yet manifests the five aggregates. In the same way he manifests the [twelve] fields and the [eighteen] spheres.

"Everything is neither existence nor nonexistence. Therefore, Buddhas and all dharmas are truly equal, with the same one appearance. Like mirages and so forth, sentient beings, Buddhas, and lands are all in one's mind, all manifestations of one's consciousness and perception. In true reality, forms projected by consciousness and perception do not exist.

"A Tathāgata is apart from consciousness and perception. Therefore, one should not see Him through imagery, knowing that imagery is produced by one's perception. This is true even for all real Buddhas [in worlds] on the tips of hairs throughout space, who are equal to and no different from the open sky. If one differentiates, one will see a Buddha; if one does not differentiate, one will not see Him. One's mind forms Buddhas. Apart from one's mind, there is no Buddha. This is true for all Buddhas of the past, present, and future, whose existence depends upon one's mind.

"Bodhisattva, if one can understand that all Buddhas and all dharmas are a measure of one's mind, one will achieve the Endurance in Accord. One can even ascend to the First Ground. After death, one will quickly be reborn in either [Akṣobhya Buddha's] Land of Embracing Joy or in [Amitābha Buddha's] Land of Ultimate Bliss. There one will constantly see the Tathāgata, serve Him, and make offerings to Him."

Then Virtue Store Bodhisattva asked Samantabhadra Bodhisattva, "If there are sentient beings that have heard this Dharma Door, whether they accept and uphold, read and recite, copy, or explain this sūtra, how much merit will they acquire?"

Samantabhadra Bodhisattva replied, "Buddha-Son, hearken! Suppose there is one who can draw in all the sentient beings in the Three Realms of Existence and enable them to leave their cycle of birth and death, becoming Arhats. Then to each of these Arhats, for one hundred kalpas, one respectfully makes various kinds of offerings, such as wonderful celestial garments, bedding, food, and medicinal potions. Moreover, after their parinirvāṇa, for each of them one erects a pagoda made of the seven treasures and respectfully makes offerings. Now suppose there is someone who observes his precepts with purity for one hundred kalpas, or cultivates endurance, diligence, and meditative concentration. Although those just mentioned will acquire immeasurable merit, they are no match for the one who, having heard this Dharma Door, esteems, believes, and accepts it, never maligning it. This one's merit exceeds that of those just mentioned. This one will quickly attain the perfect enlightenment."

Thereupon, innumerable Buddhas in all worlds in the ten directions revealed themselves and praised Samantabhadra Bodhisattva: "Very good! Very good! Buddha-Son, indeed it is as you say."

Then Śākyamuni Tathāgata emitted infinite colorful radiance from his face, illuminating everywhere in the Three Realms of Existence. Various kinds of flowers rained down, wonderful music sounded without being played, and the earth slightly trembled. In the midst of His radiance, the Buddha spoke in verse:

> If one's mind is pure upon hearing this Dharma,
> One will acquire [Bodhisattva] Grounds, samādhis, and dhāraṇīs,
> As well as precepts, endurance, and command of transcendental powers.
> One will quickly attain the unsurpassed Buddha bodhi
> And turn the wondrous Dharma wheel as never before.
> Just like past Buddhas,
> One too can include many kalpas within one thought
> And universally display innumerable worlds in a dust particle.
>
> Countless sentient beings are sinking in the Three Realms.
> Laden with afflictions and distress,
> Entangled in the wrong views, they have lost the right path.
> Thought after thought, one will liberate them all.

Because Samantabhadra Bodhisattva had gone through this Dharma Door long ago, as he spoke to the multitudes, thousands of koṭis of gods and humans were delivered from suffering. They would never regress from their resolve to attain anuttara-samyak-saṁbodhi. Virtue Store Bodhisattva and other Bodhisattvas, gods, dragons, asuras, and others in the assembly greatly rejoiced. They all believed in, accepted, and reverently carried out the teachings.

10 觀世音菩薩授記經
Sūtra of the Prophecy Bestowed upon Avalokiteśvara Bodhisattva

Translated from Sanskrit into Chinese in the Liu Song Dynasty
by
The Śramaṇa Dharmodgata from China

Thus I have heard:

At one time the Buddha was in the ṛṣi-frequented Deer Park in Vārāṇasī, together with 20,000 bhikṣus and 12,000 Bodhisattvas. Among them were Lion Bodhisattva, Lion Mind Bodhisattva, Peaceful Mind Bodhisattva, Unsurpassed Mind Bodhisattva, Upholding the World Bodhisattva, Nārada Bodhisattva, Divine God Bodhisattva, Treasure Accumulation Bodhisattva, Guhyata Bodhisattva, Worthy Protector Bodhisattva, Radiant God Bodhisattva, Loving Joy Bodhisattva, Mañjuśrī Bodhisattva, Wisdom Action Bodhisattva, Dedicated Action Bodhisattva, Displaying No Obstruction Bodhisattva, and Maitreya Bodhisattva. Bodhisattvas such these were at the head of 12,000 Bodhisattva-Mahāsattvas. Also present were 20,000 god-sons led by the god-sons Good Realm and Well Established, who all stand firm in the Mahāyāna.

At that time the World-Honored One, surrounded by His retinue in the innumerable hundreds of thousands, expounded the Dharma for their sake.

In the assembly, a Bodhisattva called Flower Virtue Store rose from his seat, bared his right shoulder, knelt on his right knee, and joined his palms, facing the Buddha. He said, "I pray only that the World-Honored One will bestow upon someone in our midst the wish to ask questions."

The Buddha told Flower Virtue Store Bodhisattva, "You may ask any question as you wish. I already know your doubts, and I will resolve them to make you happy."

Then Flower Virtue Store Bodhisattva asked the Buddha, "World-Honored One, how does one avoid regressing from the resolve to attain anuttara-samyak-saṁbodhi or from the five transcendental powers? How does one acquire the Illusion Samādhi, during which one can transform one's body by skillful means and pronounce the Dharma according to the roots of goodness of various kinds of sentient beings, enabling them to attain anuttara-samyak-saṁbodhi?"

The Buddha told Flower Virtue Store Bodhisattva, "Very good! Very good! You are able to ask about this meaning before me, the Tathāgata, Samyak-Saṁbuddha. Flower Virtue Store, you have planted your roots of goodness under past Buddhas, made offerings to a billion koṭi Buddha-Bhagavāns, and invoked the mind of great compassion for sentient beings. Very good! Hearken! Hearken! Ponder it well. I will explain it to you."

"Yes, I would be delighted to hear," the Bodhisattva responded.

The Buddha told Flower Virtue Store Bodhisattva, "If one can accomplish a particular dharma, one will acquire the Illusion Samādhi. Having acquired this samādhi, one can transform one's body by skillful means and pronounce the Dharma according to the roots of goodness of various kinds of sentient beings, enabling them to attain anuttara-samyak-saṁbodhi. What is this dharma? It is called no dependence. One does not depend on the Three Realms of Existence, the within, or the without. That there is nothing to depend on is the right observation. This right observation leads to the right eradication [of one's afflictions], with no impairment to perception. Then, from one's true mind, which never changes, one's true wisdom arises, penetrating that dharmas born through causes and conditions have illusory existences. As causes and conditions too are illusory, no dharma can be born through them. Although dharmas appear to be born through causes and conditions, nothing comes into being. One who realizes the no birth of dharmas has entered the Bodhisattva Way and invoked the mind of great lovingkindness and compassion. Out of sympathy, one will deliver all sentient beings. Having acquired a deep understanding of this meaning, one knows that all dharmas are illusory. One simply constructs dharmas with one's thoughts and words. These dharmas constructed by thoughts and words are nevertheless empty. This realization of the emptiness of dharmas is called the acquiring of the Illusion Samādhi. Having acquired this samādhi, one can transform one's body by skillful means and pronounce the Dharma according to the roots of goodness of different kinds of sentient beings, enabling them to attain anuttara-samyak-saṁbodhi."

Flower Virtue Store Bodhisattva asked the Buddha, "In this assembly, are there Bodhisattvas who have acquired this samādhi?"

The Buddha replied, "Yes, there are. In this assembly, including Maitreya Bodhisattva and Mañjuśrī Bodhisattva, there are sixty Upright Ones who, adorned with their inconceivable great vows, have acquired this samādhi."

Flower Virtue Store Bodhisattva next asked the Buddha, "World-Honored One, have Bodhisattvas acquired this samādhi in this world only? Are there Bodhisattvas in other worlds who have also acquired this Illusion Samādhi?"

The Buddha told Flower Virtue Store Bodhisattva, "West of here, beyond 100,000 koṭi lands is a land called Peace and Bliss. In that land is a Buddha called Amitābha, the Tathāgata, Arhat, Samyak-Saṁbuddha. He is now expounding the Dharma. He is attended by Bodhisattvas, and among them are two Upright Ones: Avalokiteśvara and Great Might Arrived. Both of them have acquired this samādhi. Moreover, Flower Virtue Store, Bodhisattvas will acquire this Illusion Samādhi right after they hear and accept this Dharma from those two Upright Ones for seven days and seven nights."

Flower Virtue Store Bodhisattva said to the Buddha, "World-Honored One, that land must have innumerable Bodhisattvas who have acquired this samādhi. Why? Because Bodhisattvas who have been reborn in that land should all go to those two Upright Ones, and hear and accept this Dharma."

The Buddha said, "Indeed! Indeed! Just as you say, innumerable asaṁkhyeyas of Bodhisattva-Mahāsattvas have acquired this samādhi from those two Upright Ones."

Flower Virtue Store Bodhisattva asked the Buddha, "Very good! World-Honored One, the Tathāgata, Arhat, Samyak-Saṁbuddha, I pray that You will use Your spiritual powers to have those two Upright Ones come to this world and to enable [the inhabitants of] the two worlds to see each other. Why? Because if those two Upright Ones come to this world, good men and good women who have developed their roots of goodness will hear them pronounce the Dharma and will acquire this samādhi. I also pray that we will see Amitābha Buddha in the land called Peace and Bliss, so that the good men and good women in this world will activate the anuttara-samyak-saṁbodhi mind and resolve to be reborn in His land. Once reborn there, they will never regress from their resolve to attain anuttara-samyak-saṁbodhi."

The World-Honored One accepted this request, and He emitted light from the white hair between His eyebrows, illuminating everywhere in this Three-Thousand Large Thousandfold World. The grass, trees, earth, and stones in this world, as well as Sumeru, king of mountains, the Mucilinda Mountain, the Great Mucilinda Mountain, the Cakravāla Mountain, and the Great Cakravāla Mountain, and even the dark and hidden places in this world, all turned golden and bright. As the glowing, awesome light of the sun and the moon disappeared, the radiance even illuminated everywhere in 100,000 koṭi lands in the west, including the land called Peace and Bliss, and all turned golden. This great flood of light circled Amitābha Buddha to the right seven times then vanished before Him, the Tathāgata. The sentient beings, Bodhisattvas, and voice-hearers in that land could all see this world and see Śākyamuni Buddha expounding the Dharma, surrounded by huge multitudes. It was as clear as if each of them were seeing a mango in his hand. With adoration and delight in their hearts, they chanted these words: "Namo Śākya, the Tathāgata, Arhat, Samyak-Saṁbuddha!"

In the assembly here, the bhikṣus, bhikṣuṇīs, upāsakas, upāsikās, gods, yakṣas, gandharvas, asuras, garuḍas, kiṁnaras, mahoragas, humans, nonhumans, and others, as well as the Brahma-kings, the god-king Śakra, the four god-kings, Bodhisattvas, and voice-hearers, all saw Amitābha Buddha in the Land of Peace and Bliss, surrounded by His retinue of Bodhisattvas and voice-hearers. He was as radiant as an extraordinary high treasure mountain. His glowing awesome radiance illuminated all lands. All could see Him, just as a clear-eyed person could see without difficulty the features of another person within eight feet. Having seen Him, they were joyful and exuberant, and they chanted these words: "Namo Amitābha Buddha, the Tathāgata, Arhat, Samyak-Saṁbuddha!" Then, 84,000 sentient beings in this assembly activated the anuttara-samyak-saṁbodhi mind, planted roots of goodness, and resolved to be reborn in that land.

Meanwhile the Bodhisattvas and voice-hearers in the Land of Peace and Bliss, having seen this land, marveled at it as something that never existed before. They joyfully joined their palms, made obeisance to Śākyamuni, the Tathāgata, Arhat, Samyak-Saṁbuddha, and spoke these words: "Namo Śākyamuni Buddha! He can expound the Dharma to Bodhisattvas and voice-hearers!" Then the Land of Peace and Bliss quaked in six different ways: everywhere moving, everywhere equally moving, everywhere shaking, everywhere equally shaking, everywhere quaking, and everywhere equally quaking.

Avalokiteśvara Bodhisattva and Great Might Arrived Bodhisattva said to Amitābha Buddha, "How amazing, World-Honored One! Śākyamuni Tathāgata manifested such extraordinary events. Why? Because saying the name of Śākyamuni Buddha, the Tathāgata, Arhat, caused the immeasurable great earth to quake in six different ways."

Amitābha Buddha told those two Bodhisattvas, "Śākyamuni's name is said not only in this land but also in innumerable other Buddha Lands. The same is true for the display of the shining of great radiance and the quaking of the earth in six different ways."

Innumerable asaṁkhyeyas of sentient beings in that land, upon hearing Śākyamuni Buddha's name and epithets, formed their roots of goodness. They all would never regress from their resolve to attain anuttara-samyak-saṁbodhi. In addition, forty koṭi Bodhisattvas in the assembly there, upon hearing the name and epithets of Śākyamuni, the Tathāgata, Arhat, Samyak-Saṁbuddha, made a vow with one voice, transferring their roots of goodness to their attainment of anuttara-samyak-saṁbodhi. Immediately, Amitābha Buddha bestowed upon them the prophecy of attaining anuttara-samyak-saṁbodhi.

Then Avalokiteśvara Bodhisattva and Great Might Arrived Bodhisattva went to Amitābha Buddha and bowed their heads down at His feet. Reverently joining their palms and stepping to one side, they asked that Buddha, "For what reason is Śākyamuni Buddha emitting this radiance?"

Amitābha Buddha told Avalokiteśvara Bodhisattva, "A Tathāgata, Arhat, Samyak-Saṁbuddha, would not emit radiance without reason. Today, Śākyamuni, the Tathāgata, Arhat, Samyak-Saṁbuddha, will pronounce the *Sūtra of the Bodhisattva Treasure Samādhi*. Hence He first displayed this auspicious sign."

Then Avalokiteśvara Bodhisattva and Great Might Arrived Bodhisattva said to Amitābha Buddha, "We would like to visit the Sahā World, to make obeisance and present offerings to Śākyamuni Buddha, and to hear Him expound the Dharma."

Amitābha Buddha responded, "Good men, now is the right time."

Those two Bodhisattvas said to each other, "Today we will definitely hear the wondrous Dharma expounded by Śākyamuni Buddha."

Having received the approval from Amitābha Buddha, each of those two Bodhisattvas told his retinue of forty koṭi Bodhisattvas: "Good men, together we should visit the Sahā World, make obeisance and present offerings to Śākyamuni Buddha, and hear and accept the true Dharma. Why? Because Śākyamuni, the Tathāgata, Arhat, Samyak-Saṁbuddha, was able to forego a wondrous Pure Land, so that He could do a difficult thing. By the power of His original vows, He has invoked the mind of great compassion and attained anuttara-samyak-saṁbodhi in that turbid and evil world, which has little virtue and meager merit, but has increasing greed, anger, and delusion. And He is expounding the Dharma there."

As soon as these words were spoken, Bodhisattvas and voice-hearers praised with one voice, "The sentient beings in that world can receive excellent benefits quickly even from hearing the name of Śākyamuni, the Tathāgata, Arhat, Samyak-Saṁbuddha. How many more benefits [must they receive] from seeing Him and kindling joy in their hearts? World-Honored One, we all should visit that world, and make obeisance and present offerings to Śākyamuni Buddha."

Amitābha Buddha responded, "Good men, now is the right time."

At that time, in that land, Avalokiteśvara Bodhisattva and Great Might Arrived Bodhisattva were each surrounded by forty koṭi Bodhisattvas. Using his transcendental powers, each of them conjured up forty koṭi well-adorned treasure platforms for his retinue. Each wonderful, splendid treasure platform was twelve yojanas in length and width. Each treasure platform was made of gold, silver, aquamarine, crystal, ruby, conch shell, or emerald. Some platforms were made of two treasures: gold and silver; some, three treasures: gold, silver, and aquamarine; some, four treasures: gold, silver, aquamarine, and crystal;

some, five treasures: gold, silver, aquamarine, crystal, and ruby; some, six treasures: gold, silver, aquamarine, crystal, conch shell, and ruby; and some, seven treasures, including emerald. These platforms were further adorned with red sandalwood and flowers of utpala, padma, kumuda, and puṇḍarīka. Down from the sky rained blooms of sumana, campaka, pāṭali, atimuktaka, raṇi, gauraṇi, māndarāva, mahā-māndarāva, palāśa, mahā-palāśa, mañjūṣaka, mahā-mañjūṣaka, locana, mahā-locana, cāka, mahā-cāka, suloci-cāka, caṇa, mahā-caṇa, suloci-caṇa, canuttara, tāla, and mahā-tāla. Each treasure platform was a carnival of colors, splendid, bright, pure, and radiant.

On these treasure platforms stood 84,000 magically conjured exquisite maidens, holding fiddles, sitars, lutes, guitars, flutes, violins, drums, or conch shells. They stood elegantly, playing wonderful music on such musical instruments made with innumerable jewels. Some exquisite maidens stood elegantly, holding incense of red sandalwood, agalloch sandalwood, or black agalloch sandalwood. Some exquisite maidens stood elegantly, holding flowers of utpala, padma, kumuda, and puṇḍarīka. Some exquisite maidens stood elegantly, holding blooms of māndarāva, mahā-māndarāva, palāśa, mahā-palāśa, locana, mahā-locana, caṇa, mahā-caṇa, suloci-caṇa, cāka, mahā-cāka, suloci-cāka, tāla, mahā-tāla, and suloci-tāla. Some exquisite maidens stood elegantly, holding flowers and fruits.

On these treasure platforms sat lion thrones adorned with jewels. Seated on each throne was a magically manifested Buddha, adorned with the thirty-two physical marks and eighty excellent characteristics. Hanging over each treasure platform were 84,000 assorted precious gems in blue, yellow, red, and white. On each treasure platform sat 84,000 wonderful jeweled vases, filled with powdered incense. Covering each treasure platform were 84,000 wonderful jeweled canopies. Hovering over each treasure platform were nets from which hung 84,000 jeweled bells. Standing on each treasure platform were 84,000 jeweled trees. Among the jeweled trees were ponds made of the seven treasures and filled with water with the eight virtues. In the ponds were diverse jeweled lotus flowers in blue, yellow, red, and white. Their colors were vibrant and radiant. As breezes blew, all the jeweled trees in lines rustled with wonderful tones, the harmony of which surpassed celestial music. Connecting all the trees on each treasure platform were 84,000 ropes made of wonderful treasures. Each treasure platform radiated light, reaching a distance of 84,000 yojanas, illuminating everywhere.

Then Avalokiteśvara Bodhisattva and Great Might Arrived Bodhisattva, together with their retinues of eighty koṭi Bodhisattvas, standing on equally splendid treasure platforms, disappeared from that land and arrived in this world. It happened in an instant, as quickly as a strong man could bend or extend his arm. Upon arrival, surrounded by eighty koṭi Bodhisattvas, those two Bodhisattvas, using their transcendental powers, made the ground of this world as level as the surface of water. Their attainments were adorned with great merits, their extraordinary majesty was beyond analogy, and their radiance illuminated everywhere in this Sahā World. Those two Bodhisattvas went to Śākyamuni Buddha, bowed their heads down at the Buddha's feet, and circled Him to the right seven times. Stepping back to one side, they said to the Buddha, "World-Honored One, Amitābha Buddha sends greetings to the World-Honored

One. Are Your illnesses few and Your troubles few? Is Your daily life easy and smooth? Are Your activities peaceful and blissful?"

When that land displayed those splendid, wonderful things, the Bodhisattvas and voice-hearers here in this world, seeing the splendors of the treasure platforms, marveled at them as something that never existed before. They each thought: "These splendid, wonderful treasure platforms have come from the Land of Peace and Bliss to this world. Was it by the power of the Buddha or the power of these two Bodhisattvas?"

Flower Virtue Store Bodhisattva, by virtue of the Buddha's spiritual power, asked the Buddha, "How amazing, World-Honored One! This is unprecedented. By whose awesome power are these wonderful treasure platforms of such splendor now present in this Sahā World?"

The Buddha replied, "It is by the transcendental powers of Bodhisattvas Avalokiteśvara and Great Might Arrived that such great splendor is displayed in this world."

"How amazing, World-Honored One! It is inconceivable. These two good men, whose vows and actions are pure, can use their transcendental powers to adorn the treasure platforms and to make them appear in this world."

The Buddha said, "Indeed! Indeed! It is just as you say. These two good men have purified their roots of goodness in innumerable hundreds, thousands, nayutas, and koṭis of kalpas, and have acquired the Illusion Samādhi. Abiding in this samādhi, they can manifest these things through their transcendental powers. Now, Flower Virtue Store, behold the worlds in the east. What do you see?"

Flower Virtue Store Bodhisattva used his eye, a Bodhisattva's god-eye, to observe the Buddha Lands in the east, which are as numerous as the sands of the Ganges. He saw that before each of the Buddhas there, present as well were Bodhisattvas Avalokiteśvara and Great Might Arrived, both as sublime as described before. They also paid respects and made offerings [to each Buddha], and said, "Amitābha Buddha sends greetings to the World-Honored One. Are Your illnesses few and your troubles few? Is Your daily life easy and smooth? Are Your activities peaceful and blissful?" The same display could be seen in all the worlds in the south, west, and north, as well as in the worlds toward the zenith and toward the nadir.

Flower Virtue Store Bodhisattva, having seen these things, was joyful and exuberant, as if he had gained something that never existed before. He asked the Buddha, "How amazing! World-Honored One, how did these Great Ones acquire such a samādhi? How do these Upright Ones adorn those Buddha Lands with their presence?"

Then the World-Honored One, using his spiritual power, enabled all in the assembly to see the displays. Then 32,000 members of the assembly activated the anuttara-samyak-saṁbodhi mind.

Flower Virtue Store Bodhisattva asked the Buddha, "World-Honored One, these two Upright Ones must have activated the anuttara-samyak-saṁbodhi mind long ago. In the land of which Buddha? I pray that you will tell us, to enable other Bodhisattvas to train themselves and fulfill their vows."

The Buddha said, "Hearken! Ponder it well! I will explain it to you."

"Very good! World-Honored One, I would be delighted to hear."

The Buddha said, "Far back in the past, in inconceivable, innumerable asaṁkhyeyas of kalpas, I had been king 100,000 times. The first time was near the end of the Great King Kalpa. There was a world called Display of Immeasurable Aggregate of Virtue, Peace, and Bliss. In that land was a Buddha called Golden Light Lion Frolic, the Tathāgata, Arhat, Samyak-Saṁbuddha, Knowledge and Conduct Perfected, Sugata, Understanding the World, Unsurpassed One, Tamer of Men, Teacher to Gods and Humans, Buddha the World-Honored One. I now tell you about the pure and splendid things in His Buddha Land. What is your opinion? Are there not many pure and splendid things in Amitābha Buddha's Land of Peace and Bliss?"

"A great many! They are so inconceivable that it is too difficult to describe them all."

The Buddha asked Flower Virtue Store, "Suppose one cuts a hair into one hundred pieces. One then takes a piece of this hair to draw water from the immense ocean. What is your opinion? Compare the water on the tip of that hair with that in the immense ocean. Which water is more?"

"The water in the ocean is more. It is beyond comparison," he replied.

[The Buddha continued] "Indeed, Flower Virtue Store, you should have this understanding. The splendid things in Amitābha Buddha's land are like the water on the tip of a hair while those in Golden Light Lion Frolic Buddha's land are like the water in the immense ocean. The disparity in the numbers of voice-hearers and Bodhisattvas between these two lands is of a similar order. Golden Light Lion Frolic Tathāgata also expounded the Dharma of the Three Vehicles to sentient beings. Even in kalpas as numerous as the sands of the Ganges, I will not be able to finish describing the virtues and splendors of that Buddha Land, and the joyful things about its Bodhisattvas and voice-hearers.

"In the Dharma of Golden Light Lion Frolic Tathāgata was a king named Awesome Virtue. Because he ruled the Thousandfold World with the true Dharma, he was called Dharma King. King Awesome Virtue had many sons, each endowed with a great man's twenty-eight marks. These princes all stood firm in the unsurpassed Way. That king had 76,000 gardens, in which his sons frolicked."

Flower Virtue Store asked the Buddha, "Were there women in that Buddha Land?"

The Buddha replied, "That land did not even have the word 'woman,' much less a real one. Sentient beings of that land practiced the Brahma way of life with purity. They all were born through miraculous formation and nourished by the bliss of meditation. King Awesome Virtue served Golden Light Lion Frolic Tathāgata for 84,000 koṭi years, never pursuing other ways. Then, that Buddha, knowing the king's earnestness, expounded to him the immeasurable Dharma Seal.

"What is the immeasurable Dharma Seal? Flower Virtue Store Bodhisattva, one's spiritual training should arise from one's immeasurable vows. Why? Because as a Bodhisattva-Mahāsattva, one's almsgiving is immeasurable; one's observance of the precepts is immeasurable; one's endurance of adversity is immeasurable; one's energetic progress is immeasurable; one's meditative concentration is immeasurable; and one's wisdom is immeasurable. In all, one should practice the six pāramitās through one's immeasurable cycle of birth and death. One should have lovingkindness and compassion for innumerable sentient beings. One should adorn innumerable Pure Lands. One should sound innumerable tones and command immeasurable eloquence. Flower Virtue Store, even one's transference of the merit of only one good thought is immeasurable. What is meant by the immeasurable transference of merit? Transferring one's merits to sentient beings, wishing them all to realize the no birth of all dharmas and to enter parinirvāṇa as Buddhas, is called the immeasurable transference of merit.

"Moreover, immeasurable are [the Three Liberation Doors:] emptiness, no appearance, and no wish, as well as no act. Also immeasurable are the true reality of no desire, the no birth of dharma nature, the liberation without captivation, and nirvāṇa. Good man, I have only mentioned in brief the immeasurability of dharmas. Why? Because dharmas [with neither birth nor death] have no measure.

"Then, Flower Virtue Store, as King Awesome Virtue entered samādhi in his garden, two lotus flowers emerged from the ground, one at each side of the king. They had splendid mixed colors, and their scent was as fragrant as that of celestial sandalwood. Inside each flower, seated cross-legged, a boy was born through miraculous formation. When King Awesome Virtue rose from his meditation and saw these two boys sitting in the lotus flowers, he asked them in verse:

Are you gods, dragons, spirits,
Yakṣas, kumbhāṇḍas,
Humans, or nonhumans?
I hope you will reveal your names.

"Then the boy on the king's right answered in verse:

All dharmas are empty.
Why do you ask for names?
Past dharmas have perished,
Future dharmas have not arisen,
And present dharmas do not stay.
Whose names are you asking for?
In the dharma of emptiness, there are neither humans
Nor dragons, nor rakṣasas.
Whether humans, nonhumans, or others,
None can be captured.

"The boy on the king's left spoke in verse:

A name and the object named are both empty.
Giving a name and the name given cannot be captured.
All dharmas have no names that
One can ask for.
Their true names
Have never been seen or heard.
As dharmas have neither birth nor death,
Why ask for their names?
Names and words

Are all fabrications.
My name is Jewel Adornment.
His is Jewel Superior.

"Flower Virtue Store, the two boys, having spoken these stanzas, together with King Awesome Virtue, went to Golden Light Lion Frolic Buddha. They bowed their heads down at that Buddha's feet and circled Him to the right seven times. They joined their palms respectfully and stood on one side. Then the two boys spoke with one voice, asking that Buddha in verse:

How does one make offerings
To the unsurpassed Two-Footed Honored One?
I pray that You will explain the meaning.
The hearer will carry out Your teachings.

Flowers, incense, and instrumental music,
Clothing, food, medicine, and bedding:
Of offerings such as these,
Which one is supreme?

"Golden Light Lion Frolic Buddha answered the boys in verse:

One should activate the bodhi mind
And widely rescue sentient beings.
These are the offerings to the Perfectly Enlightened One
With the thirty-two physical marks.
Suppose one offers the Tathāgata
Precious, wonderful, splendid objects,
Filling lands as numerous as the sands of the Ganges,
And joyfully carries Him on one's head.

These offerings cannot be compared with transferring with lovingkindness
One's merits to everyone's attainment of bodhi.
This merit is supreme,
Immeasurable, and boundless.
No other offerings can surpass it.
Its supremacy cannot be calculated.
A bodhi mind such as this
Will certainly attain samyak-saṁbodhi.

"The two boys spoke again in verse:

Gods, dragons, ghosts, and spirits,
Listen to my lion's roar!
Now before the Tathāgata,
I solemnly vow to activate the bodhi mind.

The cycle of birth and death turns for innumerable kalpas,
Its primordial origin unknowable.
Even for only one sentient being,
You have walked the Way for kalpas.
During these kalpas,
You have delivered innumerable multitudes.
Training in the Bodhi Way,
[You never] had mental fatigue.

From now on, if ever I were to
Allow the mind of greed to arise,
I would be cheating
All Buddhas [in worlds] in the ten directions.
Similarly, with respect to anger and delusion.
Similarly, with respect to stinginess and jealousy.
Now I speak the truth
That I will keep far away from falsehood.

Starting from today, if ever I were to
Entertain the mind of a voice-hearer,
Not delighting in training for the great bodhi,
I would be cheating Tathāgatas.
I will never seek to be a Pratyekabuddha,
For saving and benefiting myself only.
I should, for 10,000 koṭi kalpas,
Deliver sentient beings with great compassion.

As this Buddha Land here and now
Is pure, wondrous, and splendid,
May my land, after I have attained bodhi,
Surpass it 100,000 koṭi times.
There will be no voice-hearers in my land,
Nor the Pratyekabuddha Vehicle,
But Bodhisattvas only,
Whose numbers will be infinite.
The sentient beings there will be pure and untainted.
They all will have superb, wonderful bliss.
They all will attain the perfect enlightenment
And will retain and uphold the Dharma store.

If my vow is sincere,
It should shake the Great Thousandfold World.

"After these stanzas were spoken, forthwith quakes were everywhere. As 100,000 kinds of music played in harmonious, exquisite tones, radiant, wonderful garments fell spiraling down from the sky. Gods in the sky showered down powdered incense. Its fragrance wafted everywhere, delighting sentient beings' hearts."

The Buddha said to Flower Virtue Store, "What is your opinion? Was King Awesome Virtue then a different person? He is none other than I. The two boys then are now Bodhisattvas Avalokiteśvara and Great Might Arrived. Good man, it was under that Buddha that these two Bodhisattvas first activated the anuttara-samyak-saṁbodhi mind."

Flower Virtue Store said to the Buddha, "How amazing! World-Honored One, these two good men, even before they made their resolve, had already developed such profound wisdom. They thoroughly understood that names could never be captured. World-Honored One, these two Upright Ones must have made offerings to past Buddhas and acquired merits."

[The Buddha said] "Good man, you can know the number of grains of sand in the Ganges. However, the number of Buddhas to whom these two Great Ones had made offerings, and the roots of goodness they had planted, are beyond reckoning. Even before they activated the bodhi mind, they adorned themselves with what was inconceivable. Among sentient beings, they were the most boldly valiant."

Flower Virtue Store Bodhisattva then asked the Buddha, "World-Honored One, where was that land called Display of Immeasurable Gathering of Virtue, Peace, and Bliss?"

The Buddha replied, "Good man, at that time this Western Land of Peace and Bliss was called Display of Immeasurable Gathering of Virtue, Peace, and Bliss."

Flower Virtue Store Bodhisattva asked the Buddha, "World-Honored One, I pray that You will explain to us, to enable innumerable sentient beings to receive great benefits. In what land will Avalokiteśvara attain samyak-saṁbodhi? What will be the name of his world adorned with radiance? What will be the lifespan of the voice-hearers and Bodhisattvas there until they attain Buddhahood? How will these events unfold? If the World-Honored One will tell this Bodhisattva's original vows, then other Bodhisattvas, having heard his vows, will definitely train themselves to fulfill them."

The Buddha replied, "Very good! Hearken! I will tell you."

"Yes, I would be delighted to hear."

The Buddha said, "Good man, although Amitābha Buddha's lifespan will last innumerable hundreds, thousands, and koṭis of kalpas, it will finally come to an end. Good man, after incalculable distant kalpas to come, Amitābha Buddha will enter parinirvāṇa. After His parinirvāṇa, the true Dharma will continue for as long as His lifespan. The number of sentient beings that will be delivered will equal that during His life. After Amitābha's parinirvāṇa, some sentient beings there will not be able to see a Buddha. However, Bodhisattvas who have attained the Thinking-of-Buddhas Samādhi will constantly see Amitābha Buddha. Furthermore, good man, after His parinirvāṇa, all the precious things, such as bathing ponds, lotus flowers, and jeweled trees in lines, will continue to sound Dharma tones, in the same way as during that Buddha's life.

"Good man, [the night] Amitābha Buddha's true Dharma ends, after the midnight period, when the dawn breaks, Avalokiteśvara Bodhisattva, seated cross-legged under the bodhi tree made of the seven treasures, will attain anuttara-samyak-saṁbodhi. He will be called Universal Radiance Virtue Mountain King, the Tathāgata, Arhat, Samyak-Saṁbuddha, Knowledge and Action Perfected, Sugata, Understanding the World, Unsurpassed One, Tamer of Men, Teacher to Gods and Humans, Buddha the World-Honored One. His Buddha

Land will be naturally made of the seven treasures. Even in kalpas as numerous as the sands of the Ganges, Buddha-Bhagavāns will not be able to finish describing its splendors. Good man, I now give you an analogy. As Golden Light Lion Frolic Tathāgata's land was magnificent, Universal Radiance Virtue Mountain King Tathāgata's land will surpass it billions of times, koṭis of times, koṭis of billions of times, even beyond reckoning. The names 'voice-hearers' and 'Pratyekabuddhas' will be nonexistent in that Buddha's land. Only Bodhisattvas will fill His land."

Flower Virtue Store Bodhisattva asked the Buddha, "World-Honored One, will that Buddha's land still be called Peace and Bliss?"

The Buddha replied, "Good man, that Buddha's land will be called Adorned with Gathering of Multitudinous Treasures. Good man, until His parinirvāṇa, Universal Radiance Virtue Mountain King Tathāgata will be attended personally by Great Might Arrived Bodhisattva and will receive his offerings. After His parinirvāṇa, His true Dharma will be upheld [by Great Might Arrived Bodhisattva] until its end. After the end of the true Dharma, Great Might Arrived Bodhisattva will, in that land, attain anuttara-samyak-saṁbodhi. He will be called Well Established Virtue Treasure King, the Tathāgata, Arhat, Samyak-Saṁbuddha, Knowledge and Action Perfected, Sugata, Understanding the World, Unsurpassed One, Tamer of Men, Teacher to Gods and Humans, Buddha the World-Honored One. His land, His radiance, His lifespan, His Bodhisattvas, and even the duration of His Dharma will be just like those of Universal Radiance Virtue Mountain King Tathāgata. If, among good men and good women, there are those who have heard the name Well Established Virtue Treasure King Tathāgata, they will not regress from their resolve to attain anuttara-samyak-saṁbodhi.

"Moreover, good man, if there are good women who have heard the names of Golden Light Lion Frolic Tathāgata of the past and Well Established Virtue Treasure King Tathāgata [of the future], they will not assume the female form again, and their sins which would entail forty koṭi kalpas of birth and death will be expunged. They will never regress from their resolve to attain anuttara-samyak-saṁbodhi. They will see Buddhas, hear and accept the true Dharma, and make offerings to Saṅghas. In a life after the present one, they will be able to renounce family life, command unimpeded eloquence, and quickly acquire the retention of all dharmas."

Then sixty koṭi people in this assembly praised with one voice: "Namo Buddhas in parinirvāṇa [in worlds] in the ten directions!" They unanimously decided to activate the anuttara-samyak-saṁbodhi mind. The Buddha immediately bestowed upon them the prophecy of attaining anuttara-samyak-saṁbodhi. Moreover, 84,000 nayuta sentient beings, in the midst of dharmas, shunned dust and filth [their afflictions], and acquired the pure dharma-eye. Seven thousand bhikṣus eradicated their afflictions and liberated their minds.

Then Bodhisattvas Avalokiteśvara and Great Might Arrived, using their spiritual powers, enabled all in the assembly to see innumerable Buddha-Bhagavāns [in worlds] in the ten directions bestowing upon both of them the prophecy of attaining anuttara-samyak-saṁbodhi. Having seen this, they all marveled, saying, "How amazing, World-Honored One, those Tathāgatas all bestow such a prophecy upon these two Great Ones!"

Flower Virtue Store Bodhisattva said to the Buddha, "World-Honored One, suppose, among good men and good women, there are those who can accept and uphold this profound sūtra of the Tathāgata. If they read and recite it, explain and copy it, pronounce and circulate it, how much merit will they acquire? I pray only that the Tathāgata will explain in detail. Why? Because in the evil times to come, sentient beings with a meager stock of merits will not believe or accept this profound sūtra of the Tathāgata. For this reason, they will undergo suffering through the long night. It will be too difficult for them to achieve liberation. World-Honored One, I pray that, out of sympathy, You will explain, to benefit sentient beings. Besides, World-Honored One, in this assembly there are good men and good women of excellent ability, who will serve as the great light in future times."

The Buddha said, "Flower Virtue Store, Very good! Hearken! I will explain to you."

"Your instruction accepted, I would be delighted to hear," he responded.

The Buddha said, "Suppose there is a good man who carries on his shoulders all the sentient beings in the Three-Thousand Large Thousandfold World and, till the end of his life, offers them all that they desire, such as food, clothing, beds, bedding, and medicinal potions. Is the merit he has earned great?"

"Very great, World-Honored One! One's merit will be immeasurable if one makes offerings, with lovingkindness, to even one sentient being according to his needs, much more making offerings to all sentient beings."

The Buddha said, "Suppose, among good men and good women, there are those who activate the bodhi mind. If they accept and uphold this sūtra, read and recite it, explain and copy it, make various kinds of offerings to it, and widely pronounce and circulate it, their merit acquired will be a billion times greater. It will be beyond analogy."

Flower Virtue Store Bodhisattva said to the Buddha, "World-Honored One, from today on, I will accept and uphold this sūtra pronounced by the Tathāgata, and will uphold the names of these three Buddhas: one of the past and two of the future. I will read and recite this sūtra, explain and copy it, and widely pronounce and circulate it. I will keep far away from the mind of greed, anger, and delusion. Never being false, I will activate the anuttara-samyak-saṁbodhi mind. World-Honored One, when I become a Buddha, if there are women who have heard this Dharma, they will abandon the female form [in a rebirth]. After it is changed, I will bestow upon them the prophecy of attaining anuttara-samyak-saṁbodhi. They all will be called Away from Defilement, the Tathāgata, Arhat, Samyak-Saṁbuddha."

After the Buddha finished pronouncing this sūtra, Flower Virtue Store Bodhisattva-Mahāsattva, bhikṣus, bhikṣuṇīs, Bodhisattvas, voice-hearers, as well as gods, dragons, yakṣas, gandharvas, asuras, garuḍas, kiṁnaras, mahoragas, humans, nonhumans, and others, having heard the Buddha's words, greatly rejoiced.

PART III

The Patriarchs
Ancient Translators
Prayers
Mantras

The Patriarchs of the Pure Land School

The Indian Patriarchs

Nāgārjuna

Ācārya Nāgārjuna (龍樹菩薩, circa 150–250) was born into a Brahmin family in southern India. He converted to Buddhism early in life then mastered the Mahāyāna doctrine.

In India, Nāgārjuna is the founder of the Madhyamaka School, which is referred to as the Emptiness School in China because his treatises expound emptiness in the Mahāyāna perspective. In China, he is revered as the distant originating patriarch of eight Mahāyāna Schools. In particular, the Three Treatises School is founded on the *Middle Treatise* (T30n1564) and the *Twelve Doors Treatise* (T30n1568) by Nāgārjuna, and the *Treatise in One Hundred Verses* (T30n1569) by his disciple Deva. This school has grown a branch called The Four Treatises School, which adds Nāgārjuna's *Treatise on the Sūtra of Mahā-Prajñā-Pāramitā* (T25n1509) to its scope of study.

Evidence of Nāgārjuna's connection with the Pure Land School is found in fascicle 9 of the 10-fascicle version of the *Laṅkāvatāra Sūtra* (T16n0671, 0569a23–27) and in fascicle 6 of the 7-fascicle version of the *Laṅkāvatāra Sūtra* (T16n0672, 0627c17–22). In each text, the Buddha prophesies Nāgārjuna's arrival and achievements:

> Mahāmati, hearken! After the Sugata's parinirvāṇa, in times to come, in southern India, a bhikṣu of great virtue, called Nāgārjuna Bodhisattva, will be able to shatter the view of existence and nonexistence and to expound my Dharma, the unsurpassed Dharma of the Mahāyāna. He will ascend to the Joyful Ground [First Bodhisattva Ground] and will be reborn in the Land of Peace and Bliss.

In his *Comprehensive Treatise on the Ten Grounds* (Daśabhūmika-vibhāṣā-śāstra), Nāgārjuna replies to a request for an easy path to avinivartanīya (the spiritual level of no regress). In fascicle 5, chapter 9, "The Easy Path," he says, "There are difficult and easy worldly paths. While taking a land path on foot is painful, sailing down a waterway by boat is joyful. Likewise is the Bodhisattva Way: some may achieve avinivartanīya through diligent training and energetic progress while others may achieve it quickly through the Easy Path of faith. . . . Bodhisattvas who wish to attain avinivartanīya in their present life then attain anuttara-samyak-saṁbodhi should think of Buddhas [in worlds] in the ten directions and say Their names" (T26n1521, 0041b2–17). He then gives many Buddhas' names, including Amitābha Buddha. Nāgārjuna says that one should always think of Amitābha Buddha and praise Him in verse because His original vows promise that those who think of Him, say His name, and willingly take refuge in Him will definitely attain anuttara-samyak-saṁbodhi (T26n1521, 0043b10–12).

Nāgārjuna greatly influenced the development of the Pure Land School. Based on his statement, Dharma Master Tanluan (曇鸞, 476–542 or after 554) initiated the theory of the two paths and two powers, as discussed in the translator's introduction.

Vasubandhu

Vasubandhu (世親, circa 320–80) was the second of the three sons of a Brahmin named Kauśika, in the ancient kingdom of Gandhāra, in northwestern India. He and his older brother Asaṅga (無著, 4th century) laid down the foundation of Yogācāra doctrine, which is based on six Mahāyāna sūtras and eleven treatises. A major work of Asaṅga titled *Yogācārya-bhūmi-śāstra* (T30n1579) is reputed to have been imparted by Maitreya Bodhisattva, the next Buddha to come.

Vasubandhu authored many treatises, including *Abdhidharma-kośa-bhāṣya* (T31n1605), *Mahāyāna-saṅgraha-bhāṣya* (T31n1596), and *Thirty Verses on Consciousness-Only* (T31n1586). The commentaries by ten Indian masters, including Dharmapāla as the principal commentator, on these thirty verses were translated from Sanskrit into Chinese by the Chinese master Xuanzang (玄奘, 600– or 602–664) and integrated in his book *Cheng Weishi Lun* 成唯識論 (T31n1585), which means completing the doctrine of consciousness-only. It is an important text for the Faxiang (dharma appearance) School of China.

Vasubandhu is revered in China not only as the originating patriarch of the Faxiang School, but also as an originating patriarch of the Pure Land School because of his definitive treatise, *Upadeśa on the Sūtra of Amitāyus Buddha* (Sūtra 6 in this book). Of all the Pure Land texts in the Chinese Canon, this is the only treatise composed by an Indian master. In the first stanza of this treatise, Vasubandhu says that he single-mindedly takes refuge in the Tathāgata Amitāyus, wishing to be reborn in His Land of Peace and Bliss. The five doors of vigilance in his treatise have laid down the training ground for those who aspire to the Pure Land.

The Chinese Patriarchs

Although the Pure Land School has neither a guru-to-disciple lineage nor a centralized institution, it does have a line of thirteen patriarchs, honored posthumously for their achievements and for their auspicious signs of rebirth in the Pure land. Chen Chien-huang 陳劍鍠 (2001) cites ten historical texts, each with a list of proposed patriarchs. As stated by Chen, the process of electing the patriarchs of the Pure Land School began in the Southern Song Dynasty (1127–1279) by Dharma Master Zongxiao (宗曉, 1151–1214), who first recognized six patriarchs. During the following seven hundred years, the number of proposed patriarchs grew, with variations in the inclusion and exclusion of a few masters. The honor roll became definite only in 1940, when Dharma Master Yinguang (印光, 1861–1940) after his passing was honored by unanimous accolade as the thirteenth patriarch.

Because a booklet titled *Lianzong shisanzu zhuanlue* 蓮宗十三祖傳略 [Brief biographies of the thirteen patriarchs of the Lotus School] began widely circulating in China, Chinese Buddhists have accepted these thirteen Dharma masters as patriarchs of the Pure Land School. All of them demonstrated their faith and resolve, and their training in meditation, and left a legacy of words, spoken or written, and deeds. Their biographies, both in this booklet and in documentations of rebirth stories mentioned in the translator's introduction, reflect the historical development of the Pure Land School. One can see how the Buddha's teachings have taken root and flourished in China, blending into Chinese culture.

Their names are given below, followed by the biography of each patriarch. As is customary, each patriarch is identified by his name (omitting the common surname Shi),[1] the given Dharma name or a popular epithet, and by his place, to avoid confusion with another Dharma master by the same name.

> First, Huiyuan of the Lu Mountain (廬山慧遠, 334–416); second, Shandao of the Guangming Temple (光明善導, 613–81); third, Chengyuan of the Bozhou Bodhi Place (般舟承遠, 712–802); fourth, Fazhao of the Zhulin Temple (竹林法照, circa 747–821?); fifth, Shaokang of the Wulong Mountain (烏龍少康, ?–805); sixth, Yanshou of the Yongming Temple (永明延壽, 904–75); seventh, Xingchang of the Zhaoqing Temple (昭慶省常, 959–1020); eighth, Zhuhong of the Yunqi Temple (雲棲袾宏, 1535–1615); ninth, Zhixu of the Lingfeng Temple (靈峰智旭, 1599–1655); tenth, Xingce of the Puren Temple (普仁行策, 1626–82); eleventh, Shixian of the Fantian Temple (梵天實賢, 1686–1734); twelfth, Chewu of the Zifu Temple (資福徹悟, 1740–1810); thirteenth, Yinguang of the Lingyanshan Temple (靈巖印光, 1861–1940).

The First Patriarch, Huiyuan

Huiyuan of the Lu Mountain (廬山慧遠, 334–416) lived during the Eastern Jin Dynasty (317–420), which ruled southern China. His family name was Jia (賈), and he was from Yanmen (燕門) in present-day Dai County (代縣), Shanxi Province. A serious student at a young age, he studied Chinese classical texts, especially the teachings of Laozi (circa 600–470 BCE) and Zhuangzi (circa 369–286 BCE). At age twenty-one, he and his younger brother went to visit Dharma Master Dao-an (道安, 312–85) of the Heng Mountain (恒山) in Shanxi Province. After hearing Dao-an's exposition of the *Prajñā-Pāramitā Sūtra,* with a good understanding, Huiyuan marveled, "By comparison, all other doctrines are like grain husks." Both he and his brother became monks under Dao-an.

Huiyuan diligently studied and recited sūtras day and night. At age twenty-four, he began to expound sūtras to others. With special permission from Dao-an, he cited words of Zhuangzi, to which Chinese people could relate.

During the turmoil of the Sixteen Kingdoms (304–439) in northern China, Huiyuan and fellow disciples traveled with Dao-an to Xinye County (新野縣), Henan Province, then in 366 arrived in Xiangyang (襄陽), Hubei Province, where they stayed for twelve years. In 378, Xiangyang was captured by the Former Qin (前秦), one of the Sixteen Kingdoms. Dao-an was taken to its capital city, Chang-an (長安), Shănxi Province,[2] and his disciples dispersed. Huiyuan and his brother Huichi (慧持) went to Jingzhou (荆州), Hubei Province, and stayed at the Shangming Temple (上明寺) for five years.

Remembering the plan he had made with his friend Huiyong (慧永) to stay at the Luofu Mountain (羅浮山) in Guangdong Province for their spiritual training, Huiyuan headed south. On his way, he stopped at Lushan (廬山), the Lu Mountain, in Jiangxi Province. Unexpectedly, he found Huiyong there at the Xilin (west grove) Temple (西林寺), and Huiyong invited him to stay.

One day, Huiyuan went to the east side of the mountain. He touched the ground with his staff and said, "If this place is habitable, let a spring rise from the dry soil." Immediately, a spring emerged and formed a stream. There he had a hut built as his shelter. It was then 384, the ninth year of the Taiyuan years (太元) of Emperor Xiaowu (晉孝武帝), and Huiyuan was fifty-one years of age.

Huiyuan had a commanding presence, and awed people were attracted to him. Once he expounded the *Mahāparinirvāṇa Sūtra* (T12n0374) to a large crowd. As if spirits were moved by the teachings, a thunder storm felled trees and cleared the grounds. This auspicious sign was reported to the state official Hengyi (恒依). In 386, under his auspices, the Donglin (east grove) Temple (東林寺) was built on that site. The images of the Three Holy Ones were enshrined, two lotus ponds were built, and white lotuses were planted.

In 402, together with 123 monks and laymen training for rebirth in the Pure Land, Huiyuan founded a White Lotus Society. For this reason, the Pure Land School was initially called the Lotus School.

When Master Kumārajīva (鳩摩羅什, 344–413) arrived in China, Huiyuan sent a letter to greet him. They found Dharma friendship through their common understanding of the essence of the Mahāyāna. Kumārajīva translated into Chinese Nāgārjuna's *Treatise on the Sūtra of Mahā-Prajñā-Pāramitā* (T25n1509) in 100 fascicles. Huiyuan wrote a foreword and condensed this treatise into 20 fascicles.

After Huiyuan moved to the Lu Mountain, he stayed there for thirty-two years. When he saw friends off, he never crossed Huxi (虎溪), the Tiger Stream, in the mountain. He and his disciples mainly practiced thinking of Amitāyus Buddha in accordance with the *Amitāyus Sūtra* (Sūtra 1) in order to attain the Thinking-of-Buddhas Samādhi.

On the last day of the seventh month of 416, the twelfth year of the Yixi (義熙) years of Emperor An (晉安帝), Huiyuan rose from samādhi and saw Amitābha Buddha in His reward body (saṁbhogakāya) filling the sky, attended by Bodhisattvas Avalokiteśvara and Mahāsthāmaprāpta, with magically manifested Buddhas present in His radiance. He also saw waters flowing in channels, emitting Dharma tones. He then saw Huiyong and Huichi, who predeceased him, standing beside Amitābha Buddha. They greeted him and said, "You made your resolve first. Why are you tardy in homecoming?" He heard Amitābha Buddha say, "By the power of my original vows, I have come to comfort you. Seven days later, you will be reborn in my land."

Knowing that his time was near, Huiyuan manifested illness. He revealed to his disciples that during the first eleven years of his stay there, three times he had visions of Amitābha Buddha, and that this latest vision meant that he would definitely be reborn in the Pure Land. He asked them to leave his body in the pine forest, and let the mountain be his tomb.

On the sixth day of the eighth month of that year, Huiyuan sat cross-legged and passed away for rebirth in the Pure Land, at the age of eighty-three. His disciples could not bear to leave his body exposed, so they buried it on the west side of the mountain. Steles and a memorial pagoda were erected in his honor.

Huiyuan teaches all to train diligently with the understanding that dharma nature means no self-essence because dharmas are born through causes and conditions, and that nirvāṇa is the changeless ultimate. To carry on the great Dharma, one must comprehend that a person or a dharma has no self, and must treat others with benevolence.

The Second Patriarch, Shandao

Shandao of the Guangming Temple (光明善導, 613–81) was born in 613, the ninth year of the Daye (大業) years of Emperor Yang (隋煬帝) of the Sui Dynasty (581–618), and lived during the early Tang Dynasty (618–907), his family name and hometown unknown. At age ten, he became a novice monk under Dharma Master Mingsheng (明勝). He studied sūtras, including the *Lotus Sūtra* (T09n0262) and the *Vimalakīrti-nirdeśa Sūtra* (T14n0475), and the texts of the Three Treatises School. After coming of age, he was fully ordained by Vinaya Master Miaokai (妙開).

Concerned about finding in the vast Buddha Dharma a Dharma Door for him to transcend his cycle of birth and death, he went to the temple library and, with a sincere prayer, arbitrarily took a text from a shelf. It was the *Visualization Sūtra* (Sūtra 3). From then on, he diligently practiced the visualizations taught in that sūtra, thinking of the splendid adornments in the Western Pure Land.

Shandao made a pilgrimage to the Lu Mountain and paid homage to Huiyuan's place. Feeling blessed, he began a meditation retreat at the Wuzhen Temple (悟真寺) on the north side of Zhongnanshan (終南山), the Zhongnan Mountain in Shǎnxi Province. In a few years, his meditation became profound and stable, and he clearly saw jeweled towers, ponds, and flowers in the Pure Land. Then he began to travel, visiting accomplished masters.

In 641, the fifteenth year of the Zhenguan (貞觀) years of Emperor Taizong (唐太宗, 627–49), Shandao heard that Dharma Master Daochuo (道綽, 562–645) was teaching the Dharma Door of the Pure Land at the Xuanzhong Temple (玄中寺) in present-day Jiaocheng County (交城縣), Shanxi Province. Shandao went to him and asked about the essentials of this Dharma Door. Daochuo gave him a copy of the *Amitāyus Sūtra* (Sūtra 1). As they carefully studied it together, the sights of the Pure Land became so vivid to Shandao that he entered samādhi and remained in it for seven days. At that time, Shandao was twenty-nine and Daochuo was eighty.

Having witnessed Shandao's samādhi power, Daochuo asked whether he would be able to be reborn in the Pure Land. Shandao told him to place a lotus flower before the Buddha statue, then practice walking meditation for seven days, circling the statue. If the lotus flower did not wilt after seven days, Daochuo would be reborn in the Pure Land. Daochuo carried out Shandao's instruction, and was delighted to see that the lotus flower did not wilt.

Daochuo next asked Shandao to enter samādhi to make certain that he would be reborn in the Pure Land. After a few moments' samādhi, Shandao said to him,

"Master, you need to repent of three sins. First, you once placed a Buddha statue on a window ledge while you stayed inside the room. You need to repent of this sin before Buddhas in worlds in the ten directions. Second, you drove Saṅgha members to work. You need to repent of this sin before Saṅghas in the four directions. Third, temple construction work under your charge cost the lives of insects. You need to repent of this sin before all sentient beings."

Daochuo recollected his past and recognized the truth of Shandao's words. He sincerely repented of his sins in accordance with the Dharma. After his repentance, Shandao said to him, "Master, your sins have been expunged. White light will shine when you are being reborn in the Pure Land."

Earlier, Daochuo had already received a sign. In 628, the second year of the Zhenguan years of Emperor Taizong, during a group practice, all participants saw in the sky Dharma Master Tanluan in a boat made of the seven treasures, together with magically manifested Buddhas and Bodhisattvas, celestial flowers showering down. Daochuo heard Tanluan say to him, "Your palace in the Pure Land has been completed, but your life in this world is not yet spent."

In 645, the nineteenth year of the Zhenguan years of Emperor Taizong, Daochuo passed away at the age of eighty-four, as three beams of white light received him for rebirth in the Pure Land.

After the passing of Daochuo, Shandao went to Chang-an, China's capital, and began his Dharma work, inspiring people to train through the Dharma Door of saying Amitābha Buddha's name. In the Buddha Hall, on his knees, with his palms joined, he single-mindedly kept saying "amituo fo" (Amitābha Buddha) until he was exhausted. He never saved any money, and he gave to others most of the offerings he received, keeping only a few necessities for his use. He delighted in begging for food instead of waiting for offerings. He never slept lying down, and he always traveled alone, to avoid distracting conversation with companions.

To introduce to the multitudes the Dharma Door of the Pure Land, Shandao had over 100,000 copies of the *Amitābha Sūtra* (Sūtra 2) made and given to people for them to recite. He asked artists to paint pictures of the Pure Land, and gave away over 300 pictures. For over thirty years, Shandao diligently trained himself and transformed others. People called him Shandao, which means good guide. All his disciples were also very diligent. Some recited the *Amitābha Sūtra* 100,000 to 500,000 times in life. Some said Amitābha Buddha's name 10,000 to 100,000 times a day. Many attained the Thinking-of-Buddhas Samādhi and, at death, had auspicious signs of rebirth in the Pure Land.

Shandao did not advise people to practice visualization. He only taught them to say Amitābha Buddha's name. When he said "amituo fo" any number of times, each time a beam of light issued from his mouth. Emperor Gaozong (唐高宗) conferred upon his temple the name Guangming (radiance) Temple (光明寺). People also called him Guangming Master.

In 681, the second year of the Yonglong (永隆) years of Emperor Gaozong (唐高宗), Shandao passed away for rebirth in the Pure Land, at the age of sixty-nine. The three versions of this event differ significantly. But in any case, he knew his time. After passing, his body remained flexible and his face radiant, and extraordinary fragrance and celestial music lasted for a long time. His disciples enshrined his remains in a pagoda at the foot of the Zhongnan Mountain, near the city of Chang-an.

In Shandao's view, ordinary beings have severe karma hindrances, and their minds are too coarse to visualize the splendid adornments in the Land of Ultimate Bliss. It would be too hard for them to become accomplished in visualization. By contrast, it would be easy for anyone to say Amitābha Buddha's name, thought after thought. If one can continue training for life through this one Dharma Door, one's rebirth in the Pure Land will be assured. If ten people train in this way, ten will be reborn there. If one hundred people train in this way, one hundred will be reborn there.

However, if this Dharma Door is used along with other Dharma Doors, then perhaps three or four out of a thousand people will be able to be reborn there. The reason is that other Dharma Doors do not respond to the original vows of Amitābha Buddha, and that one's concentration on His name will be interrupted. One should be wary of the undesirable consequence of diversified training.

Shandao encourages those who are dying to prepare themselves for rebirth in the Pure Land. One should remember that one's karmic body is a burden, and that one's rebirth in the Pure Land will be as pleasant as changing into new clothes. One should drop all concerns about the illusory world of one's body and mind, and should single-minded say Amitābha Buddha's name, trusting that He will come to receive one into His land.

The Third Patriarch, Chengyuan

Chengyuan of the Bozhou Bodhi Place (般舟承遠, 712–802) lived during the Tang Dynasty (618–907). His family name was Xie (謝), and he was from Hanzhou (漢州), present-day Jinzhu County (錦竹縣), Sichuan Province. Unsatisfied with the teachings in Chinese classical texts, he turned to the Buddha Dharma. He first studied under Chan Master Tang (唐公) then under Dharma Master Shen (詵公).

At age twenty-four, Chengyuan became a monk under Dharma Master Huizhen (惠真) of the Yuquan Temple (玉泉寺) in Hubei Province. Following Master Huizhen's instruction, he went to Hengshan (衡山), the Heng Mountain in Hunan Province. In that area, Chengyuan was fully ordained by Dharma Master Tongxiang (通相), and he diligently studied the sūtras and the precepts. Then he went south to Guangzhou (廣州), Guangdong Province, to study under the illustrious Tripiṭaka Master Huiri (慧日). It was through the guidance of Huiri that Chengyuan entered the Dharma Door of the Pure Land, and he intensely trained in the Thinking-of-Buddhas Samādhi.

In 742, the first year of the Tianbao (天寶) years of Emperor Xuanzong (唐玄宗), at age thirty-one, Chengyuan returned to the Heng Mountain. He lived in a cave under the cliff on the southwest side of the mountain, near the city of Hengyang (衡陽). He gathered firewood and subsisted on the food offered to him. When there was no offering, he ate grass, soil, and stones. Later on, townspeople carried building materials there and built a simple temple near his cave. Chengyuan named it Amitābha Platform, a name later changed to Amitābha Temple (present-day Zhusheng Temple [祝聖寺]).

Chengyuan diligently practiced the Bozhou Samādhi, the intense ninety-day meditation taught in the *Pratyutpanna Samādhi Sūtra* (Sūtra 7), where the Chinese word *bozhou* (般舟) is a phonetic translation of the Sanskrit word *pratyutpanna*. He also energetically propagated the Dharma. He first taught people the view of the Middle Way, in the Mahāyāna doctrine, then gave them the skillful means for spiritual training, leading them into the Dharma Door of saying Amitābha Buddha's name. He wrote Amitābha Buddha's name on walls throughout the city's streets and alleys, and carved it on rocks along river banks, encouraging people to say "amituo fo." Eventually, those who accepted his teachings numbered in the tens of thousands.

On the nineteenth day of the seventh month of 802, the eighteenth year of the Zhenyuan (貞元) years of Emperor Dezong (唐德宗), Chengyuan sat cross-legged facing the west, and passed away for rebirth in the Pure Land, at the age of ninety-one.

Earlier, Dharma Master Fazhao (covered in the next biography), while residing on the Lu Mountain, in his meditation saw Amitābha Buddha attended by a monk in worn clothes. Amitābha Buddha told him that this monk was Dharma Master Chengyuan of the Heng Mountain. Fazhao moved to the Heng Mountain in 765, and became Chengyuan's disciple.

During the Dali years (大曆, 766–79) of Emperor Daizong (唐代宗), Fazhao became the Imperial Teacher. He told the emperor about Chengyuan's virtues and ascetic life. Respectfully the emperor bowed toward the south, and conferred upon Chengyuan's Amitābha Platform the name Bozhou Bodhi Place.

The Fourth Patriarch, Fazhao

Fazhao of the Zhulin (bamboo grove) Temple (竹林法照, circa 747–821?) lived during the Tang Dynasty (618–907), his family background and early years unknown. In 765 he went to Hengshan (衡山), the Heng Mountain in Hunan Province, and became a disciple of Chengyuan. On the fifteenth day of the fourth month of 766, the second year of the Yongtai (永泰) years of Emperor Daizong (唐代宗), at the Amitābha Platform, Fazhao vowed that, for the sake of bodhi and all sentient beings, he would train for life through the Dharma Door of the Pure Land, and that every summer he would do the intense ninety-day meditation retreat in accordance with the *Pratyutpanna Samādhi Sūtra* (Sūtra 7).

In that first summer, on the fourteenth day of his intense meditation, he had a vision of Amitābha Buddha, who taught him the Dharma Door of chanting a Buddha's name in five parts. He was told, "Chanting in this way accords with the five tones emitted by the jeweled trees in my land . . . Sentient beings in this Dharma-ending age that have encountered this Dharma treasure will be enabled to keep saying a Buddha's name. After death, they will definitely be reborn in my land. . . . They will cross the ocean of suffering in this life, arrive at the Ground of No Regress . . . , and quickly attain Buddhahood" (T85n2827, 1253c18–22, 26–28).

In 767, the second year of the Dali (大曆) years of Emperor Daizong (唐代宗), Fazhao was staying at the Yunfeng Temple (雲峰寺) in the city of Hengyang (衡陽). One day, in his bowl of porridge, he saw colorful clouds from which emerged a temple. To the northeast of the temple was a mountain, under which was a stream. On the north bank of the stream was a stone gate, inside which was another temple. It had a sign, which read "Zhulin Temple of the Great Holy." At another time, in his bowl of porridge, he saw several temples in the clouds, together with palaces, towers, and ponds, and the presence of tens of thousands of Bodhisattvas. Fazhao consulted learned fellow monks about his visions. He was told that this place would very likely be Wutaishan (五臺山), the Wutai (five-platform) Mountain, in Shanxi Province, which is one of the four mountains sacred to Chinese Buddhists.[3]

In the summer of 769, in a Dharma assembly at the nearby Hudong Temple (湖東寺), Fazhao led a group practice of chanting Amitābha Buddha's name in five parts. Their sincere calls were answered by the appearance of colorful clouds all over the sky. In the clouds stood towers, temples, and the Three Holy Ones—Amitābha Buddha, flanked by Bodhisattvas Avalokiteśvara and Mahāsthāmaprāpta. The people of Hengyang all witnessed this display, which lasted for a long time. They all burned incense and made obeisance.

That evening, Fazhao came across an old man, who said to him, "You made a wish to visit the golden world on Wutaishan, to make obeisance to Mañjuśrī Bodhisattva. Why do you linger here?"

Fazhao answered, "The times are hard and the journey is rough."

The old man said, "If one has strong aspiration, what difficulty can there be?"

Then the old man disappeared.

On the thirteenth day of the eighth month of 769, Fazhao, together with a team of fellow monks, set off on a pilgrimage to the Wutai Mountain. On the sixth day of the fourth month of 770, they safely arrived at the Foguang (Buddha light) Temple (佛光寺) in Wutai County.

Before dawn, Fazhao saw a beam of white light shining on him. He followed it for fifty lis, and arrived at a mountain, under which was a steam. On the north bank of this stream was a stone gate, at which stood two youths. They introduced themselves as Sudhana and Nanda. Escorted by them, Fazhao went inside the gate and walked five lis to a temple which bore a sign that read "Zhulin Temple of the Great Holy." The ground there was gold and adorned with jeweled flowers and trees, just as he had seen in his vision.

Fazhao entered the auditorium of the temple and found Bodhisattvas Mañjuśrī and Samantabhadra, each seated on a jeweled lion throne and surrounded by a multitude of Bodhisattvas. Fazhao approached them, made obeisance, and said, "Ordinary beings in this Dharma-ending age have low capacities and severe hindrances. They are unable to uncover their Buddha nature. Which Dharma Door can easily lead them to the essence of the vast Buddha Dharma?"

Mañjuśrī Bodhisattva replied, "Your question is opportune. In this Dharma-ending age, no Dharma Door can better fulfill one's wisdom and merit than the double Dharma Door of thinking of Buddhas and making offerings to the Three Jewels. In past kalpas, through thinking of Buddhas and making offerings to the Three Jewels, I acquired [sarvajña-jñāna] the knowledge of all knowledge. All good dharmas, such as pāramitā and profound dhyāna, are born from thinking of Buddhas, which is the king of dharmas."

Fazhao asked, "How does one think of Buddhas?"

Mañjuśrī Bodhisattva replied, "West of here is a world in which resides Amitābha Buddha. The power of His vows is inconceivable. You should think of Him without interruption. After death, you will definitely be reborn in His land, standing on the Ground of No Regress."

Bodhisattvas Mañjuśrī and Samantabhadra both extended their golden arms and rubbed the crown of Fazhao's head. They said, "Because you think of

Buddhas, you will soon attain anuttara-samyak-saṁbodhi. If good men and good women single-mindedly think of Buddhas, they too will quickly attain anuttara-samyak-saṁbodhi."

Exultantly and exuberantly Fazhao made obeisance to them. He left the auditorium, and the two youths escorted him outside the temple. No sooner did he raise his head than the temple vanished. Fazhao then made a pile of stones to mark the site.

On the eighth day of that month, Fazhao and his group went to the Huayan Temple (華嚴寺) and settled down. On the thirteenth day, he and fifty or so fellow monks went to the Vajra Cave of the Wutai Mountain. They reverently chanted thirty-five Buddhas' names, making obeisance to each name. After only ten prostrations, Fazhao saw the cave turn into a vast clean place where stood a palace made of pure aquamarine. Present inside were holy Bodhisattvas, including Mañjuśrī and Samantabhadra.

Hoping to see Mañjuśrī Bodhisattva once again, Fazhao later returned to the cave alone. He prostrated himself on the ground and prayed. Suddenly he saw an Indian monk who called himself Buddhapāla (his story in Rulu 2012a, 43–44). Buddhapāla led him to a sparkling jeweled temple with a sign above its door, the golden words on which read "Vajra Prajñā Temple." In the temple compound stood hundreds of majestic towers and mansions, and Mañjuśrī the Great Holy was surrounded by the multitudes. Fazhao wanted to stay there, but Buddhapāla did not permit him. He led Fazhao outside and said, "Train assiduously. When you return, you may stay."

In the twelfth month of that year, Fazhao began a meditation retreat at the Huayan Temple. He fasted and vowed to be reborn in the Pure Land. On the evening of the seventh day, an Indian monk entered the hall and asked him, "Why do you not tell people what you have experienced here on Wutaishan?" Then the Indian monk vanished.

Next day, in the afternoon, Fazhao saw another Indian monk, about eighty years of age, who sternly said to him, "If you share with sentient beings your extraordinary experiences on Wutaishan, they will be inspired to activate the bodhi mind. Why do you not do it?"

Fazhao replied, "I do not dare to conceal the holy Way. However, I fear that people might doubt my words and slander me."

The old monk said, "Even Mañjuśrī the Great Holy, who resides on this mountain, cannot avoid slanders. It is more important to induce sentient beings to activate the bodhi mind than to save yourself."

After his retreat ended, Fazhao wrote down his experiences, and circulated his stories for the world to know.

In the first month of 771, over thirty monks of the Huayan Temple went with Fazhao to visit the Vajra Cave and the site he had marked. As they were reminiscing about Fazhao's stories, they suddenly heard bells chiming in clear rhythm. Amazed and delighted, they all were convinced that what Fazhao had claimed to have seen was true. Then they recorded his stories on the walls of the Vajra Cave. Later, on the marked site, about fifteen lis south of the Huayan Temple, a small temple was built, and it was named Zhulin Temple of the Great Holy.

In the ninth month of 777, the twelfth year of the Dali years of Emperor Daizong, Fazhao and eight disciples went to the east platform of Wutaishan, the

Wutai (five-platform) Mountain. They first saw beams of white light shining. Then in the midst of colorful clouds emerged a disc of red light, in which Mañjuśrī Bodhisattva was seated on a blue lion. As snowflakes floated down from the sky, discs of colorful light showered all over the mountain valley.

For the rest of his life, with unwavering faith, Fazhao assiduously kept saying Amitābha Buddha's name. He also taught people to chant Amitābha Buddha's name in five parts. During the Dali years (大曆, 766–79), Emperor Daizong invited him to Chang-an, China's capital, to teach people his five-part chanting practice. Then, in 784, the first year of the Xingyuan (興元) years, Emperor Dezong (唐德宗) also invited him to Chang-an to teach this five-part chanting practice.

One day, in his meditation, Fazhao saw Buddhapāla again, who said to him, "Your lotus flower in the Pure Land is ready. It will bloom in three years."

Three years later, Fazhao bid farewell to the multitudes. He sat cross-legged and passed away for rebirth in the Pure Land.

Fazhao's teachings are simple and direct. He teaches people not to allow anger to arise as they train for bodhi, but to remember that in dharmas there is neither self nor others. Those who seek the Pure Land in the west should remain untainted in the midst of sense objects.

His special teaching for people to attain the Thinking-of-Buddhas Samādhi is to chant Amitābha Buddha's name in five parts with different speeds and volumes (T47n1983, 0476b27–c2): first, in a slow level tone (the first tone in Chinese); second, in a slow falling tone (the third tone in Chinese); third, at a moderate speed; fourth, at an accelerated speed; fifth, at a fast speed. All participants chant the six syllables "namo amituo fo" in the first four parts, but chant the four syllables "amituo fo" in the fifth part. Although the exact tones taught by Fazhao have been lost, modern Chinese Buddhists in group practice chant Amitābha Buddha's name in several ways as they do walking meditation, ending with fast-speed chanting after they sit down, followed by silent meditation.

The Fifth Patriarch, Shaokang

Shaokang of the Wulong Mountain (烏龍少康, ?–805) lived during the Tang Dynasty (618–907). His family name was Zhou (周), and he was from Xiandushan (仙都山), Jinyun County (縉雲縣), Zhejiang Province. Before he was born, his mother dreamed that she visited a nearby mountain called Dinghufeng (鼎湖峰), where an exquisite maiden gave her a blue lotus flower and told her, "This auspicious blue lotus is in your care. You will have a noble son. Take good care of him." When Shaokang was born, the room was filled with blue light and the fragrance of lotus flowers.

For the first seven years of his life, Shaokang did not speak a word. One day, he was taken by his mother to the Lingshan Temple (靈山寺) to make obeisance to the Buddha statue. Pointing at the statue, his mother asked him, "Who is this?" Shaokang suddenly opened his mouth for the first time and answered, "Śākyamuni Buddha."

Hence, his parents gave their permission for him to become a novice monk. At age fifteen, he already understood the meaning of several Mahāyāna sūtras, including the *Lotus Sūtra* (T09n0262) and the *Śūraṅgama Sūtra* (T19n0945). Then he studied the 80-fascicle version of the *Mahāvaipulya Sūtra of Buddha Adornment* (T10n0279), diligently learning the tenets of the Buddha Dharma.

In 785, the first year of the Zhenyuan (貞元) years of Emperor Dezong (唐德宗), Shaokang went to visit the Baima (white horse) Temple in Luoyang (洛陽), Henan Province. He saw light radiating from an essay posted on a wall, an essay titled "Xifang huadaowen" 西方化導文 [Guide to the west], by Shandao. Shaokang prayed, "If I have the conditions for the Pure Land, may this text emit light again."

Forthwith, the words again emitted shimmering light, in which Shaokang saw images of Bodhisattvas. Deeply moved by this auspicious sign, Shaokang prostrated himself on the floor and vowed, "While huge boulders lasting for a kalpa can be destroyed, my resolve to be reborn in the Western Pure Land will never change."

He then went to the Guangming (radiance) Temple (光明寺) in Chang-an (長安), Shǎnxi Province, and made obeisance to Shandao's picture in the memorial hall. Suddenly, he saw Shandao's image floating in the air. The image said to him, "Follow my teachings and transform all sentient beings. When your meritorious work for the Pure Land is completed, you will definitely be reborn there."

Heading south, in Jiangling (江陵), Hubei Province, Shaokang encountered a monk who said to him, "To transform sentient beings, you should go to Xinding (新定), Zhejiang Province. The people spiritually connected to you are there." Then the monk vanished.

So Shaokang went to Xinding and settled down. He used the offerings he received to entice children to say Amitābha Buddha's name. Initially, if a child said "amituo fo" once, he gave the child a coin. Then, a child had to say it ten times to receive a coin. In a year, people young and old all learned to say "amituo fo." The sound of Amitābha Buddha's name filled the streets of Xinding.

In 795, the tenth year of the Zhenyuan years of Emperor Dezong, on the Wulong Mountain (烏龍山), Shaokang had a three-tier stadium built, which served as a bodhi place for the Pure Land. Each lunar month, on the six purification days, male and female believers went to this bodhi place to chant Amitābha Buddha's name. On every such day, well over three thousand people participated in group practice. Shaokang took his seat and chanted Amitābha Buddha's name aloud, and the multitudes followed him in harmony. Each time Shaokang said "amituo fo," the image of a Buddha issued from his mouth. When he said it ten times, ten images successively issued from his mouth, like strung beads. Shaokang told the multitudes, "If you can see these Buddhas, you will definitely be reborn in the Pure Land." Those who saw them were delighted; others who did not began to train even harder.

In the tenth month of 805, the twenty-first year of the Zhenyuan years of Emperor Dezong, Shaokang instructed his monastic and lay disciples: "You should delight in the Dharma Door of the Pure Land and diligently train yourselves through this door. You should feel disgusted with this impure Sahā World and strive for liberation. Those who can see my radiance are my true disciples."

Then he emitted beams of light, and peacefully passed away for rebirth in the Pure Land. After cremation, his relics were enshrined in a pagoda atop a cliff called Taiziyan (臺子巖).

Many believe that Shandao was a manifestation of Amitābha Buddha, and that Shaokang was the second coming of Shandao.

The Sixth Patriarch, Yanshou

Yanshou of the Yongming Temple (永明延壽, 904–75) lived from the rule of the Wuyue Kingdom (吳越, 904–78), one of the Ten Kingdoms in southern China in the period of the Five Dynasties and the Ten Kingdoms (907–960), into the early Song Dynasty (960–1279). His family name was Wang (王), and he was from Qiantang (錢塘), present-day Hangzhou (杭州), Zhejiang Province. He started reciting the *Lotus Sūtra* (T09n0262) from memory when he was a child.

Yanshou worked as a tax collector in the government of King Wenmu (文穆王), and he often used money in the coffer to buy animals that were to be slaughtered and eaten, then set them free. For the crime of embezzlement, he was sentenced to death and taken to the public square for execution. The king sent an agent to observe his reaction. Completely serene and at ease, he told the agent, "Because thousands of lives have been saved, I can die with no regret." The king pardoned him because of his compassion for animals, and gave him permission to become a monk. That year, in 933, Yanshou, at age thirty, went to the Siming Mountain (四明山) in Zhejiang Province, and became a monk under Chan Master Cuiyan (翠巖).

Then he practiced Chan contemplation under the Imperial Teacher, Deshao (德韶, 891–972) of the Tiantai Mountain (天台山), in Zhejiang Province, who was a lineage holder of the Fayan (dharma-eye) branch of the Chan (dhyāna) School. Yanshou realized his true mind, and became the third-generation holder of this lineage.

During his seven-year stay on the Tiantai Mountain, Yanshou often practiced the Dharma Flower Samādhi[4] at the Guoqing Temple (國清寺). Then he went to the Tianzhu Mountain (天柱山) in Anhui Province. There he recited the *Lotus Sūtra* for three years. One day, in his meditation, he saw Avalokiteśvara Bodhisattvas pour sweet nectar into his mouth. After that, he acquired unimpeded eloquence. One night, when he was doing walking meditation, he suddenly found in his hand a flower that had been held by Samantabhadra Bodhisattva in his meditation.

Undecided about his spiritual path, Yanshou wrote two lots, one to focus on meditation and the other to adorn the Pure Land with myriads of goodness. In the meditation hall, after praying sincerely, he tossed these two lots seven times. Each time he drew the second lot. So Yanshou began to train single-mindedly for rebirth in the Pure Land.

In 961, the second year of the Jianlong (建隆) years of Emperor Taizu (宋太祖) of the Song Dynasty, King Zhongyi (忠懿王) appointed Yanshou to be the abbot of the Yongming Temple (永明寺) on the Nanping Mountain (南屏山), in Zhejiang Province, and conferred upon him an honorary title, Chan Master Zhijue (智覺禪師). Yanshou stayed there for fifteen years. By day he did 108 lessons, such as reciting sūtras and mantras, making obeisance, circling the Buddha statue, repenting, and saying Amitābha Buddha's name. By night he chanted Amitābha Buddha's name as he did walking meditation, traveling to other mountains. Hundreds of people followed him, and celestial music accompanied their chanting along the way.

On the twenty-sixth day of the second month of 975, the eighth year of the Kaibao (開寶) years of Emperor Taizu, in the morning, after offering burning incense and making obeisance to the Buddha statue, Yanshou said to the multitudes, "With the mind of no regress, saying 'amituo fo' word after word and thinking of the white hair between His eyebrows thought after thought, I will definitely be reborn in the Land of Peace and Bliss." He sat cross-legged and passed away peacefully for rebirth in the Pure Land, at the age of seventy-two.

During his life, Yanshou recited the *Lotus Sūtra* 13,000 times and accepted 1,700 disciples. He often imparted the Bodhisattva precepts to the multitudes. He regularly gave food to ghosts and spirits, and bought doomed animals and set them free. He always transferred his merits from all his good karmas to adorn the Pure Land.

Yanshou was a prolific writer. His major work, *Zongjinglu* 宗鏡錄 [School mirror] in 100 fascicles (T48n2016), maintains that the thesis of the Chan (dhyāna) School is the mind, which, like a mirror, reflects all manifestations. Citing hundreds of texts, he unifies in the one mind the thoughts of the Huayan School, Chan School, and the Pure Land School.

In his time, there seemed to be a wall between the Chan School and the Pure Land School. Some took the Chan path; others took the Pure Land path. The former, through Chan contemplation, seek to realize their true mind and see their Buddha nature, relying on their self-power. The latter, through thinking of Amitābha Buddha by saying His name, seek to be reborn in the Pure Land, relying on both their self-power and the other-power, the power of Amitābha's original vows.

Yanshou rebuked the Chan extremists, who disparaged the sacred texts and disdained doing good karma. In his 3-fascicle work, *Wanshan tongguiji* 萬善同歸集 [Homecoming of myriads of goodness], he says that spiritual realization must be supported by myriads of goodness, all of which come home to the Pure Land (T48n2017). Over time, the Western Pure Land has become the common destination of all Mahāyāna Schools.

As a Chan master who earnestly trained for rebirth in the Pure Land, Yanshou recommends double training through both Dharma Doors, as stated in his poem "Four Choices" (X78n1549, 0244c19–23), paraphrased below:

> With Chan training but without training for the Pure Land, nine out of ten people will go astray. When the interim state appears after one's death, with a glance one will follow it through.
>
> With training for the Pure Land but without Chan training, ten thousand out of ten thousand people will get there. Upon seeing Amitābha Buddha, why should one worry about not realizing one's true mind?
>
> With both Chan training and training for the Pure Land, one is like a tiger with horns. In the present life, one is a teacher to men. In a future life, one will be a Buddha.
>
> Without Chan training and without training for the Pure Land, one may encounter the iron bed and the copper pillars in hell. One will undergo myriad rebirths for tens of thousands of kalpas, finding nobody to rely on.

The Seventh Patriarch, Xingchang

Xingchang of the Zhaoqing Temple (昭慶省常, 959–1020) lived during the Song Dynasty (960–1279). His family name was Yan (顏), and he was from Qiantang (錢塘), present-day Hanzhou (杭州), Zhejiang Province. At age seven, he became a novice monk; at age seventeen, he was fully ordained. Observing the precepts with purity, he studied the Mahāyāna doctrine, and trained through both the Dharma Door of the Tiantai School and that of the Pure Land School.

During the Chunhua years (淳化, 990–94) of Emperor Taizong (宋太宗), at the Zhaoqing Temple (昭慶寺) in Hangzhou (杭州), Zhejiang Province, Xingchang began to promote the Dharma Door of the Pure Land. Following the way of the Lu Mountain, he founded a Lotus Society. Its members consisted of eighty monks and one thousand laypeople, including intellectuals and state officials.

Using his blood as ink, Xingchang copied the chapter "The Pure Actions" in fascicle 14 of the 80-fascicle version of the *Mahāvaipulya Sūtra of Buddha Adornment* (T10n0279). After writing each word, three times he made prostrations, circled the desk, and said Amitābha Buddha's name. He had one thousand copies of this chapter printed and gave them to one thousand people. Then he changed the name of the society to Pure Actions Society, and its members called themselves pure actions disciples. Kneeling before a sandalwood image of Amitābha Buddha, they all vowed to activate the bodhi mind and train for rebirth in the Pure Land.

On the twelfth day of the first month of 1020, the fourth year of the Tianxi (天禧) years of Emperor Zhenzong (宋真宗), Xingchang sat cross-legged in the hall, saying Amitābha Buddha's name. After a while, he announced loudly, "Buddha has come." Then he peacefully passed away for rebirth in the Pure Land, at the age of sixty-two. The multitudes saw the floor turn golden, and the color lasted for a long time. Twenty-one days later, his body was enshrined in a pagoda on the Lingyin Mountain (靈隱山), fifteen lis west of Hangzhou.

Xingchang made significant contributions to the propagation of Pure Land teachings during the Song Dynasty. Through his promotion, saying Amitābha Buddha's name came to be accepted by people in all walks of life. Following his example, other Dharma masters also founded lotus societies for people to do group practice.

The Eighth Patriarch, Zhuhong

Zhuhong of the Yunqi Temple (雲棲袾宏, 1535–1615) lived during the Ming Dynasty (1368–1644). His family name was Shen (沈), and he was born into a family of renown in Renhe (仁和), present-day Hang County, Zhejiang Province. At age seventeen, he passed a county examination and was designated a scholar (秀才). He had a neighbor, an old lady who said Amitābha Buddha's name thousands of times a day. Zhuhong asked her for the reason. She replied, "My late husband upheld Amitābha Buddha's name for life. With no illness or pain, after bidding farewell to others, he peacefully passed away for rebirth in the

Western Pure Land. So I know that the merit of saying Amitābha Buddha's name is inconceivable."

Then, Zhuhong's mind turned toward the Pure Land. To keep himself vigilant, he wrote four words "shengsi shida" 生死事大 (birth-death matters greatly) and kept the reminder on his desk.

At age twenty-seven, Zhuhong lost his father. Then his new-born son died, followed by his wife. Pressed by his mother, he married a maiden whose surname was Tang (湯). At age thirty-one, he lost his mother. After the death of four family members, Zhuhong saw through the impermanence of life.

In 1566, the forty-fifth and last year of the Jiajing (嘉靖) years of Emperor Shizong (明世宗), at age thirty-two, Zhuhong told his young wife that he decided to renounce family life. Graciously she responded, "You go first. I will follow at my own pace."[5]

Zhuhong then composed a poem of seven obliterations, renouncing seven worldly pursuits and concerns, such as family, glory, and wealth. He became a monk under Dharma Master Xingtianli (性天理) of the Wumen (doorless) Temple (無門寺), and was fully ordained by Vinaya Master Wuchenyu (無塵玉) at the Zhaoqing Temple (昭慶寺).

Then Zhuhong traveled north, seeking beneficent learned teachers. Still within the period of mourning for his mother, he carried with him his mother's name plaque. As a form of filial devotion, before eating a meal, he made an offering to her name plaque. On his visit to the Wutai Mountain, in Shanxi Province, he had a vision of Mañjuśrī Bodhisattva emitting radiance. Then he followed two elder Chan Masters Bianrong (徧融) and Xiaoyan (笑巖), and contemplated the Chan question of "who is saying that Buddha's name."

On his return trip, upon hearing the drum from a drum tower, Zhuhong suddenly realized his true mind. Heading south, exhausted from his travels, he lay unconscious at the Waguan Temple (瓦官寺) in Jinling (金陵, present-day Nanjing), Jiangsu Province. He narrowly escaped being cremated when he suddenly came to and managed to say, "I still have a breath." Before fully recovering from his illness, he continued south and finally arrived in his hometown Hangzhou (杭州), Zhejiang Province.

In 1571, the fifth year of the Longqing (隆慶) years of Emperor Muzong (明穆宗), Zhuhong went begging for food on the outskirts of Hangzhou, and was attracted to the beauty of the Yunqi Mountain (雲棲山). Back in 967, the tiger-taming Chan master of the Song Dynasty had moved there and built a temple, which was later destroyed by torrential rains. In this secluded environment, a few laymen built a three-room hut for Zhuhong. He lived there alone, pondering the Dharma and saying Amitābha Buddha's name.

For years, tigers ravaged villagers in the surrounding areas of the Yunqi Mountain. Out of compassion for them and the deceased, Zhuhong recited sūtras, said prayers, made food offerings, and transferred merit to them all. Then tigers no longer harmed people.

Villagers asked Zhuhong to relieve the severe drought. He replied, "This monk knows only how to say Amitābha Buddha's name. He has no other skills." However, people insisted that he do something. So Zhuhong walked all the lanes in the parched fields, saying "amituo fo" and striking a wooden fish (a Buddhist percussion instrument). The drought immediately ended with downpours of rain.

Joyful and grateful, villagers carried building materials to the Yunqi Mountain. As they broke ground and dug down, they discovered the foundation of the ancient Yunqi Temple. Feeling inspired and blessed, they built upon it a plain temple compound consisting of a Dharma hall, a meditation hall, and living quarters.

As Zhuhong promoted the Dharma Door of the Pure Land, monks and laypeople from the four directions flocked there to follow him, honoring him as the Yunqi Bodhisattva. Their main practice of saying "amituo fo" was supplemented by sitting meditation and scripture study.

Zhuhong revived the system of imparting precepts, and he edited the texts of ceremonial practices for delivering sentient beings in all forms. He established strict rules for his temple. Administrators, resident monks, and visitors lived in separate quarters, and the old and the sick were cared for. Twice a month, on new-moon and full-moon days, all monks were required to recite their monastic precepts and the Bodhisattva precepts in the *Brahma Net Sūtra* (T24n1484), and to repent of their transgressions. At night, watchmen patrolled the grounds, each striking a wooden fish and chanting Amitābha Buddha's name. The sound resonated across the mountain valleys.

In the middle of the sixth month of 1612, the forty-third year of the Wanli (萬曆) years of Emperor Shenzong (明神宗), Zhuhong went to the city to visit his friends and disciples, and he told them that he would go to another place. Then he returned to his temple and treated people to tea, telling them that he would no longer reside there.

On the second day of the seventh month of that year, Zhuhong manifested illness, and he sat in meditation in his room. When his disciples in the city arrived and gathered around him, Zhuhong opened his eyes and said, "You each should faithfully say Amitābha Buddha's name without thought of defection. Do not compromise my rules."

On the fourth day of that month, at noontime, amid the sound of disciples chanting "amituo fo," Zhuhong peacefully passed away for rebirth in the Pure Land, at the age of eighty-one. When the news broke, people's cries were heard tens of lis from the mountain. Forty-nine days later, his body was enshrined in a pagoda at the foot of the mountain.

Zhuhong was a prolific writer, under his well-known epithet Lianchi (lotus pond). His discourses on training for the Pure Land are collected in the Extension of the Chinese Canon. Although he approves of double training in Chan contemplation and in thinking of Amitābha Buddha, he shifts the weight to the latter. He advises Chan students to resolve to be reborn in the Pure Land. As long as rebirth is unavoidable even for one who has realized one's true mind, why not choose to be reborn in Amitābha Buddha's land, to follow the highest teacher (X62n1170, 0016-c2)?

He affirms that the Three Learnings—precepts, meditation, and wisdom—are the essence of the Buddha Dharma. As one single-mindedly thinks of that Buddha, no evil arises from one's mind. This is observance of precepts. As one single-mindedly thinks of Amitābha Buddha, one's mind does not pursue other objects. This is meditation. As one penetrates the true reality of one thought of that Buddha, one realizes that subject and object cannot be captured. This is wisdom. Thus, thinking of Amitābha Buddha is learning precepts, meditation, and wisdom (X62n1170, 0003c8–16).

Zhuhong recommends saying Amitābha Buddha's name as the best method to attain the Thinking-of-Buddhas Samādhi because this is the simplest and most brilliant way. As birth-death is not apart from one thought, likewise myriad dharmas are not apart from one thought. It is sensible to use this one thought to think of that Buddha. If one can discover the source of this thought, one will realize that Amitābha Buddha is one's true nature. Even if one fails, through the power of one's thinking, one can be reborn in the Pure Land, and come to a great realization (X62n1170, 0006c23–0007a5).

The Ninth Patriarch, Zhixu

Zhixu of the Lingfeng Temple (靈峰智旭, 1599–1655) lived from the ending of the Ming Dynasty (1368–1644) into the early Qing Dynasty (1644–1912). His family name was Zhong (鍾), and his ancestors, originally domiciled in Kaifeng (開封), Henan Province, moved south and settled in Wu County (吳縣), Jiangsu Province. For ten years, his father regularly recited the Great Compassion Mantra (Mantra 10) and, one night, dreamed of Avalokiteśvara Bodhisattva giving him a son. Soon afterward, Zhixu was born on the third day of the fifth month of 1599, the twenty-seventh year of the Wanli (萬曆) years of Emperor Shenzong (明神宗).

At a young age, Zhixu prided himself on his understanding of the philosophies of Confucius (circa 511–479 BCE) and Mencius (circa 372–289 BCE), and wrote thousands of words criticizing the Buddha Dharma. At age seventeen, he came across Zhuhong's work "Zhuchuang suibi" 竹窗隨筆 [Casual writings at the bamboo window], which is now included in text 1170 (X62n1170) in the Extension of the Chinese Canon. He immediately realized his blunder and burned all his essays that slandered the Buddha. At age twenty, his father died, for whose benefit he recited the *Sūtra of the Original Vows of Earth Store Bodhisattva* (T13n0412), and his mind turned toward transcending the worldly life. Zhixu began to say Amitābha Buddha's name every day.

At age twenty-four, three times in a month, Zhixu dreamed of Chan Master Deqing (德清, 1546–1623). However, Deqing had moved away to the Nanhua Temple (南華寺) in Caoxi (曹溪), Guangdong Province. Zhixu then became a monk under Deqing's disciple Dharma Master Xueling (雪嶺).

Zhixu went to the Jing Mountain (徑山) to practice Chan contemplation. The following summer, in deep meditation, suddenly he found the world of his body and mind disappeared, and he came to understand that all are projections of the tenacious thinking mind, moving thought after thought. His earlier perception of contradiction between dharma nature and dharma appearance fell away, and all the public cases of the Chan School that had puzzled him became clear.[6]

At age twenty-eight, after his mother died, Zhixu went to Songling (松陵), Jiangsu Province, and began another meditation retreat. During this retreat, he fell severely ill and almost died. Then he single-mindedly resolved to be reborn in the Pure Land. When his illness abated, he earnestly recited the rebirth mantra (Mantra 5) for seven days, and transferred this merit to his rebirth in the Pure Land.

After his three-year retreat ended, Zhixu studied the Vinaya and felt strongly that the precepts were the foundation of one's spiritual training. He was determined to promote the Vinaya. At age thirty-two, he began to study the doctrine of the Tiantai School, and taught it at several temples, but he did not regard himself as an exponent of the Tiantai School.

For the following twenty-four years, Zhixu stayed and taught at several temples, including the Lingfeng Temple (靈峰寺) in Anji County (安吉縣), Zhejiang Province. In 1654, at age fifty-six, Zhixu returned to the Lingfeng Temple. In the eleventh month, he fell ill. On the third day of the twelfth month, he told his disciples that, after cremation, his remains should be crushed and mixed with flour and water, and be fed to land and aquatic animals.

On the twenty-first day of the first month of 1655, the twelfth year of the reign of Emperor Shunzhi (清順治帝) of the Qing Dynasty, around noontime, seated cross-legged on his bed, Zhixu raised his hands toward the west and passed away for rebirth in the Pure Land, at the age of fifty-seven.

Three years later, his disciples opened the cubic casket[7] and found Zhixu looking fresh and alive, his hair having grown to cover his ears. After cremating his body, instead of crushing his relics, they enshrined them in a pagoda on the Lingfeng Mountain.

Zhixu is honored as one of the four great masters of the Ming Dynasty.[8] A prolific writer, under his well-known epithet Ouyi (蕅益) he annotated several sūtras and wrote on various topics. For example, his work *An Essential Explanation of the Amitābha Sūtra* (T37n1762) is a text studied by most aspirers to the Pure Land. His anthology, *Ten Essentials for the Pure Land* (X61n1164), provides another good source of learning.

During his days, the Chan path was considered elite, and saying Amitābha Buddha's name was considered a shallow business for the stupid. Chan exponents generally advised those who were saying Amitābha Buddha's name to contemplate the Chan question of "who is saying that Buddha's name."

In Zhixu's view, there is no need to contemplate who is saying His name. This and other intriguing Chan questions are for those of low capacity.[9] Even if one can eloquently deliver the teachings in all sūtras in the twelve categories and solve 1,700 public cases, these achievements are matters on the shore of saṁsāra and will be absolutely useless at one's death.

He teaches that one should believe that one's mind forms a Buddha and that one's mind is the Buddha. The present mind with the one thought of Amitābha Buddha is pure in dharma nature. Thinking of Amitābha Buddha is the unsurpassed profound Chan training. Saying His name in order to be reborn in His land is like the sobering blow to one's head dealt by a Chan master.

In his view, there is no need to abandon Amitābha Buddha in the west in order to find another Amitābha Buddha in one's mind, or to abandon His Pure Land in the west in order to find another Pure Land in one's mind, because it is impossible to find a Buddha or a Pure Land outside one's mind. Furthermore, rebirth in Amitābha Buddha's Pure Land is rebirth in all Buddhas' Pure Lands.

Zhixu urges all to set a daily schedule for saying "amituo fo." Beginners should use a mālā (strand of beads) to track one's repetitions. Through persistent training, one will be able to say it thought after thought without using the beads. Through faith and resolve, and training in thinking of Amitābha Buddha by saying His name, one will be reborn in His land, standing on the Ground of No Regress.

The Tenth Patriarch, Xingce

Xingce of the Puren Temple (普仁行策, 1626–82) lived from the ending of the Ming Dynasty (1368–1644) into the early Qing Dynasty (1644–1912). His family name was Jiang (蔣), and he was from Yixing (宜興), Jiangsu Province. His father was a good friend of Chan Master Deqing (德清, 1546–1623). Three years after the passing of Deqing, Xingce's father dreamed of Deqing entering his bedroom. Soon afterward, Xingce was born. It was 1926, the sixth year of the Tianqi (天啓) years of Emperor Xizong (明熹宗) of the Ming Dynasty.

At age twenty-three, after the death of his parents, Xingce became a monk under Dharma Master Wen (問公) of the Li-an Temple (理安寺), in Hangzhou (杭州), Zhejiang Province. He stayed there for five years, diligently training in meditation, and he never slept lying down. One day, he suddenly realized the true reality of dharmas.

In 1651, the eighth year of the reign of Emperor Shunzhi (清順治帝) of the Qing Dynasty, after the passing of Wen, Xingce went to stay at the Bao-en Temple (報恩寺). There, persuaded by Dharma Master Ying (瑛), he began to train for rebirth in the Pure Land. Then he met Dharma Master Qiaoshi (樵石), who introduced to him the doctrine of the Tiantai School, and they both practiced the Dharma Flower Samādhi. His wisdom unfolded, Xingce came to a thorough understanding of the essence of the Tiantai doctrine.

In 1663, the second year of the reign of Emperor Kangxi (清康熙帝), Xingce began a meditation retreat, staying alone in a hut on an islet in a stream in Xixi (西溪), present-day Xixi Wetland Park in Hangzhou (杭州). He trained through the Dharma Door of the Pure Land for seven years, and attained the Thinking-of-Buddhas Samādhi.

In 1670, he moved to the Puren Temple (普仁院) in Changshu County (常熟縣), Jiangsu Province. There he founded a Lotus Society to promote the Dharma Door of the Pure Land. During his thirteen-year stay, he often led a seven-day group practice of saying Amitābha Buddha's name. To this day, this group meditation retreat called Buddha Seven is still sometimes scheduled in Chinese Temples.

On the ninth day of the seventh month of 1682, the twenty-first year of the reign of Emperor Kangxi, Xingce passed away for rebirth in the Pure Land, at the age of fifty-seven.

At about the same time, a person named Sun Han (孫翰) died, and then came back to life. He reported his after-death experience: "I was taken by death agents to King Yama's palace. Suddenly, darkness was broken by bright light, and I saw flowers all over the sky. King Yama prostrated himself on the ground, in obeisance to a great master going home to the west. I asked for the name of the great master. King Yama answered, 'Xingce.' Because his radiance shone on me, I was sent back to this world."

People believe that Xingce was the second coming of Deqing. Like Deqing, Xingce first realized his true mind through Chan contemplation then trained for rebirth in the Pure Land. Also like Deqing, he promoted the Dharma Door of saying Amitābha Buddha's name.

Xingce teaches that, during a Buddha Seven retreat, one should single-mindedly say Amitābha Buddha's name. One should say it steadily, neither too fast nor too slow. This great name should continue like one's breath, neither disorderly nor interrupted. During all activities, such as dressing, eating, walking, sitting, lying down, or standing still, one should be aware that His name is present in one's mind. This is the way to train for the manifestation of the one mind (事一心). Then one has a good chance to be reborn in the Pure Land. If one can further realize one's thinking of that Buddha in true reality, then one will understand the perfect oneness of principle and manifestations.

Excerpted from his *Counsels about the Pure Land* is his exhortation for all to elicit the right faith, as paraphrased below:

> First, one should believe that minds, Buddhas, and sentient beings are not three different things. Although one is a Buddha to be and Amitābha is a Buddha fully realized, they are the same in bodhi nature. Although one is captivated [by sense objects] and deluded, one's bodhi nature is never lost. Although one has been transmigrating for kalpas, one's bodhi nature never moves. Therefore, by shining on oneself the light of the one thought [of Amitābha Buddha], one can see what one already has.
>
> Second, one should believe that one is a Buddha only in principle and in name while Amitābha is a Buddha in fulfillment. Although they are the same in bodhi nature, their states are as different as are abyss and sky. If one does not intently think of that Buddha, wishing to be reborn in His land, one will continue to drift in accordance with one's karma, undergoing immeasurable suffering. When the dharma body is transmigrating through the five life-paths, it is not called a Buddha, but called a sentient being.
>
> Third, one should believe that although one is laden with sinful karma and severe hindrances, one is a sentient being in Amitābha Buddha's mind. Although Amitābha, adorned with myriad virtues, is 100,000 koṭi lands away, He is a Buddha in one's mind. Because minds are the same in nature, minds naturally respond to one another. Like magnet drawing iron, He can feel one's pain and respond with His compassion. If sentient beings' minds remember and think of Buddhas, in the present or a future life, they will definitely see Buddhas and will never be far from Buddhas.
>
> Those with these three right beliefs should always transfer to others their merits, however slight, for all to be reborn in the Pure Land and to adorn the Pure Land. Even more so should one transfer one's merits from all good karmas, such as reciting Mahāyāna sūtras, observing the precepts with purity, setting doomed animals free, and giving alms, which serve as the provisions for one's rebirth in the Pure Land. (X62n1174, 0130b6–24)

The Eleventh Patriarch, Shixian

Shixian of the Fantian Temple (梵天實賢, 1686–1734) lived during the Qing Dynasty (1644–1912). His family name was Shi (時), and he was from Changshu (常熟), Jiangsu Province. He was born on the eighth day of the eighth month of 1686, the twenty-fifth year of the reign of Emperor Kangxi (清康熙帝), and he was a vegetarian from birth. His father died when he was young. At age seven, he was taken by his mother to the Qingliang Abbey (清涼庵) to study under Dharma Master Rongxuan (容選). At age fifteen, he became a novice monk. Then his mother died, for whose benefit Shixian recited on his knees for forty-nine days the *Sūtra of the Kindness of Parents Too Difficult to Requite* (T16n0684). On each anniversary of her passing, he made offerings before her name plaque and recited sūtras for her deliverance.

One day, on his visit to the Puren Temple (普仁院), Shixian happened to see a monk suddenly drop dead on the floor. Alarmed by the impermanence of life, he trained even harder. He observed his precepts with purity, ate only one meal a day, and never slept lying down.

In 1710, at age twenty-five, he studied many texts under Dharma Master Shaotan (紹曇) of the Longxing Temple (隆興寺) in Hangzhou (杭州). Shixian mastered the Tiantai doctrine and was recognized by Shaotan as the fourth generation of the Lingfeng (靈峰) lineage of the Tiantai School.

Then Shixian went to Chan Master Lingjiu (靈鷲) and contemplated the Chan question of "who is saying that Buddha's name." After four months of intense contemplation, he suddenly realized his true mind. He declared, "I have awakened from my dream." After that, he acquired unimpeded eloquence. Master Lingjiu offered to bestow his robe and duster on Shixian, but Shixian declined to be a lineage carrier of the Chan School.

Then Shixian went to the Zhenji Temple (真寂寺) and did a three-year retreat. By day he studied the texts in the Chinese Canon, and by night he kept saying Amitābha Buddha's name. After his retreat ended, at the request of the monks at the Zhenji Temple, he expounded the *Lotus Sūtra* (T09n0262) to them and won their appreciation. Then he went back to the Longxing Temple. He often imparted the meanings of sūtras and precepts on behalf of Shaotan, and was praised by Shaotan for his excellent explanations.

In 1719, the fifty-eighth year of the reign of Emperor Kangxi, Shixian made a pilgrimage to the Ayuwang Temple (阿育王寺), in Ningpo (寧波), Zhejiang Province. Before the pagoda enshrining the Buddha's relics, on his knees, he burned his fingers as an offering of his determination to attain Buddhahood, and made forty-eight vows. Seeing radiance issue from the relics, he composed a poem of gratitude. Each year, on the day commemorating the Buddha's parinirvāṇa, Shixian expounded to his monastic and lay disciples the *Amitābha Sūtra* (Sūtra 2) and the *Sūtra of the Buddha's Brief Final Instructions before His Parinirvāṇa* (T12n0389).

Then, Shixian stayed successively at three temples and served as the abbot. To multitudes with different preferences, he taught the ways of the Tiantai School, the Chan School, and the Pure Land School. In 1724, the second year of the reign of Emperor Yongzheng (清雍正帝), Shixian settled down in the Fantian Temple (梵天寺) in Hangzhou. In 1929, he founded a Lotus Society and encouraged its members to train for life through the Dharma Door of the Pure Land. In the last month of 1733, the eleventh year of the reign of Emperor Yongzheng, Shixian told his disciples that he would be reborn in the Pure Land the following year, on the fourteenth day of the fourth month. He then began a meditation retreat, during which he said Amitābha Buddha's name ten thousand times every day.

On the second day of the fourth month of 1734, he completed his retreat. On the twelfth day, he told the multitudes, "Ten days ago, I saw the Three Holy Ones in the sky. I just saw them again today." Paraphrased below is his farewell poem, which is collected in his discourses (X62n1179, 0259a9–10).

My body inside the flower, that Buddha appears.
His radiance shines on the purple-tinged golden lotus flower.
My mind follows that Buddha in order to be reborn.
Neither coming nor going [in true reality], vividly manifested are events.

On the thirteenth day, he stopped eating. On the morning of the fourteen day, Shixian bathed and changed into clean clothes. He sat cross-legged, facing the west. Near noontime, multitudes of believers gathered around, beseeching him to stay. He opened his eyes and said, "I will return soon. Birth-Death matters greatly. You each should say Amitābha Buddha's name with a pure mind."

Joining his palms, he closed his eyes and kept saying Amitābha Buddha's name. Then he passed away for rebirth in the Pure Land, at the age of forty-nine. In the last month of that year, his relics were enshrined in a pagoda atop Fushuiyan (拂水巖), a cliff on the north side of the Yu Mountain (虞山) in Changshu (常熟), Jiangsu Province. In the seventh year of the reign of Emperor Qianlong (清乾隆帝), his relics were moved to a new pagoda to the right of the Ayuwang Temple, and the old pagoda was used to enshrine his clothes and begging bowl.

Shixian teaches that activation of the bodhi mind is the essential first step in one's spiritual training. One should distinguish among the eight ways to activate the bodhi mind: (1) wrong, (2) right, (3) false, (4) true, (5) small, (6) great, (7) askew, (8) perfect. If one pursues sense objects, fame, benefits, or better future lives, it is the wrong way. If one seeks to end one's cycle of birth and death and to realize the unsurpassed bodhi, it is the right way. If one neither repents of one's evils nor corrects one's faults, it is the false way. If one resolves to attain Buddhahood and deliver sentient beings, it is the true way. If one seeks liberation only for oneself, it is the small way. If one considers one's wish fulfilled only upon attainment of bodhi, it is the great way. If one sees sentient beings existing outside one's mind and sees bodhi to attain, it is the askew way. If one trusts one's Buddha nature and does not see a single dharma existing outside one's mind, it is the perfect way. Such a person uses his empty mind to make an empty resolve, and takes empty actions to achieve the empty fruit, and he does not even see the appearance of emptiness. One should use the right, true, great, and perfect ways to activate the bodhi mind.

The bodhi mind is the king of all good dharmas. One can activate it through ten causes and conditions: (1) thinking of the kindness of the Buddha; (2) thinking of the kindness of one's parents; (3) thinking of the kindness of one's teachers; (4) thinking of the kindness of one's benefactors; (5) thinking of the kindness of sentient beings; (6) thinking of the pain of repeated birth and death; (7) respecting one's own spiritual nature; (8) repenting of one's evil karmas; (9) wishing to be reborn in the Pure Land; and (10) seeking to enable the true Dharma to remain in the world for a long time.

Shixian advises Chan students to turn to the Pure Land as he has done. In his view, the words "namo amituo fo" encompass 84,000 Dharma stores, and they cut through 1,700 public cases, like chopping all tangling vines with one blow. One should single-mindedly think of Amitābha Buddha and ignore Chan extremists, who do not like to hear the word Buddha.

He advises all to train assiduously for life because one's karmic rebirths for millions of kalpas cannot be ended by doing good karmas only casually and occasionally. While indolence in one's present life is temporary ease that will lead to suffering in many future lives, spiritual training is meaningful work that will lead to peace and bliss in the Pure Land and eventually to Buddhahood.

The Twelfth Patriarch, Chewu

Chewu of the Zifu Temple (資福徹悟, 1740–1810) lived during the Qing Dynasty (1644–1912). His family name was Ma (馬), and he was from Fengrun County (豐潤縣), Hebei Province. He started studying Chinese classical texts as a child. At age twenty-two, because of a severe illness, he realized the impermanence of the illusory body. Upon recovery, he went to the Sansheng Abbey (三聖庵) and became a monk under Dharma Master Lirongchi (禮榮池). At age twenty-three, he was fully ordained by Vinaya Master Hengshi (恒實) of the Xiuyun Temple (岫雲寺).

Following learned teachers, Chewu acquired a good understanding of the Mahāyāna doctrine. He studied the *Perfect Enlightenment Sūtra* (T17n0842) under Dharma Master Longyi (隆一) of the Xiangjie Temple (香界寺), and he studied the consciousness-only doctrine under Dharma Master Hui-an (慧岸) of the Zengshou Temple (增壽寺). He also heard Dharma Master Biankong (徧空) of the Xinhua Temple (心華寺) explain the *Lotus Sūtra* (T09n0262), the *Śūraṅgama Sūtra* (T19n0945), and the *Diamond Sūtra* (T08n0235).

In 1768, the thirty-third year of the reign of Emperor Qianlong (清乾隆帝), Chewu went to the Guangtong Temple (廣通寺) to practice Chan contemplation under Chan Master Cuiruchun (粹如純). Subsequently, Cuiruchun validated his realization, and designated him the thirty-sixth generation of the Linji School (臨濟宗), a major branch of the Chan School.

In 1773, when Master Cuiruchun moved to the Wanshou Temple (萬壽寺), Chewu succeeded him as abbot of the Guangtong Temple. For twenty years, he guided many disciples in their practice of Chan contemplation. The way of the Chan School thrived.

Chewu had great admiration for Yanshou and Zhuhong, who were great Chan masters but turned to the Pure Land. Determined to follow their example, he began to focus his training on the Dharma Door of the Pure Land. This was a turning point in his spiritual life. He set himself a rule to receive visitors only for the duration of a stick of burning incense. For the rest of the day, he diligently kept saying Amitabha Buddha's name and trained in other ways of the Pure Land School.

In 1792, Chewu became the abbot of the Juesheng Temple (覺生寺) in Beijing, also called the Dazhong Temple (大鐘寺). During his eight years of abbotship, he was recognized as a leading teacher of the Pure Land School. Many devotees were drawn into this Dharma Door.

In 1800, the fifth year of the reign of Emperor Jiaqing (清嘉慶帝), Chewu moved to the Zifu Temple (資福寺), also called the Hongluo Temple (紅螺寺), at the foot of the Hongluo Mountain (紅螺山), north of Beijing. The multitudes followed him there, and during the following ten years, this temple became a famed bodhi place for the Pure Land.

In the second month of 1810, Chewu said to the multitudes of believers, "The illusory causes and conditions do not last. It would be a shame to waste one's life. You each should diligently say Amitābha Buddha's name. One day, we will meet in His Pure Land."

In the twelfth month of that year, he manifested illness and asked people to assist him by saying Amitābha Buddha's name. Upon seeing in the sky innumerable banners coming from the west, he bid farewell to the multitudes: "The sign of the Pure Land is at hand. I will soon go home to the west."

In the afternoon of the seventeen day of that month, Chewu told the multitudes, "Yesterday, I saw Bodhisattvas Mañjuśrī, Avalokiteśvara, and Mahāsthāmaprāpta. Today, Amitābha Buddha has come to receive me."

The multitudes earnestly said Amitābha Buddha's name aloud as Chewu sat cross-legged facing the west. He said, "Each time voicing the great name, I see a part of the excellent appearance."

With joined palms, Chewu passed away for rebirth in the Pure Land, at the age of seventy. The multitudes all smelled an extraordinary fragrance in the air. During the week when his body lay in state, he looked fresh and alive, his hair turning from white into lustrous black. On the fourteenth day, his body was placed in a cubic casket. On the twenty-first day, after cremation of his body, hundreds of colorful relics were found.

Chewu encourages all to face death and to overcome the regular karmic force. Although the regular karmic force is like the weight of one's debts dragging one down to karmic rebirth in the Three Realms of Existence, one's pure karmic force can lift one to rebirth in the Pure Land. If one does pure karma—making obeisance, praising, wishing, visualizing, and transferring merit—for rebirth in the Pure Land, with a mind of faith, resolve, and reverence, one's pure karmic force will grow. When this pure karmic force comes to maturity, one will definitely be reborn in the Pure Land, not elsewhere.

He teaches that one should believe that (1) death always follows birth; (2) life is impermanent; (3) the journeys of transmigration are perilous; (4) the lifespan of one taking an evil life-journey is very long; (5) the Buddha's words are never false; (6) Pure Lands do exist; (7) rebirth in a Pure Land is actualized by one's resolve; (8) rebirth in the Pure Land means one will never regress on one's spiritual path; (9) one will attain Buddhahood there in one lifetime; (10) dharmas are manifestations of one's mind, which forms a Buddha. The first four beliefs support one's aversion to repeated rebirths in the Three Realms; the last six beliefs support one's earnest wish for rebirth in the Pure Land.

Chewu thinks that those who aspire to the Pure Land should know that (1) the path to bodhi begins with activating the bodhi mind; (2) the true guideline from the Pure Land School is to say Amitābha Buddha's name with profound faith and resolve; (3) the skillful way is to say His name with an undistracted mind; (4) the essential training for one's mind is to subjugate afflictions; (5) the foundation of the path is to observe the precepts with purity; (6) the helpful conditions are to do ascetic practices; (7) the goal of one's training is to achieve single-mindedness; (8) the auspicious signs before or at one's passing are evidence of one's rebirth in the Pure Land.

In reply to the question of how to achieve single-mindedness, Chewu differentiates two kinds of training. First, one can train for single-mindedness through any activity, such as making obeisance, repenting, reciting sūtras, doing sitting meditation, saying Amitābha Buddha's name, and circling the Buddha statue. This is called the manifestation of the one mind (事一心). Second, one can realize one's true mind by noting that the nature and the functions of the mind are the same. For example, as one makes obeisance, does sitting meditation, or says Amitābha Buddha's name, one's mind, in its true nature, has neither birth nor death, neither subject nor object. As one continues to search for the source of one's functioning mind, one can only find the one mind, the mind of one appearance. This is called the principle of the one mind (理一心).

As one keeps saying Amitābha Buddha's name, one should drop all other objects. Keeping this one thought, one should be solemn, as if bereaved of one's parents, and be patient, like a hen keeping her eggs warm. Training single-mindedly, one should seek neither small nor quick results. Thought after thought, the world of one's body and mind will be purified by this one pure thought.

Furthermore, one should feel (1) ashamed because one has done evil karma since time without a beginning, (2) joyful because one is fortunate to have encountered this rare Dharma Door, (3) sorrowful because of one's karma hindrances since time without a beginning, and (4) grateful because of the Buddha's lovingkindness and compassion. These feelings contribute to one's pure karma as one says Amitābha Buddha's name.

Thirteenth Patriarch, Yinguang

Yinguang of the Lingyanshan Temple (靈巖印光, 1861–1940) lived from the ending of the Qing Dynasty (1644–1912) into the early years of the Republic of China (1912–). His family name was Zhao (趙), and he was from Heyang County (郃陽縣), Shǎnxi Province. Early in life, he studied Confucianism and was influenced by ancient scholars who denounced Buddhism. Blindly following their example, he also criticized the Buddha. After age fifteen, during an illness of several years, he started studying Buddhist texts. In time he embraced the Buddha Dharma and repented of his slander.

In 1881, the seventh year of the reign of Emperor Guangxu (清光緒帝), at age twenty-one, Yinguang became a monk under Dharma Master Daochun (道純) of the Lianhuadong Temple (蓮花洞寺), on the Nanwutai (南五臺) of the Zhongnan Mountain (終南山), in Shǎnxi Province. The following year, he was fully ordained by Vinaya Master Yinhaiding (印海定) of the Shuangxi Temple (雙溪寺) in Xing-an County (興安縣), Shǎnxi Province.

While Yinguang was airing musty books from the temple library, he came across a tattered book titled *Longshu Jingtuwen* 龍舒淨土文 (T47n01970). It had been written in the Southern Song Dynasty (1127–1279) by a layman named Wang Rixiu (王日休, 1127–62), who was from Longshu (龍舒), in present-day Hefei (合肥), Anhui Province. From this book, Yinguang learned that the Dharma Door of saying Amitābha Buddha's name is the key to rebirth in the Pure Land, ending one's cycle of birth and death.

Charged with the responsibility of writing Dharma programs for the temple, Yinguang wrote daily. He soon developed bloodshot eyes and could hardly see. He learned from his eye disease that the body is the root of suffering, and he resolved to be reborn in the Pure Land. He kept saying Amitābha Buddha's name incessantly, even while performing his duties. Subsequently, his eye disease was completely cured, and he recognized that the merit of saying Amitābha Buddha's name is inconceivable.

In 1886, the twelfth year of Emperor Guangxu, at age twenty-six, Yinguang went to the Zifu Temple (資福寺), at the foot of the Hongluo Mountain (紅螺山) near Beijing. During his stay at this bodhi place for the Pure Land, he not only strengthened his training in saying Amitābha Buddha's name but also studied many Mahāyāna texts.

In 1893, at age thirty-three, Yinguang was invited to go south to Putuoshan (普陀山), a mountain island in the jurisdiction of Zhejiang Province. There he stayed at the Fayu Temple (法雨寺) and concentrated on his training for rebirth in the Pure Land. Between 1897 and 1903, he twice did a three-year meditation retreat. In his room, he kept the words "saying that Buddha's name until death" as his motto.

In 1912, the first year of the Republic of China, a layman named Kao Henian (高鶴年) had some of Yinguang's writings published in Shanghai, in a Buddhist journal. They were enthusiastically received by readers. In 1918, his writings and correspondences were published in Beijing as a book titled *Yinguang fashi wenchao* 印光法師文鈔. In 1926, the expanded version of this book was published in Shanghai. Countless readers went to the Fayu Temple to take refuge in Yinguang. Following his teachings, they became vegetarians and trained in saying Amitābha Buddha's name. Many at death received auspicious signs of rebirth in the Pure Land.

In 1928, at age sixty-eight, Yinguang left Putuoshan and went to Shanghai and stayed at the Taiping Temple (太平寺). In 1930, he moved to the Baoguo Temple (報國寺) in Suzhou (蘇州), Jiangsu Province. In 1931, he founded a publishing company to print Buddhist texts for free circulation. Upon hearing news of natural disasters, he immediately donated the funds he had received as offerings, and had reserved for book printing, to people in the disaster areas. During his stay at the Baoguo Temple, he helped Dharma Master Zhenda (真達, 1870–1947) to establish the nearby Lingyanshan Temple (靈巖山寺) as a bodhi place for the Pure Land.

In 1937, Japanese troops invaded China, and the Sino-Japanese War (1937–1945) broke out. At the request of Dharma Masters Zhenda, Desun (德森, 1883–1962), and Miaozhen (妙真, 1895–1967), Yinguang moved to the Lingyanshan Temple. In 1939, Desun collected more of Yinguang's correspondences and published the second compilation of his writings. As Yinguang continued to promote the Dharma Door of the Pure Land, the Lingyanshan Temple became even more renowned than the Zifu Temple in Beijing.

On the twenty-eighth day of the tenth month of 1940, Yinguang, in a staff meeting, designated Dharma Master Miaozhen to be the abbot, and set the first day of the eleventh month for Miaozhen's installation ceremony. On the fourth day of that month, at 1:30 a.m., Yinguang sat up on his bed and said, "Thinking of that Buddha and seeing that Buddha, I definitely will be reborn in the west." Then he began to say "amituo fo" aloud.

At 3:00 a.m., Miaozhen arrived. Yinguang told him, "Maintain this bodhi place and propagate Pure Land teachings. Do not follow the pretentious way."

Shortly after 5 a.m., amid the sound of people chanting "amituo fo," Yinguang smilingly passed away for rebirth in the Pure Land, at the age of eighty.

In 1941, on the fifteenth day of the second month, the day commemorating the Buddha's parinirvāṇa, his body was cremated. His colorful relics were enshrined in a pagoda on the Lingyan Mountain (靈巖山).

Yinguang always replied to people's letters, answering their questions, resolving their doubts, and giving them comfort and courage. To this day, his book *Yinguang fashi wenchao* has continued to draw innumerable people into the Dharma Door of the Pure Land. Millions of Chinese received the benefits of the Buddha Dharma because his publishing company gave away four to five million copies of sūtras and texts, and one million Buddha images.

Yinguang does not see any conflict between Confucianism and Buddhism. His teachings are down to earth. To parents, he speaks of lovingness; to children, he speaks of filial duty; to siblings, he speaks of mutual respect; to spouses, he speaks of harmony; to employers, he speaks of kindness; to employees, he speaks of loyalty. He advises that parents should especially teach their children to hold good intentions, to say good words, and to do good deeds. He encourages all to become good people in this world and then, relying on the power of Amitābha Buddha's kindness, to become holy beings in His land.

He reminds us that wars and natural disasters are a response to sentient beings' evil karma. However, we can change our evil karma by saying Amitābha Buddha's name and by doing good karma. To avoid suffering, one must remove the cause of suffering, which is the three poisons (greed, anger, and delusion), and one must plant the cause of goodness by benefiting others and conserving resources. If everyone understands that cause and effect continues from past to present to future, then everyone will stop doing evil and will only do good. Saying Amitābha Buddha's name to eliminate the three poisons from one's mind is the fundamental way to prevent disasters, to save the country from war, and to keep people from committing crimes. As taking another's life must be repaid by one's own life being taken, reciprocation of revenge continues life after life. Therefore, students of the Buddha Dharma should stop eating flesh because flesh-eating promotes killing.

Yinguang teaches all to live a life of reverence and humility. One should regard others as holy Bodhisattvas, and regard oneself as an ordinary being. One should endure what others cannot and do what others cannot. One should reflect upon one's own faults and never discuss others' faults. From morning till night, throughout all activities, one should keep saying Amitābha Buddha's name, either silently or in a whisper.

He advises against mixing other trainings into one's training for rebirth in the Pure Land. He cautions aspirers to the Pure Land to be wary of such enticements as realizing one's true mind and attaining Buddhahood in one's present life. In his reply to a lay Buddhist, he states that Chan students do not resolve to be reborn in the Pure Land. Relying on themselves, they contemplate the question of "who is thinking of that Buddha" in order to rise above the plane of the subject-object mind. Even if they have realized their true mind, they are far from ending their cycle of birth and death. Therefore, aspirers to the Pure Land who venture into Chan contemplation have more to lose than to gain. In addition, Tibetan Tantric sects make grand claims, so their ways can be treacherous (Shi Xingfan 1997, 142).

Yinguang promotes only the Dharma Door of the Pure Land. He emphasizes that this is a Dharma Door for people of all capacities: high, middling, and low.

Through one's faith, resolve, and training, as well as the power of Amitābha Buddha's vows, one can end, in the present life, one's cycle of birth and death. Therefore, we all should faithfully say Amitābha Buddha's name without thought of defection, and resolve to be reborn in His land.

Notes

1. All Chinese Buddhist monks and nuns assume the surname Shi (釋), which means Śākya, Śākyamuni Buddha's clan name.

2. Shǎnxi Province (陝西省) and Shanxi Province (山西省) are neighboring provinces in northern China. Their names differ in the tone of pronunciation.

3. The four mountains sacred to Chinese Buddhists are Wutaishan (五臺山) in Shanxi Province, Putuoshan (普陀山) in Zhejiang Province, Emeishan (峨嵋山) in Sichuan Province, and Jiuhuashan (九華山) in Anhui Province. They are referred to as the gold Wutai, the silver Putuo, the copper Emei, and the iron Jiuhua. They are respectively the bodhi places of Bodhisattvas Mañjuśrī, Avalokiteśvara, Samantabhadra, and Kṣitigarbha.

4. The Dharma Flower Samādhi of the Tiantai School is a practice based on the *Lotus Sūtra* (T09n0262) and the *Sūtra of the Way to Visualize Samantabhadra Bodhisattva* (T09n0277). For twenty-one days, one does walking and sitting meditation, pondering the true reality of dharmas. Repentance is an important aspect of this practice.

5. Tang, whose Dharma name was Zhujing (袾錦), became a nun at age forty-seven. Later she served as the abbess of the Xiaoyi Abbey (孝義庵), and was honored as Dharma Master Taisu (太素). At age sixty-seven, she passed away for rebirth in the Pure Land, one year before Zhuhong.

6. In Chan tradition, a story of the interaction between a master and a student is called a *gong-an* (public case), and there are 1,700 documented public cases. A single word or a short question is called a *huatou* (speech head). For example, a student asked Chan Master Zhaozhou (趙州, 778–897), "Does a dog also have Buddha nature?" He replied, "None ['wu' in Chinese]." Their dialogue is a *gong-an*, and the word *wu* is a *huatou*. Another example of a *huatou* is the question of "who is thinking of that Buddha" or "who is dragging this corpse." Through contemplating a *gong-an* or a *huatou* without using the conscious mind, i.e., not allowing any word in a mental speech to emerge (poke its head out), a student may come to realize his true mind and/or see his Buddha nature. A frequently cited public case is in text 27 in the Extension of the Chinese Canon (X01n0027, 0442c16–21). Seated, the Buddha holds up a flower. While the bhikṣus and millions of gods and humans in the assembly remain silent, Mahākāśyapa responds with a smile. He rises from his seat and stands with joined palms, without saying a word. Then the Buddha makes an important announcement: "I have the store of the true dharma-eye, the wondrous mind of nirvāṇa. This

wondrous dharma of true reality is appearance free. Not set in words, it is imparted specially, outside the teachings. Through causes and conditions, those with or without wisdom can realize it. Today, I entrust it to Mahākāśyapa." Thus, Mahākāśyapa was designated the first patriarch in the Buddhist lineage. This story is the basis for the Chan School to declare that their way is "imparted specially, outside the teachings."

7. A cubic casket is a box to hold a dead body seated cross-legged.

8. The four great Buddhist masters of the Ming Dynasty are Zhuhong (袾宏, 1535–1615), Zibo (紫柏, 1543–1603), Deqing (德清, 1546–1623), and Zhixu (智旭, 1599–1655).

9. It is generally recognized that those who, through any method, have realized their true mind and seen their Buddha nature, are of high capacity. The issue is that they are still in their cycle of birth and death, and are likely to regress even as soon as in the next life.

Ancient Translators

Lokakṣema

Lokakṣema (支婁迦讖 or 支讖, 147–?) was from Gandhāra, an ancient Indian kingdom in present-day Kashmir, northern Pakistan, and eastern Afghanistan area. He was given the surname Zhi in Chinese, because he was a descendant of the Kushan (貴霜) tribe of Yuezhi ethnicity (月氏). He went to Luoyang (洛陽), China's capital, in 167, the last year of Emperor Huan (漢桓帝) of the Eastern Han Dynasty (25–220). During the last eleven years (178–89) of Emperor Ling (漢靈帝), he translated over twenty sūtras, of which twelve are extant.

Lokakṣema was the first Indian monk who went to China to propagate Mahāyāna teachings. Among the texts he translated from Sanskrit into Chinese, the *Sūtra of the Practice of Prajñā-Pāramitā* (T08n0224) was the first in a series of prajñā-pāramitā sūtras that laid the foundation of the Mahāyāna in China; the *Sūtra of Infinite Pure Equal Enlightenment* (T12n0361) was the first of the five versions of the *Amitāyus Sūtra* that arrived in China; both versions of the *Sūtra of Pratyutpanna Buddha Sammukhāvasthita Samādhi* (T13n0417–18) prescribe an intense three-month meditation retreat.

Saṅghavarman

Saṅghavarman (康僧鎧, 3rd century) was supposedly an Indian. His Sanskrit name was translated into Chinese as Saṅgha armor, and he was given the surname Kang in Chinese, which may imply his ethnic origin from Kangju (康居) nomads in central Asia. He went to Luoyang (洛陽), in 252, the fourth year of the Jiaping (嘉平) years of the Cao Wei Kingdom (220–65). He stayed at the White Horse Temple and translated, from Sanskrit into Chinese, the *Sūtra of Amitāyus Buddha* (T12n0360) and the *Sūtra of the Elder Ugra*. The latter is included in the *Great Treasure Pile Sūtra* (T11n0310) as its 19th sūtra, in fascicle 82. Scholars question the consistency in style between these two translations. Still, he has been recognized as the translator of the *Sūtra of Amitāyus Buddha*.

He is not to be confused with two other Saṅghavarmans. The same Sanskrit name was translated into Chinese as Sengqie-bamo (僧伽跋摩) for one from India, who went to China in 433, and as Sengqie-poluo (僧伽婆羅) for the other from Funan, who lived from 460 to 524 and is also known as Saṅghapāla.

Kumārajīva

Kumārajīva (鳩摩羅什, 344–413) means youth life. He lived during the turbulent period of the Sixteen Kingdoms (304–439), which posed a threat to the Eastern Jin Dynasty (317–420). He is one of the four great sūtra translators in China. His father, Kumārāyana, was from a noble family in India, who went to Kucha (龜茲,

or 庫車, in present-day Aksu Prefecture, Xinjiang, China) and married the king's sister, Princess Jīva. From their union, Kumārajīva was born.

Jīva renounced family life when Kumārajīva was seven. Mother and son traveled in India, studying under renowned Buddhist masters. Even at such a young age, Kumārajīva had already committed to memory many sūtras and texts, and his name was heard throughout the five kingdoms of India. At twelve, he traveled with his mother to Turfan (吐魯番, an oasis city in Xinjiang, China), but the king of Kucha went to Turfan to ask him to return to Kucha. So he returned to his homeland and stayed there until his destiny called.

Fujian (苻堅), ruler of the Former Qin Kingdom (前秦) in China, had heard of the marvelous Kumārajīva and wanted to bring him to China. In 382, he sent his general Luguang (呂光) to conquer Kucha. Kucha fell the next year, and Luguang captured Kumārajīva. On their way to China, Luguang got the news that Fujian had been defeated at the Battle of the Fei River. Luguang then settled in Liangzhou (涼州), in present-day Gansu Province, and founded a state called Later Liang (後涼). For seventeen years, Kumārajīva was detained there. Finally, Yaoxing (姚興), ruler of Later Qin (後秦, 384–417), conquered Later Liang and took Kumārajīva to China.

In 401, Kumārajīva arrived in Chang-an (長安), China's capital, and Yaoxing honored him as the Imperial Teacher and forced him to marry ten women for the purpose of producing descendants of his caliber. He stayed at the Xiaoyao Garden (逍遙園) and began his great translation work with a team of assistants. During the rest of his life, he translated, from Sanskrit into Chinese, seventy-four texts in 384 fascicles, including the *Amitābha Sūtra* (T12n0366), the *Mahā-prajñā-pāramitā Sūtra* (T08n0223), the *Diamond Sūtra* (T08n0235), the *Heart Sūtra* (T08n0250), the *Lotus Sūtra* (T09n0262), the *Vimalakīrti-nirdeśa Sūtra* (T14n0475), and the *Brahma Net Sūtra* (T24n1484), as well as treatises, such as the *Mahā-prajñā-pāramitā-śāstra* (T25n1509), the *Mūlamadhyamaka-kārikā* (T30n1564), and the *Dvādaśanikāya-śāstra* (T30n1568), authored by Ācārya Nāgārjuna (龍樹菩薩, circa 150–250).

Kumārajīva's fluid and elegant translations greatly contributed to the propagation of the Dharma in China. Before his death, he said that if his translations were truthful, his tongue would not be destroyed by fire. After cremation of his body, indeed, his tongue was found intact.

Kālayaśas

Kālayaśas (畺良耶舍, 383–442) means time renown (時稱). He was from India and was accomplished in the Vinaya and the Abhidharma, especially in meditation. In 424, the first year of the Yuanjia (元嘉) years of the Liu Song Dynasty (劉宋, 420–79), he went to Jianye (建業), present-day Nanjing, China, and stayed at the Daolin Ashram (道林精舍), near the Zhong Mountain (鍾山).

He translated, from Sanskrit into Chinese, the *Sūtra of Visualization of Amitāyus Buddha* (T12n0365) and the *Sūtra of Visualization of Bodhisattvas Medicine King and Medicine Superior* (T20n1161). In 442, he visited some areas of Sichuan Province and expounded the Dharma to the multitudes. He died soon after his return, at the age of sixty.

Dharmodgata

Dharmodgata (曇無竭, 4th–5th centuries) was from Huanglong (黃龍), present-day Chaoyang (朝陽), Liaoning Province, and his family name was Lee. He became a novice monk when he was just a child. He studied hard, observing the precepts and reciting sūtras, and was well regarded by his teachers. Inspired by the example of Dharma Master Faxian (法顯, circa 337–422), who went to India in 399 and brought back Sanskrit texts in 413, Dharmodgata vowed to seek the Dharma even at the cost of his life.

In 420, the first year of the Yongchu (永初) years of the Liu Song Dynasty (劉宋, 420–79), Dharmodgata set out for the western country, together with twenty-five monks who shared his aspiration. They carried with them banners and ritual objects for making offerings as well as food and utensils.

The team passed Khocho (高昌, in present-day Turfan Prefecture, Xinjiang, China), Kucha (龜茲, or 庫車, in present-day Aksu Prefecture, Xinjiang, China), and other kingdoms. Only thirteen members of the team survived climbing a cliff on their way. After crossing the snow mountain, they arrived in Kophen (罽賓, an ancient kingdom, also called Gandhāra, in present-day Kashmir, northern Pakistan, and eastern Afghanistan area). They made obeisance to the Buddha's begging bowl and received the Sanskrit text of the *Sūtra of the Prophecy Bestowed upon Avalokiteśvara Bodhisattva* (T12n0371). The team stayed there for over a year, learning Sanskrit and studying Sanskrit texts.

The team continued on west and visited the Yuezhi country (月氏, the moon people, an Indo-European people, who had established the Kushan Empire, which at its height stretched from what is now Tajikistan to Afghanistan, Pakistan, and down into the Ganges river valley in northern India), where they paid homage to a relic of the Buddha, His head bone. Then they went to northern India, present-day Pakistan, and stayed at the Pomegranate Temple for three months, passing the summer. At this temple in India, Dharmodgata accepted the complete monastic precepts and became a fully ordained monk.

Trudging south toward Śrāvastī in central India, Dharmodgata and his team crossed unforgiving terrain and relied on sugar for food. Only five of the thirteen-member team survived the ordeal. Throughout the hardships, Dharmodgata never forgot the sūtra that he was carrying with him. By invoking Avalokiteśvara Bodhisattva's help, Dharmodgata and his surviving team escaped the perils of raging elephants and then of buffaloes.

The team continued to travel in India for several years, paying homage to the sacred sites of the Buddha and visiting with illustrious masters. Finally, departing from southern India, they undertook their return journey by sea, aboard a merchant ship. Crossing the Indian Ocean and the South China Sea, they safely arrived in Guangzhou (廣州), Guangdong Province. Dharmodgata stayed in that area, propagating the Dharma until his death.

It is remarkable that Dharmodgata had gone to India, seeking the Dharma, about two hundred years earlier than Dharma Master Xuanzang (玄奘, 600– or 602–64). However, his book on his adventurous pilgrimage had been lost.

Mandra

Mandra (曼陀羅仙, 5th–6th centuries) was a Tripiṭaka master from Funan (扶南), a pre-Angkor Indianized kingdom located around the Mekong delta. In 503, the second year of the Tianjian (天監) years during the Southern Liang Dynasty (502–57), Mandra arrived in Jiankang (建康), present-day Nanjing, Jiangsu Province. With the support of Emperor Wu (梁武帝), he helped Saṅghapāla (僧伽婆羅, 460–524), who was also from Funan, translate Sanskrit texts into Chinese. In 506, Mandra translated the *Sūtra of Mahā-Prajña-Pāramitā Pronounced by Mañjuśrī Bodhisattva* (T08n0232). Nothing more is known about him.

Bodhiruci

Bodhiruci (菩提留支, 5th–6th centuries) means bodhi splendor. A Buddhist master from northern India, he was versed in mantra practices and the Tripiṭaka. Aspiring to propagate the Dharma, in 502, the first year of the Yongping (永平) years of the Northern Wei Dynasty (386–534), he arrived in Luoyang (洛陽), China's capital. Emperor Xuanwu (魏宣武帝) valued him highly and commanded him to stay in the Yongning Temple (永寧寺) to translate Sanskrit texts into Chinese. He translated thirty-nine texts in 127 fascicles, including the *Diamond Sūtra* (T08n0236), the *Buddha Name Sūtra* (T14n0440), the 10-fascicle version of the *Laṅkāvatāra Sūtra* (T16n0671), the *Sūtra of the Profound Secret Liberation* (T16n0675), the *Sūtra of Neither Increase Nor Decrease* (T16n0668), and the *Dharma Collection Sūtra* (T17n0761), as well as treatises, such as the *Treatise on the Ten Grounds Sūtra* (T26n1522), the *Treatise on the Great Treasure Pile Sūtra* (T26n1523), and the *Upadeśa on the Sūtra of Amitāyus Buddha* (T26n1524). After 537, Bodhiruci was not seen again.

Bodhiruci expressed his unique view on the Buddha's teachings. Based on the *Mahāparinirvāṇa Sūtra* (T12n0374), he said that, for the first twelve years, the Buddha gave only half-worded teachings, followed afterward by fully-worded teachings. Bodhiruci also proposed the one tone theory, saying that the Buddha pronounces teachings in one tone, and sentient beings come to a variety of understandings according to their capacities. Furthermore, based on the *Laṅkāvatāra Sūtra,* he proposed the distinction between immediate and gradual enlightenment.

Śikṣānanda

Śikṣānanda (實叉難陀, 652–710) means study joy. He was from the kingdom of Yutian (于闐), or Khotan, present-day Hetian (和田), in Xinjiang, China. He was accomplished in the doctrines of Mahāyāna and Hīnayāna as well as other studies. In 695, the first year of the Zhengsheng (證聖) years of Empress Wu (武后則天) of the Tang Dynasty (618–907), Śikṣānanda took the Sanskrit text of the *Mahāvaipulya Sūtra of Buddha Adornment* (Buddhāvataṁsaka-mahāvaipulya-sūtra) to Luoyang (洛陽), China's eastern capital. At the command of Empress Wu, in collaboration with Bodhiruci (菩提流志, 562–727) and Yijing (義淨, 635–713), he translated the text into Chinese at the Dabiankong Temple (大遍空寺) in Luoyang. This version in 80 fascicles (T10n0279) is more comprehensive than the 60-fascicle version (T09n0278) translated by Buddhabhadra (佛馱跋陀羅, 359–429) in the Eastern Jin Dynasty (316–420). Altogether, Śikṣānanda translated, from Sanskrit into Chinese, nineteen sūtras in 107 fascicles, including the *Mahāvaipulya Sūtra of the Inconceivable State of Tathāgatas* (T10n0301), the 7-fascicle version of the *Laṅkāvatāra Sūtra* (T16n0672), and the *Sūtra of the Prophecy Bestowed on Mañjuśrī*, which is included in the *Great Treasure Pile Sūtra* (T11n0310) as its 15th sūtra, in fascicles 58–60.

In 705, Śikṣānanda returned to his homeland. However, upon repeated invitations, in 708, the second year of the Jinglong (景龍) years, once again he went to China. Emperor Zhongzong (唐中宗) went outside the capital city to welcome him respectfully.

Śikṣānanda fell ill and died in the tenth month of 710, the first year of the Jingyun (景雲) years, at the age of fifty-nine. After cremation of his body, his tongue remained intact. His disciples returned his relics and tongue to Yutian and had a memorial pagoda built for enshrining them. Later on, a seven-story memorial pagoda was erected at the place where he had been cremated. It is called the Huayan Sanzang Pagoda, which means Flower Adornment Tripiṭaka Pagoda, because Śikṣānanda was the Tripiṭaka master who had translated this sūtra, the name of which in Chinese is Flower Adornment.

Pramiti

Pramiti (般剌蜜帝, 7th–8th centuries) means correct measure. He was a monk from central India. On his first attempt to carry the *Śūraṅgama Sūtra* to China, he was found out by coast guards and was turned back. More determined than ever to have the Dharma spread throughout China, he copied the sūtra onto fine white fabric and had it sewn under the skin of his arm. After his arm was healed, he passed the inspection and was allowed to leave India.

Pramiti traveled by sea and arrived in Guangzhou (廣州), Guangdong Province, in 705, the first year of the Shenlong (神龍) years of Emperor Zhongzong (唐中宗) of the Tang Dynasty (618–907). He stayed at the Zhizhi Temple (制止寺) in Guangzhou and started to translate this *Śūraṅgama Sūtra* in 10 fascicles. He was assisted by Miccaśakya (彌伽鑠佉), an Indian monk from Udyāna, who helped render the Sanskrit text into Chinese, and by Fangrong (房融), a Chinese layman, who recorded the translation. Then a learned Chinese monk named Huaidi (懷迪) reviewed the Chinese translation (T19n0945) in light of the meaning conveyed by the sūtra.

It did not take too long for the king, furious about Pramiti's taking the sūtra out of the country, to send agents to find Pramiti. He was found and, under the escort of the agents, willingly returned to India, to accept the responsibility for his action.

The story goes that Ācārya Nāgārjuna (龍樹菩薩, circa 150–250), who is revered in China as the distant originating patriarch of eight Mahāyāna Schools, in his meditation, saw the *Śūraṅgama Sūtra* and the *Mahāvaipulya Sūtra of Buddha Adornment* in the dragon-king's palace, and he memorized these texts. Then he wrote down everything from memory. The *Śūraṅgama Sūtra* was considered a national treasure and kept in the Nālandā Monastery. Though it was forbidden to take this sūtra outside the country, it was smuggled out by Pramiti.

There was another good reason for the arrival of this sūtra in China. Over one hundred years earlier, an Indian monk remarked to Master Zhiyi (智顗, 538–97), the founding patriarch of the Tiantai School of China, that the threefold meditation of his School accorded with the tenets of the *Śūraṅgama Sūtra*. Master Zhiyi was so inspired that he had a platform built on the peak of the Tiantai Mountain. For the eighteen years until his death, on this platform he routinely bowed down toward the west, requesting this sūtra to come to China. However, he was not to see this sūtra in his life. This obeisance-to-the-sūtra platform is still there today on the Huading Peak (華頂峰) of the Tiantai Mountain, in Zhejiang Province.

Prajñā

Prajñā (般若, 734–?) was from Kophen (罽賓), an ancient kingdom, also called Gandhāra, in present-day Kashmir, northern Pakistan, and eastern Afghanistan area. He became a novice monk at seven and was fully ordained at twenty. When he was twenty-three, he went to Nālandā Monastery in central India and studied, under great masters, the Yogācāra doctrine, the middle view versus the diametric views, the *Diamond Sūtra*, and more. Then he visited nations across the South China Sea.

In 781, the second year of the Jianzhong (建中) years of Emperor Dezong (唐德宗) of the Tang Dynasty (618–907), he arrived in Guangzhou (廣州), Guangdong Province. He then went to Chang-an (長安), the capital city, and started translating Sanskrit texts into Chinese. In 788, he translated the *Sūtra of the Six Pāramitās in the Tenets of the Mahāyāna* (T08n0261) in 10 fascicles. Two years later, he was conferred the title Prajñā Tripiṭaka Master and awarded the purple robe. Then, he translated the *Heart Sūtra* (T08n0253), the 40-fascicle version of the *Mahāvaipulya Sūtra of Buddha Adornment* (T10n0293), and the *Mahāyāna Sūtra of the Observation of the Original Mind Ground* (T03n0159).

Prajñā died in the city of Luoyang (洛陽), his age unknown. He was buried on the Eastern Heights of the Longmen Caves (龍門西岡).

Prayers

1 Opening the Sūtra 開經偈

The unsurpassed, profound true Dharma
無上甚深微妙法
Is hard to encounter in billions of kalpas.
百千萬劫難遭遇
This I now have seen and heard, and can accept and uphold,
我今見聞得受持
Hoping to understand the true meaning of the Tathāgatas.
願解如來真實義

2 Transferring Merit 回向偈

May the merit of my practice
願以此功德
Adorn Buddhas' Pure Lands,
莊嚴佛淨土
Requite the fourfold kindness from above,
上報四重恩
And relieve the suffering of the three life-journeys below.
下濟三途苦
Universally wishing sentient beings,
普願諸眾生
Friends, foes, and karmic creditors,
冤親諸債主
All to activate the bodhi mind,
悉發菩提心
And all to be reborn in the Land of Ultimate Bliss.
同生極樂國

3 The Four Vast Vows 四弘誓願

Sentient beings are countless; I vow to deliver them all.
眾生無邊誓願度
Afflictions are endless; I vow to eradicate them all.
煩惱無盡誓願斷
Dharma Doors are measureless; I vow to learn them all.
法門無量誓願學
Buddha bodhi is unsurpassed; I vow to attain it.
佛道無上誓願成

4 The Universally Worthy Vow of the Ten Great Actions
普賢十大行願

First, make obeisance to Buddhas.
一者禮敬諸佛
Second, praise Tathāgatas.
二者稱讚如來
Third, make expansive offerings.
三者廣修供養
Fourth, repent of karma, the cause of hindrances.
四者懺悔業障
Fifth, express sympathetic joy over others' merits.
五者隨喜功德
Sixth, request Buddhas to turn the Dharma wheel.
六者請轉法輪
Seventh, beseech Buddhas to abide in the world.
七者請佛住世
Eighth, always follow Buddhas to learn.
八者常隨佛學
Ninth, forever support sentient beings.
九者恒順眾生
Tenth, universally transfer all merits to others.
十者普皆迴向

5 Always Walking the Bodhisattva Way 常行菩薩道

May the three kinds of hindrances and all afflictions be annihilated.
願消三障諸煩惱
May I gain wisdom and true understanding.
願得智慧真明了
May all hindrances caused by sin be removed.
普願罪障悉消除
May I always walk the Bodhisattva Way, life after life.
世世常行菩薩道

6 Repenting of All Sins 懺悔偈

The evil karmas I have done with my body, voice, and mind are caused by greed, anger, and delusion, which are without a beginning in time. Before Buddhas I now supplicate for my repentance.
往昔所造諸惡業，皆由無始貪瞋癡，從身語意之所生。今對佛前求懺悔。
The evil karmas I have done with my body, voice, and mind are caused by greed, anger, and delusion, which are without a beginning in time. I repent of all sins, the cause of hindrances.
往昔所造諸惡業，皆由無始貪瞋癡，從身語意之所生。一切罪障皆懺悔。

The evil karmas I have done with my body, voice, and mind are caused by greed, anger, and delusion, which are without a beginning in time. I repent of all the roots of sin.
往昔所造諸惡業，皆由無始貪瞋癡，從身語意之所生。一切罪根皆懺悔。

7 Wishing to Be Reborn in the Pure Land 願生淨土

I wish to be reborn in the Western Pure Land.
願生西方淨土中
I wish to have as my parents a lotus flower in nine grades.
九品蓮花爲父母
When the flower opens, I will see that Buddha and realize that dharmas have no birth,
花開見佛悟無生
And I will have as my companions the Bodhisattvas who never regress.
不退菩薩爲伴侶

8 Supplicating to Be Reborn in the Pure Land 求生淨土

I single-mindedly take refuge in Amitābha Buddha in the World of Ultimate Bliss. Illuminate me with Your pure light and draw me in with Your loving, kind vows. Thinking only of You, I now call the name of the Tathāgata. For the sake of the Bodhi Way, I supplicate to be reborn in Your Pure Land.
一心皈命極樂世界阿彌陀佛。願以淨光照我、慈誓攝我。我今正念稱如來名，爲菩提道求生淨土。
Before this Buddha attained Buddhahood in the past, he made a vow: "Suppose there are sentient beings that, with earnest faith and delight, wish to be reborn in my land, even if by only thinking ten thoughts. If they should fail to be reborn there, I would not attain the perfect enlightenment."
佛昔本誓：若有衆生欲生我國，志心信樂乃至十念，若不生者不取正覺。
My thinking of this Buddha is why I have gained entrance into the Tathāgata's ocean of great vows. By the power of this Buddha's lovingkindness, my sins will be expunged and my roots of goodness will grow stronger. At the end of my life, I will know the coming of my time. My body will have no illness or suffering. My heart will have no greed or attachments. My mind will not be demented but will be peaceful as if in meditative concentration. This Buddha, holding a golden lotus-borne platform in His hands, together with a holy multitude, will come to receive me. In the instant of a thought, I will be reborn in the Land of Ultimate Bliss. When the lotus flower opens, I will see this Buddha and hear the Buddha Vehicle, and my Buddha wisdom will immediately unfold. I will widely deliver sentient beings, fulfilling my bodhi vow.
以此念佛因緣，得入如來大誓海中。承佛慈力，衆罪消滅、善根增長。若臨命終，自知時至。身無病苦、心不貪戀、意不顛倒，如入禪定。佛及聖衆手執金臺來迎接我。於一念頃，生極樂國。華開見佛，即聞佛乘、頓開佛慧、廣度衆生滿菩提願。

Homage to all Buddhas of the past, present, and future, in worlds in the ten directions!
Homage to all Bodhisattva-Mahāsattvas!
Homage to mahā-prajñā-pāramitā!
十方三世一切佛。一切菩薩摩訶薩。摩訶般若波羅蜜。

9 Ascending the Golden Steps 上金階

In the ocean-like lotus pond assembly, seated on lotus-borne platforms are Amitābha Tathāgata and Bodhisattvas Avalokiteśvara and Great Might Arrived, who welcome me to ascend the golden steps. I majestically declare my great vows, wishing to leave all afflictions behind.
蓮池海會，彌陀如來觀音勢至坐蓮臺，接引上金階。大誓弘開，普願離塵埃。

Homage to Buddhas and Bodhisattvas in the ocean-like lotus pond assembly! (Repeat three times.)
蓮池海會佛菩薩 (三稱)

10 Praising Amitābha Buddha 讚阿彌陀佛

Amitābha Buddha in a golden body is
阿彌陀佛身金色
Unsurpassed in His excellent appearance and radiance.
相好光明無等倫
The curling white hair between His eyebrows is like five Sumeru Mountains.
白毫宛轉五須彌
His blue eyes are as clear as four great oceans.
紺目澄清四大海
Present in His radiance are innumerable koṭis of magically manifested Buddhas
光中化佛無數億
And countless magically manifested Bodhisattvas.
化菩薩眾亦無邊
He has made forty-eight vows to deliver sentient beings,
四十八願度眾生
Enabling them to arrive in nine grades at the opposite shore.
九品咸令登彼岸

Namo Amitābha Buddha of great lovingkindness and great compassion, in the Western Land of Ultimate Bliss!
Namo Amitābha Buddha! (Say these words or "namo amituo fo" as many times as one wishes.)
南無西方極樂世界。大慈大悲阿彌陀佛。
南無阿彌陀佛 (多稱)

Mantras

At that time the great Brahma-king rose from his seat and arranged his attire. Joining his palms respectfully, he said to Avalokiteśvara Bodhisattva, "Very good! Great One, I have attended innumerable assemblies of the Buddha and have heard various kinds of Dharmas and various kinds of dhāraṇīs. Never have I heard such wonderful phrases as in this Hindrance-free Great Compassion-Mind Dhāraṇī. Great One, please tell us the features and characteristics of this dhāraṇī. This large assembly and I would be delighted to hear them."

Avalokiteśvara Bodhisattva said to the Brahma-king, "For the convenience and benefit of all sentient beings, you ask me this question. Now hearken well! I will briefly tell you all a few of them."

Avalokiteśvara Bodhisattva said, "They are the great loving-kind, compassionate mind, the equality mind, the asaṁskṛta mind, the no-attachment mind, the emptiness-seeing mind, the reverent mind, the humble mind, the unflustered mind, the not-taking-wrong-views mind, and the unsurpassed bodhi mind. You should know that such minds are the features of this dhāraṇī. Accordingly you should cultivate yourselves."

—*Sūtra of the Vast, Perfect, Hindrance-free Great Compassion-Mind Dhāraṇī of the Thousand-Hand Thousand-Eye Avalokiteśvara Bodhisattva*
Translated from the Chinese Canon (T20n1060, 0108a4–15)

How to Recite a Mantra

The features of the Great Compassion-Mind Dhāraṇī are true for all the mantras pronounced by Buddhas and Bodhisattvas. One would be wise to cultivate these features whether one recites a mantra, studies a sūtra, or carries on one's daily life.

Those who have contact with Tibetan Tantrism may have some concern about receiving "transmission" of a mantra from a "highly realized" lama, vested with the authority of a certain lineage. This has never been a problem in the Mahāyāna tradition. First, the Buddha has always instructed us to do our best to disseminate the mantras which He has imparted in His teachings. Second, the aspiration to recite a mantra arises from one's own Buddha mind, one's root lama. Can one find a lama higher than the Buddha or one's own Buddha mind? Given the mantra texts, one can feel authorized to enjoy mantra recitation with a peaceful and grateful mind, in addition to those minds taught by Avalokiteśvara Bodhisattva.

The mantras on the following pages contain compound words. A compound word in Sanskrit can be overwhelmingly long. To show the components of a compound word, whether created by the rule of pronunciation or other rules, hyphens are used to connect the components. For example, tathāgatāya-arhate actually should be written and pronounced as tathāgatāyārhate, bodhimaṇḍa-alaṁkāra-alaṁkṛte as bodhimaṇḍālaṁkārālaṁkṛte, sama-āśvāsa-adhiṣṭhite as samāśvāsādhiṣṭhite, and yogi-īśvarāya as yogīśvarāya. By comparing a compound word with its components, one can see that two vowels, short or long, connected by a hyphen are merged into one long vowel. One should pronounce a compound word as one word, but it is possible to steal a breath, if needed, after a long syllable.

A mantra has boundless meanings if the meanings of the words are not known. However, some of the mantra words are well known to Buddhist students, and this knowledge by no means diminishes the power of the mantra. Sanskrit students interested in the meanings of mantra words can consult the Monier-Williams Sanskrit Dictionary.

Introduction to the Eleven Mantras

Dhāraṇī, often in the form of a long mantra, means total retention, the power to unite all dharmas and hold all meanings. Mantras 2, 4, 5, and 7 are included in the ten short mantras that Chinese Buddhists recite in their morning recitation practice.

Mantras 1–4 are dhāraṇīs respectively in Sūtras 1–4 in *Teachings of the Buddha* (Rulu 2012a), in which the Buddha explains in detail their use and power.

Mantras 5 and 6 are the mantras for rebirth in Amitābha Buddha's Pure Land. The Chinese version of Mantra 5 is in text 368 (T12n0368, 0351c8–12), which was translated into Chinese by Guṇabhadra (求那跋陀羅, 394–468) from central India. In group practice, Chinese Buddhists usually recite this mantra three times immediately after their recitation of the *Heart Sūtra* or the *Amitābha Sūtra*. Not well known to them is Mantra 6, the longer of these two rebirth mantras. The Chinese version of this mantra is in text 930 (T19n0930, 0071b5–18), which was translated into Chinese by Amoghavajra (不空金剛, 705–774) from present-day Sri Lanka.

Mantra 7 is based on the *Sūtra of the Original Vows of the Seven Medicine Buddhas,* in text 451 (T14n0451, 0414b29–c3). This mantra is imparted by the seventh Medicine Buddha called Vaiḍūrya Light King Tathāgata, after He has pronounced His twelve great vows. The popular Tibetan version differs in its last phrase, which is given below for comparison.

tad-yathā oṁ bhaiṣajye bhaiṣajye mahā-bhaiṣajye rāja samudgate svāhā ||

Tibetan Buddhists and Chinese Buddhists have been reciting their respective versions of this mantra for centuries. Their testimonies provide evidence for the healing power of this mantra in both versions.

Mantra 8 is the heart mantra of the complete dhāraṇī in text 944A (T19n0944A, 0102c12–15). Another version is found in the *Śūraṅgama Sūtra* (T19n0945), which was translated into Chinese by Pramiti (般剌蜜帝, 7th–8th centuries) from central India. Although the full name of this dhāraṇī is Tathāgata-Crown White Umbrella Unsurpassed Subjugation Dhāraṇī, Chinese Buddhists just call it the Śūraṅgama Mantra because it is in the *Śūraṅgama Sūtra.*

In this sūtra the Buddha describes the inconceivable power of this dhāraṇī to annihilate hindrances, eradicate one's afflictions, and facilitate one's attainment of Buddhahood. Many Chinese Buddhists are able to recite from memory the complete dhāraṇī in their morning recitation practice. The good news is that its heart mantra, the last few phrases of the complete dhāraṇī, is just as powerful and efficacious as the full version. It is recommended that one recite it twenty-one times a day.

Mantra 9 is copied from chapter 26 of the 27-chapter version of the *Lotus Sūtra* on the website of the Digital Sanskrit Buddhist Canon. Its corresponding Chinese version is in the 28-chapter *Lotus Sūtra* (T09n0262, 0061b19–27), fascicle 7, chapter 28. Samantabhadra Bodhisattva pledges to the Buddha that he will safeguard the *Lotus Sūtra*, and protect and comfort those who recite and uphold this sūtra. Those who have heard his mantra will know the awesome spiritual power of Samantabhadra Bodhisattva and be able to carry out his great actions as well.

Mantra 10 is copied from Answers.com, and differs from the popular Chinese version in the *Sūtra of the Vast, Perfect, Hindrance-free Great Compassion-Mind Dhāraṇī of the Thousand-Hand Thousand-Eye Avalokiteśvara Bodhisattva* (T20n1060, 0107b25–c25). Well known for its healing power, this Great Compassion Mantra is most popular among Chinese Buddhists, as Guanyin (Avalokiteśvara) is their favorite Bodhisattva.

Different versions of this mantra are in texts 1061–64, 1111, 1113A, and 1113B. Texts 1061 and 1113B also include the mantra in Siddham. However, these texts are too corrupt to transliterate into Sanskrit. There exists an English version of this mantra, phonetically translated from the version in text 1060. As intended, it sounds like Chinese.

In this sūtra Avalokiteśvara Bodhisattva teaches us to make a vow to attain the ultimate enlightenment and rescue other sentient beings with great compassion. One should chant his name and Amitābha Buddha's name, then recite this mantra. Upon completion of only five repetitions of this mantra, one's grave sins which would entail 100,000 koṭi kalpas of birth and death will all be expunged. If one recites this spiritual mantra as one's regular practice, upon one's death, Buddhas will come from worlds in the ten directions to extend their helping hands, and one will be reborn in a Buddha Land according to one's wish. Recitation of this mantra will be the distant cause for one's ultimate attainment of bodhi. On the worldly level, those who recite this mantra will not die an evil death, and they will live a good life with fifteen benefits. Not only can they ward off evil forces by reciting this mantra, but Avalokiteśvara Bodhisattva will dispatch guards to protect them from such forces.

Mantra 11 is the Prajñā-Pāramitā Mantra included in any version of the *Heart Sūtra*. The Sanskrit word *pāramita* means gone across to the opposite shore. This mantra affirms the crossing—from "gate gate" (gone, gone) to "pāragate" (gone across to the opposite shore), then to "pāra-saṁgate" (completely gone across to the opposite shore)—and ends with "bodhi svāhā" (enlightenment hail). This crossing is achieved through one's prajñā (wisdom) in the true reality of all dharmas.

Corrections of typographical or grammatical errors in the source texts of these eleven mantras are bolded and italicized.

The Eleven Mantras

1 Buddha-Crown Superb Victory Dhāraṇī (Uṣṇīṣa vijaya dhāraṇī) 佛頂尊勝陀羅尼

namo bhagavate trai-lokya prativiśiṣṭāya buddhāya bhagavate | tad-yathā oṁ viśodhaya viśodhaya | asamasama samanta-avabhāsa spharaṇa gati gahana svabhāva viśuddhe | abhiṣiñcatu māṁ | sugata vara vacana | amṛta-abhi***ṣeke*** mahāmantra ***pāne*** | āhara āhara āyuḥ sandhāraṇi | śodhaya śodhaya gagana viśuddhe | uṣṇīṣa vijaya viśuddhe | sahasra-raśmi saṁcodite | sarva tathāgata-avaloka***na*** ṣaṭ-pāramitā paripūraṇi | sarva tathāgata hṛdaya-adhiṣṭhāna-adhiṣṭhita mahāmudre | vajra-kāya saṁha***ra***ṇa viśuddhe | sarva-āvaraṇa-apāya-durgati pari-viśuddhe | prati-nivartaya-āyuḥ śuddhe | samaya-adhiṣṭhite maṇi maṇi mahāmaṇi | ta***thātā*** bhūta koṭi pariśuddhe | visphuṭa buddhi śuddhe | jaya jaya vijaya vijaya smara smara | sarva buddha-adhiṣṭhita śuddhe | vajre vajra-garbhe vajraṁ bhavatu mama śarīraṁ | sarva sattvānāṁ ca kāya pari-viśuddhe | sarva gati pariśuddhe | sarva tathāgatāśca me sama-āśvāsayantu | sarva tathāgata sama-āśvāsa-adhiṣṭhite | budhya budhya vibudhya vibudhya | bodhaya bodhaya vibodhaya vibodhaya | samanta pariśuddhe | sarva tathāgata hṛdaya-adhiṣṭhāna-adhiṣṭhita mahāmudre svāhā ||

The Heart Mantra

oṁ amṛta tejovati svāhā ||

2 Great Cundī Dhāraṇī 准提神咒

namaḥ saptānāṁ samyak-saṁbuddha koṭīnā***ṁ*** | tad-yathā oṁ cale cule cundi svāhā ||

3 Whole-Body Relic Treasure Chest Seal Dhāraṇī 全身舍利寶篋印陀羅尼

namas tryadhvikānāṁ sarva tathāgatānāṁ | oṁ bhuvi-bhavana-vare vaca***na***-vaca***ti*** | suru suru dhara dhara | sarva tathāgata dhātu dhare padmaṁ bhavati | jaya vare mudre | smara tathāgata dharma-cakra pravartana vajre bodhimaṇḍa-alaṁkāra-alaṁkṛte | sarva tathāgata-adhiṣṭhite | bodhaya bodhaya bodhi bodhi budhya budhya | saṁbodhani saṁbodhaya | cala cala calantu sarva-āvaraṇāni | sarva pāpa vigate | huru huru sarva śoka vigate | sarva tathāgata hṛdaya vajriṇi | saṁbhāra saṁbhāra | sarva tathāgata guhya dhāraṇī mudre | bhūte subhūte | sarva tathāgata-adhiṣṭhita dhātu garbhe svāhā | samaya-adhiṣṭhite svāhā | sarva tathāgata hṛdaya dhātu mudre svāhā | supratiṣṭhita stūpe tathāgata-adhiṣṭhite huru huru hūṁ hūṁ svāhā | oṁ sarva tathāgatoṣṇīṣa dhātu mudrāṇi sarva tathāgata sadhātu vibhūṣita-adhiṣṭhite hūṁ hūṁ svāhā ||

4 Dhāraṇī of Infinite-Life Resolute Radiance King Tathāgata 聖無量壽決定光明王如來陀羅尼

namo bhagavate aparimita-āyur-jñāna-suviniścita-tejorājāya | tathāgatāya-arhate samyak-saṁbuddhāya | tad-yathā [oṁ puṇya mahā-puṇya | aparimita-puṇya | aparimita-āyuḥ-puṇya-jñāna-saṁbhāropacite |] oṁ sarva saṁskāra pariśuddha dharmate gagana samudgate | svabhāva viśuddhe mahānaya parivāre svāhā ||

5 Dhāraṇī for Rebirth in the Pure Land 拔一切業障根本得生淨土陀羅尼

namo amitābhāya tathāgatāya | tad-yathā oṁ amṛtod bhave | amṛta siddhaṁ bhave | amṛta vikrānte | amṛta vikrānta-gāmini | gagana-kīrti-kare svāhā ||

6 Root Dhāraṇī of Infinite-Life Tathāgata 無量壽如來根本陀羅尼

namo ratna trayāya | nama ārya-amitābhāya tathāgatāya-arhate samyak-saṁbuddhāya | tad-yathā oṁ amṛte amṛtod bhave | amṛta saṁbhave | amṛta garbhe | amṛta siddhe | amṛta teje | amṛta vikrānte | amṛta vikrānta-gāmini | amṛta gagana kīrti-kare | amṛta dundubhi svare | sarvārtha sādhane | sarva karma kleśa kṣayaṁkare svāhā ||

The Heart Mantra
oṁ amṛta teje hara hūṁ ||

7 Mantra of Medicine Master Tathāgata 藥師灌頂真言

namo bhagavate bhaiṣajya-guru-vaiḍūrya-prabhā-rājāya | tathāgatāya-arhate samyak-saṁbuddhāya | tad-yathā oṁ bhaiṣajye bhaiṣajye bhaiṣajya samudgate svāhā ||

8 The Tathāgata-Crown White Umbrella Unsurpassed Subjugation Dhāraṇī (Tathāgatoṣṇīṣāṁ sitāta patraṁ aparājitaṁ pratyuṅgiraṁ dhāraṇī) 大佛頂首楞嚴神咒

The Heart Mantra 楞嚴咒心
tad-yathā oṁ anale anale viśada viśada bandha bandha bandhani bandhani vaira-vajrapāṇi phaṭ hūṁ bhrūṁ phaṭ svāhā ||

9 Samantabhadra Bodhisattva's Mantra 普賢菩薩所説咒

adaṇḍe daṇḍapati daṇḍa-āvartani daṇḍa-kuśale daṇḍa-sudhāri | sudhārapati buddhapaśyane sarvadhāraṇi | āvartani saṁvartani saṁgha-parīkṣite saṁgha-nirghātani | dharma-parīkṣite sarva-sattva ruta kauśalya-anugate | siṁha-vikrīḍite anuvarte vartani vartāli svāhā ||

10 Great Compassion-Mind Dhāraṇī (Nīlakaṇṭha dhāraṇī) 大悲咒

namo ratna-trayāya | nama ārya-avalokiteśvarāya bodhisattvāya mahāsattvāya mahākāruṇikāya | oṁ sarva-bhaya-śodhanāya tasya namaskṛtvā | ***idam***_ārya-avalokiteśvara tava namo nīlakaṇṭha | hṛdayaṁ vartayiṣyāmi sarvārtha-sādhanaṁ śubham_ajeyaṁ sarva-bhūtānāṁ bhava-mārga-viśodhakaṁ | tad-yathā oṁ āloka-adhipati loka-atikrānta | ehi mahā-bodhisattva sarpa sarpa smara smara hṛdayaṁ | kuru kuru karma | dhuru dhuru vijayate mahā-vijayate | dhara dhara dhāraṇī-rāja | cala cala mama vimala-amūrtte | ehi ehi ***cīrṇa cīrṇa ārṣaṁ*** pracali | vaśa***ṁ*** vaśaṁ pranāśaya | hu***ru*** hu***ru*** smara | huru huru sara sara siri siri suru suru | ***budhya budhya*** bodhaya bodhaya | maitreya nīlakaṇṭha [dehi me] darśanaṁ | praharāyamānāya svāhā | siddhāya svāhā | mahā-siddhāya svāhā | siddha-yogi-īśvarāya svāhā | nīlakaṇṭhāya svāhā | varāha-mukhāya svāhā | nara-siṁha-mukhāya svāhā | gadā-hastāya svāhā | cakra-hastāya svāhā | padma-hastāya svāhā | nīlakaṇṭha-pāndarāya svāhā | mahāta***la***-śaṁkarāya svāhā | namo ratna-trayāya | nama ārya-avalokiteśvarāya bodhisattvāya svāhā | oṁ siddhyantu mantra-padā***ni*** svāhā (This concluding phrase appears in another text.) ||

The Heart Mantra
oṁ vajra dharma hrīḥ ||

11 The Prajñā-Pāramitā Mantra 般若波羅蜜多咒

gate gate pāragate pāra-saṁgate bodhi svāhā ||

Appendix

Table A. The Sanskrit Alphabet

	33 Consonants							13 Vowels			
	Unvoiced			Voiced				Voiced			
	Un aspirate	Aspirate	Sibilant (aspirate)	Un aspirate	Aspirate	Nasal	Semi-vowel	Simple		Diphthong	
								Short	Long	Long	
1 Velar	ka	kha	ha	ga	gha	ṅa		a	ā	a+i	ā+i
2 Palatal	ca	cha	śa	ja	jha	ña	ya	i	ī	=e	=ai
3 Cerebral	ṭa	ṭha	ṣa	ḍa	ḍha	ṇa	ra	ṛ	ṝ		
4 Dental	ta	tha	sa	da	dha	na	la	ḷ		a+u	ā+u
5 Labial	pa	pha		ba	bha	ma	va	u	ū	=o	=au
Anusvāra						ṁ					
Visarga			ḥ								

Note:

1. The sounds of the twenty-five consonants are formed by *complete* contact of the tongue with the palate.
2. The four semi-vowels are voiced and unaspirated, and their sounds are formed by *slight* contact.
3. Three of the four sibilants (excepting *ha*) are unvoiced and aspirated, and their sounds are formed by *half* contact. Note that *ha* is a voiced velar sound but classified as a sibilant.
4. Voiced consonants are low and soft; unvoiced consonants are crisp and sharp. To feel the difference between a voiced and an unvoiced sound, hold the front of your throat with your hand and pronounce a syllable. It is a voiced sound if your hand detects a vibration in your throat, an unvoiced sound if no vibration. To know the difference between an aspirated and an unaspirated sound, place your palm in front of your mouth and pronounce a syllable. It is an aspirated sound if your breath hits your palm, an unaspirated sound if there is no hit. Native English speakers may find it difficult to pronounce the five unvoiced, unaspirated syllables in column one. This difficulty can be overcome once you understand the difference.
5. In Table A, each consonant is followed by the short vowel *a* to facilitate pronunciation. To learn the Sanskrit alphabet, follow the pronunciation guideline in Table B and Table C. Recite the thirteen vowels in Table B row by row. Recite the thirty-three consonants in the first column of Table C, also adding the short vowel *a* to each. Unlike the consonants, the sounds of anusvāra and visarga in the last two rows of Table A or Table C depend on the vowel preceding them. Textbooks include them with the vowels.

Table B. Pronunciation of the 13 Vowels

5 short vowels (Each lasts one count)		8 long vowels (Each lasts two counts)	
a	atra (here), like *a*bout or *a*like	ā	mahā (great), like f*a*ther
i	iva (as if, like), like ***ea***sy but not like ***i*** t or ***i*** s	ī	kīrti (fame), like ***ea***se
u	guru (heavy), like p*u*ll	ū	bhūta (reality, being), like p*oo*l
ṛ	amṛta (nectar for immortality), like p*re*tty but not like p*ri*ck	ṝ	pitṝn (fathers, accusative case), like p*re*tty lengthened
ḷ	kḷpta (arranged), like app***le*** or kett***le***		
		e = a+i	ehi (come near!), like s*a*fe
		ai = ā+i	maitreya (benevolent), like ***ai***sle
		o = a+u	namo (homage), like *o*cean without bunching the lips as if to pronounce the word *woe*
		au = ā+u	kauśalya (skillfulness), like l*ou*d

Table C. Pronunciation of the 33 Consonants

1. Velar or guttural sounds are produced by touching the rear of the tongue to the soft palate near the throat.	
k	kāya (body), like s*k*ill or s*k*in
kh	sukha (happiness), like *k*ill or *k*in
g	gagana (sky), like *g*azelle or *g*o
gh	gharma (heat), like do*gh*ouse
ṅ	gaṅgā (the Ganges), like mi*n*gle or hu*n*ger
2. Palatal sounds are produced by touching the blade of the tongue to the front palate.	
c	cakra (wheel), like *ch*uck or *ch*oke, but without aspiration
ch	chāya (shadow), like *ch*uck or *ch*oke
j	jaya (victory), like *j*ug or *j*oke
jh	nirjhara (waterfall), like *j-h*ug or fu*dge-h*ome
ñ	jñāna (wisdom), like ca*ny*on. Some people change the sound of *j* and pronounce this word like g*ny*āna, or like d*ny*āna.
3. Cerebral sounds are produced by retroflexing the tongue to touch the hard palate.	
ṭ	koṭi (ten million, the edge), like s*t*ar or s*t*ow, with the tongue retroflexed
ṭh	adhiṣṭhāna (rule over), like *t*ar or *t*ow, with the tongue retroflexed
ḍ	vaiḍūrya (aquamarine), like *d*ouse or *d*ead, with the tongue retroflexed
ḍh	mūḍha (perplexed), like ma*dh*ouse or re*dh*ead, with the tongue retroflexed
ṇ	maṇi (jewel), like *n*ativity or *n*ote, with the tongue retroflexed
4. Dental sounds are produced by touching the tip of the tongue to the back of the front teeth near their roots.	
t	tad (he, she, or it), like s*t*ar or s*t*ow
th	tathāgata (the thus-come one), like *t*ar or *t*ow
da	dāna (the act of giving), like *d*ouse or *d*ead
dh	dhāranī (retention), like ma*dh*ouse or re*dh*ead
n	nāga (dragon), like *n*ativity or *n*ote
5. Labial sounds are produced by closing and opening the lips.	
p	padma (red lotus), like s*p*in or s*p*oke
ph	phala (fruit), like *p*in or *p*oke
b	bodhi (enlightenment), like *b*ore or *b*out
bh	bhagavān (the world-honored one), like a*bh*or or ho*bh*ouse
m	mudrā (seal), like *m*agenta or *m*ode

Table C Continued

6. Four semi-vowels, the sounds of which are formed by slight contact	
y	hṛdaya (heart, mind), like yeast or yoga
r	ratna (jewel), like **r**ite or **r**ote, with the tongue slightly tapping the front palate. Avoid bunching the lips for the implicit *w* before the r-syllable as in English, which causes **r**ite to be pronounced as write, **r**ote as wrote.
l	loka (world), like **l**agoon or **l**otus
v	If not preceded by a consonant, it is pronounced as *v;* e.g., avidyā (ignorance). If preceded by a constant, it may be pronounced as *w*. Thus, sattva (being, creature) may be pronounced as sa-ttwa, sarva (all) as sar-wa, adhvan (time) as a-dhwan, and svāhā (hail) as swā-hā.
7. Four sibilants, the sounds of which are formed by half contact	
ś	śuddha (pure), like ***sh***ip or ***sh***ow
ṣ	uṣṇīṣa (crown of the head), like ***sh***ip or ***sh***ow, with the tongue retroflexed
s	sama (equal), like **s**alute or **s**olo
h	sahasra (thousand), like **h**abituate or **h**oly
8. Other sounds	
Anusvāra (ṁ)	The preceding verb is nasalized; e.g., saṁskāṛa (formation) is pronounced as sa*ng*-skā-ra, and hūṁ (a mantra syllable) as hū*ng*.
Visarga (ḥ)	The preceding verb is faintly echoed; e.g., namaḥ (homage) is pronounced as nama***ha***, narayoḥ (of the two men) as narayo***ho***, naraiḥ (with the men) as narai***hi***, and duḥkha (sorrow) as du***hu***kha.

Note:

1. A vowel as the first letter of a word, or a consonant followed by a vowel, forms a syllable, which is short or long, depending upon the vowel. All consonants are pronounced. For example, tadyathā is pronounced as tad-ya-thā, ratna as rat-na, and sattva as satt-va or sa-ttwa.
2. The stressed syllable, or guru syllable, in a multi-syllable word is the penultimate syllable if (1) it has a long vowel, or (2) it has a short vowel followed by two or more consonants. For example, the stressed syllable in bālābhyām (with, for, or from the two boys) is *lā* because it meets the first condition, and in saṁyukta (complex) is *yu* because it meets the second condition. If the penultimate syllable meets neither condition, then check the anti-penultimate syllable, and so on. For example, the stressed syllable in udbhavakara (productive) is *u*, the fifth syllable from the last.
3. The nasal sound of anusvāra (ṁ) may extend a count or two. For example, the mantra syllable hūṁ or oṁ can last two to four counts.

Glossary

affliction (kleśa, 煩惱). Something that agitates one's mind, resulting in evil karmas done with one's body and/or voice. The three root afflictions, called the three poisons, are (1) greed, (2) anger, and (3) delusion. Derived from these three are (4) arrogance, (5) doubt, and (6) wrong views. The list can be extended to ten by distinguishing five kinds of wrong views: (6) the self-view that an embodied self exists in a person composed of the five aggregates and that this self owns the five aggregates and things considered as external; (7) the diametric view of perpetuity or cessation; (8) the evil view of no causality; (9) the preceding three wrong views, plus certain inferior views; (10) observance of useless precepts, such as staying naked, covering oneself with ashes, imitating cows or dogs, and self-harm, futilely hoping to achieve a better rebirth. These ten afflictions drive sentient beings. The first five are called the chronic drivers (鈍使), which can be removed gradually; they are also called thinking confusions (思惑) because they arise from one's thinking of self, others, or both. The last five are called the acute drivers (利使), which can be removed quickly; they are also called view confusions (見惑). Ignorance of the truth is the root of all afflictions.

agalloch (沉水). The fragrant, resinous wood of an East Indian tree, aquilaria agallocha, also called agarwood, used as incense in the Orient. It is called in China the sink-in-water fragrant wood.

Akaniṣṭha Heaven (阿迦尼吒天), or Ultimate Form Heaven (色究竟天). It is the top heaven (有頂天) of the eighteen heavens in the form realm (see Three Realms of Existence).

ālaya-vijñāna (阿賴耶識). The store consciousness (藏識), also known as the eighth consciousness, which stores the pure, impure, and neutral seeds of one's experience since time without a beginning. These seeds manifest as causes and conditions that lead to karmic events in one's life, which in turn become seeds. Maintaining the physical and mental life of a sentient being, ālaya is neither different from nor the same as the physical body. As the base of the other seven consciousnesses (see eighteen spheres), ālaya is the root consciousness (mūla-vijñāna). After one's death, ālaya may either immediately manifest a rebirth according to karmic forces and conditions or first produce an ethereal interim body, which can last up to forty-nine days, pending the right karmic conditions for a rebirth. Ālaya is also identified with the thus-come store (tathāgata-garbha) as well as Buddha nature (see true suchness). The seeds in a Buddha's mind are all pure seeds which no longer change, and the name ālaya-vijñāna is then changed to amala-vijñāna, the stainless consciousness.

Anāthapiṇḍika (給孤獨). Provider for the Deprived, a name given to the Elder Sudatta for his generosity to the poor and forlorn. He bought a garden from Prince Jeta as an offering to the Buddha.

anuttara-samyak-saṁbodhi (阿耨多羅三藐三菩提). The unsurpassed, equally perfect enlightenment (無上正等正覺). *Anuttara* means unsurpassed; *samyak* is derived from the stem *samyañc*, which means same or identical; *saṁbodhi* means perfect enlightenment. *Equally* means that the perfect enlightenment of all Buddhas is the same. The third epithet of a Buddha is Samyak-Saṁbuddha, the Equally, Perfectly Enlightened One.

anuttara-samyak-saṁbodhi mind (阿耨多羅三藐三菩提心). The resolve to attain the unsurpassed, equally perfect enlightenment, to benefit self and others.

Arhat (阿羅漢). A voice-hearer who has attained the fourth and highest fruit on the Liberation Way (see voice-hearer fruits) by shattering his fixation on having an autonomous self and eradicating all his afflictions. A Buddha is also an Arhat, but not vice versa (see bodhi). As the second of a Buddha's ten epithets, Arhat means worthy of offerings.

arrogance (慢). Arrogance has seven types: (1) arrogance (慢) is vaunting one's superiority over inferiors; (2) over-arrogance (過慢) is asserting one's superiority over equals; (3) arrogant over-arrogance (慢過慢) is alleging one's superiority over superiors; (4) self-arrogance (我慢) is the root of all other arrogances, considering oneself by definition to be superior to others; (5) exceeding arrogance (增上慢) is alleging realization of truth one has not realized; (6) humility-camouflaged arrogance (卑慢) is admitting slight inferiority to those who are much superior; and (7) evil arrogance (邪慢) is boasting of virtues one does not have.

asaṁkhyeya (阿僧祇). Innumerable, or an exceedingly large number.

asaṁskṛta (無爲). Not formed or made through causes and conditions. Although *asaṁskṛta* is an antonym of *saṁskṛta* (有爲), the asaṁskṛta dharma is the true reality of saṁskṛta dharmas, not their opposite.

asura (阿修羅). A sub-god or non-god. An asura may assume the form of god, human, animal, or hungry ghost. Given to anger and jealousy, an asura is considered more an evil life-journey than a good one.

attuning thought (一念相應). Actually not a thought. In a flash of attunement, one enters a non-dual state, realizing one's true mind and/or seeing one's Buddha nature. In Chan Buddhism, experiencing an attuning thought means breaking through the first or the second gateless gate.

Avīci Hell (阿鼻地獄). The last of the eight hot hells. It is a hell of uninterrupted suffering for those who have committed grave sins, such as the five rebellious sins.

avinivartanīya (阿鞞跋致). The spiritual level from which a Bodhisattva will never regress (不退). Bodhisattvas with the first six or more of the ten faithful minds will never regress from faith; Bodhisattvas at the seventh level of abiding or above will never abandon the Mahāyāna; Bodhisattvas on the First Ground or above will never lose their spiritual realization; Bodhisattvas on the Eighth Ground or above will never lose their mindfulness, and their progress will be effortless (see stages of the Bodhisattva Way).

Bhagavān (薄伽梵). The tenth epithet of a Buddha is Buddha-Bhagavān, or Buddha the World-Honored One.

bhikṣu (比丘). A fully ordained monk in the Buddha's Order, who observes, in the Mahāyāna tradition, 250 monastic precepts.

bhikṣuṇī (比丘尼). A fully ordained nun in the Buddha's Order, who observes, in the Mahāyāna tradition, 500 monastic precepts.

birth-death (jāti-maraṇa, 生死). See saṁsāra.

bodhi (菩提). Enlightenment or unsurpassed wisdom. There are three kinds of bodhi, corresponding to the enlightenment of the holy beings of the Three Vehicles: (1) the bodhi of a voice-hearer who has attained Arhatship; (2) the greater bodhi of a Pratyekabuddha; (3) the greatest bodhi of a Buddha. In old translations, bodhi is translated into Chinese as the Way (道), which should be distinguished from the path (mārga).

bodhi mind (bodhi-citta, 菩提心). See anuttara-samyak-saṁbodhi mind.

bodhimaṇḍa (道場). The bodhi place, which refers to the vajra seat of a Buddha sitting under the bodhi tree where He attains Buddhahood. In a general sense, it is a place for spiritual learning and practice, such as a temple or one's home. In a profound sense, since the Way to Buddhahood is one's mind, all sentient beings are bodhi places.

Bodhisattva (菩薩). A bodhi being who rides the Mahāyāna and delivers sentient beings along the Way. He will eventually attain Buddhahood, to benefit himself and others.

Bodhisattva-Mahāsattva (菩薩摩訶薩). A holy Bodhisattva who is a mahāsattva (great being) because of his great vows, great actions, and the great number of sentient beings he delivers.

Bodhisattva precepts (菩薩戒). Precepts for both lay and monastic Buddhists who ride the Mahāyāna. They are called the three clusters of pure precepts (三聚淨戒), consisting of (1) restraining precepts, (2) precepts for doing good dharmas, and (3) precepts for benefiting sentient beings. The first cluster is to prevent negative actions, and the other two are to cultivate the positive qualities essential to the development of a Bodhisattva. Bodhisattva precepts vary with their sources. In the *Brahma Net Sūtra* (T24n1484), there are ten major and forty-eight minor precepts; in the *Sūtra of the Upāsaka Precepts* (T24n1488), there are six major and twenty-eight minor precepts. Chinese monastic Buddhists observe the former set of Bodhisattva precepts. Lay Buddhists may choose to accept either set of Bodhisattva precepts.

Brahmā (梵). Purity, or freedom from desire. It is deified in Hinduism as the Creator. The Brahma way of life in the desire realm is celibacy.

Brahma gods (梵天). Gods, who have only pure desires, reside in the Brahma World (brahma-loka), i.e., the first of the four dhyāna heavens in the form realm. The first dhyāna heaven comprises three heavens: Brahma Multitude (Brahma-pāriṣadya), Brahma Minister (Brahma-purohita), and Great Brahmā (Mahābrahmā). The Brahma-king Śikhin, assisted by his ministers, rules all Brahma gods in these three heavens (see Three Realms of Existence).

Brahmin (婆羅門). A member of the highest of the four Indian castes. As a priest, a Brahmin officiates at religious rites and teaches Vedic literature.

Buddha (佛). The Enlightened One. According to the Mahāyāna tradition, Śākyamuni Buddha (circa 563–483 BCE) is the present one in a line of past and future Buddhas. Each Buddha has a particular name, such as Śākyamuni, to suit the needs of sentient beings of His time. The ten epithets common to all Buddhas are (1) Tathāgata (Thus-Come One or Thus-Gone One), (2) Arhat (Worthy of Offerings), (3) Samyak-Saṁbuddha (Equally, Perfectly Enlightened One), (4) Vidyācaraṇa-Sampanna (Knowledge and Conduct Perfected), (5) Sugata (Well-Arrived One or Well-Gone One), (6) Lokavid (Understanding the World), (7) Anuttara (Unsurpassed One), (8) Puruṣa-

Damya-Sārathi (Tamer of Men), (9) Śāstā Deva-Manuṣyāṇām (Teacher to Gods and Humans), and (10) Buddha-Bhagavān (Buddha the World-Honored One).

Buddha-crown (buddhoṣṇīṣa, 佛頂), or Tathāgata-crown (tathāgatoṣṇīṣa). A fleshy mound on the crown of a Buddha's head, which is one of the thirty-two physical marks of a Buddha, a sign resulting from countless lives of doing good dharmas and teaching others to do so. The same term also refers to the invisible top of a Buddha's head, which is one of the eighty excellent characteristics of a Buddha, a sign resulting from countless lives of venerating, praising, and making obeisance to innumerable holy beings, teachers, and parents. The invisible Buddha-crown signifies one's true mind, which is free from causes and conditions.

Buddha Vehicle (Buddha-yāna, 佛乘). The destination of the Great Vehicle (Mahāyāna) is Buddhahood, so it is also called the Buddha Vehicle. In the *Lotus Sūtra* (T09n0262), the Buddha introduces the One Vehicle (eka-yāna, 一乘), declaring that not only riders of the Two Vehicles but all sentient beings will eventually attain Buddhahood.

bhūta (部多). A living being or the ghost of a deceased person.

Cause Ground (因地). It means the training ground of a Bodhisattva before attaining Buddhahood, the Fruit (Result) Ground, or the Buddha Ground. It may also refer to the training ground of a Bodhisattva before ascending to the First Ground (see stages of the Bodhisattva Way).

character-type (gotra, 種性). The Sanskrit word *gotra* means family. According to the *Garland Sūtra* (T24n1485), Bodhisattvas are classified into five character-types, corresponding to the middle five of the seven stages of the Bodhisattva Way: (1) the learning character-type (習種性) is developed through the ten levels of abiding; (2) The nature character-type (性種性) is developed through the ten levels of action; (3) the bodhi character-type (道種性) is developed through the ten levels of transference of merit; (4) the holy character-type (聖種性) is developed through the Ten Grounds; (5) the virtually perfect enlightenment nature (等覺性) is developed when a Bodhisattva attains enlightenment nearly equal to that of a Buddha. At the seventh stage, a Bodhisattva becomes a Buddha, whose perfect enlightenment nature (妙覺性) is fully revealed. Besides, those with affinity for the Voice-Hearer Vehicle are called the voice-hearer character-type; those with affinity for the Pratyekabuddha Vehicle are called the Pratyekabuddha character-type (see Two Vehicles).

Command of the Eight Great Displays (八大自在). According to the *Mahāparinirvāṇa Sūtra* (T12n0375), fascicle 23, the true self of a Buddha has total command of the eight great displays: (1) one physical body can manifest many copies; (2) one physical body can fill a Large Thousandfold World; (3) this vast body can lift off and travel far; (4) it can remain in one land and manifest innumerable varieties of forms in response to sentient beings; (5) the functions of its five faculties can be interchangeable; (6) He can attain all dharmas with no attachment to any attainment; (7) He can expound the meaning of one stanza for innumerable kalpas; (8) His body can pervade everywhere, like space.

deliverance (度). Liberation achieved by crossing over to that shore of nirvāṇa from this shore of saṁsāra. Those who have achieved deliverance are Arhats,

Pratyekabuddhas, and Buddhas. The first two have achieved the liberation fruit and the bodhi fruit for themselves. Buddhas have achieved not only the liberation fruit for themselves but also the great bodhi fruit of omniscience, for delivering sentient beings.

dhāraṇī (陀羅尼). Usually in the form of a long mantra, it means total retention (總持). With excellent memory, samādhi, and wisdom, A Bodhisattva has the inconceivable power to unite all dharmas and hold all meanings. He can not only retain all good dharmas but also stop the rise of evil dharmas.

dharma (法). (1) The teachings of a Buddha (the word dharma in this meaning is capitalized in English); (2) law; (3) anything (mental, physical, event); (4) a mental object of consciousness, such as a thought.

dharma-eye (法眼). The spiritual eye that not only penetrates the true reality of all things but also discriminates all things. Bodhisattvas who have realized the no birth of dharmas ascend to the First Ground and acquire the pure dharma-eye, with which they continue to help sentient beings according to their natures and preferences (see five eyes).

Dharma Seal (dharma-mudrā, 法印). Buddhist teachings are summarized in Dharma Seals, against which other doctrines should be measured. The Four Dharma Seals are as follows: (1) processes are impermanent; (2) experiences boil down to suffering; (3) dharmas have no selves; (4) nirvāṇa is silence and stillness. Because suffering is the consequence of the impermanence of everything in the life of a sentient being, including itself, the second Dharma Seal can be omitted from the list to make the Three Dharma Seals. Five Dharma Seals can be established by adding a fifth Dharma Seal: (5) dharmas are empty. In the Mahāyāna doctrine, all these seals are integrated into one, the one true reality.

Dharma vessel (法器). (1) A person capable of accepting and learning the Buddha Dharma. (2) A Buddhist ritual object, such a drum, a bell, or a wooden fish.

dhyāna (禪). Meditation. Meditation above the desire-realm level is generally classified into four levels, the four dhyānas (四禪) of the form realm. In the first dhyāna, one's mind is undisturbed by the pleasures of the desire realm, but it has coarse and subtle perception. In the second dhyāna, there is bliss in meditation. In the third dhyāna, there is subtle joy after abandoning the bliss of the second dhyāna. In the fourth dhyāna, one's mind is in pure meditation, free from any subtle feelings or movements. Each level of dhyāna is also called the Root Samādhi, from which will grow virtues, such as the Four Immeasurable Minds and the eight liberations (see the four samādhis of the formless realm).

dhyāna with appearance (有相禪). Meditation supported by the appearance of a mental object. One can focus one's attention on a point of the body, count the breaths, recite mantra syllables silently, gaze at an object, or visualize an object.

dhyāna without appearance (無相禪). Meditation unsupported by the appearance of any mental object. One can ponder true suchness without thoughts or think of a Buddha without saying His name or visualizing His body.

discharge (āsrava, 漏). Outflow of afflictions, characteristic of sentient beings engaged in their cycle of birth and death. For example, anger is an affliction in one's mind, which is discharged through one's body and voice. Any discharge is a display of one's affliction, and it does not decrease affliction.

dragon (nāga, 龍). (1) A serpent-like sea creature, which can take a little water and pour down rains. (2) A symbol of one's true mind in the statement that the great nāga is always in samādhi, never moving. An Arhat is likened to the great dragon.

eight classes of Dharma protectors (八部護法). The nonhuman protectors of the Dharma are gods, dragons, gandharvas, asuras, yakṣas, garuḍas, kiṁnaras, and mahoragas.

eight difficulties (八難). One has either no opportunity or no motivation to see a Buddha or hear His Dharma, while in any of the eight difficulties: (1) as a hell-dweller; (2) as a hungry ghost; (3) as an animal; (4) as an inhabitant of Uttarakuru, the northern continent, where life is too pleasant; (5) in deep meditation in a formless heaven; (6) being blind, deaf, or mute; (7) as a worldly eloquent intellectual; (8) in the period between the presence of one Buddha and the next.

eight holy ranks (八聖). See voice-hearer fruits.

eight liberations (aṣṭa-vimokṣa, 八解脫, 八背捨). Through samādhi power, one successively achieves eight liberations from one's greed for rebirth in the form and formless realms: (1) liberation from perceptible desires for form by visualizing the impurity of external objects; (2) liberation from imperceptible desires for form by visualizing the impurity of external objects; (3) liberation from all desires for form by visualizing the purity of external objects; (4) liberation from visualization of the purity of external objects through the mental state of boundless space; (5) liberation from the state of boundless space through the mental state of boundless consciousness; (6) liberation from the state of boundless consciousness through the mental state of nothingness; (7) liberation from the state of nothingness through the mental state of neither with nor without perception; and (8) liberation from the state of neither with nor without perception through the mental state of total suspension of sensory reception and perception. Liberations 1–2 correspond to the first two dhyānas, and liberation 3 corresponds to the fourth dhyāna. The third dhyāna is not used because one's mind is not vigilant in a subtle joyful state. Liberations 4–7 correspond to the four samādhis in the formless realm (see samādhi), and liberation 8 is the liberation samādhi attained by an Arhat.

eight precepts (aṣṭa-śīla, 八關齋戒). Besides the five precepts, which are observed for life at all times, lay Buddhists may accept the eight precepts. They should observe them regularly each lunar month on the six purification days. The eight precepts are (1) no killing; (2) no stealing; (3) no sex; (4) no lying; (5) no drinking alcohol; (6) no wearing perfumes or adornments, and no singing, dancing, or watching song-dance entertainments; (7) no sleeping on a luxurious bed; and (8) no eating after lunch, until morning. Note that the third of the eight precepts is no sex whereas the third of the five precepts is no sexual misconduct. Observing these eight prohibitions (關) for 24 hours at a time, one abstains (齋) not only from sins prohibited by the five precepts but also from sensory gratification.

eight tones (八音). The Tathāgata's Brahma tone has eight qualities: (1) fine, (2) gentle, (3) harmonious, (4) awe-inspiring, (5) manly, (6) error-free, (7) far-reaching, and (8) carrying inexhaustible meaning.

eighteen emptinesses (十八空). Given in the *Mahā-prajñā-pāramitā Sūtra* (T08n0223, 0218c17) is the emptiness of (1) the insides of the body; (2) anything outside of the body; (3) the appearance of inside or outside; (4) the preceding three emptinesses; (5) the four domains; (6) the highest truth [nirvāṇa]; (7) that which is saṁskṛta; (8) that which is asaṁskṛta; (9) the preceding eight emptinesses; (10) sentient beings without a beginning; (11) a composite thing disassembled; (12) self-essence of anything; (13) general and particular appearances of anything; (14) dharmas that make up a sentient being, such as the five aggregates, the twelve fields, and the eighteen spheres; (15) dharmas, which can never be captured; (16) existence; (17) nonexistence; and (18) the appearance of existence or nonexistence.

Eighteen Exclusive Dharmas (aṣṭādaśa-āveṇika-dharma, 十八不共法). Only Buddhas have these eighteen attainments, which Arhats, Pratyekabuddhas, and Bodhisattvas do not have. They include (1–3) perfection in conduct, speech, and mindfulness; (4) impartiality to all; (5) constant serenity; (6) equability toward sensory experiences; (7) unceasing desire to deliver sentient beings; (8) inexhaustible energy for helping sentient beings; (9) unfailing memory of the Buddha Dharma; (10) perfect wisdom in everything; (11) total liberation from afflictions and habits; (12) perfect knowledge and views of liberation; (13–15) perfect body karmas, voice karmas, and mind karmas, led by wisdom; (16–18) perfect knowledge of the past, present, and future. Another set of eighteen includes the Ten Powers, the Four Fearlessnesses, the Threefold Mindfulness of Equality, and the Great Compassion. The Threefold Mindfulness of Equality means that a Buddha's mind abides in equality toward (1) those who listen to the Dharma reverently, (2) those who listen to the Dharma irreverently, and (3) these two groups.

eighteen spheres (aṣṭādaśa-dhātu, 十八界). A sentient being is composed of the eighteen spheres: the six faculties (eye, ear, nose, tongue, body, and mental faculty [manas]), the six sense objects (sights, sounds, scents, flavors, tactile sensations, and mental objects), and the six consciousnesses (eye consciousness, ear consciousness, nose consciousness, tongue consciousness, body consciousness, and mental consciousness). Mental consciousness, the sixth consciousness, functions by itself as well as together with the first five consciousnesses. As the eye is the physical base from which eye consciousness arises, likewise manas (mental faculty) is the mental base from which mental consciousness arises. In the Mahāyāna doctrine, manas is also designated as the seventh consciousness, which has four inborn defilements: (1) self-delusion (我癡), (2) self-love (我愛), (3) self-view (我見), and (4) self-arrogance (我慢). Ālaya, the eighth consciousness, though not explicitly included in the eighteen spheres, is the root of them all.

Eightfold Right Path (八正道). This right path to one's liberation from the cycle of birth and death includes (1) right views, (2) right thinking, (3) right speech, (4) right action, (5) right livelihood, (6) right effort, (7) right mindfulness, and (8) right meditative absorption (samādhi). Paths 1–2 educate one with understanding, paths 3–5 establish one on the ground of morality, paths 7–8 develop one's mental power and wisdom through meditation, and path 6 is applied to the other seven paths of training.

emptiness (śūnyatā, 空). The lack of self-essence (independent inherent existence) of any dharma that arises and perishes through causes and conditions. Emptiness is not nothingness because it does not deny the illusory existence of all things. The non-duality of emptiness and manifestations, and of nirvāṇa and saṁsāra, is the Middle View of the Mahāyāna doctrine (see two emptinesses).

Endurance in Dharmas (法忍). It includes not only endurance of persecution or suffering but also continued acceptance of the truth that dharmas are never born.

Endurance in the Realization of the No Birth of Dharmas (無生法忍). The lasting realization of the truth that dharmas have neither birth nor death as they appear and disappear through causes and conditions (see Three Endurances in the Dharma).

Five Āgamas (五阿含). An āgama is a collection of early Buddhist scriptures. The Five Āgamas in the Chinese Canon are the Dīrgha Āgama (long discourses), the Madhyama Āgama (middle-length discourses), the Saṁyukta Āgama (connected discourses), the Ekottarika Āgama (discourses ordered by the number of dharmas in each discourse), and the Kṣudraka Āgama (minor discourses). They are parallel but not identical to the Five Nikāyas in the Pāli Canon, which are the Dīgha Nikāya, the Majjhima Nikāya, the Saṁyutta Nikāya, the Aṅguttara Nikāya, and the Khuddaka Nikāya.

five aggregates (pañca-skandha, 五蘊, 五陰). A sentient being is composed of the five aggregates: rūpa (form), vedanā (sensory reception), saṁjñā (perception), saṁskāra (mental processing), and vijñāna (consciousness). The first one is material and the other four are mental. Since these four are non-form (非色), thus present in name only, the five aggregates are summarized as name and form (名色). *Skandha* (蘊) in Sanskrit also means that which covers or conceals (陰), and the regular working of the five skandhas conceals true reality from a sentient being.

five coverings (pañca-āvaraṇa, 五蓋). One's true mind is covered up by (1) greed, (2) anger, (3) torpor, (4) restlessness, and (5) doubt.

five desires (五欲). One's desires for pleasures in the five sense objects are (1) sights, (2) sounds, (3) scents, (4) flavors, and (5) tactile sensations. One also has the desire for pleasure in (6) mental objects, verbal or nonverbal, coarse or fine. Humans are driven especially by their desires for (1) riches, (2) sex, (3) reputation, (4) food and drink, and (5) sleep. These are impure desires in the desire realm, and there are pure desires in the form and formless realms.

five eyes (pañca-cakṣu, 五眼). These are (1) the physical-eye that a sentient being is born with; (2) the god-eye that can see anything anywhere; (3) the wisdom-eye that can see the emptiness of dharmas; (4) the dharma-eye that can discriminate all dharmas; and (5) the Buddha-eye of omniscience, which includes the preceding four at the highest level (see three wisdom-knowledges).

five faculties (pañca-indrya, 五根). The first five of the six faculties.

Five Powers. See Thirty-seven Elements of Bodhi.

five precepts (pañca-śīla, 五戒). For lay Buddhists, the five precepts are (1) no killing, (2) no stealing, (3) no sexual misconduct, (4) no lying, and (5) no drinking alcohol.

five rebellious acts or sins (五逆). These are (1) patricide, (2) matricide, (3) killing an Arhat, (4) shedding the blood of a Buddha (including maligning His Dharma), and (5) destroying the harmony of a Saṅgha. They are also called the karma of the five no interruptions because any of them drives one into Avīci Hell, the hell of the five no interruptions.

Five Roots. See Thirty-seven Elements of Bodhi.

five studies (pañca-vidyā, 五明). These are (1) language and composition, (2) science and technology, (3) medical arts, (4) logic, and (5) inner knowledge in a certain discipline.

five sūtras and one treatise (五經一論). The Pure Land School follows (1) the *Sūtra of Amitāyus Buddha* (T12n0360); (2) the *Sūtra of Amitābha Buddha* (T12n0366); (3) the *Sūtra of Visualization of Amitāyus Buddha* (T12n0365); (4) "Great Might Arrived Bodhisattva's Thinking-of-Buddhas as the Perfect Passage" (a subsection in fascicle 5 of the *Śūraṅgama Sūtra* [T19n0945]); (5) "The Universally Worthy Action Vow" (fascicle 40 of the 40-fascicle version of the *Mahāvaipulya Sūtra of Buddha Adornment* [T10n0293]); and (6) the *Upadeśa on the Sūtra of Amitāyus Buddha* (T26n1524).

five tones (五音). The five pitches on the pentatonic scale. This scale is used all over the world. In Chinese music, the five tones on the major pentatonic scale are called gong (宮), shang (商), jue (角), zhi (徵), yu (羽), approximately C, D, E, G, A on the heptatonic scale.

five transcendental powers (五通). Through meditation, one can develop these powers: (1) the god-eye to see anything anywhere; (2) the god-ear to hear any sound anywhere; (3) the ability to know the past lives of self and others; (4) the ability to know the thoughts of others; (5) the ability to transform one's body and to travel instantly to any place.

five turbidities (pañca-kaṣāya, 五濁). The five kinds of degeneracy which begin, in a decreasing kalpa, when human lifespan has decreased from 80,000 years to 20,000 years, and become more severe as human lifespan decreases to 10 years. They are (1) the turbidity of a kalpa in decay, which is characterized by the next four turbidities; (2) the turbidity of views, such as the five wrong views; (3) the turbidity of afflictions, including greed, anger, delusion, arrogance, and doubt; (4) the turbidity of sentient beings that live a wicked life and are in increasing suffering; (5) the turbidity of human lifespan as it decreases to 10 years. The wrong views in (2) and the afflictions in (3) are turbidity itself, which leads to the results in (4) and (5).

Flowers mentioned in the sūtras are listed below. A question mark next to the Chinese name of a plant indicates the failure to find its corresponding Sanskrit name. Then a Sanskrit name is constructed phonetically from Chinese.

utpala (優波羅)—blue lotus
padma (波頭摩)—red lotus
kumuda (拘物頭)—white lotus
puṇḍarīka (分陀利華)—large white lotus
atimuktaka (阿提目多花)—an herbaceous plant which has fragrant red or white blooms

cāka (遮迦花?)
campaka (瞻蔔)—the champaka (玉蘭) tree which has fragrant golden or white flowers
caṇa (栴那花)—the chickpea plant
canuttara (栴奴多羅花?)
kiṁśuka (甄叔迦)—the tree butea frondosa, or its bright orange-red flowers
locana (盧遮那花)—a certain plant
māndarāva (曼陀羅花)—the red blooms of the coral tree, considered as celestial flowers
mañjūṣaka (曼殊沙花)—the white blooms of an herbaceous plant, considered as celestial flowers
palāśa (波樓沙花)—the flaming orange blooms of a tree called butea monosperma, native to India and Southeast Asia
pāṭali (波羅羅花)—a tree which has fragrant purple flowers
raṇi (羅尼花?)
gauraṇi (瞿羅尼花?)
suloci (蘇樓至?)
sumana (須曼那華)—the jasmine plant, which has fragrant white, yellow, or red blooms
tāla (他邏)—the fan palm tree
udumbara (烏曇跋羅)—the ficus glomerata, a tree that produces fruit with hidden flowers. Hence the appearance of its bloom is likened to the rare appearance of a Buddha.

four appearances (四相).

A. The four appearances of any saṁskṛta dharma are the four stages of a process: (1) arising, (2) staying, (3) changing, and (4) perishing. In the case of a sentient being, these four are (1) birth, (2) aging, (3) illness, and (4) death (see ten appearances). In the case of a world, these four are (1) formation, (2) staying, (3) destruction, and (4) void.

B. The four appearances in the *Diamond Sūtra* (T08n0235) are the self-images of a sentient being: (1) an autonomous self, which relates to everything conceived or perceived as non-self; (2) a human being with something in common with or different from other human beings; (3) a sentient being with something in common with or different from other sentient beings; and (4) a living being that has a lifespan to terminate, preserve, or prolong. The latter three are derived from the first. These are also called the four views (四見).

four continents (catur-dvīpa, 四洲). In the center of a small world in the Three Realms of Existence is Mount Sumeru. It is encircled by eight concentric mountain ranges, and these nine mountains are separated by eight oceans. Rising above the salty ocean between the outermost mountain range and the seventh inner mountain range are four large continents aligned with the four sides of Mount Sumeru. In the east is Pūrvavideha; in the south is Jambudvīpa; in the west is Aparagodānīya; in the north is Uttarakuru, where life is too pleasant for its inhabitants to seek the Dharma. Between every two large continents are two medium-sized continents and five hundred uninhabited small continents.

Four Dharmas to Rely Upon (四依法). In the *Mahāparinirvāṇa Sūtra* (T12n0375 [different from the *Mahāparinibbāna Sutta* in the Pāli Canon]), fascicle 6, the

Buddha teaches us to rely upon (1) the Dharma, not an individual; (2) sūtras of definitive meaning, not those of provisional meaning; (3) the true meaning, not just the words; (4) one's wisdom-knowledge, not consciousness. In summary, dharma means dharma nature; definitive meaning refers to Mahāyāna sūtras; true meaning refers to the eternal abiding and changelessness of the Tathāgata; wisdom-knowledge means the understanding that all sentient beings have Buddha nature.

four domains (catur-dhātu, 四界). According to ancient Indian philosophy, matter is made of the four domains—earth, water, fire, and wind—which have four corresponding appearances: solid, liquid, heat, and mobility. Hence they are also called the great seeds (mahābhūta, 大種) with the four appearances as their self-essence, or changeless qualities. In fact, these appearances are the states of matter under prevailing conditions (see six domains).

Four Drawing-in Dharmas (四攝法). To draw sentient beings into the Dharma, one should use these four skillful ways: (1) almsgiving, (2) loving words, (3) beneficial actions, and (4) collaborative work.

Four Fearlessnesses (四無畏). Only a Buddha has (1) fearlessness because knowledge of all knowledge has been acquired; (2) fearlessness because all afflictions have been eradicated; (3) fearlessness in explaining hindrances that obstruct one's realization of bodhi; and (4) fearlessness in explaining the right path to end one's suffering.

Four Foundations of Mindfulness (四念住).

A. According to the Pāli Canon of the Theravāda School, one practices (1) mindfulness of one's body in stillness and in motion; (2) mindfulness of one's sensory experience as pleasant, unpleasant, or neutral; (3) mindfulness of one's mental afflictions: greed, anger, and delusion; and (4) mindfulness of one's mental objects, including the teachings of the Buddha. Through vigilant mindfulness, one realizes that all dharmas are impermanent and that there is no self in command.

B. According to the Mahāyāna doctrine, one needs to observe these: (1) the body is impure; (2) all experiences boil down to suffering; (3) the mind is constantly changing; and (4) all dharmas have no selves (see right mindfulness).

four god-kings (四天王). They reside halfway up Mount Sumeru, in the first of the six desire heavens. As protectors of the world, they ward off the attacks of asuras. On the east side is Dhṛtarsaṣtra, the god-king Upholding the Kingdom; on the south side is Virūḍhaka, the god-king Increase and Growth; on the west side is Virūpākṣa, the god-king Broad Eye; and on the north side is Vaiśravaṇa, the god-king Hearing Much.

four grave prohibitions (四重禁). These are the prohibitions against committing the four grave root sins: (1) killing, (2) stealing, (3) sexual misconduct, and (4) lying, especially alleging spiritual attainment one does not have. The third root sin for monastic Buddhists is having sex.

four groups of disciples (四眾). See Saṅgha.

Four Immeasurable Minds (四無量心). These are (1) lovingkindness, (2) compassion, (3) sympathetic joy, and (4) equability.

four Indian castes (四姓). These are (1) Brahmin (priest), (2) kṣatriya (royalty and warrior), (3) vaiśya (farmer and merchant), and (4) śūdra (serf). The Buddha ruled that all from the four castes would be allowed to become Buddhist śramaṇas as the fifth caste, the highest of all castes.

four modes of birth (四生). Sentient beings are born through (1) the womb, such as humans and other mammals; (2) the egg, such as the birds and reptiles; (3) moisture, such as fishes and insects; (4) miraculous formation, such as gods, ghosts, and hell-dwellers.

four necessities (四事供養). Offerings to a monk, usually including (1) food and drink, (2) clothing, (3) bedding, and (4) medicine.

Four Noble Truths (四聖諦). In His first turning of the Dharma wheel, the Buddha taught the Four Noble Truths: (1) suffering (duḥkha), (2) accumulation (samudaya), (3) cessation (nirodha), and (4) the path (mārga). Suffering is the essence of repeated birth and death through the six life-journeys; accumulation of afflictions, especially thirsty love (tṛṣṇa), is the cause of suffering; cessation of suffering reveals nirvāṇa; and the Eightfold Right Path is the Path to nirvāṇa. As a condensed version of the Twelve Links of Dependent Arising, the first two truths reveal that, for continuing the flow of saṁsāra, the cause is the accumulation of afflictions and the effect is suffering. The last two truths reveal that, for terminating the flow of saṁsāra, the cause is taking the Eightfold Right Path and the effect is cessation of suffering, realizing nirvāṇa.

Four Preparatory Trainings (四加行), or Four Roots of Goodness (四善根位). According to the Consciousness-Only School, after the stage of Gathering Provisions is completed, one embarks upon the stage of Preparatory Trainings by investigating the four aspects of dharmas: name, meaning, self-essence, and differentiation, to successively develop the four roots of goodness: (1) Warmth—one realizes in the Illumination Samādhi that objects are empty; (2) Pinnacle—one affirms the same realization through the Enhanced Illumination Samādhi; (3) Endurance—one realizes in the Sealing-in-Accord Samādhi that consciousness as the agent of differentiation is empty; (4) Foremost in the World—one ascertains in the Uninterrupted Samādhi that both the object perceived and the agent that perceives are empty. With this realization, one ascends to the First Bodhisattva Ground (see stages of the Bodhisattva Way), beginning the holy stage toward Buddhahood.

fourfold kindness (四重恩). Kindness comes from (1) parents and teachers, (2) the Three Jewels, (3) country, and (4) sentient beings.

gandharva (乾闥婆). A fragrance eater who is also a celestial musician playing in the court of gods.

garuḍa (迦樓羅). A large bird-like being that eats dragons.

god (deva, 天). The highest life form in the Three Realms of Existence. According to their merits and mental states, gods reside in six desire heavens, eighteen form heavens, and four formless heavens.

Gṛdhrakūṭa Mountain (耆闍崛山). The Vulture Peak Mountain (靈鷲山), northeast of the city of Rājagṛha. There the Buddha pronounced the *Lotus Sūtra* (T09n0262) and many other sūtras.

hell of the five no interruptions (五無間獄). In Avīci Hell, sentient beings undergo suffering with no interruption in five aspects: (1) no interruption in time; (2) no unoccupied space because one or many hell-dwellers fill up the hell; (3) no interruption in torture; (4) no exception for any sentient being; and (5) no interruption from life to life.

Hīnayāna (小乘). The Small Vehicle (see Two Vehicles).

Illumination Door of the One Hundred Dharmas (百法明門).

A. According to the *Sūtra of the Garland of the Original Karmas of a Bodhisattva,* this Dharma Door refers to the ten faithful minds, each with ten levels, totaling one hundred. On the Bodhisattva Way, a Bodhisattva sage at the first level of abiding goes through this Dharma Door before ascending to next level (T24n1485, 1011c6–8). In addition, a holy Bodhisattva on the First Ground also goes through this Dharma Door before ascending to the next ground (ibid., 1014c24–25).

B. According to the *Sūtra of Visualization of Amitāyus Buddha* (T12n0365), one goes through this Dharma Door to ascend to the First Ground. The one hundred dharmas, though not explained in this sūtra, are likely to be the same as those in the *Garland Sūtra*.

C. Asaṅga (無著, circa 4th century) in his book *Yogācārya-bhūmi-śāstra* (T30n1579) classifies all dharmas, saṁskṛta and asaṁskṛta, into a total of 660. His younger brother Vasubandhu (世親, circa 320–80) condenses it into 100, in his *Mahāyāna Treatise on the Illumination Door of the One Hundred Dharmas* (T31n1614).

inversion (顛倒). The seven inversions are (1) taking the impermanence of dharmas as permanence; (2) taking misery as happiness; (3) taking impurity as purity; (4) taking no self as self; (5) inverted perceptions, which refer to the inverted differentiations in the first four inversions; (6) inverted views, which refer to the establishment of, attachment to, and delight in the first four inversions; and (7) inverted mind, which refers to afflictions arising from the first four inversions. According to the *Mahāparinirvāṇa Sūtra* (T12n0375), fascicle 7, the first four inversions also include (1) taking the eternity of the Tathāgata as impermanence, (2) taking the bliss of the Tathāgata as suffering, (3) taking the purity of the Tathāgata as impurity, and (4) taking the true self as no self.

Jambudvīpa (贍部洲). One of the four continents surrounding Mount Sumeru in a small world. Located south of Mount Sumeru and identified by the huge jambu tree, Jambudvīpa, the southern continent, is where humans and animals reside.

Jetavana (祇樹園). The Jeta Grove, a garden near Śrāvastī, presented to the Buddha by the Elder Sudatta, who purchased it from Prince Jeta with gold covering its ground. In honor of the two benefactors, the estate was henceforth known as the Garden of Jeta and Anāthapiṇḍika (祇樹給孤獨園). The Buddha spent nineteen rainy seasons with His 1,250 monks in the monastery built on the land. There he gave many of His teachings.

jīvajīva (耆婆耆婆). A legendary two-headed bird (命命鳥) with a beautiful call.

kalā (歌羅). A minute length, one hundredth or one sixteenth the length of a human body hair.

kalaviṅka (迦陵頻伽). A bird with a melodious voice, found in the Himalayas. It has beautiful black plumage and a red beak. It starts singing in the eggshell before it is hatched. Its beautiful voice surpasses that of humans, gods, kiṁnaras, and other birds, and is likened to the wondrous tones of Buddhas and holy Bodhisattvas.

kalpa (劫). An eon. A large kalpa is the long period of formation, staying, destruction, and void of a world. It is divided into eighty small kalpas, each lasting 16,800,000 years.

karma (業).

A. An action, a work, or a deed done with one's body, voice, or mind. Good and evil karmas bring corresponding requitals in one's present and/or future lives. Neutral karmas (無記業) are actions that cannot be accounted as good or evil.

B. Karma (羯磨) is also the work in a ceremony for imparting Buddhist precepts or for repentance. It includes four requirements: (1) the dharma, i.e., the procedure; (2) the purpose; (3) people meeting the quorum; (4) the designated place.

Kauśala (憍薩羅國), or Kośala. Situated in central India, it is one of the sixteen ancient kingdoms of India.

kiṁnara (緊那羅). A celestial musician that resembles human, but with horns on his head.

koṭi (俱胝). The edge, the highest point. As a numeral, koṭi means one hundred thousand, one million, or ten million.

kṣaṇa (剎那). The smallest unit of time, something like a nanosecond. According to Buddhist doctrine, a thought lasts 60 kṣaṇas. In each kṣaṇa 900 sets of arising and ceasing of mental processing take place.

kumbhāṇḍa (鳩槃荼). A ghost, shaped like a pot, which feeds on the vitality of humans.

Laṅkā (楞迦). Present-day Sri Lanka or the name of a mountain of gemstones in Sri Lanka.

li (里). A traditional Chinese unit of distance, a Chinese mile. A li now has a standardized length of 500 meters, or half a kilometer.

life-journey (gati, 趣), or life-path (道). The life experience of a life form in its cycle of birth and death. According to past karmas, a sentient being continues to transmigrate through the six life-journeys in corresponding life forms: god, asura, human, animal, hungry ghost, and hell-dweller. The first three life-journeys are considered the good (fortunate) ones; the last three, the evil (unfortunate) ones. Given to anger and jealousy, asuras may be considered the fourth evil life-journey. Sometimes, only five life-journeys are mentioned in the sūtras because asuras may assume any of the first four life forms and live among sentient beings in these forms. In comparison with life in the Pure Land of Ultimate Bliss, all life-journeys in this world are evil.

ludicrous statement (戲論). All wrong views are ludicrous statements. Furthermore, a statement is composed of words, which are empty names and appearances employed to make differentiations. It is ludicrous because in true reality it is empty.

Magadha (摩竭陀). A kingdom in central India, the headquarters of Buddhism up to year 400.

mahāvaipulya sūtras (大方廣經). Extensive Mahāyāna sūtras that are great in explaining the right principles and great in their vast scope.

Mahāyāna (大乘). The Great Vehicle that can carry many people to Buddhahood. It is also called the Bodhisattva Vehicle because its riders are Bodhisattvas, who are resolved to attain Buddhahood, to benefit themselves and others (see Buddha Vehicle). The Mahāyāna doctrine, widely followed in Northeast

Asia (China, Korea, and Japan), refers to the Theravāda School in Southeast Asia (Sri Lanka, Burma, Thailand, Laos, and Cambodia) as the Small Vehicle (Hīnayāna, 小乘), which can be either or both of the Two Vehicles (二乘).

mahoraga (摩呼洛迦). A serpent or land dragon.

mantra (咒). An esoteric incantation. Buddhist mantras are imparted by Buddhas, sometimes through holy Bodhisattvas or Dharma protectors.

māra (魔). Killer, destroyer, evil one, or devil. The four kinds of māras are (1) the celestial māra, a god named Pāpīyān, residing with legions of subordinates in Paranirmita-vaśa-vartin Heaven, the sixth desire heaven; (2) māra of the five aggregates, which conceals one's Buddha mind; (3) māra of afflictions, which drives one to do evil karma; and (4) māra of death, which ends one's life.

mudrā (印). A seal, symbolized by positions of the hands and intertwinings of the fingers, used in ritual practices. A seal possesses secret meanings and magical efficacy (see Dharma Seal).

namo (南無). Reverential homage, salutation, adoration, or obeisance. Based on the Sanskrit rule of pronunciation, this word may be spelled as namo, nama, namaḥ, namas, or namaś, according to the initial letter of the next word.

Nārāyaṇa (那羅延天). A Hindu god who has great strength. He is identified as Viṣṇu in the desire realm, and is included in the trinity of Brahmā, Nārāyaṇa, and Maheśvara (Śiva, in Hinduism).

nayuta (那由他), or niyuta. A numeral, meaning one hundred thousand, one million, or ten million.

nirvāṇa (涅槃). By taking the Eightfold Right Path, one eradicates one's afflictions and realizes nirvāṇa, liberating oneself from one's cycle of birth and death. The four nirvāṇas are (1) the inherent nirvāṇa (自性涅槃), which means true reality, the no birth and no death of all dharmas; (2) the nirvāṇa with remnant (有餘依涅槃), which means the enlightenment of an Arhat or a Pratyekabuddha who is still living; (3) the nirvāṇa without remnant (無餘依涅槃), which means the death of an Arhat or a Pratyekabuddha, who has abandoned his body, the remnant of his karmic existence; and (4) the nirvāṇa that abides nowhere (無住處涅槃), which means the supreme enlightenment of a Buddha. The great nirvāṇa of a Buddha includes the realization of the eternity, bliss, true self, and purity of the Tathāgata, and the attainment of powers unavailable to an Arhat or a Pratyekabuddha. Beyond the duality of existence and nonexistence, saṁsāra and nirvāṇa, a Buddha continues to manifest in most suitable ways in response to the needs of sentient beings, thus abiding nowhere.

no regress. See avinivartanīya.

nourishment (食). Provided by (1) ingestion of food; (2) contact with enjoyable sense objects, such as sights, sounds, scents, flavors, and tactile sensations; (3) formation of mental food, such as ideas, expectations, and recollections; and (4) ālaya consciousness that maintains one's physiological and mental processes as well as carries karmic seeds, which will lead to future rebirths. An ordinary being in the desire realm requires these four kinds of nourishment to survive.

one appearance (eka-lakṣaṇa,一相). All dharmas are in the one appearance of true suchness, which is beyond differentiation of appearances and beyond differentiation between appearance and no appearance. However, the one appearance is often referred to as the one appearance of no appearance.

one flavor (eka-rasa, 一味). (1) All dharmas are in the one flavor of true suchness. (2) The Buddha's teachings of the Three Vehicles are all in the one flavor of the One Vehicle. As the one appearance of dharmas is likened to the earth, the one flavor of the Buddha's teachings is likened to the rain nourishing all the plants on earth.

parinirvāṇa (般涅槃). It means beyond nirvāṇa, the death of an Arhat or a Buddha by entering profound samādhi. Whether or not He has abandoned His body in demonstrating parinirvāṇa, a Buddha is in the nirvāṇa that abides nowhere, beyond the duality of existence and nonexistence. A Buddha's parinirvāṇa is called mahāparinirvāṇa.

past seven Buddhas (過去七佛). The last 3 of the 1,000 Buddhas of the preceding Majestic Kalpa are Vipaśyin, Śikhin, and Viśvabhū; the first 4 of the 1,000 Buddhas of the present Worthy Kalpa are Krakucchanda, Kanakamuni, Kāśyapa, and Śākyamuni.

perfect passage (圓通). A Dharma Door, the perfect practice of meditation, through which one can pass from ignorance to significant realizations. In the *Śūraṅgama Sūtra* (T19n0945), at the Buddha's command, twenty-five Arhats and holy Bodhisattvas reveal their perfect passages.

piśāca (畢舍遮). A demonic ghost that eats human flesh and sucks human vitality.

Pratyekabuddha (緣覺佛). One who is enlightened through contemplating the Twelve Links of Dependent Arising. He is also called a solitary Buddha (獨覺佛) because, living in solitude, he has realized the truth without receiving teachings from a Buddha.

pure abode heavens (淨居天). The top five of the nine heavens that constitute the fourth dhyāna heaven in the form realm (see Three Realms of Existence).

Rājagṛha (王舍城). The capital city of Magadha in central India, near the Vulture Peak Mountain.

rakṣasa (羅刹). A demonic ghost that eats human flesh. Rakṣasas are said to be the original inhabitants of Sri Lanka.

right mindfulness (samyak-smṛti, 正念). The seventh in the Eightfold Right Path. A few examples of right mindfulness include (1) practice of the Four Foundations of Mindfulness; (2) remembrance of the Dharma, such as the no birth of all dharmas; (3) remembrance of a Buddha; and (4) the inconceivable mindfulness of a Buddha.

roots of goodness (kuśala-mūla, 善根). These are (1) no greed, (2) no anger, and (3) no delusion. The five roots in Thirty-seven Elements of Bodhi are goodness in themselves and can grow other good dharmas (also see Four Preparatory Trainings).

ṛṣi (仙人). An ascetic hermit considered to be an immortal or a godlike human. Śākyamuni Buddha is also revered as the Great Ṛṣi. In the *Śūraṅgama Sūtra* (T19n0945), the Buddha describes ten kinds of ṛṣis, who live thousands or tens of thousands of years, with the five transcendental powers, such as walking on land, traveling across sky, changing themselves into any form, etc.

Sahā World (sahā-lokadhātu, 娑婆世界). The endurance world. It refers to Jambudvīpa or the Three-Thousand Large Thousandfold World, where its inhabitants are able to endure their suffering and may even find their lives enjoyable.

śakrābhi-lagna-ratna (釋迦毘楞伽寶). The precious jewel worn on the neck of the god-king Śakra, which illuminates all of the Thirty-three Heavens (Trayastriṁśa Heaven) constituting the second desire heaven under his rule. It is likened to the wisdom of Bodhisattvas, which can manifest myriad things.

Śakro-Devānām-Indra (釋提桓因). The title of the god-king of Trayastriṁśa Heaven, often abbreviated as Śakra or Indra. The Buddha calls the incumbent Śakra by his family name, Kauśika.

samādhi (定). A state of mental absorption in meditation. Above the level of the desire realm, there are eight levels of worldly samādhi (八定). The first four levels are the four dhyānas (四禪) of the form realm. The next four levels are the four samādhis of the formless realm (四空定): Boundless Space (空無邊), Boundless Consciousness (識無邊), Nothingness (無所有), and Neither with Nor without Perception (非有想非無想). A Buddhist or non-Buddhist who has attained any of the eight levels of meditation can be reborn in a corresponding heaven in the form or formless realm. Only an Arhat can attain the ninth level called the Samādhi of Total Halt (滅盡定), also more appropriately called the Samādhi of Total Suspension of Sensory Reception and Perception (滅受想定). To enter the Samādhi Door of Buddhas is to attain innumerable samādhis.

śamatha (奢摩他). It means stillness, a mental state in which one's mind is in single-minded concentration (see vipaśyanā).

saṁsāra (輪迴), or jāti-maraṇa (生死). The cycle of birth and death, in which every sentient being transmigrates through the six life-journeys in the Three Realms of Existence. This endless cycle is called the hard-to-cross ocean, also called the ocean of suffering (see two types of birth and death).

saṁskṛta (有爲). Formed or made through causes and conditions. Each saṁskṛta dharma is a process with the four appearances. Sentient beings and all the things they perceive or conceive are saṁskṛta dharmas (see asaṁskṛta).

samyak-saṁbodhi (等正覺). See anuttara-samyak-saṁbodhi.

Saṅgha (僧伽). A community comprising a Buddha's four groups of disciples (四衆): monks (bhikṣu), nuns (bhikṣuṇī), laymen (upāsaka), and laywomen (upāsikā).

śārī (舍利). A mynah bird. Śārikā was the name of Śāriputra's mother because her eyes were bright and clever like those of a mynah.

sarvajña. See three wisdom-knowledges.

self-essence (svabhāva, 自性). An inherent state of being, self-made, self-determined, and changeless. This is a false reality that sentient beings attach to their perceptions. In truth, nothing has self-essence because everything is constantly changing through causes and conditions. That all dharmas are without self-essence is the true reality defined as emptiness.

Seven Bodhi Factors (七覺分). These are (1) critical examination of theories, (2) energetic progress, (3) joyful mentality, (4) lightness and peacefulness in body and mind, (5) mindfulness in all activities and remembrance of the true Dharma, (6) samādhi, and (7) equability under favorable or unfavorable circumstances.

seven noble treasures (七聖財). These are (1) faith, (2) wisdom, (3) observing the precepts, (4) hearing teachings, (5) having a sense of shame, (6) having a sense of dishonor, and (7) discarding afflictions.

seven treasures (七寶). These are (1) suvarṇa (金, gold); (2) rūpya (銀, silver); (3) vaiḍūrya (琉璃, aquamarine); (4) sphaṭika (頗梨, crystal); (5) musāragalva (硨磲, conch shell or white coral); (6) lohita-muktikā (赤珠, ruby); and (7) aśmagarbha (瑪瑙, emerald). Sometimes coral and amber are included in place of crystal and ruby. F. Max Müller cites a reference in *Buddhist Mahāyāna Texts* (Cowell et al. [1894] 1969, part 2, 92), in which vaiḍūrya is matched with lapis lazuli, and aśmagarbha with diamond. While lapis lazuli is an opaque intense blue stone, indications in the sūtras are that vaiḍūrya should be a transparent blue beryl, such as aquamarine. According to the *Monier-Williams Online Dictionary*, aśmagarbha is emerald; vajra (伐折羅) is diamond, an adamantine mineral (金剛).

siddhi (悉地). Achievement through spiritual training using one's body, voice, and mind. The ultimate siddhi is Buddhahood.

six branches of family (六親). They include father, mother, wife, sons, elder brothers, and younger brothers. Sisters and daughters are not mentioned because they will be included in their husbands' families as wives and mothers.

six desire heavens (六欲天). (1) Heaven of the Four God-Kings (Cātur-mahārāja-kāyika-deva, (四天王天); (2) Trayastriṁśa Heaven (忉利天), or Thirty-three Heavens (三十三天), ruled by Śakra-Devānām-Indra; (3) Yāma Heaven (夜摩天), ruled by Suyāma-devarāja; (4) Tuṣita Heaven (兜率天), ruled by Saṁtuṣita-devarāja; (5) Nirmāṇa-rati Heaven (化自在天), ruled by Sunirmita-devarāja; (6) Paranirmita-vaśa-vartin Heaven (他化自在天), ruled by Vaśavartti-devarāja. The first two heavens are earth-abode heavens; all other heavens are sky-abode heavens.

six domains (ṣad-dhātu, 六界, 六大). A sentient being is made of the six domains—earth, water, fire, wind, space, and consciousness—and appears to have these features: solid substance, fluid, heat, motion, space within the body, and consciousness. A non-sentient thing (plant or nonliving thing) is made of the first five domains (see four domains).

six elements of harmony and respect (六和敬). Members of a Saṅgha need to have accord among their body, voice, mind, precepts, almsgiving, and views, in order to have harmony with and respect for one another.

six faculties (ṣaḍ-indriya, 六根, 六入). These are eye, ear, nose, tongue, body, and mental faculty (manas). The first five are sense organs, which function as sensory entrances (see twelve fields).

six pāramitās (六度, 六波羅蜜). The Sanskrit word *pāramita* means gone across to the opposite shore. To succeed in crossing over to that shore of nirvāṇa, opposite this shore of saṁsāra, a Bodhisattva needs to achieve the six pāramitās: (1) dāna (almsgiving), (2) śīla (observance of precepts), (3) kṣānti (endurance of adversity), (4) vīrya (energetic progress), (5) dhyāna (meditation), and (6) prajñā (development of wisdom). See ten pāramitās.

six periods (六時). The day is divided into morning (6–10 a.m.), midday (10 a.m. – 2 p.m.), and afternoon (2–6 p.m.); the night into evening (6–10 p.m.), midnight (10 p.m.–2 a.m.), and post-midnight (2–6 a.m.). Each period has four hours.

six purification days (六齋日). On the 8th, 14th, 15th, 23rd, 29th, and 30th day of each lunar month, lay Buddhists can accept and observe the eight precepts, abstaining from committing sins that are evil by nature and from sensory gratification. The Sanskrit word *poṣadha* (齋) means fasting for purification. However, not knowing the meaning of *poṣadha*, some lay Buddhists assign these six days for eating vegetarian meals.

six remembrances (六念). Remembrances of (1) the Buddha, (2) the Dharma, (3) the Saṅgha, (4) the precepts, (5) almsgiving, and (6) heaven: ordinary beings should remember that rebirth in a heaven is acquired by purifying one's mind, observing one's precepts, and almsgiving, and that they can strive to qualify. Riders of the Mahāyāna should remember the heaven of the highest meaning (第一義天), the ultimate nirvāṇa.

six transcendental powers (六通). With no more afflictions to discharge, he has liberated himself from his cycle of birth and death. Hence, eradication of afflictions, which ends their discharges (漏盡通), is called the sixth transcendental power of an Arhat, which is unavailable to those who have not attained Arhatship. It also makes his achievement in the first five transcendental powers superior to that of those others.

śramaṇa (沙門). An ascetic or a monk, one who has renounced family life and lives a life of purity, poverty, and diligent training, seeking the truth.

śrāmaṇera (沙彌). A novice Buddhist monk, usually seven to twenty years old.

Śrāvastī (舍衛國). The capital city of the ancient kingdom of Kauśala.

stages of the Bodhisattva Way (菩薩階位). The spiritual levels of a Bodhisattva on the Way to Buddhahood. According to the 80-fascicle version of the *Mahāvaipulya Sūtra of Buddha Adornment* (T10n0279), a Bodhisattva advances through fifty-two levels, which are grouped into seven stages: (1) ten faithful minds, (2) ten levels of abiding, (3) ten levels of action, (4) ten levels of transference of merit, (5) Ten Grounds, (6) virtually perfect enlightenment, and (7) perfect enlightenment. A Bodhisattva will continue to be an ordinary being as he cultivates the ten faithful minds; he will be a sage as he practices the ten pāramitās, progressing through the ten levels of abiding, ten levels of action, and ten levels of transference of merit; and he will be a holy being as he progresses through the Ten Grounds. A Bodhisattva will ascend to the First Ground when he realizes that all dharmas have no birth. From the First Ground to the Tenth Ground, he will achieve the ten pāramitās one after another, in one-to-one correspondence with the Ten Grounds. At the fifty-first level, his enlightenment being virtually perfect, he will be in the holy position of waiting to become a Buddha in his next life. At the fifty-second level, he attains the perfect enlightenment, achieving the ultimate fruit of the aspiration and training of a Bodhisattva.

store (藏). A paraphrase of the Sanskrit word *garbha*, which means the womb or the child in the womb. Then the thus-come store (tathāgata-garbha) is one's true mind, also called the vajra (indestructible) store. One's true mind is likened to the space store in its vastness, and to the earth store in its supportiveness and hidden treasures. The realm of all dharmas is the dharma store. The aggregate of all Dharmas (Buddhas' teachings) is the Dharma store; the collection of all precepts is the precept store.

stūpa (窣堵婆). A memorial pagoda for the remains of a holy being, whether relics of bones or scriptures.

suffering (duḥkha, 苦). The first of the Four Noble Truths.

A. The eight kinds of suffering are (1) birth, (2) old age, (3) illness, (4) death, (5) inability to get what one wants, (6) loss of what one loves, (7) encounter with what one hates, and (8) the driving force of the five aggregates. Driven by the five aggregates, one experiences impermanence, pain, and sorrow in the preceding seven situations.

B. The three kinds of suffering are (1) pain brought by a cause (苦苦), (2) deterioration of pleasure (壞苦), and (3) continuous change in all processes (行苦).

sūtras in the twelve categories (十二部經). The teachings of the Buddha are classified by content and form into the twelve categories: (1) sūtra, discourses in prose; (2) geya, songs that repeat the teachings; (3) vyākaraṇa, prophecies; (4) gāthā, stanzas; (5) udāna, self-initiated utterances; (6) nidāna, causes for the discourses; (7) avadāna, parables; (8) itivṛttaka, sūtras that begin with "so it has been said"; (9) jātaka, past lives of the Buddha; (10) vaipulya, extensive teachings; (11) adbhuta-dharma, marvelous events; and (12) upadeśa, pointing-out instructions.

Tathāgata (如來). The Thus-Come One, the first of the ten epithets of a Buddha, which signifies true suchness. Although the Tathāgata never moves, a Buddha appears to have come and gone in the same way as have past Buddhas.

ten appearances (十相). As stated in the *Mahāparinirvāṇa Sūtra* (T12n0375), the appearances of a sentient being are (1) sights, (2) sounds, (3) scents, (4) flavors, (5) tactile sensations, (6) birth, (7) staying, (8) death, (9) male, and (10) female (see four appearances).

ten directions (十方). The spatial directions of east, southeast, south, southwest, west, northwest, north, northeast, the nadir, and the zenith.

ten evil karmas (十惡). These are (1) killing, (2) stealing, (3) sexual misconduct, (4) false speech, (5) divisive speech, (6) abusive speech, (7) suggestive speech, (8) greed, (9) anger, and (10) the wrong views.

ten fetters (十纏). These are (1) no sense of shame, (2) no sense of dishonor, (3) jealousy, (4) stinginess, (5) remorse, (6) torpor, (7) restlessness, (8) stupor, (9) rage, and (10) concealing one's wrongdoings.

ten good karmas (十善). The opposites of the ten evil karmas are (1) no killing, (2) no stealing, (3) no sexual misconduct, (4) no false speech, (5) no divisive speech, (6) no abusive speech, (7) no suggestive speech, (8) no greed, (9) no anger, and (10) no wrong views.

ten pāramitās (十度, 十波羅蜜). In parallel with the Ten Grounds for Bodhisattva development (see stages of the Bodhisattva Way), added to the list of six pāramitās are four more pāramitās: (7) upāya (skillful means), (8) praṇidhāna (earnest wish), (9) bala (power), and (10) jñāna (wisdom-knowledge).

Ten Powers (daśa-bala, 十力). Only a Buddha has perfect knowledge of (1) the right or wrong in every situation and its corresponding karmic consequences; (2) the karmic requitals of every sentient being in the past, present, and future; (3) all stages of dhyāna and samādhi; (4) the capacity and future attainment of every sentient being; (5) the desires and inclinations of every sentient being; (6) the nature and condition of every sentient being; (7) the consequences of all actions with or without afflictions; (8) all past lives of every sentient being and their karmic reasons; (9) all future rebirths of every sentient being and their karmic reasons; and (10) the permanent termination of all afflictions and habits upon attainment of Buddhahood.

ten precepts (daśa-śīla, 十戒). Observed by novice monks and nuns, the ten precepts include the eight precepts, but precepts 7 and 8 are renumbered 8 and 9, because precept 6 is divided into two: (6) no wearing perfumes or adornments, and (7) no singing, dancing, or watching song-dance entertainments. A tenth precept is added: (10) no touching or hoarding money or treasures.

Thirty-seven Elements of Bodhi (三十七道品). Trainings for attaining bodhi include

A. Four Foundations of Mindfulness;
B. Four Right Endeavors [(1) end forever the existing evil, (2) do not allow new evil to arise, (3) cause new goodness to arise, and (4) expand existing goodness];
C. Four Works to Attain Samādhi [(1) aspiration, (2) energetic progress, (3) focus, and (4) contemplation];
D. Five Roots [(1) faith, (2) energetic progress, (3) remembrance of the true Dharma, (4) samādhi, and (5) wisdom];
E. Five Powers [(1) power in faith, (2) power in energetic progress, (3) power in remembrance of the true Dharma, (4) power in samādhi, and (5) power in wisdom];
F. Seven Bodhi Factors;
G. Eightfold Right Path.

three ages of the Dharma (正像末期). The Dharma of Śākyamuni Buddha will end after these three ages: (1) The true Dharma age (正法) lasted 500 to 1,000 years after His passing. During this period, there were teachings, carrying out of the teachings, and attaining of fruits. (2) The Dharma-likeness age (像法) lasted 500 to 1,000 years. During this period, there were teachings and carrying out of the teachings, but no attaining of fruits. (3) The Dharma-ending age (末法) will last 10,000 years. During this period, the teachings will gradually vanish, and there will be neither carrying out of the teachings nor attaining of fruits. Because people will no longer be receptive, the Dharma will be gone for a long time until the advent of the next Buddha. In the *Bodhisattva in the Womb Sūtra* (T12n384, 1025c15–19), fascicle 2, the Buddha prophesies that, after 56 koṭi and 70 million years, which means 630 million years (if a koṭi is 10 million), Maitreya Bodhisattva will descend from Tuṣita Heaven and become the next Buddha, bringing the Dharma to a renewed world.

three bodies of a Buddha (三身). These are (1) dharmakāya (the dharma body or truth body), which is emptiness, the true reality of all dharmas; (2) saṁbhogakāya (the reward body or enjoyment body) in a sublime ethereal form, which represents the immeasurable merit of a Buddha; and (3) nirmāṇakāya (a response body through birth or a miraculously manifested body), which is the manifestation of a Buddha in response to sentient beings that are ready to accept the Dharma. The reward body and the response body are the appearances of the dharma body, and these three bodies are inseparable. According to the Tiantai School of China, of the latest Buddha, Vairocana is the dharmakāya, Rocana is the saṁbhogakāya, and Śākyamuni is the nirmāṇakāya.

three Buddha natures (三佛性). These are (1) Buddha nature inherent in all sentient beings but unknown to them, (2) Buddha nature gradually revealed through one's spiritual training, and (3) Buddha nature evident in a Buddha.

Three Clarities (三明). An Arhat has achieved (1) clear knowledge of the past lives of himself and others and their causes and conditions, (2) clarity of his god-eye that sees others' future lives and their causes and conditions, and (3) clear knowledge that his afflictions have ceased and will never arise again. The Three Clarities of a Buddha are supreme and are called the Three Thorough Clarities (三達).

Three Endurances in the Dharma (三法忍). According to the *Sūtra of Amitāyus Buddha* (T12n0360), these are (1) Endurance in Hearing the Sounds (音響忍), which means acceptance of the Dharma through hearing it; (2) Endurance in Accord (柔順忍), which means agreement with the Dharma through pondering in accord with the truth; and (3) Endurance in the Realization of the No Birth of Dharmas (無生法忍), which is the lasting realization of the truth that dharmas have neither birth nor death.

three fortune fields (三福田). These are (1) the reverence field (敬田), which means the Three Jewels; (2) the kindness field (恩田), which means one's parents and teachers; and (3) the compassion field (悲田), which means the poor, the sick, and animals. By making offerings to any of these three fortune fields, one plants seeds which will yield harvests of fortune in one's present and future lives.

three groups (三聚). Sentient beings are divided into three groups: (1) the group that definitely progresses on the right path to bodhi (正定聚); (2) the group that definitely is not on the bodhi path (邪定聚); (3) the group that is indecisive about its paths (不定聚).

Three Jewels (三寶). These are (1) the Buddha, the unsurpassed perfectly enlightened teacher; (2) the Dharma, His teachings; and (3) the Saṅgha, the Buddhist community.

three kinds of hindrances (三障). Hindrances to realization of one's true mind are (1) afflictions, such as greed, anger, and delusion, which agitate one's mind and lead to negative karmas; (2) karmas, done with one's body, voice, and mind, which lead to requitals; and (3) requitals, such as an unfortunate rebirth in human form with incomplete faculties, or in the form of animal, hungry ghost, or hell dweller.

Three Liberation Doors (trīṇi vimokṣa-mokha, 三解脫門), or Three Samādhis. These are (1) emptiness, (2) no appearance, and (3) no wish or no act. Through samādhi, one realizes emptiness, penetrating the no birth of all dharmas. One also realizes that the illusory appearances of dharmas conceived or perceived are no appearance. One makes no wish and does nothing for future rebirths in the Three Realms of Existence.

Three Realms of Existence (trayo-dhātu, 三界, 三有). The world of illusory existence, in which sentient beings transmigrate, comprises (1) the desire realm (欲界), where reside sentient beings with the full range of afflictions, such as hell dwellers, ghosts, animals, humans, asuras, and some gods; (2) the form realm (色界), where Brahma gods, who have only pure desires, reside in eighteen form heavens classified into the four dhyāna heavens (四禪天), or four levels of meditation; and (3) the formless realm (無色界), where formless gods are in mental existence in four formless heavens, or at four levels of long, deep meditative absorption (see samādhi).

Three Refuges (三皈依). One becomes a Buddhist by taking refuge, for protection and guidance, in the Three Jewels: the Buddha, the Dharma, and the Saṅgha. In the *Sūtra of the Upāsaka Precepts* (T24n1488), the Buddha teaches the Four Refuges, and the fourth one is the Precepts.

Three Samādhis (三三昧). See Three Liberation Doors.

three turnings of the Dharma wheel in the twelve appearances (三轉法輪十二行相). The Buddha turned three times the Dharma wheel of the Four Noble Truths. During the first turning for indication, the Buddha revealed, "This is suffering; this is accumulation of afflictions; this is cessation of suffering; this is the path." During the second turning for persuasion, He advised, "This is the suffering you should know; this is the accumulation of afflictions you should destroy; this is the cessation of suffering you should achieve; this is the path you should take." During the third turning for confirmation, He testified, "This is the suffering I have known; this is the accumulation of afflictions I have destroyed; this is the cessation of suffering I have achieved; this is the path I have completed."

Three Vehicles (三乘). The Great Vehicle (Mahāyāna) and the Two Vehicles.

three wisdom-knowledges (三智). These are (1) the overall wisdom-knowledge (sarvajña, 一切智), which is the emptiness of everything, realized by an Arhat, a Pratyekabuddha, and a holy Bodhisattva; (2) discriminatory wisdom-knowledge (道種智), which is developed in a holy Bodhisattva, who differentiates all displays of illusory existence in order to deliver sentient beings; and (3) knowledge of all knowledge (sarvajña-jñāna, 一切種智), or omniscience (sarvajñatā), which is a Buddha's perfect wisdom-knowledge of all beings and all things in their general and particular aspects, and of the non-duality of emptiness and myriad displays.

Three-Thousand Large Thousandfold World (三千大千世界). A galaxy, the educational district of a Buddha. It consists of a billion small worlds, each including a Mount Sumeru surrounded by four continents and interlaying circles of eight oceans and eight mountain ranges. One thousand such small worlds constitute a Small Thousandfold World. One thousand Small Thousandfold Worlds constitute a Medium Thousandfold World. Finally, one thousand Medium Thousandfold Worlds constitute a Large Thousandfold World. Therefore, *Three-Thousand* does not mean 3,000, but 1,000 raised to the power of 3, as described above. It can also mean that there are three kinds of Thousandfold World: small, medium, and large.

total retention (總持). See dhāraṇī.

Trayastriṁśa Heaven (忉利天). The second of the six desire heavens. It is on the top of Mount Sumeru, and the first desire heaven is halfway up Mount Sumeru, while all other heavens are up in the sky. Trayastriṁśa Heaven means Thirty-three Heavens, all ruled by the god-king Śakro-Devānām-Indra, who is commonly called Śakra or Indra.

Tripiṭaka (三藏). The three collections of texts of the Buddhist canon: (1) the Sūtra-piṭaka, discourses of the Buddha; (2) the Vinaya-piṭaka, rules of conduct; and (3) the Abhidharma-piṭaka, treatises on the Dharma. A Tripiṭaka master is accomplished in all three areas.

true suchness (bhūta-tathatā, 真如). The changeless true reality of all dharmas, the absolute truth that dharmas have neither birth nor death. It has other names, including emptiness, true emptiness, ultimate emptiness, one appearance, one flavor, true reality, ultimate reality (bhūta-koṭi), primal state, Buddha mind, true mind, inherent pure mind, the Thus-Come One (Tathāgata), the thus-come store (Tathāgata-garbha), vajra store, dharma-kāya, Buddha nature, dharma nature, dharma realm, the one true dharma realm, the highest truth (paramārtha), the great seal, and the great perfection. One's body and mental states, and objects perceived as external, are all manifestations of one's true mind, projected through causes and conditions from the pure, impure, and neutral seeds stored in ālaya consciousness.

twelve fields (dvādaśa-āyatana, 十二處, 十二入). A sentient being is composed of the twelve fields: the six faculties (eye, ear, nose, tongue, body, and mental faculty [manas]) and their six objects (sights, sounds, scents, flavors, tactile sensations, and mental objects). The six faculties are also called the six internal fields, and their objects are called the six external fields. The Consciousness-Only School calls the latter "projected appearances" (影像相分). And modern neurologists recognize that percepts are "brain representations" (see eighteen spheres).

Twelve Links of Dependent Arising (十二因緣法). The principle that explains why and how a sentient being continues to be reborn according to karma. Each link is the main condition for the next one to arise. These twelve links are (1) ignorance, (2) karmic actions, (3) consciousness, (4) name and form, (5) six faculties, (6) contact with sense objects, (7) sensory reception, (8) love, (9) grasping, (10) karmic force for being, (11) birth, and (12) old age and death. Links 1–2 refer to the afflictions and karmic seeds from previous lives, links 3–7 refer to the karmic fruit in the present life, links 8–10 refer to karmas in the present life, and links 11–12 refer to the karmic fruit in the next life. In this sequence, the twelve links connect one's lives from the past to the present, continuing to the future. With ignorance, one goes from affliction to karma to suffering, continuing the endless spiral of birth and death. By ending ignorance one will disengage the remaining eleven links and end one's cycle of birth and death.

twenty-five forms of existence (二十五有). There are fourteen in the desire realm (欲界), seven in the form realm (色界), and four in the formless realm (無色界).

two emptinesses (二空). (1) The emptiness of a sentient being (人空) composed of dharmas, such as the five aggregates, and dependent on causes and conditions; (2) the emptiness of a dharma (法空) dependent on causes and conditions (see eighteen emptinesses).

Two Paths (二道).

A. (1) The Path with Discharges (有漏道) is the worldly path taken by those with afflictions, as they follow the first two of the Four Noble Truths and transmigrate in the Three Realms of Existence; (2) the Path without Discharges (無漏道) is the holy path taken by those who follow the last two of the Four Noble Truths, in order to eradicate their afflictions and transcend the Three Realms (see discharge).

B. (1) The Difficult Path (難行道) to Buddhahood is through repeated birth and death in the Three Realms of Existence; (2) the Easy Path (易行道) to Buddhahood is through rebirth in a Pure Buddha Land to train there.

two types of birth and death (二種生死). (1) An ordinary being, whose lifespan and life form are governed by the law of karma, repeatedly undergoes karmic birth and death (分段生死). (2) A holy Bodhisattva on any of the Ten Grounds, whose lifespan and mind-created body (意生身) are changeable at will, undergoes changeable birth and death (變易生死). Only a Buddha has ended both types of birth and death.

Two Vehicles (二乘). The Voice-Hearer Vehicle that leads to Arhatship and the Pratyekabuddha Vehicle that leads to Pratyekabuddhahood, for one's own liberation only. The Mahāyāna doctrine refers to the Theravāda School in Southeast Asia (Sri Lanka, Burma, Thailand, Laos, and Cambodia) as the Small Vehicle (Hīnayāna), which can be either or both of these Two Vehicles.

Two-Footed Honored One (dvipadottama, 兩足尊). A Buddha is the most honored one among sentient beings standing on two feet, i.e., gods and humans. Moreover, the two feet of a Buddha are compared to meditation and moral conduct, merit and wisdom, knowledge in the relative and absolute truth, knowledge and action, or vow and action. A Buddha has perfected both.

unimpeded eloquence (無礙辯). This includes (1) unimpeded understanding of dharmas, (2) unimpeded interpretation of their meanings, (3) unimpeded forms of expression, and (4) unimpeded delight in articulation according to the capacity of the listeners.

upadeśa (優波提舍). A pointing-out instruction, usually interpreted as a treatise (see sūtras in the twelve categories).

upaniṣad (優波尼薩曇). Sitting down at the feet of another to listen to his words. It suggests secret knowledge given in this manner. It may be an esoteric unit of measure.

upāsaka (優婆塞). A Buddhist layman (see Saṅgha).

upāsikā (優婆夷). A Buddhist laywoman. (see Saṅgha).

Vairocana (毘盧遮那). The name of the dharmakāya or saṁbhogakāya of a Buddha (see three bodies of a Buddha). Vairocana means pervasive radiance, and signifies the universal equality of everything in true suchness as well as the all-encompassing wisdom of a Buddha. According to the *Mahāvaipulya Sūtra of Buddha Adornment* (T09n278) in 60 fascicles, Vairocana is the name for a Buddha's dharmakāya. According to the *Brahma Net Sūtra* (T24n1484), Rocana is the name for a Buddha's saṁbhogakāya. Śākyamuni Buddha, in his nirmāṇakāya, is sometimes referred to as Vairocana Buddha or Rocana Buddha.

Vaiśālī (毘舍離). The domicile of the Licchavi clan, one of the sixteen great city kingdoms of ancient India. One hundred years after the Buddha's parinirvāṇa, in this city, 700 sages gathered in the second assembly for the compilation and revision of the Buddhist Canon.

vajra (伐折羅, 金剛). (1) Adamantine and indestructible, a description of the true suchness of all dharmas. (2) Diamond, considered to be as hard as the thunderbolt. (3) A ritual object, as a symbol of skillful means for delivering oneself and others from the cycle of birth and death.

Vārāṇasī (波羅奈國). An ancient city state on the Ganges, the present-day city of Benares. Nearby is Deer Park, where the Buddha gave His first teachings to five monks.

Veda (吠陀). Sacred knowledge, the general name of the Hindu canonical sacred texts. The four Vedas are the Ṛg-veda, Sāma-veda, Yajur-veda, and Athara-veda. They include mantras, prayers, hymns, and rituals. The Ṛg-veda is the only original work of the first three Vedas. Its texts are assigned to a period between 1400 and 1000 BCE. The fourth Veda, Athara-veda, emerged later.

vessel world (器世間). The living environment of a sentient being, e.g., a birdcage holding a bird. For this sentient being, assuming the life form of a bird is the main requital (正報), and living in a birdcage, its vessel world, is the reliance requital (依報). Alhough the main requital does not change during the life of a sentient being, its reliance requital may change, e.g., the bird may be released from its cage.

view of void (空見). The wrong view that the emptiness of dharmas means nothingness and that therefore causality can be ignored.

vipaśyanā (毗婆舍那). Correct observation or clear seeing, which leads to insight. Śamatha-vipaśyanā has been translated as stillness and observation (止觀), or as silent illumination (默照). When śamatha and vipaśyanā are balanced in power, one may realize the non-dual state of one's mind.

voice-hearer (śrāvaka, 聲聞). One who has received oral teachings from a Buddha. The four groups of disciples of Śākyamuni Buddha were all voice-hearers. In the *Lotus Sūtra* (T09n0262), the Buddha bestows upon 1,200 Arhats and 2,000 voice-hearers the prophecy of attaining Buddhahood. Listed below are a few disciples of the Buddha:

Ājñātakauṇḍinya (阿若憍陳如) was one of the first five disciples of the Buddha. He is well regarded as an Elder.

Ānanda (阿難) was the younger brother of Devadatta. As the Buddha's attendant, he is noted for hearing and remembering all the teachings of the Buddha. Ānanda became an Arhat after the Buddha's parinirvāṇa. In the first assembly of Arhats, he recited from memory all the teachings for the compilation of the sūtras. Succeeding Mahākāśyapa, he is reckoned as the second patriarch of the Buddhist lineage.

Aniruddha (阿那律) became a disciple soon after the Buddha's enlightenment. He used to fall asleep when the Buddha was teaching and was reproved by the Buddha. Ashamed, he practiced day and night without sleep and lost his eyesight. However, he was able to see with his god-eye.

Cullapatka (周梨槃陀迦), also called Śuddhipanthaka, and his twin brother, Patka (Panthaka), were born on a roadside while their parents were traveling. He was forgetful of the Buddha's teachings. Then the Buddha told him to remember the short phrase "remove the dust and filth" as he did cleaning work in his daily life. He then attained Arhatship and transcendental powers.

Devadatta (提婆達多) was a cousin of the Buddha, with whom he had competed since childhood. He became a disciple after the Buddha had attained perfect enlightenment. He trained hard for twelve years but did not attain Arhatship. Disgusted, he studied magic and formed his own group. Devadatta beat a nun to death and made several attempts to murder the Buddha and destroy the Saṅgha. He fell into hell after his death. However, in a previous life he had given the Buddha Mahāyāna teachings. Despite the wicked deeds in his life, the Buddha prophesies in the *Lotus Sūtra* (T09n0262) that Devadatta will become a Buddha called Devarāja.

Gavāṁpati (憍梵波提) had been a cow for 500 lives because of his past karma. As a disciple of the Buddha, he still ruminated like a cow, and he was mocked by people as the cow-faced bhikṣu. Out of compassion, the Buddha sent him to a garden in Trayastriṁśa Heaven to train in meditation. He returned to Earth after the Buddha's parinirvāṇa, and he too entered parinirvāṇa soon afterward.

Kālodāyin (迦留陀夷) was a disciple whose skin was very black. He used to beg for food at night. A pregnant woman miscarried when she saw him in a flash of lightning in the dark of the night. Then the Buddha stipulated that no one should beg for food after noontime.

Kapphiṇa (劫賓那) was born under the constellation Scorpio. He is said to have understood astronomy, been the king of Southern Kauśala, and then become a disciple of the Buddha, receiving his monastic name Mahākapphiṇa. In the *Lotus Sūtra* (T09n0262), the Buddha prophesies that Kapphiṇa will become a Buddha called Samanta-prabhāsa.

Kāśyapa brothers (三迦葉) were Uruvilvākāśyapa (優樓頻螺迦葉), Nadīkāśyapa (那提迦葉), and Gayākāśyapa (伽耶迦葉). Initially fire-worshippers, they joined the Buddha's Order together with their 1,000 followers.

Mahāculla (摩訶周那), also called Patka, Panthaka, or Mahāpanthaka, was the elder twin brother of Cullapatka. More intelligent than his twin, he soon attained Arhatship after joining the Buddha's Order.

Mahākāśyapa (摩訶迦葉) was initially a Brahmin in Magadha. He became a disciple three years after the Buddha had attained enlightenment. In eight days, Mahākāśyapa attained Arhatship. He is considered foremost in ascetic practices. When the Buddha held up a flower, only Mahākāśyapa in the huge assembly understood the meaning and responded with a smile (X01n0027, 0442c16–21). Then the Buddha entrusted him with the continuation of the lineage, and he became the first patriarch after the Buddha's parinirvāṇa. After entrusting the lineage to Ānanda, Mahākāśyapa went to the Vulture Peak (Gṛdhrakūṭa) Mountain. There he has remained in samādhi. He will enter parinirvāṇa after the advent the next Buddha, Maitreya.

Mahākātyāyana (摩訶迦旃延) was born into the Brahmin caste in the kingdom of Avanti in western India. He studied the Vedas under his uncle Asita, a ṛṣi, who foresaw that Prince Siddhārtha would attain Buddhahood. Mahākātyāyana then followed the Buddha in honor of Asita's death wish. Through diligent training under the Buddha, Mahākātyāyana attained Arhatship. After the parinirvāṇa of the Buddha, he often debated with non-Buddhists, and is considered foremost in polemic.

Mahākauṣṭhila (摩訶拘絺羅) joined the Buddha's Order after his nephew Śāriputra did. He soon attained Arhatship and acquired unimpeded eloquence. The Buddha praised him as foremost in eloquence.

Mahāmaudgalyāyana (大目揵連), together with his own disciples, following his good friend Śāriputra, became a disciple of the Buddha and attained Arhatship in a month. Śāriputra is portrayed as standing on the Buddha's right, with Maudgalyāyana on His left. Maudgalyāyana was stoned to death by Brahmins shortly before the Buddha's parinirvāṇa. He is considered foremost in transcendental powers.

Nanda (難陀). (1) Nanda was the half brother of the Buddha. He was also called Sundara-Nanda (孫陀羅難陀), with his wife's name Sundarī added to differentiate him from Nanda the Cattle Herder. He was tall and handsome, with thirty marks of a great man. After becoming a monk under the Buddha, he was still attached to his wife. Through the Buddha's skillful teachings, he ended his love and desire and attained Arhatship. (2) Nanda was the Cattle Herder who offered milk every day to the Buddha and His disciples during their three-month summer retreat. Assuming that the Buddha knew nothing about cattle herding, he asked Him questions. After the Buddha told him eleven things about cattle herding, Nanda was deeply moved and joined the Buddha's Order.

Patka (半託迦), also called Panthaka or Mahāpanthaka, was the elder twin brother of Cullapatka. More intelligent than his twin, he was accomplished in the five studies. He attained Arhatship soon after joining the Buddha's Order.

Piṇḍola-Bharadvāja (賓頭盧頗羅墮) is also called the Long-Eyebrowed Arhat, and Bharadvāja is one of the six famous family names of Brahmins. He is one of the sixteen great Arhats who remain in the world for various reasons. Piṇḍola was the son of a state minister and attained Arhatship at a young age. However, after he flaunted his transcendental powers, the Buddha rebuked him and forbade him to enter parinirvāṇa. So he is still in the world, delivering sentient beings.

Pūrṇa (富樓那) is also called Pūrṇa-Maitrāyaṇīputra, under his mother's family name Maitrāyaṇī. He was the son of a minister of King Śuddhodana of the kingdom of Kapilavastu. He was very intelligent, and studied the Vedas at a young age. On the night Prince Siddhārtha left the palace to seek the truth, he too left with thirty friends to practice asceticism in the snow mountain. He attained the four dhyānas and the five transcendental powers. After Siddhārtha attained Buddhahood and did the first turning of the Dharma wheel in Deer Park, he became a monk in the Buddha's Order and soon attained Arhatship. He is considered foremost in expounding the Dharma because some 99,000 people were delivered through his teachings.

Rāhula (羅睺羅) was the only son of Śākyamuni Buddha and Yaśodharā. He had been in gestation for six years and was born on the lunar eclipse after the Buddha had attained perfect enlightenment. Rāhula was six years old when the Buddha returned to the city kingdom of Kapilavastu, and he became a novice monk at the command of the Buddha. Foremost in secret training, he is to be reborn as the eldest son of every future Buddha.

Revata (離婆多) is the younger brother of Śāriputra. In his meditation at a temple, he saw two ghosts fighting to eat a corpse. Realizing the illusoriness of the body, he renounced family life and became a disciple of the Buddha. Traveling barefoot in a snow country, his feet were frostbitten. The Buddha praised him for his contentment with few material things and allowed him to wear shoes.

Śāriputra (舍利弗), together with his own disciples, joined the Buddha's Order soon after the Buddha's enlightenment. After being a principal disciple for forty-four years, to avoid his grief over the Buddha's parinirvāṇa, he requested and received the Buddha's permission to enter parinirvāṇa sooner than the Buddha. He is considered foremost in wisdom among the disciples.

Subhūti (須菩提) is foremost among the disciples in understanding the meaning of emptiness. He is the principal interlocutor in the *Prajñā-Pāramitā Sūtra*.

Svāgata (莎伽陀). In the *Buddha Pronounces the Sūtra of the Bhikṣu Svāgata's Merit* (T14n0501), this bhikṣu named Svāgata lay drunk under a tree. The Buddha praised his merit for subjugating a vengeful dragon and explained that Svāgata was not really drunk but pretended drunkenness for a purpose.

Upāli (優波離) had been a barber in the royal court. He became a disciple, together with Ānanda, six years after the Buddha had attained perfect enlightenment. Foremost in observing the precepts, he contributed to the compilation of the Vinaya in the first assembly of the Arhats after the Buddha's parinirvāṇa.

Upananda (跋難陀) and his brother Nanda (難陀) often caused disciplinary problems. Because of their misconduct, the Buddha had to add a few more precepts to the collection. Upananda rejoiced over the Buddha's parinirvāṇa because in his opinion it freed the disciples from restraint.

Vakkula (薄拘羅), or Vakula, was a disciple who lived to age 160 without a moment's illness or pain.

voice-hearer fruits (聲聞果).

A. The four holy fruits achieved by voice-hearers on the Liberation Way are (1) Srotāpanna, the Stream Enterer, who will attain Arhatship after at most seven times being reborn as a god then a human; (2) Sakṛdāgāmin, the Once Returner, who will be reborn as a human only once more before attaining Arhatship; (3) Anāgāmin, the Never Returner, who will not be reborn as a human but will attain Arhatship in a pure abode heaven in the form realm; and (4) Arhat, the Foe Destroyer, who has attained the nirvāṇa with remnant by annihilating his fixation on having an autonomous self and eradicating all his afflictions.

B. These four holy fruits and the corresponding nearness to them are called the eight holy ranks (八聖). Actually, one who is in the first rank, nearing the first holy fruit, is only a sage, and those in the higher seven ranks are holy beings. Those who are still learning (śaikṣa, 有學) are in the first seven ranks. Only Arhats, in the eight rank, are those who have nothing more to learn (aśaikṣa, 無學).

Vulture Peak Mountain. See Gṛdhrakūṭa Mountain.

water with the eight virtues (八功德水). According to the *Praising the Pure Land Sūtra* (T12n0367), these eight virtues are (1) purity and clarity, (2) coolness, (3) sweetness, (4) lightness and softness, (5) soothing, (6) peace and harmony, (7) quenching of thirst, and (8) nourishing and vitalizing.

Way (道). The Way in the Mahāyāna doctrine is to find the ultimate truth within one's own mind. Those who see objects as existing outside their minds are considered not on the Way. The word *Way* (Dao or Tao) in Chinese Daoism means the natural order of things in the world, contrary to its meaning in Buddhist doctrine.

Wheel-Turning King (cakra-vartī-rāja, 轉輪王). A ruler, the wheels of whose chariot roll everywhere unimpeded. The wheel (cakra), one of the seven precious things he owns, comes in four ranks: iron, copper, silver, and gold. The iron wheel king rules over one continent, the south; the copper wheel king, over two, east and south; the silver wheel king, over three, east, west, and south; the gold wheel king, over all four continents. A Buddha, the universal Dharma King, turns the Dharma wheel, giving teachings to sentient beings.

yakṣa (夜叉). A demonic ghost that eats human flesh.

Yama (夜摩). The king of the underworld and superintendent of the karmic punishment of hell-dwellers.

yojana (由旬). The distance covered by one day's march of an army or by one day's walk of a yoked bull. One yojana may equal 4 or 8 krośas, each krośa being the distance at which a bull's bellow can be heard. The estimated distance of a yojana varies from 8 to 19 kilometers.

Reference

In English

Buddhist Text Translation Society, trans. 2009. *The Śūraṅgama Sūtra: A New Translation with Excerpts from the Commentary by the Venerable Master Hsüan Hua*. Talmage, CA: Buddhist Text Translation Society.

Chang, Garma C. C., ed. 1985. *A Treasury of Mahāyāna Sūtras*. University Park and London: Pennsylvania State University Press.

Harrison, Paul, trans. 1998. *The Pratyutpanna Samādhi Sutra;* and John McRae, trans. 1998. *The Śūraṅgama Samādhi Sutra*. Berkeley, CA: Numata Center.

Inagaki, Hisao, and Harold Stewart, trans. 1995. *The Three Pure Land Sutras: A Study and Translation from Chinese*. Berkeley, CA: Numata Center.

Luk, Charles, trans. 1966. *The Śūraṅgama Sūtra*. New Delhi: Munshiram Manoharlal Publishers, 2001.

Müller, F. Max, trans. 1894. The larger Sukāvatī-vyūha. In *Buddhist Mahāyāna Texts*, edited by E. B. Cowell and Others, pt. 2, 1–75. New York: Dover Publications, 1969. (An unabridged and unaltered republication of Volume XLIX of *The Sacred Books of the East*. Oxford: Clarendon Press, 1894.)

———, trans. 1894. The smaller Sukāvatī-vyūha. In *Buddhist Mahāyāna Texts*, edited by E. B. Cowell and Others, pt. 2, 89–103. New York: Dover Publications, 1969. (An unabridged and unaltered republication of Volume XLIX of *The Sacred Books of the East*. Oxford: Clarendon Press, 1894.)

Rulu, trans. 2012a. *Teachings of the Buddha*. Bloomington, IN: AuthorHouse. (Orig. pub. 2009.)

Tasakusu, J., trans. 1894. The Amitāyur-dhyāna-sūtra. In *Buddhist Mahāyāna Texts*, edited by E. B. Cowell and Others, pt. 2, 161–201. New York: Dover Publications, 1969. (An unabridged and unaltered republication of Volume XLIX of *The Sacred Books of the East*. Oxford: Clarendon Press, 1894.)

In Chinese

Chinese Electronic Tripiṭaka Collection 電子佛典集成. DVD-ROM, 2009 version. Containing the Taishō Tripiṭaka 大正藏, vols. 1–55, 85, and the Shinsan Zokuzōkyō 卍續藏, vols. 1–88. Taipei, Taiwan: Chinese Buddhist Electronic Text Association. Also available online at http://cbeta.org/

Foguang dacidian 佛光大辭典 [Buddha's light dictionary]. 1988. Kaoshiung, Taiwan: Buddha's Light Publishing. Also available online at http://www.fgs.org.tw/fgs_book/fgs_drser.aspx

Lianzong shisanzu zhuanlue 蓮宗十三祖傳略 [Brief biographies of the thirteen patriarchs of the Lotus School]. 1983. Hongkong: Chongde Publishing 崇德出版社

Lin Qi-an 林祺安, comp. 2002. *Hanyi wuliang shoujing huiyi duizhao* 漢譯無量壽經會譯對照 [Matching the integrated text with the Chinese translations of the Amitāyus Sūtra]. Taipei, Taiwan: Daqian Publishing 大千出版社

Shi Huilu 釋慧律, comp. 1995. *Jingtu shengxianlu yijie* 淨土聖賢錄易解 [Easily comprehensible records of holies and sages of the Pure Land]. 6 vols. Kaoshiung, Taiwan: Wenshu Wenjiao Jijinhui 文殊文教基金會.

Shi Xingfan 釋性梵. 1997. *Foshuo wuliangshoujing jiangyi* 佛說無量壽經講義 [Lecture notes on the Amitāyus Sūtra]. Tainan, Taiwan: Heyu Publishing 和裕出版社.

———, comp. 1997. Wangsheng jingtuzhuan jiyiao 往生淨土傳輯要 [Important stories of rebirth in the Pure Land]. Kaoshiung, Taiwan: Shi Xingfan

Shi Yinguang 釋印光. 1993. *Yinguang fashi wenchao sanbian* 印光法師文鈔三編 [The third compilation of the writings of Dharma Master Yinguang]. 2 vols. Taizhong, Taiwan: Qinglian Publishing 青蓮出版社

Soothill, W. E., and Lewis Hodous, comps. 1962. *A Dictionary of Chinese Buddhist Terms* 中英佛學辭典. Kaoshiung, Taiwan: Buddhist Culture Service. Also available online at http://ybh.chibs.edu.tw/2L_data_ybh/dict/dict-s/soothill-hodous.htm

On the Internet

Chen Chien-huang 陳劍鍠. 2001. "Jindai queli lianzong shisanwei zushidi guocheng jiqi shiyi" 近代確立蓮宗十三位祖師的過程及其釋疑 [The process of electing the thirteen patriarchs of the Lotus School and the resolution of doubts]. http://www.confucius2000.com/scholar/chenjh2.htm

Online Buddhist Dictionary 在線佛學辭典. http://www.baus-ebs.org/fodict%5Fonline/

Online Buddhist Sutras. http://www.fodian.net/world/

Rulu. Mahayana Buddhist Sutras and Mantras. http://www.sutrasmantras.info/

Sanskrit, Tamil and Pahlavi Dictionaries. http://webapps.uni-koeln.de/tamil/

Shi Da-an 釋大安. Jingtuzong jiaocheng 淨土宗教程 [Teachings of the Pure Land School]. http://www.daanfs.cn:8080/dianziwendang/jtzjc.doc

University of the West. Digital Sanskrit Buddhist Canon. http://www.uwest.edu/sanskritcanon/dp/

WIKIPEDIA: The Free Encyclopedia. http://en.wikipedia.org/